C000041510

"In this eloquent and timely book, Curtis Freeman reminds us that protecting the right to dissent is both a civic and sacred duty. Freeman traces the roots of certain traditions of dissent, with a particular focus on the work and witness of John Bunyan, Daniel Defoe, and William Blake. He rightly argues that commitments to protect the right to protest against prevailing secular and religious orders have not only admirably respected liberty of conscience, they have also strengthened the institutions of church and state. All who care about the health of nations and the integrity of faith will want to read this important book."

—Melissa Rogers, *Nonresident Senior Fellow,*
Brookings Institution

"Protestant Dissent has been a powerful countercurrent within English-speaking culture, but it is often poorly understood. Curtis Freeman illuminates the tradition through absorbing case studies of three iconic writers: John Bunyan, Daniel Defoe, and William Blake. Each study explores their sources, their most famous text— *Pilgrim's Progress, Robinson Crusoe,* and *Jerusalem*—and their reception. Weaving together history, literature, and theology, this book offers a rich account of an important subject. It makes a compelling case for rediscovering dissent as a living tradition."

—John Coffey, *Professor of Early Modern History,*
University of Leicester

"A lively and captivating study of seventeenth-century nonconformity and its afterlives, *Undomesticated Dissent* attends foremost to the creative power of dissent in theology, politics, and fiction, as well as its import to communities of resistance across the globe. Refusing to surrender diverse nonconformist projects to the past, Freeman looks forward to their postapocalyptic future, urging readers to reconsider the history as well as the ongoing work of dissent. This is an ambitious and important book that offers a vital alternative political imaginary."

—Russ Leo, *Assistant Professor of English,*
Princeton University

"This is a groundbreaking book in Baptist studies, bringing new perspectives as the author sets Baptist life in the wider context of dissent, both past and present. He admirably succeeds in distilling a great deal of learned commentary on traditions of dissent into a flowing argument which grips the reader's interest and provokes thought about Baptist dissenting identity in the modern world. The book itself, like its subject matter, has the character of a prophetic word."

—Paul S. Fiddes, *Professor of Systematic Theology, University of Oxford*

UNDOMESTICATED DISSENT
Democracy and the Public Virtue of Religious Nonconformity

CURTIS W. FREEMAN

BAYLOR UNIVERSITY PRESS

Cover Design by Will Brown
Cover image: "Christian Beaten Down by Apollyon," watercolor painting by William Blake, c. 1824, illustration XX of John Bunyan's *The Pilgrim's Progress*.

An earlier version of some material that appears in chapter 3 was previously published and is used with permission: "The True Knowledge of Religion and of the Christian Doctrine: Robinson Crusoe as Catechist and Theologian," *Horizons* 59 (2013): 163–83.

Library of Congress Cataloging-in-Publication Data

Names: Freeman, Curtis W., author.
Title: Undomesticated dissent : democracy and the public virtue of religious nonconformity / Curtis W. Freeman.
Description: Waco, Texas : Baylor University Press, [2017] | Includes bibliographical references and index.
Identifiers: LCCN 2016057178 (print) | LCCN 2017026382 (ebook) | ISBN 9781481307277 (ebook-Mobi/Kindle) | ISBN 9781481306904 (ePub) | ISBN 9781481307284 (web PDF) | ISBN 9781481306881 (hardback : alk. paper)
Subjects: LCSH: Dissenters, Religious—England—History. | Bunyan, John, 1628-1688. Pilgrim's progress. | Defoe, Daniel, 1661?-1731. Robinson Crusoe. | Blake, William, 1757-1827. Jerusalem.
Classification: LCC BX5203.3 (ebook) | LCC BX5203.3 .F74 2017 (print) | DDC 280/.40942—dc23
LC record available at https://lccn.loc.gov/2016057178

Printed in the United States of America on acid-free paper with a minimum of 30 percent postconsumer waste recycled content.

For Jim McClendon, of blessed memory,
ever undomesticated in dissent

We must not confuse dissent with disloyalty. We must remember always that accusation is not proof and that conviction depends upon evidence and due process of law. We will not walk in fear, one of another. We will not be driven by fear into an age of unreason, if we dig deep in our history and our doctrine, and remember that we are not descended from fearful men—not from men who feared to write, to speak, to associate, and to defend causes that were, for the moment, unpopular.

~ Edward R. Murrow

CONTENTS

ACKNOWLEDGMENTS

I want to offer thanks to the many people who have encouraged and supported my work on this book. I am especially grateful to Parush Parushev, Stuart Blythe, and the International Baptist Theological Seminary in Amsterdam, Holland, who invited me to give the Hughey Lectures on November 3, 2014, where this project began. I am also grateful to Roger Ward and the members of the seminar of the Young Scholars in the Baptist Academy meeting on June 12–15, 2015, at Regent's Park College in Oxford University, who offered a helpful critique on the Bunyan chapter. I owe much to William Portier and the College Theology Society, who asked me to give a plenary address at the 2013 annual meeting, which led me to begin thinking about Defoe and *Robinson Crusoe*. I would also like to offer my sincere appreciation to President Joshua W. T. Cho and the faculty of the Hong Kong Baptist Seminary, who invited me to give the Baptist Heritage Lectures on October 13–15, 2015; to Provost Ben Leslie for giving me the honor of delivering the Joyce Compton Brown Lecture at Gardner-Webb University on October 26, 2015; and to Rektor Michael Kißkalt, who asked me to present a lecture to the faculty and students of the Theologische Hochschule in Elstal, Germany, on February 2, 2016. I also want to thank my former dean Richard Hays and colleagues of Duke University Divinity School for making it possible for me to be on academic leave in the spring semester of 2016, which enabled me to complete this manuscript, and to thank the Advisory Board and staff of the Baptist House of Studies (especially Callie Davis, Kiki Barnes, Randy Carter, and Adam English) for their excellent work during my absence. I owe a special thanks to Gregory Williams for preparing the bibliography and to Judith Heyhoe for the index. I am deeply grateful for contributions by the people who read earlier drafts of these chapters and offered suggestions about how I might improve them. I particularly want to thank Robert Collmer, David Aers, Christopher Rowland, Kate Bowler, Paul Fiddes, Ralph Wood, Brian Giemza, William Willimon, Kevin Georgas, Stanley Hauerwas, David Marshall, David Toole, Aaron Griffith, Judith Heyhoe, Darryl Powell, and Debra Freeman. They have helped me write a much better book than I ever could have written alone. Finally, to Carey Newman, who believed in this project from the beginning and encouraged its completion all along the way.

PREFACE

Here lyes interred the body of Mr. Edward Bagshaw
Minister of the Gospel who received from God
   Faith to embrace it,
   Courage to defend it,
   And Patience to suffer for it;
When by the most despised, and by many persecuted,
esteeming the Advantages of Birth, and Education,
and Learning (all eminent to him) as Things of Worth,
to be accounted Loss for the Knowledge of Christ.
From the Reproaches of professed Adversaries
He Took Sanctuary, by the Will of God, In Eternal Rest,
the 28th of December 1671.[1]

I did not choose my subject. It, or rather they, chose me. Late one evening in the summer of 2005 I found myself, quite by accident, in Bunhill Fields, the old nonconformist burial ground on the far north end of London. Earlier in the day, our little band of pilgrims had visited Westminster Abbey and St. Paul's Cathedral, and we had hoped

---

[1] Inscription on the tomb of Edward Bagshaw, in *The Inscriptions Upon the Tombs, Grave-Stones, &c. in the Dissenters Burial-Place Near Bunhill-Fields* (London: E. Curll, 1717), 26.

to see Wesley's Chapel, but upon arriving we discovered to our disappointment it had closed for the day. Someone suggested that we might walk across the street to the cemetery where Susannah Wesley was buried. As we made our way to the small marker beside her grave, we discovered ourselves in the midst of a cloud of witnesses, who though dead still speak through the faithful testimony they have left behind (Heb 11:4). Located outside the city walls, Bunhill (Bone-hill) Fields was the burial site of preference for nonconformists, who because of their undomesticated dissent were not interred on land owned by the Church of England. The grounds were enclosed by a wall in 1665, and by the time the final plot was filled in 1854 it included an estimated 123,000 graves.[2] Memorials for some of the most honored names of English dissent are to be found here: John Foxe, Praise-God Barebones, Vavasor Powell, John Owen, Thomas Goodwin, Isaac Watts, Samuel Stennett, William Kiffin, Hanserd Knollys, Francis "Elephant" Smith, John Gill, John Rippon, and Daniel Williams, to name but a few. The community of saints here gathered awaiting the resurrection of the dead consists not only of Independents (Congregationalists), Baptists, and Presbyterians but also of Unitarians, Free Thinkers, and more. Some were ministers, but most were common folk—tailors and haberdashers, soldiers and sailors, physicians and printers, merchants and mechanics.

Though the established church regarded this place to be unconsecrated, for our company it was holy ground, confirming what the poet Robert Southey said about Bunhill Fields being "the Campo Santo of the Dissenters."[3] It was hallowed not by the triumph of Christian knights, who died in battle defending the true faith against the false religion of the beast, but by faithful witnesses who suffered for the gospel, like the Oxford-educated clergyman Edward Bagshaw, whose unswerving loyalty to King Jesus caused him to be arrested by King Charles II for "treasonable practices" and imprisoned for much of the

---

[2] Charles Reed, *History of the Bunhill Fields Burial Ground* (London: Charles Skipper & East, 1893).

[3] Robert Southey, *Common-Place Book*, ed. John Wood Warter, 4 vols. (London: Longman, Brown, Green & Longmans, 1849–1851), 3:161, no. 405.

last decade of his life.[4] The inscription on the grave of the publisher and preacher Francis Smith reads like an obituary, telling his life story:

> Here lyeth the Body of FRANCIS SMITH,
> Bookseller, who in his youth was settled in a separate
> Congregation, where he sustained, between the Years
> of 1659 & 1688, great Persecution by imprisonments,
> Exile, and large Fines laid on Ministers and Meeting-
> Houses, and for printing and promoting Petitions
> for calling of a Parliament, with several things
> against Popery, and after near 40 Imprisonments, he
> was fined 500*l*. for printing and selling the Speech
> of a Noble Peer, and Three times Corporal Punish-
> ment. For the said Fine, he was 5 Years Prisoner in
> the *King's-Bench*: His hard Duress there, utterly
> impaired his health. He dyed House-keeper in the
> Custom-House, *December* the 22d, 1691.[5]

Those buried here have passed on a rich but neglected legacy of sermons, hymns, histories, experiences, biblical commentaries, and theological writings, but what impressed us most were the simple markers that endured wind and weather as a sign for future generations to ask what these stones mean. The inscription on the grave of Margaret Bagshaw attests to the voices of dissent that refused to be domesticated by the oppressive powers that be:

> Here the Wicked cease from Troubling,
> And here the Weary be at Rest;
> Here the Prisoners rest together,
> They hear not the Voice of the Oppressor.[6]

In one sense, these tributes are "monuments of tradition" that bear witness to how Christians in earlier times lived out the faith, and so

---

[4] *Oxford Dictionary of National Biography* (Oxford: Oxford University Press, 2004–2014), s.v. "Edward Bagshaw," by N. H. Keeble.

[5] Inscription on the grave of Francis Smith, December 22, 1691, in *Inscriptions Upon the Tombs*, 17.

[6] Inscription on the tomb of Margaret Bagshaw, February 20, 1692, in *Inscriptions Upon the Tombs*, 27.

they invite contemporary believers to participate with a living tradition by telling the stories of those buried here and learning from their examples.[7] In his elegy on Bunhill Fields, Thomas Gutteridge likened the dissenters' burial grounds to Westminster Abbey and invited visitors to attend to the story told by these monuments:

> Survey the Ground bestrew'd with Tombs and Stones,
> Within it's lin'd with Bodies, Sculls, and Bones.
> What Place with this can run a Parallel?
> Its like an Abbey or Cathedral,
> The Tombs so thick, and Graves the Stones do tell.[8]

But with such a diversity of voices, it might well be asked where to begin such a story. Here the genius of the place provides a clue. At the center of Bunhill Fields, there is a courtyard with three memorials: one for John Bunyan (1628–1688), a second for Daniel Defoe (1660?–1731), and a third for William Blake (1757–1827). As I stood in the fading light, I wondered why these three were chosen to be remembered in the poet's corner of this dissenters' sanctuary and what they might say to those who step into this sacred space. The book of Hebrews concludes with the declaration that since "Jesus also suffered outside the city gate in order to sanctify the people by his own blood," those who follow him must go outside the city "and bear the abuse he endured" (Heb 13:12-13, NRSV). These monuments remembered the lives of saints who suffered because they followed Jesus and like him were forced outside walls in search of another city. I wanted to know how to tell this story.

When Bunhill Fields was preserved by the city of London in 1867 it was noted that the graves of Bunyan and Defoe—"the writers of the two most popular works in the English language"—are here.[9] At the

---

[7] Yves Congar, *The Meaning of Tradition* (San Francisco: Ignatius, 2004), 129–55. James Wm. McClendon Jr. suggests that the telling of the life stories of the saints "can be made to serve as an encouragement and guidance for our own lives in the presence of God." McClendon, *Biography as Theology: How Life Stories Can Remake Today's Theology* (Nashville: Abingdon, 1974), 210.

[8] Thomas Gutteridge, *The Universal Elegy; or A Poem on Bunhill Burial Ground* (London, 1735?), 13, 17.

[9] *Bunhill Fields Burial Ground: Proceedings in Reference to its Preservation* (London: Hamilton, Adams, 1867), 27.

centenary of his death, when the significance of Blake had grown, a new headstone was commissioned and later moved to join the memorials to Bunyan and Defoe. These three have left an influential and enduring literary legacy. Other dissenting voices of note are surely worthy of remembering, but attending to these three, who in history's judgment stand at the center of the dissenting tradition, honors what G. K. Chesterton once called "the democracy of the dead."[10] Yet such a starting point is more than democracy extended through time.[11] It is an attempt to follow the guidance of their wisdom. These monuments in the central courtyard seem to suggest that anyone seeking to understand dissent would do well to start here, for the story waiting to be told bears witness to an identifiable tradition that is more about "the living faith of the dead" than "the dead faith of the living."[12] But for that living faith to be kept alive, it must be remembered.

This book is an exercise in remembering that engages three classic texts of dissent by Bunyan, Defoe, and Blake—*The Pilgrim's Progress*, *Robinson Crusoe*, and *Jerusalem*. Classics like these are inexhaustible. They generate a surplus of meanings and are always in need of deeper and closer readings. They are not mere objects of hermeneutical inquiry but instead possess the power to provoke, challenge, and transform the imagination. And by shattering the boundaries that limit religious experience, they become paradigmatic among the wider community of readers.[13] Yet, unlike monuments etched in stone that offer the same face to those that view them in different times and circumstances, literary works are more like musical orchestrations that resonate in new ways

---

[10] Gilbert K. Chesterton, *Orthodoxy* (New York: Image/Doubleday, 1959), 48.

[11] The description of tradition as "democracy extended through time" belongs to Chesterton, *Orthodoxy*, 47. Alasdair MacIntyre similarly described a tradition as a lively argument extended over time about how the goods and values of that tradition are best understood and defended. MacIntyre, *After Virtue: A Study in Moral Theory* (Notre Dame, Ind.: University of Notre Dame Press, 1981), 175.

[12] Jaroslav Pelikan, *The Christian Tradition: A History of the Development of Doctrine*, vol. 1, *The Emergence of the Catholic Tradition (100–600)* (Chicago: University of Chicago Press, 1971), 9.

[13] The suggestion of *The Pilgrim's Progress*, *Robinson Crusoe*, and *Jerusalem* as classic texts of dissent follows the description by David Tracy, *Analogical Imagination: Christian Theology and the Culture of Pluralism* (New York: Crossroad, 1981), 108–9.

with readers each time they are read. This study then is more than an act of remembering. It is a kind of performance, or perhaps it might more accurately be described as an experiment in reception history that not only examines how these texts were produced and first received but also attends to the evolutionary history of how they have been received in new times and contexts against the shifting horizon of expectations.[14]

These classic works by Bunyan, Defoe, and Blake attest to a tradition of dissent that demands more than attention to the textual structure and the contextual production, for their literary history presupposes an ongoing conversation between the present and the past.[15] And because *The Pilgrim's Progress*, *Robinson Crusoe*, and *Jerusalem* were so portable—and consequently so widely read by popular audiences in times, languages, and cultures very different from the contexts that produced and first received them—these three works became instrumental in disseminating the message of the dissenting tradition far and wide from England to India, China, Africa, North America, the

[14] Reception history as a critical theory has its roots in the work of Hans Robert Jauss, especially his essay "Literary History as a Challenge to Literary Theory," *New Literary History* 2, no. 1 (1970): 7–37; a revised and expanded version appears in *Toward an Aesthetic of Reception*, trans. Timothy Bahti (Minneapolis: University of Minnesota Press, 1982), 3–45. Jauss was a student of Hans Georg Gadamer and was one of the founding members of the Constance school of literary criticism. He shared much in common with his colleague Wolfgang Iser, whose synchronic focus analyzes the phenomenology of the reading experience, but Jauss' primary concern is the diachronic dimension of reading and reception in which a work awakens old memories, stirs hidden emotions, and arouses new expectations. He contends that a text evokes for the readers the "horizon of expectations" that may change over time through the further reception. The chief value of reception history, and in particular by attending to the "changes of horizon," is to enrich the understanding of the text by incorporating new levels of consciousness produced through its impact on subsequent generations of readers. For an excellent collection of essays that address the adaptation of reception from literary theory to cultural and historical studies, see James Machor and Philip Goldstein, eds., *Reception Study: From Literary Theory to Cultural Studies* (New York: Routledge, 2001). For an example of how historians have employed reception theory, see Polly Ha and Patrick Collinson, eds., *The Reception of Continental Reformation in Britain* (New York: Oxford, 2010).

[15] Alasdair MacIntyre described a tradition as a lively argument extended over time about how the goods and values of that tradition are best understood and defended. MacIntyre, *After Virtue*, 175.

Caribbean, and beyond. It might even be argued provocatively that these works do not so much constitute a dissenting tradition as much as they invent one.[16] Tracing the reception of these texts makes a more modest claim than suggesting causality or influence, for, as the history of their reception will show, the dissenting tradition itself is not so much fixed as it is essentially contested.[17] So this study seeks to attend to the horizons of expectation that generated these works and by which they were initially received, but also to the shifting horizons of their continuing reception.

This work, however, is not primarily an exercise of literary interpretation, or critical theory, or historical analysis, as important as those efforts have been to deepening the understanding of these three writers and their writings. This book seeks to tell the story of religious dissent as a polemical and dialectical argument from the seventeenth century to the present, from Bunhill Fields to Plymouth Rock. Its narrative displays the ongoing contestation about the proper mode of dissent from evangelical to political to radical, and more importantly it places Bunyan, Defoe, and Blake, and their writings, within this extended argument. Yet to offer such an account of the past is not motivated simply by a curiosity about what happened, or how to properly situate these authors, or even what might be learned by reading these texts.[18] It begins with the conviction that an understanding of this particular history, one that has been often ignored and diminished as belonging to the losers of history, is necessary for living at this particular moment. It operates with the understanding that the past is not really past but rather is constitutive of the present. To put it simply, this book seeks to

[16] Here I am alluding to a process of invention described by Terrence W. Tilley in which he argues that "traditions are neither made nor found, yet both constructed and given." Tilley, *Inventing Catholic Tradition* (Maryknoll, N.Y.: Orbis, 2000), 15.

[17] W. B. Gallie described an "essentially contested concept" as one for which its definition and use is determined by ongoing disputes and continuing disagreement. Gallie, "Essentially Contested Concept," in *The Importance of Language*, ed. Max Black (Englewood Cliffs, N.J.: Prentice-Hall, 1962), 121-46.

[18] Rowan Williams, *Why Study the Past? The Quest for the Historical Church* (Grand Rapids: Eerdmans, 2005), 6; and Stanley Hauerwas, "The Past Matters Theologically: Thinking Tradition," in *Theologies of Retrieval: An Exploration and Appraisal*, ed. Darren Sarisky (London: T&T Clark, 2017).

show how and why dissent matters, not only as a historical movement that has been laid to rest and memorialized on stone and in texts, but as a vital practice for the good of Christianity today, and, indeed, for the flourishing of free societies.

One of the recurrent themes throughout these chapters is what I call "the apocalyptic imagination." Such an outlook too often gets labeled as "chiliastic," "millenarian," or "otherworldly," and the perspectives of those so motivated are dismissed as wild speculations of overheated brains, producing more heat than light. I challenge that claim by showing the constructive connections between eschatology and politics in the history of dissent. It is the apocalyptic imagination that provides dissenters with a subversive social vision and strengthens their conviction to resist the powers of domestication.[19] Readers will want to be particularly attentive to the differing ways in which Bunyan, Defoe, and Blake reconceive their theological accounts of political nonconformity for new contexts, as well as asking how such a vision might serve as a resource for contemporary Christianity. Yet eschatologically guided imagination has not always resulted in productive social engagement. Even as apocalyptic can be a generative source of democracy, as it will become abundantly clear, its eschatological vision also provides an energetic force for anarchy. The story of dissent, therefore, is both cautionary and instructive. I offer these reflections, not that readers would stop here, but with the hope that they might be moved to engage anew these texts that have the capacity to expand the limits of experience and open the horizons of the imagination to a transformed vision that the voices of undomesticated dissent might arise afresh.

---

[19] As Anathea E. Portier-Young shows, the politics of apocalyptic literature were embedded in an alternative vision of reality that countered the imperial domination system and undercut its ultimacy. Portier-Young, *Apocalypse Against Empire: Theologies of Resistance in Early Judaism* (Grand Rapids: Eerdmans, 2011), 35. This apocalyptic imagination animated the everyday practices employed by dissenters to resist being determined by, and even to subvert, the powers of the dominant culture. For a theoretical account of the subversive tactics of resistance, see Michel de Certeau, *The Practice of Everyday Life*, trans. Steven F. Rendall (Berkeley: University of California Press, 1984), xiv, 18, passim.

1

DOMESTICATING DISSENT

But we simple shepherds that walk on the moor,
In faith, we are near-hands out of the door,
No wonder, as it stands, if we be poor,
For the tith of our lands lies as fallow as the floor,
As ye ken,
> *We are so lamed,*
> *Overtaxed and shamed,*
> *We are made hand-tamed,*
By these gentry-men.[1]

The restoration of the monarchy in England proved to be a time of testing for dissenters, especially those like Vavasor Powell whose Baptist and millenarian convictions threatened the powers of church and state. Refusing to swear an oath of allegiance to any king but Jesus and rejecting the authority of diocesan bishops and the imposition of a common prayer book, Powell was arrested and imprisoned in the summer of 1660.[2] He followed a long line of Baptist dissenters, begin-

---

[1] Wakefield Master, *Second Shepherd's Play*, adapted by Ian Borden (Vancouver: Revelry Theater, 1991), scene 1.14–26.

[2] Powell argued that, in regard to worship, "the Scriptures themselves are a sufficient Directory and Rubrick to the Church of God." He contended that there is no pattern for diocesan bishops in Scripture and more importantly that

ning with Thomas Helwys, who declared that Christians should not avoid persecution, "for the disciples of Christ cannot glorify God and advance his truth better, then by suffering all manner of persecution for it."[3] Powell remained undomesticated in his dissent. Writing to his friends from his cell in Fleet Prison, he urged, "Let us not be troubled that the winde now blowes in our faces, or that like Lazarus we receive our evil things in this world." For, he continued, "[a] day of close discovery and through tryal is come, or coming upon us, and the leaves of profession are like to hide hypocrisy no longer." The only refuge for the coming danger, he warned, was for each Christian to "get Christ . . . to bind thy conscience to peace, and thy affections and flesh to the good Behaviour." Resting in the confidence that his conscience was securely bound, he concluded, "If I may not have liberty to serve Christ, I would have the Glory to suffer for Christ."[4] And suffer he did, remaining a prisoner of conscience for seven long years. When he was finally released, Powell immediately returned to preaching, which again resulted in his arrest and imprisonment. He died in Fleet Prison on October 27, 1670, having spent most of his last eleven years in jail. He was laid to rest in the dissenter burial ground at Bunhill Fields. Etched on his gravestone were these lines, composed by his friend and fellow prisoner Edward Bagshaw, who followed him to a grave in Bunhill Fields the following year:

> In vain oppressors do themselves perplex,
> To find out acts how they the Saints may vex;
> Death spoils their plots, and sets th' oppressed free,
> Thus Vavasor obtained true liberty,
> Christ him releas'd and now he's join'd among
> The martyr'd-souls, with whom he cries, how long?[5]

---

episcopal polity is actually forbidden by the clear teaching of Scripture. Vavasor Powell, *Common-Prayer-Book No Divine Service* (London: Livewell Chapman, 1660), 2 and 16–17.

[3] Thomas Helwys, *A Short Declaration of the Mystery of Iniquity* (1611/1612), ed. Richard Groves (Macon, Ga.: Mercer University Press, 1998), 69 and 209.

[4] Vavasor Powell, *The Bird in the Cage Chirping* (London: L.C., 1661), Epistle Dedicatory and 71–74.

[5] *Bunhill Fields Burial Ground: Proceedings in Reference to its Preservation* (London: Hamilton, Adams, 1867), 83; Thomas Crosby, *The History of the English Baptists*

Milton's account of the angel Abdiel in *Paradise Lost*, who faced Satan and his demonic legions all alone, might have been chosen as a fitting description of undomesticated dissent:

> Among innumerable false, unmov'd,
> Unshak'n, unseduc'd, unterrfi'd
> His Loyaltie he kept, his Love, his Zeale;
> Nor number, nor example with him wrought
> To swerve from truth, or change his constant mind
> Though single. From amidst them forth he passd,
> Long way through hostile scorn, which he susteind
> Superior, nor of violence fear'd aught;
> And with retorted scorn his back he turn'd
> On those proud Towrs to swift destruction doom'd.[6]

This thinly disguised contempt for the ecclesiastical establishment identified Abdiel's faithful stand against Satan as "dissent" and the loyal angels of heaven as his "sect," leaving no doubt in his conviction that truth was on the side of the dissenting minority, for "few sometimes may know, when thousands err."[7] Yet Powell's epitaph bears witness to a different sort of dissenter, not a zealous enthusiast who confronts the hosts of evil all alone, but one of a righteous remnant whose body like the Master was laid to rest with a communion of persecuted saints outside the walls of the city and beyond the reach of the state-established church. Yet it is also an apocalyptic vision of undomesticated dissent rooted in an abiding hope in the victory and vindication of the Lamb who was slain and ever lives, as the lone dissenting voice is joined with the prayers of the martyrs who cry out,

---

(London: The Editor, 1738), 1:381; David Davies, *Vavasor Powell: The Baptist Evangelist of Wales in the Seventeenth Century* (London: Alexander & Shepheard, 1896), 159; Michael Watts, *The Dissenters*, vol. 1: *From the Reformation to the French Revolution* (Oxford: Clarendon, 1978), 237–38.

[6] Milton, *Paradise Lost*, V.899–907, in *John Milton Complete Poems and Major Prose*, ed. Merritt Y. Hughes (New York: Macmillan, 1957), 323.

[7] Milton, *Paradise Lost*, VI.143–49, in *John Milton Complete Poems*, 327. Milton observed, "I never knew that time in England when men of truest religion were not counted secretaries [sectaries]." *Eikonoklastes, Preface*, in *John Milton Complete Poems*, 787.

"How long, O Lord, holy and true, dost thou not judge and avenge our blood on them that dwell on the earth?" (Rev 6:10[8]).

THE DISSENTER TRADITION

Dissent has proven notoriously difficult to define. Along with its synonyms "separatist" and "nonconformist," the term "dissenter" covers a wide range of groups from Presbyterians on the right flank to Quakers on the left with Baptists and Independents in the middle. It also includes more radical movements from Familists and Fifth Monarchists, to Levellers and Diggers, as well as Ranters and Muggletonians.[9] Dissenters diverged widely in theological outlook, often within the same group, though they all shared a common bond as minorities who were first persecuted and later tolerated by the dominant majority in the established church. Through the centuries, the basic request of dissenters has simply been "to be left alone to worship God in their own way."[10] This negative way of understanding dissent has its roots in "Protestantism," which received its name on April 19, 1529, when John of Saxony read a letter dissenting from the majority decision at the Second Diet of Speyer, saying:

> We protest by these present, before God, our only Creator, Preserver, Redeemer, and Saviour, and who will one day be our Judge, as well as before all men and all creatures, that we, for us and for our people, neither consent nor adhere in any manner whatsoever to the proposed decree, in anything that is contrary to God, to His Holy Word, to our right conscience, to the salvation of our souls, and to the last decree of Speyer.[11]

---

[8] Unless otherwise noted, all biblical translations are from the KJV.

[9] Geoffrey F. Nuttall, *The Holy Spirit in Puritan Faith and Experience* (Oxford: Basil Blackwell, 1946), 1–19.

[10] Watts, *Dissenters*, 1:2.

[11] James Aitken Wylie, *History of Protestantism* (London: Cassell, 1800), 1:550–51. There is no full English translation of *Die Bescherung und Protestation*, written to protest the majority edict of the Second Diet of Speyer in 1529. The German text of the *Protestation* may be found in Julius Ney, *Geschichte des Reichstages zu Speyer im Jahre 1529: Mit einem Anhange ungedruckter Akten und Briefe* (Hamburg: Angentur des Rauhen Hauses, 1880), 50–51. Paul Tillich argued that the Protestant principle that had its origins in the Second Diet of Speyer "contains the divine and human protest

To be sure, dissent entails the courage to say "No!" But it is about more than just the "No!" Dissent is not simply a case of whining against oppression, resisting institutional corruption, demurring against the affirmations of others.[12] To define dissenters merely as "noisy nay-sayers" supposes that if all oppressive restraints were removed, then dissent would simply fade away. Such an account ignores the deep underlying beliefs and practices that not only united historic dissenting communities but were shared across communities. Dissent is also grounded in a profound "Yes!" to Jesus Christ as Lord, to God alone as sovereign over the conscience, and to the gathered community where Jesus Christ reigns and is discerned together.[13]

Dissent in the context of English Protestantism has roots in a particular understanding of the royal office of Christ to whom all, even earthly monarchs, are accountable. This theological conviction of Christ as King gave rise to the dissenting practice of resisting and being subject to "the powers that be" (Rom 13:1). It is exemplified by the Scottish Presbyterian Henry Melville, who once, in a private meeting with James VI of Scotland (later James I of England), upbraided the king, calling him "God's sillie vassal." Taking James by the sleeve, he declared:

> I mon [must] tell yow, thair is twa Kings and twa Kingdomes in Scotland. Thair is Chryst Jesus the King, and his Kingdome the Kirk, whase subject King James the Saxt is, and of whose kingdome nocht a king, nor a lord, nor a heid, bot a member.[14]

---

against any absolute claim made for a relative reality, even if this claim is made by a Protestant church." He continued, "[T]he Protestant principle is the judge of every religious and cultural reality including the religion and culture which calls itself 'Protestant.'" Tillich, *The Protestant Era*, trans. James Luther Adams (Chicago: University of Chicago Press, 1957), 163.

[12] Edwin Scott Gaustad, *Dissent in American Religion*, rev. ed. (Chicago: University of Chicago Press, 2006), 4.

[13] Lee Canipe defines religious dissent along similar lines, as "faithful, conscientious obedience to God." Canipe, *Loyal Dissenters: Reading Scripture and Talking Freedom with 17th-Century English Baptists* (Macon, Ga.: Smyth & Helwys, 2016), 139 and 146–47.

[14] Mellvill, *The Autobiography and Diary of Mr. James Mellvill*, ed. Robert Pitcairn (Edinburgh: Woodrow Society, 1842), 370.

Protestant dissenters like Melville followed this Reformed tradition that strictly limited the power of secular authorities. Robert Browne, the first dissenter to call for separation from the Church of England, took this conviction of reformation a step further, acknowledging the sovereignty of the queen in civil matters, but he argued that the power keys of the kingdom to bind and loose, to retain and remit, were given not to civil magistrates but to gospel ministers (Matt 18:18; John 20:23). Browne believed that the ecclesial government could not be reformed from within because the established church was under the sway of popish powers, so he argued for establishing independent congregations without waiting for the support of the civil authorities.[15] The parish churches "are not Jerusalem," he exclaimed. "For beholde, can they be Jerusalem, which is called the Throne of the Lorde, when there the Bishops sitt as on the Throne of Antichriste?"[16] Though Browne later returned to the Church of England, many of his followers remained in separation.

The most articulate voice of early English dissent was Henry Barrow, who rejected the imperial establishment of the church and contended instead for the church as a gathered community that lived under the reign of Christ and maintained discipline according to Christ's rule.[17] He was arrested in 1587 for his dissenting views and locked away in London's Fleet Prison. The separation of powers affirmed by Barrow stands in stark contrast to the magisterial flattery of Lancelot Andrewes, the preeminent English preacher of the day and avowed monarchist, who averred:

> They that rise against the King, are God's enemies; for God and the King are so in league, such a knot, so straight between them, as one

---

[15] Robert Browne, *A Treatise of Reformation without Tarying for Anie*, in Harrison and Browne, *The Writings of Robert Harrison and Robert Browne*, ed. Albert Peel and Leland H. Carlson, vol. 2 of *Elizabethan Nonconformist Texts* (London: George Allen & Unwin, 1953), 152–70.

[16] Robert Browne, *A Treatise upon the 23. of Matthewe*, in Harrison and Browne, *Writings of Robert Harrison and Robert Browne*, 206.

[17] Henry Barrow, *A True Description Out of the Worde of God, Of the Visible Church* (1589), A2; reprinted in Barrow, *The Writings of Henry Barrow*, ed. Leland H. Carlson, vol. 3 of *Elizabethan Nonconformist Texts* (London: Allen & Unwin, 1962), 214–16.

cannot be enemy to the one, but he must be to the other. This is the knot. They are by God, of or from God, for or instead of God. . . . In His place they sit, His person they represent, they are taken into the fellowship of the same name. *Ego dixi*, He hath said it, and we may be bold to say it after him, They are gods; and what would we more? Then must their enemies be God's enemies.[18]

It was a remarkable statement that identified an inseparable unity between God and the king, but more importantly it offered a theological support for an established national church under the control of a divinely ordained national monarch.[19] According to this rule, to reject the sovereignty of the crown over the church was tantamount to rejecting Christ and his church.

Andrewes and other clergy called on Barrow and his fellow dissenters in jail several times during March 1590, not to make pastoral visits, but, as Barrow later observed, "to fish from them som matter, wheruppon they might accuse them to theire holy fathers the bishops, who thereupon might delyver them, as convicts of heresie unto the secular powers."[20] The meeting on March 18 began cordially, but,

---

[18] Lancelot Andrewes, sermon August 5, 1607, in *Ninety-Six Sermons*, 5 vols. (Oxford: John Henry Parker, 1841), 4:3–14. The sermon text was, "And Cushi answered, The enemies of my lord the King, and all that rise against thee to do thee hurt, be as that young man is" (2 Sam 18:32).

[19] In his commentary on Ps 82:6 ("I have said, Ye are gods"), John Calvin states that rulers are bestowed with both God's authority and name, but he adds that the dignity with which rulers are invested is temporal, and thus wicked rulers cannot escape judgment, because like all other human beings they stand under the judgment of God. Calvin writes, "The government of the world has been committed to them upon the distinct understanding that they themselves also must one day appear at the judgment-seat of heaven to render up an account. The dignity, therefore, with which they are clothed is only temporary, and will pass away with the fashion of the world." Henry Melville's warning to James VI followed Calvin's teaching on the judgment of secular authorities, whereas Lancelot Andrewes regarded the divine authority of the king to be more than a mere temporal arrangement. Calvin, *Commentary on the Book of Psalms*, trans. James Anderson (Grand Rapids: Eerdmans, 1949), 335.

[20] Henry Barrow, "A Collection of Certaine Sclaunderous Articles Gyven out by the Bisshops Against Such Faithful Christians," in Greenwood and Barrow, *The Writings of John Greenwood 1587–1590, together with the Joint Writings of Henry Barrow and John Greenwood 1587–1590*, ed. Leland H. Carlson, vol. 4 of *Elizabethan Nonconformist Texts* (London: Allen & Unwin, 1962), 110.

when Barrow asked that their conference be determined by Scripture, Andrewes unleashed a torrent of hostile questions, accusing Barrow of savoring "a pryvat spyrit." Barrow answered, "This is the spirit of Christ and his apostles, and moste publique they submitted theire doctrines to the trial of all men," and, he continued, "so do I." But then Andrewes crossed beyond the pale, suggesting that Barrow should actually be happy for his imprisonment, adding that "the solitarie and contemplative life" is the one he himself would choose. It was a clever but cruel comment. Barrow had spent three years in deplorable conditions, separated from his family, friends, and church. "You speak philosophically," Barrow replied, "but not christianly." For, he explained, "[s]o sweete is the harmonie of God's grace unto me in the congregation, and the conversation of the saints at all tymes, as I think my self as a sparrow on the howse toppe when I am exiled from them." Then, like Nathan the prophet before King David, Barrow asked, "But could you be content also, Mr. Androes, to be kept from exercise and ayre so long together?"[21] It was for want of witty rhetoric that dissenters like Barrow used plain speech, lacking "that glib and oily art" that court preachers like Andrewes had mastered.[22] Yet, unlike them, he spoke the unvarnished truth.

The ranks of dissenters were soon to swell as a result of the conference at Hampton Court called in January 1604 by King James I. The so-called Millenary Petition presented to the king by "the godly" clergy upon his ascension to the throne of England objected to such practices as the wearing of the surplice, making the sign of the cross at baptism, and kneeling at communion as remnants of Roman Catholicism that

---

[21] Henry Barrow, Conference No. 3 (March 18, 1589/1590), in Greenwood and Barrow, *Writings of John Greenwood 1587–1590*, 141–43.

[22] Borrowing a line from Cordelia, the youngest daughter of King Lear in Shakespeare's play, who unlike her duplicitous sisters told her father the truth that she loved her father "according to [her] bond, no more nor less." When pressed why she did not fawn over her father as her sisters did, she answered, "I want that glib and oily art." *King Lear*, act 1, scene 1, lines 93 and 226, in *The Complete Works of Shakespeare*, ed. David Bevington (Glenview, Ill.: Scott, Foresman, 1980), 1176. The play ends tragically with Edgar's speech: "The weight of this sad time we must obey, / Speak what we feel, not what we ought to say." *King Lear*, act 5, scene 3, line 330, in *Complete Works of Shakespeare*, 1215.

must be purged from the Church of England. Over the course of the conference, it became increasingly clear that James had no patience for "troublesome spirits" who seemed never content with civil or ecclesiastical matters. It also became clear that the Geneva Bible favored by puritans was a peculiar source of irritation for the king. He especially took umbrage with its antiroyalist explanatory notes, like the one in Acts 5 that suggested that "when they commande, or forbid us anything contrary to the worde of God," the Christian's duty is "to obey God then men," or the declaration that the disobedience of the Hebrew midwives to Pharaoh was "lawful."[23] Here, the Geneva Bible followed the line of John Calvin that "earthly princes lay aside all their power when they rise up against God"—Calvin added, "We ought rather utterly to defy than to obey them."[24] James preferred the Royalist renderings of Romans 13 that called for obedience to the higher powers and ascribed damnation to those who resist them. It was a tradition of interpretation stated classically in the homily "Against Disobedience and Willful Rebellion" appointed to be read in the churches throughout England, which, citing Deuteronomy 26, described the earthly monarch as "the Lord's anointed" who could not be opposed. It further asserted that

> neither comeliness of personage, neither nobility, nor favour of the people, no nor the favour of the King himself, can save a rebel from due punishment; God the King of all kings being so offended with him, that rather than he should lack due execution for his treason, every tree by the way will be a gallows or gibbet unto him, and the hair of his own head will be unto him instead of an halter, to hang him up with, rather than he should lack one: a fearful example of God's punishment, good people, to consider![25]

James left no room for doubt when on the final day of the conference he announced his plan for uncompromising puritans, famously

---

[23] *The Bible and Holy Scriptures* (Geneva: Rouland Hall, 1560; repr., Madison: University of Wisconsin Press, 1969), Acts 5:29 and Exod 1:19-21.

[24] John Calvin, *Commentary on Daniel* (Grand Rapids: Eerdmans, 1948), 382.

[25] John Griffiths, ed., *The Homilies Appointed to Be Read in Churches* (London, 1623; repr., Brynmill, U.K.: Preservation Press, 2006), 420. The sermon invokes Rom 13 and 1 Sam 26 as biblical warrant for divinely ordained monarchy.

decrying, "I will make them conform themselves, or else I will harry them out of the land, or else do worse."[26]

The enactment of the *Constitutions and Canons* of the church in 1604 closed the loopholes for Presbyterians and provided an effective tool for expelling nonconformists, requiring all ministers to subscribe to the supremacy of the crown, the Book of Common Prayer and the Bishops, and the Thirty-Nine Articles.[27] It also called for reporting on private conventicles, declaring:

> No Priests or Ministers of the word of God, nor any other persons, shall meete together in any private house, or elsewhere, to consult upon any matter or course to bee taken by them, or upon their motion or direction by any other, which may any way tend to the impeaching or depraving of the doctrine of the Church of England, or of the Booke of Common Prayer, or of any part of the government and Discipline now established in the Church of England, under paine of Excommunication.[28]

For nonconformist ministers like John Smyth and John Robinson, who had gathered a separate congregation in 1606 at Gainsborough, near Lincoln, the pressures of imperial and ecclesial surveillance became too much. They decided to make haste out of Babylon seeking the liberty of the New Jerusalem.[29] The Robinson group, known as the Pilgrim

---

[26] William Barlow, *The Summe and Substance of the Conference* (London: V[alentine] S[immes], 1604), 83. Mark H. Curtis, "The Hampton Court Conference and Its Aftermath," *History* 46, no. 156 (1961): 1–16; Frederick Shriver, "Hampton Court Revisited: James I and the Puritans," *Journal of Ecclesiastical History* 33, no. 1 (1982): 48–71; and Patrick Collinson, "The Jacobean Religious Settlement: The Hampton Court Conference," in *Before the English Civil War: Essays in Early Stuart Politics and Government*, ed. Howard Tomlinson (New York: St. Martin's, 1984), 27–51.

[27] *Constitutions and Canons Ecclesiastical*, 2nd ed. (London: Robert Barker, 1604), 36 and 38.

[28] *Constitutions and Canons Ecclesiastical*, 73. Canons 11–12 proscribe maintaining religious conventicles without the king's authority or submitting to the constitutions of such assemblies or congregations under the penalty of excommunication ipso facto, adding that none shall "be restored untill they repent, and publikely revoke those their wicked and Anabaptisticall errors."

[29] Champlain Burrage, *The Early English Dissenters in Light of Recent Research* (Cambridge: Cambridge University Press, 1912), 1:231–32; and Nicholas Bunker,

Church, subsequently journeyed from Leiden to New England, where they established Plymouth Colony. The Smyth community settled in Amsterdam, where they divided, with one group remaining under his ministry and another returning home under the leadership of Thomas Helwys, a wealthy layman. They established the first Baptist congregation on English soil. Shortly after their return, Helwys made a case for their churchly status, arguing in *The Mystery of Iniquity*, published in 1612, that Christ made a new covenant with those that believe and are baptized.[30] The subversive politics of the Baptists is reflected in a note to James I that Helwys inscribed on the flyleaf. It reads, "The king is a mortal man and not God, therefore has no power over the immortal souls of his subjects, to make laws and ordinances for them, and to set spiritual lords over them."[31]

The majority of dissenters attempted to remain in the Church of England. They were often derisively characterized as "puritans," people who, as a contemporary commentator described them, held to a "strict life and precise opinions, which cannot be hated for anything but their singularity in zeal and piety."[32] Despite what others thought about them, these conforming puritans perceived themselves simply as Protestants, holding out hope of further reform of the church.[33] The more zealous among them "regarded themselves as 'the godly,' a minority of genuinely true believers in an otherwise lukewarm or

---

Making Haste from Babylon: The Mayflower Pilgrims and Their World (New York: Vintage, 2011), 170–77.

[30] Helwys, *Mystery of Iniquity*, 132.

[31] Helwys, *Mystery of Iniquity*, vi. There is no evidence that Helwys' text with its personal message ever reached the king.

[32] Henry Parker, *A Discourse concerning Puritans*, 2nd ed. (London: Printed for Robert Bostock, 1641), 58–60, 11. The suggestion that these were Protestants with "precise opinions" prompted Theodore Dwight Bozeman to suggest that "precisionism" might be a more appropriate term than "puritanism" to describe the strict Protestantism of late Tudor and early Stuart England. Bozeman, *The Precisionist Strain: Disciplinary Religion and Antinomian Backlash in Puritanism to 1638* (Chapel Hill: University of North Carolina Press, 2004), 3–7.

[33] Patrick Collinson, *From Cranmer to Sancroft* (New York: Hambledon Continuum, 2006), 122.

corrupt mass."[34] Some of these nonconforming puritans, following the example of Browne, found warrant in the call to "come out from among them, and be ye separate" (2 Cor 6:17), leading them to gather independent congregations. But dissent often had as much to do with class as with zeal and piety. Presbyterians like Thomas Edwards saw themselves closer to the Church of England, theologically and socially, and were keen to characterize Baptists and other more extreme dissenters as "Mechanicks taking upon them to preach and baptize, as Smiths, Taylors, Shoomakers, Pedlars, Weavers, &c."[35] A broadsheet published in London in 1646 provided images and descriptions of "the most dangerous and damnable tenets" spread by "mechannick spirits." It claimed that the most egregious heresies were to be found among the working class: confectioners, smiths, shoemakers, tailors, saddlers, porters, box-makers, soap-boilers, glovers, meal-men, chicken-men, and button-makers.[36] It suggested that dissent sometimes had as much to do with social location as theological vision.

Scholars seeking to tell the story of dissent face the challenge that dissenters could differ as much from one sect to another, and even among members of the same sect, as from the established church.[37]

---

[34] Peter Lake, *Anglicans and Puritans? Presbyterianism and English Conformist Thought from Whitgift to Hooker* (London: Unwin Hyman, 1988), 7.

[35] Thomas Edwards, *Gangraena: The First and Second Part*, 3rd ed. (London: Ralph Smith, 1646), I.29. See also Ann Hughes, *Gangraena and the Struggle for the English Revolution* (Oxford: Oxford University Press, 2004).

[36] *A Discovery of the Most Dangerous and Damnable Tenets That Have Been Spread Within This Few Years By Erronious, Heritical, and Mechannick Spirits* (London, 1647). The broadsheet lists forty-nine erroneous-heretical tenets of mechanic preachers. All sects are lumped together in a boiling stew of seditious and schismatic dissent.

[37] In his important study on the emergence of antinomianism, David R. Como argues against historians like Christopher Hill and Patrick Collinson, who have tried to provide a unified account of puritanism. Como contends that puritanism was not a "homogeneous ideology" but a "fractured landscape." Como, *Blown by the Spirit: Puritanism and the Emergence of an Antinomian Underground in Pre-Civil-War England* (Stanford: Stanford University Press, 2004), 10–32. Como here extends his earlier research: see David R. Como and Peter Lake, "'Orthodoxy' and Its Discontents: Dispute Settlement and the Production of 'Consensus' in the London (Puritan) 'Underground,'" *Journal of British Studies* 39, no. 1 (2000): 34–70. According to this account, dissenting movements emerged out of the unstable and volatile social and religious context of hyperstrophic puritanism that existed in the liminal space between

One way to account for a continuity among dissenters over time is to point to their shared socioeconomic context. Such an approach is offered by social historians, who hypothesize that dissenters formed a "continuing underground tradition" that flowed through English society like "leaden pipes in the ground."[38] Another way of finding commonality is to stress the family resemblance and shared traits among divergent dissenting groups.[39] Still another method is to provide an encyclopedic overview of all things pertaining to dissent.[40] Although the social, genealogical, and encyclopedic approaches have contributed significantly to an understanding of dissent, there is another mode of inquiry about the ways in which its concepts, ideas, and mind-set may be understood without reducing religious beliefs to economic realities or deconstructing a unified account of history as a chronological series of events arising from a single starting point.[41] This alternative way construes religious dissent as a particular tradition within the

orthodoxy and heresy in the seventeenth century. Peter Lake, *The Boxmaker's Revenge: "Orthodoxy," "Heterodoxy" and the Politics of the Parish in Early Stuart London* (Stanford: Stanford University Press, 2001), 397–404. Lake argues the identification of dissenting religion as a "continuing underground tradition" is reductionistic and too simplistic to account for on-the-ground expressions that were more "acts of creative bricolage, kaleidoscopic combinations and recombinations of ideological materials, drawn from a number of sources." *Boxmaker's Revenge*, 400.

[38] Hill, *The Collected Essays of Christopher Hill*, 3 vols. (Amherst: University of Massachusetts Press, 1986), 2:107. See also Edward Palmer Thompson, *The Making of the English Working Class* (Middlesex: Penguin, 1970), 28–58.

[39] Watts, *Dissenters*, vol. 1; and Irvin Buckwalter Horst, *The Radical Brethren: Anabaptism and the English Reformation* (Nieuwkoop: B. De Graaf, 1972). See also Burrage, *Early English Dissenters*; and David Bogue and James Bennett, *History of Dissenters: From the Revolution to the Year 1808*, 2nd ed. (London: F. Westley & A. H. Davis, 1833).

[40] An example of the encyclopedic approach is *Bibliotheca Dissidentium*, a series of twenty-seven completed volumes (1980–present) of sixteenth-century nonconformist writings, largely in Latin, with scholarly introductions, essays, and notations in French, German, and English (general editor André Séguenny in collaboration with Jean Rott and Martin Rothkegel, *Bibliotheca Dissidentium* [Baden-Baden: Valentin Koerner, 1980–present]). See also Robert Pope, ed., *T&T Clark Companion to Nonconformity* (London: T&T Clark, 2013).

[41] Alasdair MacIntyre, *Three Rival Versions of Moral Enquiry: Encyclopaedia, Genealogy, and Tradition* (Notre Dame, Ind.: University of Notre Dame Press, 1990).

history of the Christian church, growing out of English Protestant-ism. Such an account does not seek to explain dissent as a homogenous group with a unified set of beliefs but rather recognizes its polemical and dialectical nature. To regard dissent as a tradition in this sense is to understand it as a lively argument extended over time about how the goods and values of the tradition are best understood and defend-ed.[42] A tradition-dependent mode of inquiry therefore attends to the enacted narrative that is the embodiment, in actions and transactions, of actual social life.[43] That narrative of the dissenter tradition found expression in John Foxe's enormously popular and hugely influential book *Acts and Monuments*, first published in 1563.[44]

Not only did Foxe's book (known commonly as the *Book of Mar-tyrs*) provide dissenters with the basic source material that enabled them to tell their version of ecclesiastical history. It offered a particular theological perspective that was embodied in the lives of the Marian martyrs (1555–1558). Foxe included many documents, like John Phil-pot's "Letter to the Christian Congregation, exhorting them to refrain from the idolatrous Service of the Papists," which he wrote from King's Bench Prison in 1555 as he awaited execution. Philpot urged his readers not to be deceived by the dissimulation that they could keep their faith to themselves "and dissemble with antichrist."[45] He emphatically urged them to obey God's call to come out of Babylon (Rev 18:8)—by which he meant the false church of Rome imposed on

---

[42] Alasdair MacIntyre, *After Virtue: A Study in Moral Theory* (Notre Dame, Ind.: University of Notre Dame Press, 1981), 175.

[43] MacIntyre, *Three Rival Versions*, 80.

[44] Barrington Raymond White, *The English Separatist Tradition: From the Mar-ian Martyrs to the Pilgrim Fathers* (London: Oxford University Press, 1971), 1–19.

[45] Calvin's repeated criticism of religious dissimulation that separated faith from action, which he called Nicodemism, was perpetuated in Foxe's *Acts and Monuments*. See Kenneth Joseph Woo, "'Newter'-ing the Nicodemite: Reception of John Calvin's *Quatre* Sermons (1552) in Sixteenth-Century England" (ThD diss., Duke University, 2015); David F. Wright, "Why Was Calvin So Severe a Critic of Nicodemism?" in *Calvinus Evangelii Propugnator*, ed. David F. Wright, A. N. Lane, and Jon Balserak (Grand Rapids: CRC Product Services, 2006), 66–90; Carlos Eire, "Calvin and Nico-demism: A Reappraisal," *Sixteenth Century Journal* 10, no. 1 (1979), 45–69; and Eire, "Prelude to Sedition: Calvin's Attack on Nicodemism and Religious Compromise," *Archiv für Reformationsgeschichte* 76 (1985): 120–145.

England by Queen Mary—and to withdraw from those who walk disorderly (2 Thess 3:9). He also admonished them not to trust that their conscience would properly guide them if they continued to worship in the idolatrous (Roman Catholic) Church, because a good conscience would not permit true Christians to participate in such false worship. He exhorted them to remember that the conscience "cannot be good, unless it be directed after the knowledge of God's word."[46] Foxe's *Book of Martyrs* became standard reading for puritans, both privately and in communal gatherings. It was important because its chronological apocalyptic framework based on the book of Revelation enabled dissenters to tell their story in such a way that connected their struggles back to the apostles and to Jesus himself. It also provided an account of congregations that met secretly during the time of Mary's apostate rule, giving later separatists analogues for their congregational ecclesiology.[47] But, most importantly, it established the apocalyptic imagination within the dissenting tradition as the primary means of resistance to the powers of the beast.[48]

THE APOCALYPTIC IMAGINATION

Arthur Dent was the rector of a parish church in Essex. He was a popular preacher, but he was no extreme puritan. Dent prayed for God's blessings and protection of the king and his government.[49] But the seeds of dissent continued to grow, and by 1584 he ran into trouble with the diocesan bishop John Aylmer for refusing to wear the surplice or to make the sign of the cross at baptism. Dent was one of twenty-seven

[46] Foxe, *The Acts and Monuments of John Foxe: A New and Complete Edition*, ed. Stephen Reed Cattley, 7 vols. (London: Seeley & Burnside, 1837–1841), 7:686–90.

[47] Patrick Collinson, *The Elizabethan Puritan Movement* (Oxford: Clarendon, 1967), 24; and White, *English Separatist*, 14–18.

[48] Richard Bauckham, *Tudor Apocalypse: Sixteenth Century Apocalypticism, Millennarianism and the English Reformation* (Abingdon, Oxford: Sutton Courtenay, 1978), 11–14; Paul Christianson, *Reformers and Babylon: English Apocalyptic Visions from the Reformation to the Eve of the Civil War* (Toronto: University of Toronto Press, 1978), 39–46; and Katharine R. Firth, *The Apocalyptic Tradition in Reformation Britain, 1530–1645* (Oxford: Oxford University Press, 1979), 69–110.

[49] Arthur Dent, *The Plaine Mans Path to Heaven*, 15th ed. (Belfast: North of Ireland Book and Tract Depository, 1859), 318–19, 326–27.

ministers who refused to subscribe the declaration "that there is nothing contained in the Book of Common Prayer contrary to the word of
God." The dissenters declaimed, "We do protest in the sight of God,
who searcheth all hearts, that we do not refuse from a desire to dissent,
or from any sinister affection, but in the fear of God, and from the
necessity of conscience."[50] Dent's book *The Plaine Mans Path-way to
Heaven* (1601) was influential for generations of dissenters, including
John Bunyan. In it Dent pleaded with God Almighty to pour down
the vials of wrath upon the kingdom of the beast so that "their riches,
wealth, credit, and authority dry up every day more and more as the
river Euphrates."[51] He was thinking of the Roman Catholic Church
and its allied states of Italy and Spain. Dent later published *The Ruine
of Rome*, a commentary on the book of Revelation, in which he argued
that Rome was Antichrist.[52] Though the apocalyptic imagination of
puritans like Dent was fixed on the Church of Rome, it was not long
before dissenters began to see Antichrist in the Church of England.
The pattern for dissenters like Dent seeing history in apocalyptic terms
began with John Bale's book *The Image of Bothe Churches* (1548).[53] Following an earlier Wyclifite tradition, Bale described the millennium
as a period of a thousand years beginning with Christ's birth when
Satan was bound. After this time of restraint, the devil was loosed in
the papacy. According to this narration of history, the book of Revelation tells the ongoing story of how this false church of Antichrist
continues to persecute the true church that loves and teaches the word
of God until the final defeat of Satan. Bale's apocalyptic outlook found
expression in Foxe's *Acts and Monuments*, which became the basic hermeneutical lens for generations of dissenting Protestants.[54]

One of the most significant influences on the apocalyptic imagination of dissenters on both sides of the Atlantic was Thomas Brightman's

---

[50] "To the Reader," in Dent, *Plaine Mans Path to Heaven*, vi.

[51] Dent, *Plaine Mans Path to Heaven*, 317–18, 324.

[52] Arthur Dent, *The Ruine of Rome* (London: W.I. for Simon Waterson and
Richard Banckworth, 1607).

[53] John Bale, *The Image of Bothe Churches* (1548), in *Select Works of John Bale*, ed.
Henry Christmas (Cambridge: Cambridge University Press, 1849), 249–640.

[54] Bauckham, *Tudor Apocalypse*, 28–33, 60–64, and 73–88.

Apocalypsis Apocalypseos.[55] Brightman was a fellow at Queens' College, Cambridge, in the 1580s, where he was associated with a group of dissenters, including the controversial Francis Johnson. Though Brightman was a proponent of the reform of the English church along Presbyterian lines, he served as rector of a church in Bedfordshire from 1592 until his death in 1607. His posthumously published *Revelations on Revelation* first appeared in English in 1611 and went through multiple editions until 1644. It drew from the apocalyptic imagination of Bale and Foxe but adapted their millennial expectations to an Augustinian historicism.[56] Brightman's account divided church history into seven periods from the apostolic era to the present. The Laodicean age represented the lukewarm, half-reformed Church of England. These periods depicted the gradual corruption of the church that began with Constantine and continued until it became fully apostate in the Roman Catholic Church. Brightman saw, enacted in the apocalyptic visions of John, the slow process toward a recovery of apostolic faith begun by Wycliffe and the Protestant Reformers, but the work was not yet complete, for vestiges of Antichrist still held sway in episcopal polity, formal liturgy, and lax discipline. Brightman believed that the way to retrieve apostolicity was through the recovery of an apocalyptic

---

[55] Thomas Brightman, *Apocalypsis Apocalypseos, a Revelation of the Apocalypse* (Amsterdam: Iudocus Hondius & Hendrick Laurenss, 1611).

[56] Augustine rejected both the chiliastic view of the early church and the Eusebian realized eschatology in favor of his dynamic eschatology of the two cities. Augustine, *City of God*, 15.2, trans. Henry Bettenson (New York: Penguin Books, 1984), 597–98. He suggested the millennium might be identified with the entire Christian era. Augustine, *City of God*, 20.7, 908. Drawing from the Donatist theologian Tyconius, Augustine developed an eschatological ecclesiology that described the church as a mixed body (*corpus permixtum*). Augustine, *On Christian Doctrine*, 3.32, trans. Marcus Dods, in *Nicene and Post-Nicene Fathers*, 1st series (Grand Rapids: Eerdmans, 1979), 2:569. The two cities are intermingled in the temporal age (*saeculum*) as wheat and tares, and they must await the eschaton for separation. Here, the eschatology of the two cities overlaps with the ecclesiology of two bodies as Augustine identified the church (*ecclesia*) and the kingdom (*regnum*). The mixed kingdom is the church "as it now is" in this evil age, and the unmixed kingdom is the church "as it will be" destined for the eternal age to come (20.9). Thus, the church is the city of God in pilgrimage. So when Augustine identified the church and the millennium, it was in this mixed eschatological sense.

view of the New Jerusalem on earth. Yet, in this vision of the apocalypse, looming on the horizon was not an imminent end of history but rather the complete conquest of the Catholic Church, the conversion of the Jews, and the restoration of apostolic Christianity, which would result in a millennium of true religion on earth and the fulfillment of the Presbyterian mission.[57]

Whereas Brightman located the millennium in the past, Joseph Mede contended that it described events yet to come in the future. His influential work *Clavis Apocalyptica* (the Latin edition was published in 1627, and an English translation was published posthumously in 1643) declared that the prophecy of the New Jerusalem would be imminently fulfilled, with the expectation that Christ would return and reign with the saints on earth for a thousand years.[58] Though Mede shared with puritans the view of Rome as Antichrist and the necessity of godliness, he remained loyal to the Church of England and supportive of Archbishop Laud. Yet his millennial scheme, while politically restrained, provided a framework for more extreme and seditious expressions of chiliastic interpretation.[59] Mede did not

---

[57] *Oxford Dictionary of National Biography*, s.v. "Thomas Brightman," by Theodore Dwight Bozeman; Peter Toon, *Puritans, the Millennium, and the Future of Israel* (Cambridge: James Clarke, 2003), 26–32; and Bauckham, *Tudor Apocalypse*, 222–24.

[58] Joseph Mede, *The Key of the Revelation*, trans. Richard More (London: R.B., 1643), part 2, 122–23. Christianson, *Reformers and Babylon*, 124–29.

[59] Chiliasm was the prevailing view among Christians for the first three centuries. They believed that the physical return of Christ to earth would be followed by a literal thousand-year reign with the saints (Rev 20:1–10). Papias was exuberant in his vision of the millennial kingdom where each grape vine will have "ten thousand branches, and in each branch ten thousand twigs, and in each true twig ten thousand shoots, and in every one of the shoots ten thousand clusters, and on every one of the clusters ten thousand grapes, and every grape when pressed will give five-and-twenty metretes of wine." Papias, *Fragments*, IV, in *The Ante-Nicene Fathers* (Grand Rapids: Eerdmans, 1979), 1:153. Irenaeus defended Papias' chiliasm against the gnostics who denied the resurrection of the body and the earthly kingdom. Irenaeus of Leon, *Against Heresies*, 5.33.4, in *Ante-Nicene Fathers*, 1:563. Tertullian likewise averred the chiliastic view of a physical kingdom in Jerusalem. He stated that "we do confess that a kingdom is promised to us upon the earth, although before heaven, only in another state of existence; inasmuch as it will be after the resurrection for a thousand years in the divinely-built city of Jerusalem, 'let down from heaven,' which the apostle also calls 'our mother from above;' and, while declaring that our *politeuma*, or citizenship, is in

think himself to be promoting heterodoxy, but rather he believed he was retrieving the faith of the early church. His ideas were mediated through his students: Thomas Goodwin, the popular preacher and Cromwell's chaplain; Henry More, author of *A Modest Enquiry into the Mystery of Iniquity*, which curated and developed his teacher's writings; and to a lesser extent even the eminent poet and politician John Milton, who though not Mede's pupil was a student at Cambridge when he taught.[60] The popular appeal of the millennialism that Mede propagated soon led to it becoming the prevailing eschatological outlook among English Protestants. In most respects the eschatology of nonseparating and separating puritans was very much alike.[61] Yet there was one significant difference that marked the divide between them. Conforming puritans equated Rome with Babylon, the false church of Antichrist, but nonconforming separatists ascribed these same images to the Church of England, with some suggesting that it epitomized the lukewarm church of Laodicea or that the bishops were Antichrist.[62]

John Wilkinson, a dissenter and disciple of Henry Barrow, described himself in 1613 as "a prisoner for the patience and faith of the Saints."[63] Wilkinson, like Barrow, suffered and died for his convictions

---

heaven, he predicates of it that it is really a city in heaven." Tertullian, *Against Marcion*, 3.25, in *Ante-Nicene Fathers*, 3:342.

[60] Goodwin, *The Works of Thomas Goodwin*, 12 vols. (Edinburgh: James Nichol, 1861–1866), 3:1–226; and Henry More, *A Modest Enquiry into the Mystery of Iniquity* (London: James Flesher, 1664). Christopher Hill makes the connection between Milton and Mede, in *Milton and the English Revolution* (Harmondsworth, Middlesex: Penguin, 1979), 281.

[61] Richard L. Greaves, "The Puritan-Nonconformist Tradition in England," *Albion* 17, no. 4 (1985): 449–86.

[62] Christianson, *Reformers and Babylon*, 246.

[63] John Wilkinson, *A Reproof of Some Things Written by John Morton, and Others of His Company and Followers, to Prove That infants Are Not in the State of Condemnation, And That Therefore They Are Not to Be Baptized* (1613). Wilkinson identifies himself on the title page as "a Prisoner at Colchester for the Patience and Faith of the Saints." Reprinted as Wilkinson, *The Sealed Fountaine Opened to the Faithfull, and Their Seed* (London, 1646 [1613]). Little is known about Wilkinson. Some have inferred from his arguments against baptism that he may have been a Seeker and perhaps even regarded himself as one of the Messengers (Apostles), who would reestablish the church anew. Burrage, *Early English Dissenters*, 1:192–94.

that the established church in England was held under the sway of the false worship of the beast. In his exposition of the thirteenth chapter of Revelation, Wilkinson declaimed,

> The Church of England . . . is unworthy to be adorned with the title of the Church of Christ, but ought to be accounted the image of the first Beast, that is of great Babylon which is an habitation of divells, an hold of fowle spirits, and a cage of every uncleane and hatefull Bird.[64]

The final words of his pamphlet envisioned the coming millennium, where the souls of the martyrs, who (like himself) were faithful witnesses to Jesus and the Word of God, and who refused to worship the beast, "lived and reigned with Christ a thousand years."[65] John Smyth—a Jacobean exile who fled to Amsterdam and gathered the first congregation of English Baptists—went even further, arguing that, because they baptized infants, even Independent Congregationalists bore the mark of the Beast (Rev 13:11-18) and were "of the same constitution with England and Rome," being "a most unnatural daughter" to their "mother England" and their "grandmother Rome."[66] Smyth's erstwhile partner in separation Thomas Helwys argued similarly, identifying the first beast of Revelation 13 with the Roman Catholic Church and the second beast (which imitated the first) with the Church of England, and arguing that the other separating congregations were false churches because they mimicked the bishops and presbyters and made covenant with the children of the flesh.[67]

Even more dangerous than these debates about eschatologically inspired ecclesial separation were the populist conversations about how an apocalyptic imagination might evoke economic and political revolution as a means of bringing about the kingdom of God on earth. One such prophet was an itinerant tinker from Northamptonshire

---

[64] John Wilkinson, *An Exposition of the 13: Chapter of the Revelation of Iesus Christ* (Amsterdam: G. Thorp, 1619), 34–35.

[65] Wilkinson, *Exposition of the 13*, 37.

[66] Smyth, *The Character of the Beast*, in *The Works of John Smyth*, ed. W. T. Whitley, 2 vols. (Cambridge: Cambridge University Press, 1915), 2:565.

[67] Helwys, *Mystery of Iniquity*, 117–25.

named John Reynolds, affectionately known as Captain Pouch. In May 1607, Reynolds found himself at the head of a popular revolution in the English midlands, inspired by his claim that the Lord of heaven had directed him to "throw down" all land enclosures. Reynolds garnered huge support among the working class, who gathered by the thousands to follow his vision of religious reformation and social equality. The revolt was suppressed, and Reynolds was executed, but the unrest continued.[68] Levellers like John Lilburne threatened the social order by arguing that the absolute sovereignty of God as Lord and King demanded the equality of all people and government by mutual agreement or consent.[69] Diggers like Gerrard Winstanley and William Everard went further, envisioning the coming of the New Jerusalem and the restoration of all things in which "the whole earth shall be a common treasury," for "the earth and the blessings of the earth shall be common to all."[70] What made Levellers and Diggers dangerous to the powers was not just the threat of equalizing economic resources and land redistribution but the eschatological conviction that Christ alone is the King and Lord of heaven and earth. The widespread appeal of apocalyptic imagery among common people was due to its powerful narrative of cosmic struggle between good and evil, identifying the forces of Antichrist with those who persecute the saints.

On the eve of revolution, the Independent London minister Thomas Goodwin preached a sermon entitled *A Glimpse of Syons Glory* in which he announced that he would show "how upon the destruction of Babylon Christ shall reign gloriously, and how we are to further it." Goodwin declaimed that God had already begun the overthrow of the beast and that Babylon was falling. "The work of the day," Goodwin argued, is "to cry down Babylon, that it may fall

[68] John Stow and Edmund Howes, *Annales; or, Generall Chronicle of England* (London: Richard Meighen, 1631), 890; also Christopher Hill and Edmund Dell, eds., *The Good Old Cause: The English Revolution of 1640–1660* (New York: Routledge, 2012), 22a.

[69] John Lilburne, *The Free-Mans Freedome Vindicated* (London, 1646), 11.

[70] Winstanley, *The New Law of Righteousness*, VII (1649), in *The Works of Gerrard Winstanley*, ed. George H. Sabine (Ithaca, N.Y.: Cornell University Press, 1941), 184, and 152–53.

more and more," and "to give God no rest, till he sets up Jerusalem as the praise of the whole world." The anticipation of Babylon's fall and Christ's coming could be heard in the voices of the multitude crying out, "Down with Antichrist! Down with Popery!" The sermon laid out the millennial hope in vivid images, describing how Christ would reign on earth with the saints for a thousand years. It concluded with an exhortation for faithful Christians to be patient, laying the foundation for the New Jerusalem soon to come.[71] The next year, just days before the first battle of the Civil War, another Independent minister, John Goodwin, struck an apocalyptic note in a sermon, declaring that the forces of Antichrist were "about to be destroyed and cast out of the world."[72] On October 23, 1642, the theater of the apocalyptic imagination spilled over onto the stage of history in the struggle between Royalist and Parliamentary forces at the Battle of Edgehill. Dissenters like the Goodwins were concerned that the influence of Antichrist was growing throughout Europe and encroaching on Protestant England in the uprising of Catholic Ireland. A popular ballad warned of the coming danger:

> But Pope his Vicar commands all estates,
> Kings, Emperors, and greatest Potentates,
> And turnes his power to furious tyranny,
> Against that Christ and all his company:
> And by his rage they now abide affliction,
> He's *Antichrist* without all contradiction.[73]

In a sermon delivered to Parliament in 1644, Presbyterian Stephen Marshall charged the army soldiers present to "Goe on and fight the Battells of the Lord Jesus Christ," adding, "Doe now see, that the

---

[71] Thomas Goodwin, *A Glimpse of Syons Glory* (London: Printed for William Larnar, 1641), 2, 6, 32–33; in *Works of Thomas Goodwin*, 12:65–79.

[72] John Goodwin, *Anticavalierism; or, Truth Pleading as Well the Necessity as the Lawfulnesse of This Present Warre for the Suppressing of that Butcherly Brood of Cavaliering Incendiaries* (London: Henry Overton, 1643), 21. George Thomason collected Goodwin's tract on October 21, 1642. John Coffey, *John Goodwin and the Puritan Revolution* (Woodbridge, Suffolk: Boydell, 2006), 85–89.

[73] *A True and Plaine Genealogy or Pedigree of Antichrist* (London: For Samuell Rande, 1634).

question in England is, whether Christ or Antichrist shall be Lord or King."[74] It is not surprising that Christians who heard sermons and sang songs like these perceived the events unfolding before their eyes to be an enactment of the apocalyptic drama of the forces of Antichrist making war on the saints (Rev 13:7). Yet they also understood that the danger of impending disaster was not entirely from outside the realm. It was being promoted from within by the high church policies of Archbishop William Laud, who was by then imprisoned in the Tower of London. Godly contempt for Laud found a surprising herald in Archibald Armstrong, the court jester to King Charles I, who reportedly once offered grace for a banquet at Whitehall, saying, "Great praise be given to God and little Laud to the devil."[75] But John Goodwin went a step further, fueling antimonarchical fires by arguing that there is a sense in which "Kingly government is no Ordinance of God." He explained that kings who make unjust commands, and those who enforce them, have no lawful authority. They may be—indeed, must be—righteously resisted.[76] Goodwin announced that God was awakening the saints to the truth of "the just bounds and limits of authority, and power" and "the just and full extent of the lawfull liberties of those that live in subjection." And the good news, he declared, was that God had chosen not the gentry but "Christians of ordinary rank and quality" to "have the principall hand in executing the judgements of God upon the *Whore*."[77]

Swarms of dissenters like John Bunyan rushed out to enlist in the New Model Army to fight against the king, motivated in significant

[74] Stephen Marshall, *A Sacred Panegyrick, or a Sermon of Thanksgiving* (London, 1644), 21.

[75] John Southworth, *Fools and Jesters at the English Court* (Stroud, Gloucestershire: History Press, 1998), 148. Laud, who like Armstrong was short in stature, took great offence at the joke. Armstrong's unrelenting ridicule finally reached a breaking point, and Laud had the king's fool removed from the court. The fool, with Presbyterian support, had the last laugh, as he published a pamphlet entitled *Archy's Dream* in which he envisioned Laud in hell.

[76] John Goodwin, *Anticavalierism*, 4–5, 10–12. Goodwin subverts the established church reading of Rom 13 and 2 Sam 1 that were used as biblical warrant for absolute obedience to the monarchy.

[77] John Goodwin, *Anticavalierism*, 12.

part by a sense that the struggle was not merely with flesh and blood "but against principalities, against powers, against the rulers of the darkness of this world, against spiritual wickedness in high places" (Eph 6:12).[78] Yet Baptist preacher Christopher Blackwood warned that Antichrist could not be finally defeated on the battlefield, for his garrisons must be stormed by further reformation. Presbyterians argued that the fall of Antichrist would commence with abolishing episcopacy, but Blackwood and the Baptists contended that the spiritual warfare must lay siege to his last and greatest strongholds: the compulsion of conscience and infant baptism.[79] Henry Denne, another Baptist, offered a more subtle argument that it was a mistake to identify Antichrist simply with a single figure like the pope, the bishops, or the Turks, but rather it should be understood as a complex constellation of forces that comprise "that mysticall body of iniquity, which opposeth Jesus Christ."[80] The apocalyptic imagination of dissenters grew increasingly more intense in the late 1640s, during the course of the Civil War. Fifth Monarchists like William Aspinwall and Mary Cary equated King Charles I with the little horn of the beast prophesied in Daniel 7:8 and 8:9-10.[81] The execution of the king on January 30, 1649, led many to believe that the coming of the Christ was imminent.

[78] Richard Baxter complained that there were "swarms of Anabaptists" in the armies. Cited in William Orme, "The Life and Times of Richard Baxter," in Baxter, *The Practical Works of the Rev. Richard Baxter*, 23 vols. (London: James Duncan, 1830), 1:44. Baxter states that Baptists and Independents were most prevalent, but he noted that there were significant numbers of Antinomians and Arminians.

[79] Christopher Blackwood, *The Storming of Antichrist* (London: S.N., 1644).

[80] Henry Denne, *The Man of Sin Discovered* (London: John Sweeting, 1646), 15. Denne's mystical view of Antichrist was a gesture toward John Bale's earlier account of two churches. Bunyan adopted Denne's interpretation of Antichrist as a "mystical man." He proposed that Antichrist is a complex figure, with a head, a body, and a soul: "The devil *he* is the head; the synagogue of Satan, *that* is his body; that wicket spirit of iniquity, *that* is the soul of Antichrist." Bunyan, *Of Antichrist, And His Ruin* (1692), in *The Works of John Bunyan*, ed. George Offor, 3 vols. (Glasgow: W. G. Blackie and Son, 1854; repr., Carlisle, Penn.: Banner of Trust, 1991), 2:46.

[81] William Aspinwall, *An Explication and Application of the Seventh Chapter of Daniel* (London: R.I., 1654), 26–30; and Mary Cary, *The Little Horns Doom and Downfall; or, A Scripture-Prophesie of King James, and King Charles, and of This Present Parliament, Unfolded* (London, 1651). Prominent Fifth Monarchist ministers Christopher Feake and Henry Jessey wrote endorsements for Carey's book.

Eschatological speculation continued in the early days of the Commonwealth, as some saw Cromwell to be continuing the battle against Antichrist and preparing for the reign of the saints. After the dismissal of the Rump Parliament, many dissenters grew disenchanted with Cromwell's leadership. Vavasor Powell, Christopher Feake, and Anna Trapnel went so far as to openly suggest that Cromwell, not King Charles I, was the little horn of the beast.[82] Quakers like James Naylor urged the Saints to join the Lamb's War and fight against the forces of the dragon, the beast, and the false prophet with the weapons of the Spirit.[83] The apocalyptic expectation continued to expand and evolve with the changing events.

It is an odd history that a desire for greater godliness in the church resulted in violent revolution and the execution of the king. Yet puritanism was a complex phenomenon that cannot be reduced to a theological program or a social agenda.[84] It was a religious mindset committed

[82] Louise Fargo Brown, *The Political Activities of the Baptists and Fifth Monarchy Men In England during the Interregnum* (Washington, D.C.: American Historical Association, 1912), 44–46; Bernard S. Capp, *The Fifth Monarchy Men: A Study in Seventeenth-Century English Millenarianism* (Totowa: Rowman & Littlefield, 1972), 99–114. See Christopher Feake, *A Beam of Light, Shining in the Midst of Much Darkness and Confusion* (London: J.C., 1659); and Anna Trapnel, *The Cry of a Stone* (London, 1654), 6–13; in Curtis W. Freeman, ed., *A Company of Women Preachers: Baptist Prophetesses in Seventeenth-Century England* (Waco, Tex.: Baylor University Press, 2011).

[83] James Naylor, *The Lambs Warre against the Man of Sinne* (London: Thomas Simmons, 1657); Douglas Gwyn, "The Early Quaker Lamb's War: Secularisation and the Death of Tragedy in Early Modern England," in *Towards Tragedy/Reclaiming Hope: Literature, Theology and Sociology in Conversation*, ed. Pink Dandelion (Aldershot, U.K.: Ashgate, 2004), 33–56; and David Lowenstein, "The War of the Lamb: George Fox and the Apocalyptic Discourse of Revolutionary Quakerism," in *The Emergence of Quaker Writing: Dissenting Literature in Seventeenth-Century England*, ed. Thomas N. Corns and David Lowenstein (London: Frank Cass, 1995), 25–41.

[84] Classic studies by Perry Miller focused more on the mental and theological dimension of puritanism, whereas Michael Walzer attended to the social and political aspects. Perry Miller, *The New England Mind: From Colony to Province*, 2 vols. (Cambridge, Mass.: Belknap, 1953); and Michael Walzer, *The Revolution of the Saints: A Study in the Origins of Radical Politics* (Cambridge, Mass.: Harvard University Press, 1965). Like Max Weber, Walzer emphasizes the moral discipline and worldly asceticism of puritanism, describing them as alienated revolutionaries animated by moral zeal. Cf. Max Weber, *The Protestant Ethic and the Spirit of Capitalism*, trans. Talcott Parsons (New York: Charles Scribner's Sons, 1958), 145 and 254–55n173.

to ecclesial reformation as well as a social movement aimed toward political reconstruction. Godly Christians viewed both priestcraft and monarchy as obstacles to the changes they believed were needed in church and society. But these parallel agendas had a common source in the shared tradition that viewed history as the unfolding drama of apocalyptic theater. Independents like John Owen and Presbyterians like Stephen Marshall imagined the New Jerusalem being built within the revised political structures by creating a holy commonwealth. Levellers, Diggers, Quakers, Fifth Monarchists, and many Baptists envisioned a more subversive view of the apocalypse where the existing institutions must be overturned for the New Jerusalem to come on earth. Moderates and radicals alike rejected the politics of Antichrist that dominated the English church and state (and subsequently the Tory Party), in favor of the Protestant (and later Whig) politics. Yet it was an uneasy alliance in which dissenters of the more subversive sort never felt quite at home. Despite the differences, in the eyes of both the state and its established church, all dissenters were seen (at least potentially) as troublesome spirits, disorderly enthusiasts, deluded fanatics, and seditious revolutionaries. Their beliefs and practices were regarded as the seeds of both religious chaos and social anarchy. They were wild and untamed creatures who must be domesticated to serve the purposes of the greater good of England. It is not surprising, then, that John Bunyan wrote from his jail cell in Bedford that God's people have ever been looked upon as "a turbulent, seditious, and factious people."[85]

THE POWERS OF DOMESTICATION

Edward Wightman was put to death in Lichfield, England, on April 11, 1612. The former cloth merchant, sometime alehouse keeper, and itinerant lay preacher was charged with holding the "Damnable and Heretical Opinions" of Ebionism, Cerenthianism, Valentinianism, Arianism, Macedonianism, Simony, Manichaeism, Photinianism, and Anabaptism, as well as "other cursed Opinions belched by the instinct

---

[85] Bunyan, *I Will Pray with the Spirit*, in *Works of John Bunyan*, 1:630. This quote inspired Christopher Hill's biography of Bunyan.

of Satan." It seems likely that his main crime lay in the final charge and that the other allegations were mostly rhetorical excess.[86] Simply stated, he was a dissenter. Upon examination by church officials, it was confirmed that Wightman indeed maintained and propagated the aforesaid "Blasphemies and Errours stubbornly and partinaciously, knowingly, maliciously, and with an hardened heart." By order of James I, king of England, under the authority of *de haeretico comburendo* (the anti-Lollard statute passed in 1401 by Henry IV), and with the approval of Richard Neile, bishop of Coventry and Lichfield, Wightman was handed over to the sheriff of Lichfield, where he was condemned "to be Burned in the detestation of the said Crime and for manifest example of other Christians, that they may not fall into the same Crime." After being put to the flames, Wightman cried out that he would recant and was returned to prison. When he subsequently refused to renounce his heresy in writing, he was taken again to the stake, where he cried out again that he would recant. But the sheriff is said to have replied that Wightman "showld cosen him no more." His pleas ignored, Edward Wightman was "burned to ashes" by a roaring fire.[87]

---

[86] Curtis W. Freeman, "Last Heretic and/or First Baptist? Reflections on the Burning of Edward Wightman in 1612," in *Mirrors and Microscopes: Historical Perspectives of Baptists*, ed. C. Douglas Weaver (Milton Keynes: Paternoster, 2015), 74–86.

[87] James R[ex]., "A Narration of the Burning of Edward Wightman," in *A True Relation of the Commissions and Warrants for the Condemnation and Burning of Bartholomew Legatt and Thomas Withman* [*sic*] (London: Michael Spark, 1651), 7–13. See also Burrage, *Early English Dissenters*, 1:216–20; and Ian Atherton and David Como, "The Burning of Edward Wightman: Puritanism, Prelacy, and the Politics of Heresy in Early Modern England," *English Historical Review* 120, no. 489 (2005): 1215–50. The 1401 statute *de haeretico comburendo* (Regarding the Burning of Heretics) declared that anyone who promulgated "wicked Preachings, Doctrines, Opinions, Schools, and heretical and erroneous Informations" was to be brought first before a diocesan church court. If found guilty of heresy, the accused was permitted the opportunity to abjure. Heretics who refused to recant were to be delivered over to the local civil authorities, who were responsible for overseeing the burning of the heretic in a public place "that such Punishment may strike Fear into the Minds of other, whereby, no such wicked Doctrine and heretical and erroneous Opinions, nor their Authors and Fautors, in the said Realm and Dominions, against the Catholic Faith, Christian Law, and Determination of the Holy Church, which God prohibit, be sustained or in any way suffered."

Wightman's fame (or infamy) lies not in being the worst of heretics. Others were far more notorious. Yet his place in history is nevertheless secure as the last heretic executed in England, though in this honor he edged out Bartholomew Legate by a mere three weeks.[88] His death coincided with the authorized King James Version of the Bible, which solidified the Jacobean establishment by silencing dissenters and empowering the emerging voices of high church theology. It is not surprising, then, that William Laud and Lancelot Andrewes, whose sacramental piety and Arminian theology came to characterize the high church vision, both participated in Wightman's trial and were instrumental in his death. Wightman was an ideal scapegoat for James, who was eager to demonstrate himself to be the defender of the faith.[89] In a more pragmatic sense Wightman's execution demonstrated to the audience of Protestants in Europe the willingness of James to use harsh discipline without really angering any of the key players, either the Anti-Calvinists, the Remonstrants, or Counter Remonstrants.[90] In this sense, Wightman might be viewed as the perfect political sacrifice, a figure whom no party or congregation was willing to defend.

Statutes of the Realm: Printed by Command of His Majesty King George the Third, 11 vols. (London: Dawsons, 1963), 2:127–28.

[88] Twenty-five Catholics were put to death during the reign of James I. The last one was William Southerne in 1618, six years after Edward Wightman. Catholics continued to be executed during the Protectorate, although they were charged with sedition, not heresy, and sentenced to die by hanging, not burning. On Catholic deaths, see John Coffey, *Persecution and Toleration in Protestant England, 1558–1689* (New York: Longman, 2000), 117–21, 134, and 157–58; and Brad S. Gregory, *Salvation at Stake: Christian Martyrdom in Early Modern Europe* (Cambridge, Mass.: Harvard University Press, 1999), 250–314. Catholics in England from about 1570 to 1791 who refused to attend services in the Church of England were regarded as recusants rather than dissenters and punished by fines, confiscation of property, and imprisonment.

[89] Renè Girard, *The Scapegoat*, trans. Yvonne Freccero (Baltimore: Johns Hopkins University Press, 1986), 14–23.

[90] Wightman's execution was played out against the backdrop of an international and ecumenical challenge to orthodoxy in the appointment of the Socinian theologian Conrad Vorstius to the chair of divinity at the University of Leiden in 1611. Sarah Mortimer, *Reason and Religion in the English Revolution: The Challenge of Socinianism* (Cambridge: Cambridge University Press, 2010), 46–49; H. John McLachlan, *Socinianism in Seventeenth-Century England* (London: Oxford University Press, 1951), 36–37; and Atherton and Como, "Burning of Edward Wightman," 1241–45.

According to a political construal of events, by executing Wightman, James was able to dispense with a heretic who seemed to be dangerously close to moderate puritans (appeasing Andrewes and company) and, at the same time, one who was obviously something other than a puritan, which was clear to anyone versed in puritan theology.

Public executions of dissenters like Wightman were not only judicial performance. They were also political ritual. On the scaffold, the power of the sovereign over against the anger of the people was mediated in the body of the victim. The punishment of the accused was carried out as public spectacle, intended as an exhibition of absolute power. And because the body of the condemned belonged to a king, it was subjected to extreme abuse as a demonstration of royal authority. The theater of public spectacle was performed before a cheering audience, manifesting the power of the sovereign.[91] The aim of punishment, however, was not death but a demonstration of complete and total domination. Dissenters that played too important of an economic role in the workforce needed to keep the engines of empire running, but the power to punish served the purpose of social order.[92] Lesser forms of punishment were also used to punish. Bunyan was jailed for twelve years. Defoe was imprisoned and pilloried. And even after the age of spectacle had past, its specter haunted Blake, as he mentioned "The Wound" he still saw near his London home, which he described as "Tyburn's fatal Tree," where large crowds once gathered to witness mass executions. Alluding to the punitive, even redemptive, effect of such arbitrary and absolute violence, he asked, "Is that Calvary and Golgotha?"[93] It is a question that rose up from the experience of dissenters who long stood under the power of English empire.

[91] Michel Foucault, *Discipline and Punish* (New York: Vintage Books, 1977), 32–69.

[92] The use of the term "empire" denotes the colonies and territories gathered under rule of the United Kingdom from the late sixteenth through the mid-twentieth centuries. The story is told by Niall Ferguson, *Empire: The Rise and Demise of the British World Order and the Lessons for Global Power* (New York: Basic Books, 2004). But it also is used more generally in a postcolonial sense: see Michael Hardt and Antonio Negri, *Empire* (Cambridge, Mass.: Harvard University Press, 2000), xi–41.

[93] William Blake, *Jerusalem*, 72.54, 12.26,28, 13.54, and 63.33, in *Blake Complete Writings*, ed. Geoffrey Keynes (London: Oxford University Press, 1969), 715, 632, 665, and

The *Second Shepherd's Play* of the Wakefield Master voices the sense of subjugation that dissenters felt under the powers of domestication. Like the livestock on the land where they labored, they were lamed, shamed, and tamed by rent, taxes, and tithes owed to the gentry, the crown, and the church. Dissenters, like the shepherds, by and large were composed of working-class folk. In the view of "the powers that be," they were wild and untamed spirits that had to be subdued, tamed, and domesticated. Yet domestication required more than simply the taming of captive individuals to become habituated to the master's presence. To be successful, domestication required an evolutionary process of adaption to the captive environment, so that over generations it resulted in developmental changes in the whole species of domesticated individuals, who became interdependent with their masters.[94] One of the most important tools in the process of domesticating dissenters was the King James Bible, which as it turned out was as much about making the English language godly as it was about putting the Bible into words capable of being understood in English.[95] As Miles Smith, one of the King James translators, elegantly explained:

> Translation it is that openeth the window, to let in the light; that breaketh the shell, that we may eat the kernel; that putteth aside the curtaine, that we may looke into the most Holy place; that remooveth the cover of the well, that wee may come by the water, even as *Jacob* rolled away the stone from the mouth of the well, by which meanes the flockes of *Laban* were watered.[96]

Though initially opposed by the godly, who preferred the Geneva Bible, the King James Version eventually became the Bible of choice

---

698. After his return from Felpham (1803–1821), Blake lived at South Moulton Street in London, near the "Tyburn Tree," which was the principal place for mass executions in London. The "Tree" was erected in 1571, and the last execution was held in 1783.

[94] Charles Darwin, *The Origin of Species* (London: John Murray, 1859; repr., Chicago: Encyclopedia Britannica, 1952), chap. 1, "Variation under Domestication," 9–23; and E. O. Price, *Animal Domestication and Behavior* (New York: CABI, 2002), 10–12.

[95] Adam Nicolson, *God's Secretaries: The Making of the King James Bible* (New York: HarperCollins, 2003), 211.

[96] Miles Smith, "The Translators to the Reader," in *The Holy Bible: Conteyning the Old Testament, and the New* (London: Robert Barker, 1611).

for church and chapel, and in so doing it succeeded where the Book of Common Prayer had failed, by giving England a common religious language.

Dissenters according to the biological analogy were seen as beastly and dangerous but also potentially useful if their energy could be subdued, tamed, and domesticated. Yet not all dissenters proved to be domesticable. Some were capable of being hand-tamed by the gentry, but others were too wild and incorrigible to submit to the service of empire. They suffered for their stickling. It is not surprising to observe human subjects refusing to conform, no matter how absolute the master, just as not all animal species have proven to be domesticable.[97] Nevertheless, empire exerted its power by issuing decrees and codes that over the years landed huge numbers of undomesticable dissenters in jails and prisons, not for days, or weeks, or months, but years. They were separated from domestic society and incarcerated like wild animals in cells with iron bars. This carceral logic became one of the key elements of social control, which empire used as a strategy that stood behind the threat and exercise of discipline. Its aim was to create a space in which prisoners were subjugated to a virtual sovereignty so that they internalized the discipline within themselves.[98] Other tactics of domestication included prohibiting dissenters from admission to university study or employment, blocking paths of upward mobility. They were left with the choices of attending dissenting academies or self-education and with the growing opportunities for social advancement in the emerging mercantile economy. In order to restrict political participation, dissenters were excluded from holding public office by various iterations of the Test and Corporation Acts, unless in violation of conscience they conformed to the established church. Some dissenters saw occasional conformity as mortgaging the conscience, while others regarded it as a matter of the liberty.[99]

[97] Jared Diamond points out that of all the big herbivorous mammalian species in history, only fourteen have been domesticated. Some like zebras have proven too wild to tame and hopelessly undomesticable. Others like elephants can be tamed but not domesticated. Diamond, *Guns, Germs, and Steel: The Fates of Human Societies* (New York: W. W. Norton, 1999), 157–75.

[98] Hardt and Negri, *Empire*, 330.

[99] See chapter 3, p. 97.

Such strategies of domestication were focused on docile and compliant dissenters. Wild, fanatical, incorrigible dissenters were regarded by the establishment powers in church and state as "proud, wicked, deceived, deluded, lying, mad, melancholy, crackbrained, self willed, conceited Fool[s], and black Sinner[s], led by whimsies, notions, and knif-knafs of [their] own head[s]."[100] Those that could not be domesticated and made useful to the service of the empire had to be eliminated. The execution of the king, the growing power of the landed gentry, and the rising economic force of the merchant class demonstrated the diffusion of power.[101] With the dawning of modernity, the modality of state power shifted from spectacle to surveillance and from punishment to discipline.[102] This migration of the absolute sovereignty of the monarch to more decentralized expressions of state power conveyed an increased role for the enforcement of discipline by the gentry, especially to those who served as magistrates. Yet, as Defoe perceptively observed, though the names of these power arrangements changed over the years from "Cavalier and Roundhead" to "Royalists and Rebels" to "Tories and Whigs," the real division remained between "Church and Dissent."[103] In this one distinction, political, social, and religious lines of demarcation converged.

Contestation between dissenters and the gentry, and later between dissenters and the rising merchant class, played out a Hobbesian struggle of each against all in the increasing enclosure of common land.[104] The argument for general enclosure depicted the poor as a "wild race" of "barbarians" and the commons as a "wild country" that served as

---

[100] Anne Wentworth, *The Revelation of Jesus Christ* (1679), 19, in Freeman, *Company of Women Preachers*, 712.

[101] Robert Brenner, *Merchants and Revolution: Commercial Change, Political Conflict, and London's Overseas Traders, 1550–1653* (New York: Verso, 2003). Brenner's massive study shows by a close and careful reading of archival sources that the Civil War was the result of a political collision between the monarchy and the landowning class with the catalyst being the new London merchants.

[102] Foucault, *Discipline and Punish*, 216–17.

[103] Daniel Defoe, *A New Test of the Church of England's Loyalty* (London, 1702), 3.

[104] Thomas Hobbes, *Leviathan; or, The Matter, Forme and Power of a Common Wealth Ecclesiasticall and Civil*, 1.13 (London: Andrew Crooke, 1651; repr., Chicago: University of Chicago Press, 1952), 84–87.

their "breeding ground." Land enclosure became a way of enforcing social discipline.[105] Though it would be an overgeneralization simply to identify the poor with dissenters, there was significant overlap. As earlier working-class dissenters found themselves alienated from the gentry and high church politics, later landless dissenters not only similarly experienced conflict with the established church and Tory politicians but frequently were disaffected by the emerging market economy and its Whig representatives, which viewed property as a commodity and wealth not as a right of birth but as a reward of work and vocation. It was not only Levellers and Diggers who challenged the dangers of the accumulation of wealth and property but even the middling sort, like the Baptist printer Francis "Elephant" Smith, who portrayed the dying Christian as turning back from heaven's reward with eyes on worldly wealth and power.[106]

Though dissenters were seen by the established order of state and church as wild and dangerous people that must be domesticated, dissenters saw the world in precisely opposite terms. For them it was the institutions and personalities of empire that were beastly, subjecting the righteous to abuse and domination. They intuitively recognized that the descriptions of evil in the books of Daniel and Revelation depicted imperial power, collectively personified in singular imagery of beastly figures.[107] They perceived empire as being animated by an array of human and supra-human forces the Bible calls the "principalities and powers," which coalesce to destroy life.[108] Yet they anticipated a time coming when:

---

[105] E. P. Thompson, *Making of the English Working Class*, 239–43.

[106] Francis Smith, *Symptoms of Growth and Decay in Godliness* (London: Francis Smith, 1673).

[107] Henry More, *Synopsis Prophetica; or, The Second Part of the Enquiry Into the Mystery of Iniquity* (London: James Flesher, 1664), 1.3.3–8, 218–19. More called this form of representation *henopoeia*.

[108] Hendrik Berkhof, *Christ and the Powers* (Scottdale, Penn.: Herald, 1962); Walter Wink, *Engaging the Powers: Discernment and Resistance in a World of Domination* (Minneapolis: Fortress, 1992); John Howard Yoder, *The Politics of Jesus* (Grand Rapids: Eerdmans, 1972), chap. 8; Daniel Coluccielo Barber, *Deleuze and the Naming of God* (Edinburgh: Edinburgh University Press, 2014), 112–13.

The wolf shall live with the lamb,
the leopard shall lie down with the kid,
the calf and the lion and the fatling together,
and a little child shall lead them.
The cow and the bear shall graze,
their young shall lie down together;
and the lion shall eat straw like the ox. (Isa 11:6-7, NRSV)

In the New Jerusalem, unruly and disordered aspects of creation would be brought into harmony, and even wild, incorrigible creatures would be tamed and domesticated by the hands of Jesus the Christ, the Lamb of God.[109] It was this apocalyptic imagination that enabled dissenters to suffer unjust violence with patience, awaiting God's ultimate and final triumph over the powers.

At no point was the hierarchy of power more asserted or the claims of authority more disputed than in death. In early modern England, Christian burial was an entitlement guaranteed by ecclesiastical and common law, as much a civil right as an ecclesial privilege. Prior to the seventeenth century, burial inside the church, near the altar, was restricted to the landed gentry and clergy. Others were interred outside. The churchyard served as a visible manifestation of the church catholic, extending the boundary of the parish beyond the congregation of the living to the community of the dead. It was a liminal space between the gathering of the faithful and the communion of saints. It was holy ground shared by both the quick and the dead. It was the penultimate resting place for the bodies of the faithful awaiting the

---

[109] Quakers envisioned a coming time when "the earth would be full of the knowledge of the Lord as the waters cover the sea" (Isa 11:9). The American Quaker painter Edward Hicks vividly portrayed this vision in his sixty-two versions of *Peaceable Kingdom*. Hicks explained the underlying meanings of his artistic symbolism in a sermon on February 22, 1837, in Loudon County, Virginia. He described an elaborate cosmological and anthropological account of the imagery of his paintings. It weaves together the four humors (melancholic, sanguine, phlegmatic, and choleric) with the four elements (air, earth, water, and fire), typified in unregenerate creatures (wolf, leopard, bear, and lion) and regenerate animals (lamb, kid, cow, and ox). Hicks, "Goose Creek Sermon," in *Memoirs of the Life and Religious Labors of Edward Hicks* (Philadelphia: Merrihew & Thompson, 1851), 263–331.

hope of resurrection, elegantly expressed by Robert Blair in his poem *The Grave*, where he declaimed:

When the dread trumpet sounds, the slumb'ring dust,
Not unattentive to the call, shall wake;
And every joint possess its proper place,
With a new elegance of form, unknown.[110]

Refusal of the right of burial in the parish churchyard was the exception reserved for dangerous people: the unbaptized, excommunicants, schismatics, and criminals.[111] To be denied a place of rest among the communion of saints was to suffer permanent exclusion from the cultural and political order, amounting to the virtual obliteration of personhood after death. Separation from the community of those who had died in Christ put in question the hope of resurrection. It was the politics of exclusion written in stone.[112]

The question of the necrogeography of dissenters became a highly contested matter. Though they met in their own separate gatherings, the great majority of dissenters still expected that they and their children would be buried in the parish churchyard. Yet some clergy still refused to bury them on the grounds that they were unbaptized. In 1808, John Wight Wickes, the rector of a church in Wardley, Rutland-shire, refused to bury the infant child of two of his parishioners, John and Mary Swigler. The Swiglers were poor dissenters, yet when their young daughter Hannah died, even though she had been baptized by a dissenting minister, they sought to bury her in the parish church-yard. The case was finally resolved in 1809 in favor of the dissenters by the highest ecclesiastical court in Canterbury. The ruling declared that the baptism of a child by a dissenting minister was sufficient to warrant a Christian burial by the established church, and consequently

[110] Robert Blair, *The Grave* (London: Printed for M. Cooper, 1743). The most popular edition of Blair's poem was published in 1808 by Robert Cromek with twelve illustrations based on original engravings by William Blake.

[111] *Constitutions and Canons Ecclesiastical*, 68.

[112] Thomas W. Laqueur, *The Work of the Dead: A Cultural History of Mortal Remains* (Princeton, N.J.: Princeton University Press, 2015), 112–73.

it acknowledged the validity of nonconformist baptisms.[113] But while many outside the established church were seeking to claim their right to be buried within the geographic scope of its communion, others chose for their bodies to be laid to rest in dissenter burial grounds associated with meeting houses or public places like Bunhill Fields.[114]

That Bunyan, Defoe, and Blake were buried among dissenting Christians and not in a parish churchyard is significant. It signifies their rejection of a state-established and geographically delineated church in favor of a Free Church defined by personal conviction, a community of saints sustained in death, not by its proximity to the altar, but by the faithfulness of its witnesses. Those buried in that earth chose to be laid to rest in the dissenter's necropolis, beyond the boundaries of ecclesiastical community, outside the walls of civil society, in unconsecrated ground where the bones of plague victims were once disposed, to await the hope of the resurrection of the dead. In his 1735 elegy to Bunhill Fields, Thomas Gutteridge wrote:

> In Bunhill Burial Ground crumbling to Dust,
> There lies two Generations of the Just;
> Part the last Age, and Part the present Day,
> Blend there their Dust into one blessed Clay:
> Who knows what Generations there may rise
> When the last Trump shall rend and tear the Skies;
> A large Assembly in this Ground does lie,
> When rais'd with streaming glory that shall fly.[115]

There, in that enclosed space, separated in death from the established church, unmixed with the bodies of those with rank and privilege, they were buried where, it was thought, their fanatical dreams could

---

[113] *A Sketch of the History and Proceedings of the Deputies Appointed to Protect the Civil Rights of Protestant Dissenters* (London: Samuel Burton, 1813), 65–72; Joseph Butterworth and Son, *A General Catalogue of Law Books*, 20.41, 6th enlarged ed. (London: Butterworth, 1819), 162; *Parish Law: Being a Digest of the Law Relating to Parishes* (Cambridge: Cambridge University Press, 1830), 52–53; Laqueur, *Work of the Dead*, 175–82.

[114] Laqueur, *Work of the Dead*, 298–305.

[115] Thomas Gutteridge, *The Universal Elegy; or, A Poem on Bunhill Burial Ground* (London, 1735?), 13, 15.

no longer contaminate citizens or threaten the social order. But their dreams lived on. The apocalyptic imagination that animated dissenters and troubled the state and its established church could not be so easily suppressed by the politics of exclusion. It survived the dead through their monuments of witness and memory, and also in the consciousness, conscience, and convictions of individuals and communities who lived on to tell the story. But perhaps most importantly for the purpose of this study, the apocalyptic imagination was handed on in a living tradition of dissent, transmitted in hymns, sermons, histories, and particularly in literary works like Bunyan's *Pilgrim's Progress*, Defoe's *Robinson Crusoe*, and Blake's *Jerusalem*.

2

SLUMBERING DISSENT
John Bunyan

Well, Faithful, thou hast faithfully profest
Unto thy Lord: with him thou shalt be blest,
When faithless ones, with all their vain delights,
Are crying out under their hellish plights.
Sing, Faithful, sing; and let thy name survive;
For though they kill'd thee, thou art yet alive.[1]

John Bunyan had spent nearly twelve years in prison by the time part 1 of *The Pilgrim's Progress* was published in 1678. He was arrested on November 12, 1660, and found guilty of "[d]evilishly and perniciously abstaining from coming to church to hear divine service, and . . . being a common upholder of several unlawful meetings and conventicles."[2] Before going to prison, he struggled with "how to be able to endure," if his imprisonment turned out to be "long and tedious," and "how to be able to encounter death," should that be his portion. He came to see that he must have patience to suffer joyfully

---

[1] John Bunyan, *The Pilgrim's Progress*, ed. N. H. Keeble (New York: Oxford University Press, 1984), 80. Subsequent citations are to this edition.

[2] Elizabethan Conventical Act of 1593, 35; cited by W. R. Owens, in John Bunyan, *Grace Abounding to the Chief of Sinners*, ed. W. R. Owens (London: Penguin, 1987), 127n137.

(Col 1:11) and that he must "pass a sentence of death upon everything that can properly be called a thing of this life," including his wife, his children, his health, and even his own life (2 Cor 1:9).[3] During his time in the Bedford jail, Bunyan kept his copy of John Foxe's *Book of Martyrs* with him, which next to the Bible was his primary source of reading.[4] So he learned to understand that his imprisonment along with subsequent dissenters who suffered under the Clarendon Code was part of a long story stretching back to the first Christian martyrs. But he wondered how to understand what God was doing in history given this new change events.

CHRIST THE KING

Bunyan's song to Faithful might well have been written as a eulogy for one of these early Christian martyrs. It placed him in the crimson trail of those whose voices could not be silenced even in death, and yet Bunyan imagined a very different world coming to be than did earlier dissenters. The exuberant hope of the past had been mugged by the political reality of present. No longer did he expect the imminent coming of Christ to establish his kingdom on earth where Christ would reign as the Lord omnipotent with the saints. For dissenters in earlier generations, such millennial expectations had political implications. In his millennial manifesto on the *Mystery of Iniquity*, Thomas Helwys declared that "Christ only" is King and that James was merely "an earthly king" having "no power to rule in this spiritual

---

[3] Bunyan, *Grace Abounding*, §§324–25, Owens, 79.

[4] John Foxe, *Acts and Monuments* (London: John Day, 1563). Four editions were published in Foxe's lifetime (1563, 1570, 1576, and 1583), and it went through multiple editions over the years. More popularly known as Foxe's *Book of Martyrs*, its plain language and vivid account of the Protestant martyrs under the reign of Mary Tudor appealed to working-class folk like Bunyan, who kept his copy with him during his imprisonment. For the influence and reception of Foxe by Bunyan, see John R. Knott, *Discourses of Martyrdom in English Literature, 1563–1694* (Cambridge: Cambridge University Press, 1993), 179–215; and Thomas S. Freeman, "A Library in Three Volumes: Foxe's 'Book of Martyrs' in the Writings of John Bunyan," *Bunyan Studies* 5 (1994): 47–57.

kingdom of Christ" or to "compel any to be subjects thereof."[5] Fifth Monarchists went further, rejecting the authority of all earthly sovereigns and looking for openings to hasten the soon coming reign of King Jesus.[6] The most radical and ultimately regicidal voices supported prophecies like those of Mary Cary, which identified Charles I as the little horn of the beast predicted in Daniel 7:8 and 8:9-10.[7] Even after the execution of the king, chiliastic speculations continued to energize the political imagination. But as the Protectorate began to resemble monarchy, radicals lost confidence. After the Barebones Parliament was dissolved in December of 1653, Vavasor Powell told the saints to go home and pray, "Lord, wilt Thou have Oliver Cromwell or Jesus Christ to reign over us?"[8] When Powell was arrested and examined before the Council of State on charges of treason in 1654, millennial hopes were kept alive by voices like the London prophetess Anna Trapnel, who fell into a trance and prophesied for twelve days, including a suggestion that Oliver Cromwell, not King Charles, was Antichrist.[9]

The millennial zeal that inspired the Civil War of the 1640s and the Protectorate of the 1650s was quenched by the return of Charles II to the throne. As Powell, the old but undaunted Fifth Monarchist, lay dying in Fleet Prison in the fall of 1670, any dream of the saints reigning on earth had vanished. But the spirit of undomesticated

---

[5] Thomas Helwys, *A Short Declaration of the Mystery of Iniquity* (1611/1612), ed. Richard Groves (Macon, Ga.: Mercer University Press, 1998), 34 and 39. See also Brian Haymes, "On Religious Liberty: Re-reading *A Short Declaration of the Mystery of Iniquity* in London in 2005," *Baptist Quarterly* 42, no. 3 (2007): 197–217.

[6] Louise Fargo Brown, *The Political Activities of the Baptists and Fifth Monarchy Men in England during the Interregnum* (Washington, D.C.: American Historical Association, 1912), 44–46; Bernard S. Capp, *The Fifth Monarchy Men: A Study in Seventeenth-Century English Millenarianism* (London: Faber & Faber, 1972), 99–114.

[7] Mary Cary, *The Little Horns Doom and Downfall; or, A Scripture-Prophesie of King James, and King Charles, and of This Present Parliament, Unfolded* (London, 1651). Christopher Feake and Henry Jessey wrote letters of endorsement for Cary. See Jane Baston, "History, Prophecy, and Interpretation: Mary Cary and Fifth Monarchism," *Prose Studies* 21, no. 3 (1998): 1–18.

[8] *Calendar of State Papers, Domestic, 1653–1654* (London: Longmans, 1875–1876), 306.

[9] Anna Trapnel, *The Cry of a Stone* (London, 1654), 6–13.

dissent began a prolonged hibernation with the restoration of the monarchy. Yet this slumbering radicalism found vital expression among the gathered congregations, which (though they no longer embraced militant millenarianism) continued to affirm the closely related ecclesial conviction that Christ reigned as King with the saints in the visible community of the church.[10] In this new social world, dissenters renounced their earlier militant hope of attaining control of government and resolved to suffer patiently in the world. In so doing, they combined political quietism with a slumbering radicalism that remained latently present in their faith and practice and might "in any more hopeful context, break into fire once more."[11] The Baptist leader and London pastor William Kiffin intoned that all the gathered churches avowed together "this great truth, [that] Christ is the King of his church; and that Christ hath given this power to his church, not to a hierarchy, neither to a national presbytery, but to a company of saints in a congregational way."[12] But, in the eyes of both civil and ecclesiastical authorities, even the old moderate dissenting sects were seen as a threat to the fragile establishment of order, as "every Presbyterian was a potential rebel and every Independent a regicide at heart."[13]

In his pamphlet *Some Gospel Truths Opened*, published in 1656, just one year after being received into the Bedford congregation, Bunyan expressed his conviction that "the coming of the Lord Jesus Christ is . . . nigh, even at the doors."[14] Though he admitted that no one can know the day or the hour, he added that "the scriptures will give us

[10] The phrase "slumbering radicalism" belongs to Edward Palmer Thompson, *The Making of the English Working Class* (Middlesex: Penguin, 1970), 30–34.

[11] E. P. Thompson, *Making of the English Working Class*, 30.

[12] William Kiffin, in the preface to Thomas Goodwin's 1641 sermon *A Glimpse of Syons Glory*, in Goodwin, *The Works of Thomas Goodwin* (Edinburgh: James Nichol, 1866), 12:63; cited in Murray Tolmie, *The Triumph of the Saints: Separate Churches in London 1616–1649* (Cambridge: Cambridge University Press, 1977), 85.

[13] Michael Watts, *The Dissenters*, vol. 1: *From the Reformation to the French Revolution* (Oxford: Clarendon, 1978), 222.

[14] Bunyan, *Some Gospel Truths Opened* (1656), in *The Works of John Bunyan*, ed. George Offor, 3 vols. (Glasgow: W. G. Blackie & Son, 1854; repr., Carlisle, Penn.: Banner of Trust, 1991), 2:168.

light into the nearness of his coming."[15] As evidence, he cited the fulfillment of signs such as the falling away of faith, wars and rumors of wars, lukewarm love for the coming of Christ, and false prophets and scoffers, especially the Quakers who denied that the fleshly body of Jesus ascended into heaven. Instead, they maintained that Christ had ascended into the saints, and so they did not look forward to his bodily return to earth but rather believed that the second advent had already occurred as Christ the true light spiritually indwelt each individual Christian (John 1:9). Moreover, they believed that the immediate presence of the inward light enabled the saints to fight against the beast in the Lamb's War as described in the Apocalypse of John (Rev 14–19). The intense opposition to their movement was seen by the Friends as the fulfillment of the apocalyptic vision.

Bunyan's early concerns were directed to immature Christians who might be drawn to the immediacy of the realized eschatology of the Quakers, which he vigorously rejected on the basis that it rested on a Christology that lacked the fullness of the incarnation. Pointing to the vision of Christ in the fifth chapter of the book of Revelation, in which the Lamb appears in the midst of both the throne of God and the twenty-four elders, Bunyan declaimed that the risen and ascended Lord was both divine and human.[16] He urged his readers to reject the spiritualized eschatology of the Quakers and remain steadfast in the blessed hope of Christ's coming, challenging them to discern the signs of the times and to look for the bodily return of the risen Lord who had ascended bodily into heaven. To wait expectantly for the imminent coming of Christ, Bunyan argued, the saints must separate from false professors, hypocrites, and all ungodly, so as to be ready to receive their coming King and to join him in his thousand-year reign on earth. Bunyan's tract was not well received among Quakers. George Fox denounced him as a liar and suggested

---

[15] Bunyan, *Some Gospel Truths Opened*, in *Works of John Bunyan*, 2:162–63.

[16] Bunyan, *Grace Abounding*, §§122–24, Owens, 33. Richard L. Greaves, *Glimpses of Glory: John Bunyan and English Dissent* (Stanford: Stanford University Press, 2002), 75–77. In Bunyan's list of errors of the Quakers, number seven states they held that the human Jesus who was crucified did not ascend into heaven. *Grace Abounding*, §24, Owens, 33.

that he "had better keep silent, than to fight against the Lord, the Lamb and his Saints."[17] But Fifth Monarchists like Vavasor Powell would have found little with which to quibble.

Fifth Monarchists took their name from Daniel 2:44, which described five world empires, the last of which would "break in pieces" the other four (viz., Babylon, Assyria, Greece, and Rome) and "stand for ever." The fifth monarchy, they believed, described the kingdom of Jesus Christ. Their belief in a literal earthly millennium led them to take direct political action aimed at transforming England into a kingdom of saints awaiting the imminent return of King Jesus, who would reign on earth with him for a thousand years (Rev 20:4). Fervent millennialists supported the execution of King Charles I, opposed the Protectorate of Oliver Crowell, and even called for armed rebellion against the restoration of King Charles II. It is not surprising, then, that when the Bedford clerk of the peace came to visit Bunyan in jail, he inquired about the recent armed insurrection in London led by Thomas Venner and other Fifth Monarchists, instigated to hasten the return of Christ. Bunyan disavowed any connection with the revolt and proclaimed his loyalty to the king.[18] The powers that be, however, remained suspicious that his millennialism harbored seeds of radical politics as questions about his allegiance continued to follow him throughout his life.[19] Bunyan, to be sure, had Fifth Monarchy associations and shared much of their theology, but more than a decade of imprisonment tempered his millennial enthusiasm.[20] Even though Bunyan did not share their militant politics, he

---

[17] Fox, *The Great Mistery of the Great Whore Unfolded* (London, 1659), in *The Works of George Fox*, 8 vols. (Philadelphia: Marcus T. C. Gould; New York: Isaac T. Hopper, 1831), 3:338 and 346.

[18] Bunyan, *A Relation of the Imprisonment of Mr. John Bunyan*, in *Grace Abounding*, 100. See also Capp, *Fifth Monarchy Men*, 199–201.

[19] Bunyan, *Of Antichrist, and His Ruin*, in *Works of John Bunyan*, 2:45.

[20] Richard L. Greaves, "John Bunyan and the Fifth Monarchists," *Albion* 13, no. 2 (1981): 83–95. George Offor identified the man in the iron cage at Interpreter's House as Bunyan's friend John Child, a Fifth Monarchist and former member of the Bedford congregation who conformed to the Church of England after the restoration. Bunyan, *Works of John Bunyan*, 3:72; and Christopher Hill, *A Turbulent, Seditious, and Factious People: John Bunyan and His Church, 1628–1688* (Oxford: Oxford University Press, 1998), 119. Child argued with his former dissenting colleagues, insisting in *A*

maintained the common conviction of Jesus Christ as King.[21] And though he still retained diminished millennial expectations, he no longer looked for the action of the saints to bring down Antichrist.[22] Yet Bunyan believed that until the day of Antichrist's fall, the saints would surely undergo great persecution.

A CROWN OF LIFE

Bunyan laid out this new eschatological outlook in *The Pilgrim's Progress*, retaining much of the apocalyptic imagery from which earlier dissenters had drawn, although it was part of a very different eschatological narrative. As Faithful and Christian prepare to enter the town of Vanity Fair, Evangelist again appears and discloses to them that they will be "beset with enemies, who will strain hard" to kill them. He tells them that one (or both) of them will seal their testimony in blood, but he admonishes them, "Be you faithful unto death, and the King will give you a Crown of life."[23] It is an image drawn from the

---

Second Argument for a More Full and Firm Union amongst All Good Protestants (London: J. How, 1684) that the state church was an acceptable and perhaps even preferable alternative to nonconformity because of its learned teachers and sound doctrine. A delegation of Baptists that included Benjamin Keach, (Hercules?) Collins, and Mr. B. (John Bunyan) met with Child, seeking to restore him to their fellowship. They were unsuccessful, as Child reportedly declaimed, "I shall go to hell; I am broken in judgment." He committed suicide in 1684. See Greaves, *Glimpses of Glory*, 517.

[21] William Robert Owens argues that it is unreasonable to think that Bunyan's repeated expressions of loyalty to the crown were purely pragmatic and that he concealed a "deep and natural hatred of both king and government, like any normal Baptist of the time." Owens, "Bunyan and the Millennium," in *John Bunyan and His England, 1628–88*, ed. Anne Laurence, W. R. Owens, and Stuart Sim (London: Hambledon, 1990), 90–91; quoting William York Tindall, *John Bunyan: Mechanick Preacher* (New York: Columbia University Press, 1964), 136–37.

[22] It is likely that Bunyan's description of the Delectable Mountains as Immanuel's Land is his allusion to the earthly millennium. Bunyan, *Pilgrim's Progress*, 97. Bunyan explicitly rejects the millennialist conviction that the saints shall bring down Antichrist, arguing, "That Antichrist shall not down, but by the hand of kings." *Of Antichrist, and His Ruin*, in *Works of John Bunyan*, 2:61. W. R. Owens (editor) shows that Bunyan is not alone but is voicing the growing conviction of other dissenting Christians, in *The Miscellaneous Works of John Bunyan* (Oxford: Clarendon, 1994), 13:xxxi–xxxiv.

[23] Bunyan, *Pilgrim's Progress*, 72.

message of the risen Christ to the church of Smyrna in the book of Revelation, whose members were to suffer and be imprisoned. Yet, it promised, to those who were faithful unto death that they would receive the crown of life (Rev 2:10). The image of the King granting a crown to those who persevere unto death occurs only three times in Bunyan's narrative. The first is at the beginning when Christian sets out, and Pliable asks him about the end of the journey. "There are Crowns of Glory to be given us," Christian replies, but, when he and his companion fall into the miry Slough of Despond, Pliable quickly gets out and turns back.[24] The crown imagery also appears in the final scene as Christian and Hopeful cross the River of Death and arrive at the heavenly city. Two angels appear and tell them that because of their sufferings for the King they will wear crowns of gold. As they enter the gate, they are met by others with crowns, and the bells of the city ring with joy.[25] The most prominent instance of the crown imagery is in the trial and martyrdom of Faithful, which stands not only in the center of the story's plot but at the crucial point in the characterization of Christian pilgrimage.

Evangelist urges Christian and Faithful to endure the coming trial so that like the Philadelphian Christians they may obtain the incorruptible crown and hold fast unto the end (Rev 3:11). As the pilgrims enter Vanity Fair, the narrator explains that the way to the Celestial City runs "thorow this Town" and that the only way not to pass through it is to be spared by death, adding that even Christ himself went through it, though he bought nothing at Vanity Fair despite great efforts to entice him by Beelzebub himself.[26] The locals quickly recognize Christian and Faithful as strangers by the plainness of their dress and speech. Yet the more the pilgrims resist offers by the merchants, the more agitated the townspeople become—some despising, others mocking, and still others taunting and reproaching. At last an angry mob surrounds them. After abusing, beating, and smearing them with dirt, they are thrown into a cage and later shackled in chains so they can be led through the fair to endure shame and

[24] Bunyan, *Pilgrim's Progress*, 12–13.
[25] Bunyan, *Pilgrim's Progress*, 130–33.
[26] Bunyan, *Pilgrim's Progress*, 73.

abuse. They are indicted and charged with being "disturbers" of the trade, making "commotions and divisions in the town," and holding "most dangerous opinions, in contempt of the law" of the town's prince.[27] Here, dissenters are not presented as militant revolutionaries leading an army to inaugurate the reign of the saints, but their presence is dangerous to the social and economic order nonetheless.

Christian and Faithful are arraigned before a grand jury in the court of Lord Hategood. After Faithful answers to the charges, false witnesses step forward to testify against him. Envy accuses him of being "one of the vilest men" in the country. Superstition states that he heard Faithful denounce their religion as "naught." Finally, Pickthank swears that he heard Faithful speak slanderously against their noble ruler Prince Beelzebub as well as many of the honorable residents of the town.[28] In his defense, Faithful, like Jesus before his accusers, turns the charges back on his accusers, arguing that their laws are contrary to God's word, their religion is without revelation, and their god is the devil. His testimony simply confirms their prejudice. Needing no further justification, the judge addresses the jury, suggesting that the accused is guilty of heresy and treason. Without consulting his fellow jurors, the foreman declares Faithful a heretic and a traitor, and the other members of the jury concur.[29] The mob then drags him out of the court, where they scourge, buffet, lance, stone, and stab him to death and finally burn his body to ashes.[30] Yet, like the prophet Elijah, God vindicates Faithful, taking him up

---

[27] Bunyan, *Pilgrim's Progress*, 76.

[28] Bunyan, *Pilgrim's Progress*, 77.

[29] Bunyan, *Pilgrim's Progress*, 79.

[30] That Faithful is burned at the stake is a clear indication he is regarded not just as a criminal but as a heretic, for this is the method of death prescribed in *de haeretico comburendo*, the anti-Lollard statute passed in 1401 by Henry IV, repealed in April 1677, the year before the publication of the *Pilgrim's Progress*. The last heretic to be burned at the stake in England was Edward Wightman, who was executed by order of James I on April 11, 1612. See James R[ex]., "A Narration of the Burning of Edward Wightman," in *A True Relation of the Commissions and Warrants for the Condemnation and Burning of Bartholomew Legatt and Thomas Withman* [sic] (London: Michael Spark, 1651), 7–13; and Ian Atherton and David Como, "The Burning of Edward Wightman: Puritanism, Prelacy, and the Politics of Heresy in Early Modern England," *English Historical Review* 120, no. 489 (2005): 1215–50.

in a whirlwind and carrying him away in a chariot of fire straight to the celestial city (2 Kgs 2:11). Here, in the new eschatological outlook, regicide is replaced by martyrdom as the model of Christian faithfulness.

In this remarkable scene, Bunyan continues to read his social world with an eschatological imagination in continuity with dissenters of past generations, like the anonymous author of the tract *Religion's Peace*, which appealed to King James I for full liberty of conscience, identifying the bishops as playing Antichrist by constraining the conscience of dissenters and tyrannizing them body and soul. "The king ought not any longer to give his authority and power," the voice declared, "lest he fulfill the scripture, which saith, that kings should *give their power and authority to the beast* (Rev 13)."[31] Bunyan, however, was no longer looking to the world stage of current political events for catastrophic fulfillments of the end time. Instead, he imagined the apocalyptic drama being enacted in the everyday social struggle of ordinary people who answer the gospel's call to be followers of Christ. In this narrative, Antichrist is no more the literal personification of a single sinister figure. Though evil personified may take the name Beelzebub, Apollyon, Diabolos, or Legion, he is the embodiment of the vast network of worldly "kings and kingdoms" that have been seduced by the false church, the whore of Babylon, the mother of harlots, becoming so "entangled with her beauty, and with her fornication, that they have been adulterated from God and their own salvation."[32] This unholy union of ecclesiastical and civil powers is the beast that wages war against Christ and the saints. Though the authorities of church and state may claim by the warrant of Romans 13 to be ordained by God, they are instead agents of Satan as prophesied in Revelation 13.[33] It is no surprise, then, that Vanity Fair is a place where "the Ware of Rome and her Merchandize

---

[31] *Religions Peace; or, A Plea for Liberty of Conscience*, 1614 (London: John Sweeting, 1646), in Edward Bean Underhill, *Tracts on Liberty of Conscience and Persecution, 1614–1661* (New York: Burt Franklin, 1966), 35; emphasis in original.

[32] Bunyan, *Holy City*, in *Works of John Bunyan*, 3:436.

[33] Bunyan, *The Imprisonment of Mr. John Bunyan*, in *Grace Abounding*, 104.

is greatly promoted,"[34] for the Church of England in its Erastian accommodation to worldly power is identified as the daughter of the great whore, drunk with the blood of saints (Rev 17:5-6). Neither does Bunyan conceal the resemblance of the charges against the two pilgrims and his contemporary dissenters. Nor does he disguise the fact that the judge and jury in the trial of Faithful look very much like the Bedfordshire magistrates before whom Bunyan appeared, for all of them serve the dragon and the beast who made war on the saints (Rev 13:1-10).

It is important to note that when word of the disruptive strangers gets back to "the great one of the fair" (Bunyan's epithet for Beelzebub), rather than confronting them directly, he sends several of his trusted deputies to examine Christian and Faithful in secret. These agents of Satan reach a judgment with haste, concluding that these strangers are "Bedlams and Mad."[35] And because the pilgrims are insane and disorderly, they must be locked away, not as criminals in a jail, but like wild animals in a cage. Here, Bunyan suggests the deep suspicion of empire toward dissenters, who are regarded as unreasonable enthusiasts, subversive to the establishment, and disruptive of the economy. Dissenters are considered beastly and dangerous. They must be subdued, tamed, and domesticated. But if dissenters are judged to be incorrigible and undomesticable, they must be subjected to the spectacle of public humiliation and torture. Some of the citizens of the town who are "more observing" and "less prejudiced" than the rest attempt to intervene and stop the abuse, but, when these temperate voices speak out in favor of the accused, the angry mob threatens to subject their fellow citizens to the same punishment. Then the trial proceeds without further opposition. The execution of Faithful following the guilty verdict must not be mistaken as judicial action. For it is the performance of political theater, as the body of the condemned, which the king claims as his own property, is exposed in public to extreme and excessive violence. Yet the cruel exhibition is

---

[34] Bunyan, *Pilgrim's Progress*, 73.

[35] Bunyan, *Pilgrim's Progress*, 74–75. Referring to the pilgrims as "Bedlams and Mad" is an allusion to Bethlehem Hospital in London, where the insane and disorderly were confined.

intended not merely to punish but to manifest the absolute power of the sovereign over against the limited power of the people mediated through the body of the condemned.[36]

This shift in focus from the high and mighty to the poor and humble places the eschatological outlook of Bunyan's narrative much closer to the Quakers than the millennialism of his earlier polemical writings.[37] For Faithful demonstrates that the saints will reign, but, as William Penn wrote from his cell in the Tower of London, "to reign, 'tis necessary to suffer."[38] The dangerous eschatological imagination of dissenters is outwardly visible in the economic description of the pilgrims as "poor men" and the jury as "gentlemen." Class distinctions identify the servants of the beast, recognized by their titles and land, from pilgrims, whose clothing and manners are common to tailors and weavers, box-makers and soap-boilers, and mechanics and tinkers (like Bunyan himself).[39] Class condescension toward nonconformists was a typical domesticating strategy used against dissenters by Anglicans like Edward Fowler, the former Presbyterian and latitudinarian vicar in Bedfordshire, but it occasionally appeared within the ranks of dissenters where class distinctions were less common.[40] For example, in his criticism of Bunyan's open views on bap-

[36] Bunyan, *Pilgrim's Progress*, 80. On the punitive theater of torture, see Michel Foucault, *Discipline and Punish*, trans. Alan Sheridan, 2nd ed. (New York: Vintage Books, 1995), 33–69.

[37] On the similarity of Baptists and Quakers in the seventeenth century, see Ted Leroy Underwood, *Primitivism, Radicalism, and the Lamb's War: The Baptist-Quaker Conflict in Seventeenth-Century England* (New York: Oxford University Press, 1997), 4.

[38] William Penn, *No Cross, No Crown*, 8th ed. (Leeds: James Lister, 1743), 31. Penn's book was first published in 1668 but greatly expanded in 1682, and subsequently it went through numerous editions. The title page glosses Luke 9:23 describing the way of the *cross* and 2 Tim 4:7-8 that promises a *crown* of righteousness that awaits the faithful on the day of Christ's appearing.

[39] A broadside published in 1647 entitled *A Discovery of the Most Dangerous and Damnable Tenets That Have Been Spread within This Few Yeares: By Many Erronious, Heretical and Mechannick Spirits* identified confectioners, smiths, shoemakers, tailors, saddlers, porter, box-makers, soap-boilers, glovers, meal-men, chicken-men, and button-makers as trades particularly inclined toward dissenting opinions.

[40] Edward Fowler's *The Design of Christianity* (1671) and Bunyan's *Defence of the Doctrine of Justification, by Faith in Jesus Christ* (1672), in Bunyan, *Works of John Bunyan*, 2:279–354.

tism and communion, Thomas Paul, the strict sectarian and colleague of wealthy Baptist minister and London magistrate William Kiffin, condescendingly referenced Bunyan's social rank and occupation.[41] But social class is not so much a structure or a category as it is something that simply happens in human relationships. Class formation and consciousness is based on a shared experience determined by the relations into which they were born or entered into by factors not of their own choosing.[42]

Before coming to Vanity Fair, Faithful recalls his earlier encounter in the Valley of Humiliation with a man called Shame. Shame attacked Christian's religion as weak and pitiful, pointing out that few of the "Mighty, Rich, or Wise" were pilgrims, who all seemed to be of "base and low estate." He also claimed that the poor pilgrims he had met were ignorant of the times and lacked understanding of sciences. Religion, Shame continued, makes its followers "grow strange to the great" and "respect the base," because, he added, they are simply "of the same Religious fraternity." But Faithful rejects such foolishness, reminding Christian, "That which is highly esteemed among Men, is had in abomination with God" (Luke 16:15), and concluding that "the poor man that loveth Christ, is richer then the greatest man in the world that hate him."[43] Although Bunyan was no political revolutionary, his preaching was undoubtedly regarded as dangerous rabble rousing by the Bedfordshire gentry.[44] Yet, for dissenters of the middling sort like Bunyan, the strategy of resisting the domesticating powers of class shame was not through radical politics but rather in the embodiment of the practices of congregational separatism and faithful witness. Bunyan's friend and fellow struggler William Dell declared that the enemies of Christ's true church, like the citizens of Vanity Fair, "abuse the precious saints of God," calling them sectaries, schismatics, heretics, and other reproaches for fear that they might

---

[41] Thomas Paul, *Some Serious Reflections on That Part of Mr. Bunion's Confession of Faith: Touching Church Communion with Unbaptized Persons* (London: Francis Smith, 1673), 1.

[42] E. P. Thompson, *Making of the English Working Class*, 9–10.

[43] Bunyan, *Pilgrim's Progress*, 59–60.

[44] Hill, *Turbulent, Seditious, and Factious People*, 106.

"turn the world upside down."[45] Indeed, there was good reason to be concerned, for in *The Pilgrim's Progress* Bunyan provided dissenters with an apocalyptic narrative, albeit a quietly subversive one, which held out the promise of the crown of life to those who resisted the powers and proved faithful unto death. It was such a community that John Bunyan described as ever looked upon as "a turbulent, seditious, and factious people."[46] For every congregational meeting was potentially seditious. Fitted with "the whole armor of God" (Eph 6:10-20), the saints prepared to do battle against Hobgoblins and Foul Fiends.[47]

As Christian prepares to face Apollyon, he wrestles with whether he should turn back or stand his ground. Then he remembers that "he had no Armour for his back," so that turning back is not an option. It is an image that Bunyan surely must have drawn from his experience as a soldier, but the existential struggle was more pressing and grew out of his conviction that, when he went to jail, he was determined to "pass a sentence of death upon everything that can properly be called a thing of this life."[48] He would not, and he could not, turn back. There, he faces Apollyon with no armor for the back and no plan for retreat. The description comes straight out of apocalyptic imagery describing the first beast in the thirteenth chapter of the book of Revelation: a hideous monster with wings like a dragon, feet like a bear, and a mouth like a lion (Rev 13:2). And like the rich merchants of Vanity Fair and the gentry men of Bedfordshire, he is clothed in fine dress as a prideful display of wealth. Yet his clothing covers his body like the scales of a fish. It is not surprising that Bunyan elsewhere described Antichrist as a "gentleman," who makes the saints

[45] William Dell, *Several Sermons and Discourses* (London: J. Sowle, 1709), 6, 109, 144, and 481; cited in Christopher Hill, *The World Turned Upside Down* (London: Penguin, 1972), 94.

[46] Bunyan, *I Will Pray with the Spirit*, in *Works of John Bunyan*, 1:630. This quote inspired Christopher Hill's biography of Bunyan.

[47] See William Haller, *The Rise of Puritanism* (New York: Columbia University Press, 1957), 150–72.

[48] Bunyan, *Grace Abounding*, §§324–25, Owens, 79.

his "pet."[49] He represents false religion in the trappings of polite culture. He declares Christian to be one of his subjects and himself to be "Prince" and "God" and "King" of the country from which Christian began his journey. But Christian answers that he owes allegiance to "the King of Princes." Even at this point, Apollyon offers Christian what he and those who serve him regard to be a reasonable solution to escape punishment—"turn again and go back." But with no armor for his back, Christian refuses and faces the dragon in mortal combat. Wounded by the enemy and weakened from the battle, Christian seizes his two-edged sword, the word of God (Heb 4:12), and thrusts it into the soft underbelly of the beast, who retreats shrieking in pain as one mortally wounded.[50] Bunyan's description of Christian's struggle with Apollyon bears striking resemblance to the Red Cross Knight's mortal combat with the dragon in Spenser's *Faerie Queene*, from the fire-breathing and shrieking monsters to the wounded but triumphant knights.[51] Yet the conflict in Bunyan's allegory and the

[49] Bunyan, *Of Antichrist, and His Ruin*, in *Works of John Bunyan*, 2:54; emphasis in original. Bunyan's description of Antichrist as a gentleman is strikingly similar to the denuded account of gentility criticized by Richard Braithwait, who argued that "vertue is the greatest Signal of *Gentry*." This good character is "expressed by goodness of *Person*, than greatness of *Place*." The vulgar sense of honor values "the *purple* more than *person*, *descent* more than *desert*, *title* [more] than *merit*." Such an adulterated view of gentility "generates from the *worth* of her Ancestors, derogates likewise the *birth* of her Ancestors." Braithwait, *The English Gentleman* (London: John Haviland, 1630); in The Epistle Dedicatory. However, Thomas Merton suggested that the corrupted account of gentility survived three centuries later in the vague English cultural Christianity he was taught at Oakham School by the chaplain, Buggy Jerwood, who said that the word "charity" in 1 Cor 13 describes "all that we mean when we call a chap a 'gentleman.'" Merton sarcastically reflected, "In other words, charity meant good-sportsmanship, cricket, the decent thing, wearing the right kind of clothes, using the proper spoon, and not being a cad or a bounder." Merton, *The Seven Storey Mountain: An Autobiography of Faith* (New York: Harcourt, 1948), 80–81.

[50] Bunyan, *Pilgrim's Progress*, 46.

[51] Edmund Spenser, *The Faerie Queene*, book 1, ed. George A. Wauchope (Project Gutenberg, 2005), canto 11. The parallels between *The Pilgrim's Progress* and *The Faerie Queene* are so obvious and striking that it has been suggested that, though Bunyan does not mention it, he must have read Spenser's epic poem or at least have been familiar with the plot. Harold Golder, "Bunyan and Spenser," *PMLA* 45, no. 1 (1930): 216–37.

social and political realities it addressed are more akin to Milton's account of Abdiel's confrontation with Satan in *Paradise Lost*. There, it is the faithful angel who declares to the unfaithful and erroneous legions words that surely must have been uttered by many a sectarian to leaders of the church: "How few sometimes may know, when thousands err."[52] And it is this dissenter who heroically strikes the first blow to Satan's head in the war of heaven.[53]

But it is not only the words of dissenters that appear in these literary accounts of spiritual warfare. The voice of Apollyon, though roaring in hideous serpentine dialect, was all too familiar to Bunyan. More than once he had heard it speaking through the magistrates and clergy who pleaded with him to be reasonable and simply to stop preaching. Yet Antichrist is a trope, an image, a mystical figure, not a literal person. As Bunyan explained, Antichrist represents a complex constellation of relations with the devil as its head, the synagogue of Satan as its body, and the spirit of iniquity as its soul.[54] The voice of Apollyon is also one that dissenters like Thomas Hardcastle recognized. Hardcastle was a graduate of St. John's College in Cambridge, a former Anglican priest, and the brother-in-law of the prominent Baptist evangelist and prophet Vavasor Powell. The Broadmead Baptist Church of Bristol called Hardcastle as its pastor on May 19, 1674. In February of 1675, when the government revoked the preaching licenses of all dissenters, Hardcastle was arrested and sent to London for trial. He was returned to Bristol and discharged on August 2, 1675. After preaching at Broadmead on the Sunday following his release, Hardcastle was again arrested and jailed. During his six months of confinement in Newgate Prison at Bristol, Hardcastle wrote twenty-two weekly letters, which were read to the congregation during the Sunday afternoon worship in the place of the sermon. In his first letter, written to the Bristol congregation on August 18, 1675, he intoned:

> God is with us whilst we are with him. He gives new strength according to the day. It is not holding out a while, but it is enduring

[52] Milton, *Paradise Lost*, VI.149, in *John Milton Complete Poems and Major Prose*, ed. Merritt Y. Hughes (New York: Macmillan, 1957), 327.

[53] Milton, *Paradise Lost*, VI.189–94, in *John Milton Complete Poems*, 328.

[54] Bunyan, *Of Antichrist, and His Ruin*, in *Works of John Bunyan*, 2:46.

to the end. The blessing is to him that overcometh. The greatest safety lies in duty, and keeping close to it. He is most in danger, and runs himself into it, that declines duty for fear of the cross, and suffering from men. It has been our great error that we have not trusted in the power of God. We have reasoned about the worst that men can do, but have not believed the best that God can do. Sense and carnal reason must be left behind the things of God. We must not consult in flesh and blood. "He that will come after me, let him deny himself, and take up his cross, and follow me" [Matt 16:24]. This is gospel sense. Is preaching and meeting together a duty only when men will suffer us, or is it an indispensable duty at all times, when men forbid and persecute? The gospel makes no exception or suspension, but rather a supposition that we shall be persecuted, and hurried before ruler; and therefore makes provision, not for our hiding or withdrawing, but for a mouth and wisdom, and says it shall turn to testimony. . . . Religion is still for standing and going forward.[55]

And with words that also find their way onto the lips of Bunyan's Christian, Hardcastle closed his letter, "There is no armour for the back."[56] Though he died three years later, Hardcastle never retreated. Enduring to the end, like Faithful he received his crown of life, and he was not alone.[57]

The Experience of Grace

Bunyan profoundly altered the theological outlook for dissenters in a second significant way. He inverted the eschatological vision and turned it inside out by collapsing the outer world of history into the inner world of the self. The soul becomes a liminal space to travel

[55] Thomas Hardcastle, first letter (August 18, 1675) from Newgate Prison, Bristol, in Edward Bean Underhill, ed., *The Records of a Church of Christ, Meeting in Broadmead Bristol, 1640–1685* (London: J. Haddon, 1847), 258.

[56] Keith E. Durso, *No Armor for the Back* (Macon, Ga.: Mercer University Press, 2007), 128–42.

[57] Underhill, *Tracts on Liberty of Conscience*. In his anthology, Underhill includes statements by the Baptists—Leonard Busher, Thomas Helwys, John Murton, Samuel Richardson, and others.

from the old ways of thinking toward new horizons of experience.[58] The narrative of *The Pilgrim's Progress* charts out an introspective journey of the soul "from this world to that which is to come" through which the reader is invited to follow along. As Bunyan stated in his opening apology:

> This Book will make a Travailer of thee,
> If by its Counsel thou wilt ruled be;
> It will direct thee to the Holy Land,
> If thou wilt its Directions understand.[59]

But the journey is eschatological, not merely psychological. So as to leave no room for doubt, it begins with a direct word from the narrator explaining that his inspiration comes by way of a dream, signaling that it is not simply an allegorical tale told in tropes and types but rather an apocalyptic vision following the paradigm of prophetic experience. In this respect, its opening is not unlike the Apocalypse of John the Revelator, who received an ecstatic vision while "in the Spirit on the Lord's day" and heard a voice saying, "What thou seest, write in a book" (Rev 1:10-11). Accounts of dreams and visions abound in puritan literature, especially in conversion narratives, though not all dreams were regarded as sources of divine revelation.[60] As Thomas Goodwin observed, dreams could be good or bad depending on the nature of the supernatural visitor.[61] Yet such transcendental experiences were accepted as a valid means of divine inspiration through which God communicated immediately with the soul. So when asked how she was brought to refreshing grace, Sarah Wight, a young woman in the congregation of Baptist pastor and

---

[58] Victor Turner, *The Ritual Process* (Ithaca, N.Y.: Cornell University Press, 1969), 95–97.

[59] Bunyan, *Pilgrim's Progress*, 6.

[60] On dreams and visions in puritan spiritual experience, see Nigel Smith, *Perfection Proclaimed: Language and Literature in English Radical Religion 1640–1660* (Oxford: Clarendon, 1989), 73–103.

[61] Philip Goodwin, *The Mystery of Dreames, Historically Discoursed* (London, 1658).

Bunyan's friend Henry Jessey, answered, "By visions of God."[62] These visions came to her frequently as she slept. Baptist prophetess Anna Trapnel had a vision of an angel appearing to her just before she fell asleep.[63] And Bunyan himself received visions in which God communicated directly to him.[64]

The opening scene in *The Pilgrim's Progress* portrays a man clothed in rags with a book in his hand and a burden on his back. As he reads from the book, he becomes greatly distressed by thoughts of an imminent apocalypse, when the coming wrath will collide with his heavy guilt. He cries out, "What shall I do to be saved?"[65] The energy of this question drives the characters and the plot of the story from beginning to end. Yet the answer is not something that the man can find out by himself. It will occur to him, but only after conversation with others. Enter Evangelist, who tells the poor man that the resolution to his conflict lies at the end of a dangerous journey. Though Bunyan's question can be traced back to the apostolic era, where it is found on the lips of the Philippian jailor (Acts 16:30), his answer stands in continuity with generations of English puritans, who required candidates for church membership to offer an account of "the experience of grace." This "experience" was not a psychological permutation of human affection as described by William James[66] or an anthropological feeling of absolute dependence as suggested by Friedrich Schleiermacher.[67] It was a constellation of convictions and affections that bore the evidence of the presence and activity of God in the soul.

---

[62] Henry Jessey, *The Exceeding Riches of Grace Advanced* (London: Matthew Simmons, 1647), 86; in Curtis W. Freeman, ed., *A Company of Women Preachers: Baptist Prophetesses in Seventeenth-Century England* (Waco, Tex.: Baylor University Press, 2011), 217.

[63] Anna Trapnel, *A Legacy for Saints* (London: T. Brewster, 1654), 19; in Freeman, *Company of Women Preachers*, 539.

[64] Bunyan, *Grace Abounding*, §§53–55, Owens, 18.

[65] Bunyan, *Pilgrim's Progress*, 9.

[66] William James, *Varieties of Religious Experience* (New York: Collins, 1960), 50.

[67] Friedrich Schleiermacher, *On Religion: Addresses in Response to Its Cultured Critics*, trans. Terrence N. Tice (Richmond, Va.: John Knox, 1969), 79.

So, in 1653, Vavasor Powell wrote in his popular collection entitled *Spirituall Experiences of Sundry Beleevers* that Christian "experience" is "a Copy written by the Spirit of God upon the hearts of beleevers."[68] Yet, by "copy," he did not mean a mere transcript of the original but rather meant an authentic specimen written directly by the Spirit of God, so that each specimen is evidence of the same author and each copy represents the same experience. The practice of hearing experiences is a recurrent theme in Bunyan's story. When Christian arrives at Palace Beautiful, before he can be admitted to the table for the breaking of bread, Piety, Prudence, and Charity have to hear his experience of grace.[69] And when Christian meets Faithful on the way, it is not until they share "sweet discourse of all things that had happened to them in their Pilgrimage" that they agree to walk together.[70] And when Christian and Hopeful are tempted to fall asleep in the Enchanted ground, they find strength in sharing their experience of grace.[71] Bunyan also called attention to those who lacked the experience of grace—like Ignorance (who at no time displays "convictions of sin" or "fear" of his condition),[72] or Talkative (whose "religion is only in word"), or Formalist and Hypocrisy (who seek "to make short cut" of experience).[73]

But in the work of conversion, there were no short cuts. It was a process that could last years. Among puritans there was wide agreement that converts went through a series of distinct stages from the awareness of sin to the reception of salvation, though there was no consensus about how to name the progress of pilgrims in discrete

[68] Vavasor Powell, *Spirituall Experiences, of Sundry Beleevers* (London: Robert Ibbitson, 1653). Powell does not use the term "copy" as a mere transcript of the original but uses it more in the sense of a specimen written by the Spirit of God, so that each specimen is evidence of the same author and each copy represents the same experience. *Oxford English Dictionary*, s.v. "copy."

[69] Bunyan, *Pilgrim's Progress*, 39–43.

[70] Bunyan, *Pilgrim's Progress*, 55–58.

[71] Bunyan, *Pilgrim's Progress*, 112–18.

[72] Bunyan, *Pilgrim's Progress*, 118–22.

[73] Bunyan, *Pilgrim's Progress*, 62–70.

phases.[74] Bunyan's opening scene with the man clothed in his rags of righteousness (Isa 64:6) and sinking under the burden of sin (Ps 38:4) is certainly a dramatic account of the beginnings of conversion. Christian is aware from his reading of the Scripture that he stands under condemnation, yet he does not know what to do about it. Upon the advice of Evangelist, he left his family and fled the city of destruction for the wicket gate, a door into the church large enough for only one person to enter.[75] Not long into the journey, the burdened man, now called Christian, conscious only of his sin, stumbles from despair into the Slough of Despond. As he is lifted out of the mire, Help explains that "as the sinner is awakened about his lost condition, there ariseth in his soul many fears, and doubts, and discouraging apprehensions, which all of them get together, and settle in this place."[76]

As Christian makes his way through the wicket gate to the House of Interpreter, he is guided into the second stage of conversion leading to the wall called salvation. He runs along the wall until he comes to a place where there stands a cross and below it a grave. As he stands before the cross, the burden he had been carrying is loosed and tumbles into the grave where he sees it no more. Then three angels appear and greet him, pronouncing his sins forgiven, clothing him in new garments, and giving him a scroll with a seal as a sign of his salvation.[77] But the journey of conversion is not done. He continues on to the community of faith gathered at Palace Beautiful, which lies not in the way of salvation but "just by the High-way side."[78] There, he is admitted into the House, and after examination of his experience he

[74] W. R. Owens, introduction to Bunyan, *Grace Abounding*, xxiii. For discussions of divergent morphological accounts, see Jerald C. Brauer, "Conversion: From Puritanism to Revivalism," *Journal of Religion* 58, no. 3 (1978): 233; Edmund S. Morgan, *Visible Saints* (New York: New York University Press, 1963), 90–91; Elizabeth Reis, "Seventeenth-Century Puritan Conversion Narratives," in *Religions of the United States in Practice*, ed. Colleen McDannell (Princeton, N.J.: Princeton University Press, 2001), 1:22–26; Patricia Caldwell, *The Puritan Conversion Narrative: The Beginnings of American Expression* (Cambridge: Cambridge University Press, 1983).

[75] Bunyan, *Pilgrim's Progress*, 8–9.

[76] Bunyan, *Pilgrim's Progress*, 13. Faithful and Hopeful both exhibit this sign of grace (*Pilgrim's Progress*, 68 and 114).

[77] Bunyan, *Pilgrim's Progress*, 24–31.

[78] Bunyan, *Pilgrim's Progress*, 37.

is invited to share fellowship at the table. But the journey is still not over, for Christian must pass through the Valley of Humiliation to do battle against Apollyon armed only with the weapons of the Spirit. At the very moment when Christian comes to despair of life itself, he unsheathes his two-edged sword and inflicts the beast with a mortal wound.[79] Yet the journey still not done for Christian must still pass through Vanity Fair with his fellow pilgrim Faithful and be locked in Doubting Castle with his companion Hopeful.[80] These too are part of the conversion process. When Christian finally crosses the River of Death, arrives at the Celestial City, and presents his scroll to the attendants, and the King commands that the gate be opened that he may enter—only then is the journey of salvation complete.

Even a cursory reading of *Grace Abounding* suggests that Bunyan drew from his own experience of grace for the account he offers in *The Pilgrim's Progress*. He continued over a long time "to be converted to Jesus Christ,"[81] fleeing his own city of Destruction among his ungodly companions in Elstow, listening to his own Evangelists in a group of poor women at Bedford, finding his own entrance through the narrow gap in the wall of salvation leading to the straight way, falling into his own Slough of Despond in the antinomian mire of the Ranters, being locked in his own Doubting Castle for fear of having committed the unpardonable sin of Esau, conversing with his own Interpreter in Good John Gifford, fighting his own battles with Hobgoblins and Foul Fiends in the Bedford magistrates, having his own come-to-Jesus experience with the help of his wife, and making his own entrance into the gathered community at St. John's Church. Yet the story of *The Pilgrim's Progress* is not merely an allegorized autobiography of Bunyan's conversion. It became a kind of popular epic of dissent, not for everyone, but certainly for noncomformists like Bunyan and the Baptists, who were regarded by gentry and

[79] Bunyan, *Pilgrim's Progress*, 49.

[80] John Stachniewski argues that the theology election and damnation exemplified in the struggle of the conversion process resulted in a profound sense of doubt, terror, and despair, creating a "persecutory imagination" that permeated the social life of England in the seventeenth century. Stachniewski, *The Persecutory Imagination: English Puritanism and the Literature of Despair* (Oxford: Clarendon, 1991).

[81] Bunyan, *Grace Abounding*, §73, 22.

clergy alike as a turbulent, seditious, and factious people.[82] In its dark figures and shadows, religion and politics were mixed, providing an imagination for resistance hidden deep in its secret code. And at the heart of the story is the conviction that without hope the long journey of dissent cannot be sustained.

Bunyan's depiction of Christian pilgrimage seems to confirm the suspicion that *The Pilgrim's Progress* is a story of the lone individual in search of personal salvation. Christian leaves family, home, and community to follow his own spiritual quest. It appears to present the portrait of a solitary soul scrupulously combing through inner experience in search of signs of grace while ignoring the outward social world. Such a reading might take Bunyan's story simply as another typical account of puritan introspection, anticipating the heightened sense of the self that demarcates the emerging modern consciousness. But such a conclusion would be mistaken. For Bunyan places his account of conversion within a narrative of the visible church fitly described by John Robinson (the first-generation dissenter and Jacobean exile in Leiden) as "a company, consisting though but of two or three, separated from the world . . . and gathered into the name of Christ by a covenant made to walk in all the ways of God known unto them."[83] Bunyan's vision thus depicts a pilgrim church of two or three that gathers and walks together, with an emphasis on the word *together*. Christian may set out on the journey by himself, but he never walks alone. Salvation cannot be discerned alone, nor can its process be completed alone. Christian has companions and guides along the way: Evangelist, Help, Interpreter, Piety, Prudence, Charity, and especially Faithful and Hopeful. It is not a vision of the communion of saints or the church catholic. Yet it sketches out a picture of the church as a gathered community.

Because salvation is a dangerous journey, it must be undertaken with other pilgrims. The path is filled with wind and weather, foul fiends, and great discouragement, which must be endured and resisted. Yet Bunyan was insistent that resistance without a community of

---

[82] Bunyan, *I Will Pray with the Spirit*, in *Works of John Bunyan*, 1:630; and Hill, *Turbulent, Seditious, and Factious People*, 371.

[83] Robinson, *The Works of John Robinson*, 3 vols. (London: John Snow, 1851), 2:132.

pilgrims is futile. His strategy of resistance against the forces of imperial domestication accepted that "the powers that be are ordained of God" (Rom 13:1), and so he agreed "to submit to the King as supreme, also to the governors as to them that are sent by him."[84] But he contended that though the king had power over the body, this power did not extend to the soul. He, thus, maintained a dual obedience to follow God in matters where his conscience was convinced and to submit to the king's authority by suffering when he could not obey the king in violation of his conscience. Essentially, Bunyan held this conviction: "[T]he king can take my body but not my soul, for it belongs to King Jesus."[85] This parsing of duties to God and king correlating to matters of soul and body was a common distinction among dissenters like Thomas Helwys, who, in a note to King James I inscribed on the flyleaf of his *Mystery of Iniquity*, stated, "The king is a mortal man and not God, therefore has no power over the immortal souls of his subjects, to make laws and ordinances for them, and to set spiritual lords over them."[86] For Helwys, as for Bunyan, Christ alone is Lord over the conscience, and not the king, and so the king has no prerogative to judge between God and humanity.[87] This account nevertheless had the unfortunate consequence of reifying the dichotomy between soul and body that partitioned the spiritual world from social history. Yet, whereas the slumbering dissent of Bunyan may have given the appearance of domestication like a sleeping lion may be mistaken as tame, it was a false and dangerous assumption. For the boundary between these spiritual and social worlds was permeable, and in the end he did not abide by a dichotomous anthropology of spirituality and materiality that renders resistance to the powers futile.[88]

[84] Bunyan, *Relation of the Imprisonment of Mr. John Bunyan*, in *Grace Abounding*, 104.

[85] This dichotomous anthropology is allegorically represented in Bunyan's *The Holy War*, which describes the city of Mansoul, which rejected its rightful king Shaddai, was taken captive by Dibolous, and was finally freed by Emmanuel (in *Works of John Bunyan*, 3:245–373).

[86] Helwys, *Mystery of Iniquity*, vi.

[87] Helwys, *Mystery of Iniquity*, 53.

[88] Bunyan might have sought to address this tension toward a holistic anthropology through his conviction of the divine-human union in Christ, who (as fully

Interpreters of the Dream

Bunyan concluded his story with an invitation for readers to interpret his dream.[89] His offer was surprisingly well received. *The Pilgrim's Progress* sold over one hundred thousand copies the first decade alone and has become one of the most widely read books in the world. But not everyone was so enthusiastically receptive. Edward Fowler, the latitudinarian vicar of a neighboring village in Bedfordshire during the 1660s, attacked Bunyan, calling him a rank and ranting antinomian, a wretched scribbler, grossly ignorant, a piece of proud folly, a most black-mouthed culminator, an ignorant fanatic, an impudent malicious schismatic, and a filthy libertine with mad licentious principles.[90] Even some of his fellow Baptists questioned his place within their fellowship. Thomas Paul attacked Bunyan's view of baptism as "no bar to communion" (accusing him of throwing dirt on the Baptists) and condescendingly referred to his lower social rank, suggesting that, if he were more open about his beliefs, he might gain more work than he could handle.[91] Yet, despite this opposition, Bunyan gained almost universal respect and reception among intellectuals and evangelicals. Understanding the emergence of this ironic consensus, however, requires some explanation.

The inclusion of Bunyan's works in literate circles did not happen without a struggle. His crude language and common outlook stood in the way of his reception by readers in polite culture. One of the early indications of changing attitudes was the acclaim for *The*

God) commands obedience and (as fully human) demonstrates what obedience looks like. Bunyan gestures in this direction in his appeal to the incarnation against the Quakers, in *Grace Abounding*, §§122–23, Owens, 33. The first Baptist theologian to reject explicitly the prevailing dichotomy was H. Wheeler Robinson, who recovered the holism of Hebrew psychology. He displayed that, from a biblical point of view, it is correct to think of human existence as an ensouled body or an embodied soul. Robinson, "Hebrew Psychology," in *The People and the Book*, ed. Arthur S. Peake (Oxford: Clarendon, 1925), 362, 366.

[89] Bunyan, *Pilgrim's Progress*, 134.

[90] Edward Fowler, *Dirt Wip't Off; or, A Manifest Discovery of the Gross Ignorance, Erroneousness and Most Unchristian Wicked Spirit of One John Bunyan, Lay-Preacher in Bedford* (London: Richard Royston, 1672).

[91] Paul, *Some Serious Reflections*, 1 and 42.

Pilgrim's Progress by Samuel Taylor Coleridge in his 1818 "Lectures on European Literature," in which he commended Bunyan's work as being second only to the Bible for "teaching and enforcing the whole saving truth according to the mind that was in Christ Jesus." Coleridge readily admitted that it was composed of "the lowest style of English," but he maintained that "there is a great theological acumen in the work."[92] His brother-in-law, the poet Robert Southey, was less impressed. Southey was troubled by Bunyan's feelings of torment, the "extreme ignorance out of which he worked his way, and the stage of burning enthusiasm through which he passed."[93] Coleridge shared similar concerns, yet amazingly he was able to see that the same Calvinism that gave rise to doubts of election and fits of despair had produced a work of such exquisite and delightful color. The explanation for such miraculous inspiration was, he intoned, that Bunyan's "piety was baffled by his genius, and the Bunyan of Parnassus had the better of the Bunyan of the Conventicle."[94]

Critical scholarship gradually followed the path laid out by Coleridge, but Bunyan's eventual reception into the canon of English literature did not come without a price. In order to be received as a literary classic, *The Pilgrim's Progress* had to be shown to be the work of a creative genius, not a radical dissenter. Later critics would come to see this bifurcation between the unconscious artist and the rational Calvinist as artificial and seek to hold the Parnassian and Conventicler together as one subject.[95] Yet reading Bunyan well requires more

---

[92] Coleridge, "Lectures on Literature," in *The Collected Works of Samuel Taylor Coleridge* (Princeton, N.J.: Princeton University Press, 1969–2002), 1:103.

[93] Robert Southey, "The Life of John Bunyan," in *The Pilgrim's Progress*, by John Bunyan, ed. Robert Southey (New York: Harper & Brothers, 1837), 11–74. Southey was repulsed by what John Stachniewski describes as "the persecutory imagination" of puritanism shared by Bunyan, which infiltrated the social and religious life of England in the first half of the seventeenth century. Stachniewski challenges the view of later evangelicalism that shaved off the psychic terror, arguing that the mind of Bunyan's Christian is obsessed with fears of election and reprobation. Stachniewski suggests that Bunyan's use of allegory is his attempt to exorcize the persecutory fears that he dramatized (Stachniewski, *Persecutory Imagination*, 169 and 215–16).

[94] Coleridge, "Lectures on Literature," in *Collected Works*, 1:103.

[95] Roger Sharrock, "Bunyan Studies Today: An Evaluation," in *Bunyan in England and Abroad*, ed. M. van Os and G. J. Schutte (Amsterdam: VU University

than holding these two parts together in the interpretive process. Coleridge assumed that, like the oracle of Delphi, Bunyan channeled his muse of universal (natural?) human experience, thus transcending his historical particularity and writing a popular prose epic for everyone. But this critical strategy ended up being simply another sophisticated version of domestication. Like the Bedford gentry who sought to silence Bunyan's voice, the critics ignored the tinker and poor man in favor of the voice of universal human experience, which as it turned out was not universal at all but rather a very specific voice of a very particular racial group and social class, and indeed they transformed him into one of their own. It was up to social historians of the twentieth century like Christopher Hill and E. P. Thompson to recover the slumbering radicalism at the center of Bunyan's writings that drew from the working-class animus for the gentry.[96]

But, for other readers, *The Pilgrim's Progress* was less important for its literary value than for its evangelical appeal. They came down on the side of Bunyan as a hero of nonconformity rather than as a creative genius. Joining the great company who read it attentively that began in Bunyan's own lifetime, this second group saw *The Pilgrim's Progress* as universal in a different sense from the literary critics. Nonconformists were drawn to its clear presentation of the evangelical message that was for all.[97] Yet, even among dissenters, the recep-

---

Press, 1990), 46–47; and N. H. Keeble, ed., *John Bunyan: Conventicle and Parnassus; Tercentenary Essays* (Oxford: Clarendon, 1988).

[96] Hill, *Turbulent, Seditious, and Factious People*, 373; and E. P. Thompson, *Making of the English Working Class*, 30–34.

[97] Stuart Sim argues that Bunyan's Christian in *The Pilgrim's Progress* is not just a role model for future generations of dissenters but appeals particularly to intolerant, repressive, authoritarian, and biblically literalist fundamentalists. Sim states that "Christian is utterly convinced that he is in possession of the truth and can only treat anyone who chooses to dispute the point as an enemy." Sim, "Bunyan and His Fundamentalist Readers," in *Reception, Appropriation, Recollection: Bunyan's "Pilgrim's Progress,"* ed. W. R. Owens and Stuart Sim (Oxford: Peter Lang, 2007), 213–28. But just as Bunyan's allegorical characterization is more complex than a flat reading might suggest, so is the nature and character of evangelicalism more complex than such an easy identification of Bunyan and his legacy as fundamentalist. While it may be the case that all fundamentalists are evangelical, it is not the case that all evangelicals are fundamentalists. George M. Marsden delineates the difference, explaining that

tion of Bunyan remained mixed for some time. His narrative fit into the old puritan theological pattern in which conversion was marked by at least two stages: first, *preparation*, understood as a long process whereby the unconverted person becomes awakened to the will of God and disappointed by the futility of trying to keep God's commandments in one's own strength; and, second, *conversion*, in which the regenerating work of grace becomes evident and displays that one is among the elect of God.

The underlying assumptions of this pattern reflected the theology of the Westminster Confession of Faith (1646), including inherited guilt, double predestination, and effectual calling, which maintained that the nonelect "are incapable of being outwardly called by the ministry of the Word."[98] Such an outlook was unacceptable to dissenters of a more Arminian persuasion and to other nonconformists, especially Methodists. Bunyan's portrayal of the Man in the Iron Cage, who believed his heart to be so hardened that he could never repent, suggested that some might be beyond the pale of redemption, as Bunyan once thought himself to be.[99] Descriptions of such despair could have kept John Wesley from reading *The Pilgrim's Progress*, for he believed that the good news of the gospel was for all, and he hated the Calvinist doctrine of election. Yet he saw, in its story, great grace and such necessity of new birth that (to paraphrase Coleridge)

"fundamentalists are not just religious conservatives, they are conservatives who are willing to take a stand and to fight." Marsden, *Understanding Fundamentalism and Evangelicalism* (Grand Rapids: Eerdmans, 1991), 1. Here Marsden riffs on the classic statement by Curtis Lee Laws that fundamentalists are Christians who "cling to the great fundamentals and who mean to do battle royal" for the faith. Laws, "Convention Sidelights," *Watchman-Examiner*, July 1, 1920, 834.

[98] Westminster Confession of Faith, X.3, in *Creeds of the Churches*, ed. John H. Leith, 3rd ed. (Louisville, Ky.: Westminster John Knox, 1982), 206.

[99] Bunyan, *Pilgrim's Progress*, 28–29; see Bunyan, *Grace Abounding*, §§44–45, 57–58, Owens, 16, 19. Keeble identifies the Man in the Iron Cage as John Child, a lapsed Baptist who conformed to the Church of England in 1660 (*Pilgrim's Progress*, 268n28). Keeble points out that Bunyan's language in describing the despair of the caged man mirrors Christopher Marlowe's *Dr. Faustus*, act 2, scene 1, lines 17–18, in *The Complete Plays*, ed. J. B. Steane (Harmondsworth: Penguin, 1969), 285. The Man in the Iron Cage may also reflect the story of Francis Spira, which Bunyan read. Nathaniel Bacon, *Relation of the Fearful Estate of Francis Spira in the Year 1548* (London: I[ohn] L[egat], 1638).

Bunyan's Calvinism was baffled by his sense of God's love. Wesley abridged *The Pilgrim's Progress* in 1743 and commended it for use by the Methodists.[100] George Whitefield, who found the doctrines of grace more congenial to his theological sentiments, was no less insistent on preaching the gospel of new birth to all comers. It is noteworthy, then, that in his preface written for Bunyan's *Works*, Whitefield endearingly referred to Bunyan as possessing "the catholic spirit."[101]

The major shift toward a more catholic account of evangelical faith that Whitefield alluded to occurred toward the end of the eighteenth century. Proponents of the old doctrines of grace like John Gill, a leading Baptist pastor in London, rejected any notion of an "open offer" of the gospel, reserving the invitation of grace only to the elect.[102] For high Calvinists, faith was warranted by an inner persuasion of interest in Christ, signifying regeneration and election. In 1785, Andrew Fuller published an influential book entitled *The Gospel Worthy of All Acceptation*, which shifted the warrant for faith from an inner-subjective interest in Christ to an outer-objective focus on Christ and his gospel. "If," Fuller proposed, "faith in Christ be the duty of the ungodly"—and he affirmed that it is—then "it must of course follow that every sinner, whatever be his character, is completely *warranted* to trust in the Lord Jesus Christ for the salvation of his soul." The corollary to this truth, Fuller continued, is that "it is the duty of ministers of Christ plainly and faithfully to preach the

---

[100] John Bunyan, *The Pilgrim's Progress*, abridged by John Wesley (Newcastle: John Gooding, 1743). It went through multiple editions throughout Wesley's lifetime and was widely used among Methodists. As a young man, John Wesley's father heard Bunyan preach, and his mother Susannah Wesley's grave in Bunhill Fields is not far from Bunyan's memorial. Methodist preachers made frequent reference to Bunyan, and his account of evangelical conversion exerted a formative influence on their own autobiographical narratives. N. H. Keeble, "Of Him Thousands Daily Sing and Talk: Bunyan and His Reputation," in Keeble, *John Bunyan: Conventicle and Parnassus*, 249–50; and Gordon Stevens Wakefield, *Bunyan the Christian* (London: Harper Collins, 1992), 49.

[101] Whitefield, "A Recommendatory Preface to the Works of Mr. John Bunyan," in *The Works of the Reverend George Whitefield*, 4 vols. (London: Edward & Charles Dilly, 1771), 4:307.

[102] John Gill, *A Body of Doctrinal Divinity*, 6.13 (London: M. & S. Higham, 1839), 545–52.

Gospel to all who will hear it."[103] That the influence of Robert Hall Sr. was instrumental in Fuller's gradual awareness that the doctrines of grace as explained by Gill and other high Calvinists were a stumbling block to salvation is widely recognized.[104] But an overlooked factor in this theological shift was Bunyan, who, as Fuller observed, "maintained the doctrines of election and predestination" while also holding out "the free offer to sinners without distinction."[105] A similar version of the new evangelical theology was picked up simultaneously in the United States through the revivals that swept the country. When asked to describe his theological outlook, Elder John Leland, a leading figure in the evangelical transformation of Virginia, quipped that "the preaching that has been most blessed of God, and most profitable to men, is the doctrine of sovereign grace in the salvation of souls, mixed with a little of what is called Arminianism."[106]

This evangelical paradigm shift was complete by the end of the nineteenth century and is most clear in the commendation of C. H. Spurgeon, who stated, "[N]ext to the Bible, the book I value most is John Bunyan's *Pilgrim's Progress*."[107] Spurgeon, however, was critical of Bunyan's account of the process of conversion and, in particular, the thought that Bunyan's Evangelist instructs Christian to carry the

---

[103] Fuller, *The Gospel Worthy of All Acceptation*, in *The Complete Works of Rev. Andrew Fuller*, ed. Joseph Belcher, 3 vols. (Philadelphia: American Baptist Publication Society, 1845; repr., Harrisonburg, Va.: Sprinkle, 1988), 2:383–93; emphasis in original. See Peter J. Morden, *Offering Christ to the World: Andrew Fuller (1754–1815) and the Revival of Eighteenth Century Particular Baptist Life* (Carlisle, U.K.: Paternoster, 2003), 23–51.

[104] Hall contended that "the way to Jesus is graciously laid open for everyone who chooses to come to him." Robert Hall [Sr.], *Help to Zion's Travelers* (Bristol: William Pine, 1781), 117.

[105] Fuller, *Complete Works*, 1:15.

[106] Leland, *Letter of Valediction on Leaving Virginia in 1791*, in *The Writings of the Late Elder John Leland*, ed. L. F. Greene (New York: G. W. Wood, 1845; repr., New York: Arno, 1969), 172.

[107] Charles H. Spurgeon, *Pictures from Pilgrim's Progress* (Chicago: Fleming H. Revell, 1903), 7. On Spurgeon and Bunyan, see Peter J. Morden, *Communion with Christ and His People: The Spirituality of C. H. Spurgeon* (Oxford: Regent's Park College, 2010), 26–30.

burden on his back first to the wicket gate (the church), then to the Slough of Despond, until finally coming to the cross. He exclaimed,

> We must not say to the sinner, "Now, Sinner, if you will be saved, go to the baptismal pool—go to the wicket gate—go to the church—do this or that." No, the Cross should be right in front of the wicket gate and we should say to the sinner, "Throw yourself there and you are safe! But you are not safe till you can cast off your burden and lie at the foot of the Cross and find peace in Jesus."[108]

Conversion was thus shortened from a process to an event and Arminianized, giving more emphasis to human response and laying less stress on divine enabling. Though there were differences among evangelicals, the practical effect of this consensus was an understanding that the good news was to be freely offered to all with nothing placed before the cross: in the words of the gospel hymn, "Just as I am without one plea."[109] Bunyan portrays in colorful terms a central evangelical conviction that "saving faith means a direct, individual response to the grace offered by God in Christ."[110] Yet this transformation of *The Pilgrim's Progress* from a puritan story to an evangelical classic did not come without a price either. For in the process of the inward turn toward conversion, the radical social vision that gave it such authenticity began to fall asleep.

One unforeseen uptake of this new evangelical consensus—as George Offor, the editor of the immensely popular edition of *The Works of John Bunyan*, put it—was that *The Pilgrim's Progress* "has been

---

[108] Charles H. Spurgeon, "The Dumb Become Singers," in *Metropolitan Tabernacle Pulpit*, vol. 58 (London: Passmore, 1912; repr., Pasadena, Tex.: Pilgrim Publications, 1979), 599.

[109] Charles H. Spurgeon quotes the first verse of this hymn in his sermon "None but Jesus," in *Spurgeon's Sermons* (New York: Sheldon, 1857–1860), 7:259–76. This sermon provides a clear statement by Spurgeon of the evangelical consensus on the warrant of faith.

[110] Paul S. Fiddes, *Tracks and Traces: Baptist Identity in Church and Theology* (Carlisle, U.K.: Paternoster, 2003), 228.

translated into most of the languages and dialects of the world."[111] Where Bunyan's reception into the official canon of literature was largely a national matter that concerned readers in England, the evangelical transmission of his writings was a transnational process that involved all nations. What propelled *The Pilgrim's Progress* into the awareness of global readers was the missionary conviction to go into all the world combined with the belief that Bunyan's story put forth the evangelical message in a clear and simple way. This missionary mandate made Bunyan "portable," to lift up the wonderful description by Isabel Hofmeyr.[112] Yet the complicated entanglement of the missionary enterprise with Western cultural imperialism has given grounds to postcolonial questions about the portability of *The Pilgrim's Progress*, suggesting that its so-called universality has been used to underwrite the racial uniqueness of England and its empire. Such a reading is ironically the exact opposite of Bunyan's purpose, which contained an apocalyptic vision of revolutionary politics thinly disguised as a spiritual allegory. But while the missionary employment of this document is not free of problems, the process of translation actually serves to subvert and complicate the postcolonial critique, destigmatizing the receiving culture by entrusting the gospel into new forms while also relativizing the sending culture by denying that there is only one normative expression of Christianity.[113]

Beginning with Felix Carey's work in 1821, Baptist missionaries from England produced a steady stream of translations of *The Pilgrim's Progress* into a host of languages throughout South Asia, including Hindi, Oriya (Odia), Bengali, Lushai (Mizoram), Urdu,

[111] George Offor, "A Memoir of John Bunyan," in Bunyan, *Works of John Bunyan*, 1:lvii.

[112] Isabel Hofmeyr, *The Portable Bunyan: A Transnational History of "The Pilgrim's Progress"* (Princeton, N.J.: Princeton University Press, 2004); and Hofmeyr, "Bunyan: Colonial, Postcolonial," in *The Cambridge Companion to Bunyan*, ed. Anne Dunan-Page (Cambridge: Cambridge University Press, 2010), 162–76.

[113] Lamin Sanneh, "Christian Missions and the Western Guilt Complex," *Christian Century*, April 8, 1987, 331–34; and Sanneh, *Translating the Message: The Missionary Impact on Culture* (Maryknoll, N.Y.: Orbis, 1989), 1–3.

and Sinhalese.[114] American Baptist missionaries followed suit, publishing indigenous-language versions, starting with Sarah Judson's Burmese edition of 1840, which her husband Adoniram praised as "one of the best pieces of composition which we have yet published."[115] It had a profound effect on the shape of devotion among Christians in Burma, teaching them how to read and understand the Bible and to live as Christians.[116] Jonathan Wade, who had produced a five-volume thesaurus of the Karen language, translated *The Pilgrim's Progress* into Karen in 1863.[117] It is unclear precisely how indigenous Christians may have been reading Bunyan's work, but Wade's handwritten account, "The First Seventy Years of the Mission to the Karens of Burma" gives some indication. He offers a brief but vivid report on the persecution of Karen Christians. On one occasion,

[114] The Angus Library at Regent's Park College, Oxford University, has a number of early South Asian translations. John Bunyan, *Bunyan's Pilgrim's Progress*, abridged and trans. into Hindi by Rev. W. Buyers (Calcutta: Baptist Missionary Press, 1835); *The Pilgrim's Progress*, trans. Shem Sahu (part 1), trans. Ghanu Shyam Naik (part 2) (Cuttack: Religious Tract Society and the Orissa Tract Society, 1873); *The Pilgrim's Progress*, part 1, trans. into Bengalee by F[elix] Carey (Serampore: Mission Press, 1821); *Kristian Vân Ram Kawng Zwh Thu*, trans. into Lushai (London: Religious Tract Society, n.d.); *The Pilgrim's Progress*, in Urdu (P.R.B.S., 1889); and *Bunyan's Pilgrim's Progress*, first part, in Sinhalese (Colombo: The Christian, 1907).

[115] John Bunyan, *Bunyan's Pilgrim's Progress*, part 1, trans. Sarah Judson (Maulmain: American Baptist Mission Press, 1840). The second edition was published in 1855, available in the American Baptist Historical Collection Archives, Atlanta, Georgia, hereafter simply referred to as the ABHS Archives. Sarah Judson's translation of *The Pilgrim's Progress*, part 1, continued to remain in print as late as 1906. Adoniram Judson, "Obituary—Mrs. Sarah B. Judson," *Baptist Missionary Magazine* 26, no. 2 (1846): 42; cited in Emily C. Judson, *Memoir of Mrs. Sarah B. Judson* (New York: Colby, 1849), 225.

[116] Laura Rogers Levens, "'Reading the Judsons': Recovering the Literary Works of Ann, Sarah, Emily, and Adoniram Judson for a New Baptist Mission History," *American Baptist Quarterly* 32 no. 1 (2013): 37–73.

[117] John Bunyan, *Bunyan's Pilgrim's Progress*, trans. from the London Tract Society's edition into Sgau Karen by J[onathan] Wade (Rangoon: Printed at the Mission Press; published by the Burmah Bible and Tract Society, 1863), in ABHS Archives. Jonathan and Deborah Wade came to Rangoon as new missionaries in 1823. The book contains simple black-and-white etchings of episodes from the story. The characters and scenes are English/European, and no attempt is made to make them indigenous. One thousand copies of the first edition were printed.

someone asked what might happen if the national authorities were to give an order to cut off their heads. The Karen converts replied, "Then let him cut off our heads. We believe in Jesus Christ; if we are killed we shall go directly where Jesus is, and there we shall be happy."[118] Wade relates several similar stories of harassment and intimidation, one of a man who was ordered by the head of his village to abandon the faith. The man unflinchingly replied, "I believe in the Lord Jesus Christ and no more worship Nats, or Pagodas, or Images, or drink spirits. I worship the Eternal God." He was fined. During a severe persecution in 1835, every Christian who professed faith in Jesus Christ was given a very heavy fine of four times the amount of the average Karen's total property. The result of the persecution, Wade observed, was that 167 Karens came forward for baptism.[119]

It is not hard to imagine that episodes from *The Pilgrim's Progress* like the martyrdom of Faithful served as models of Christian discipleship for indigenous Christians in Burma and elsewhere.[120] Nor should it be surprising that this tradition of dissent fostered resistance to empires old and new. In her first visit to the United States in more than four decades, Nobel Laureate Aung San Suu Kyi explained that the seeds of democracy in Burma cannot be explained simply as a result of geopolitics but rather must be seen in the light of the educational and humanitarian work of the Baptist missionaries, who labored hard to preserve Burmese culture and manners while also introducing evangelical Christianity of the sort exemplified by

[118] Jonathan Wade, "The First Seventy Years of the Mission to the Karens of Burma," handwritten manuscript in Jonathan Wade Papers, 38–39, in ABHS Archives.

[119] Wade, "First Seventy Years," 39, in ABHS Archives.

[120] The ABHS Archives contain additional translations in Bengali, Cantonese, and Fiji. John Bunyan, *The Pilgrim's Progress from This World to That Which Is to Come*, part 1 (Calcutta: Printed at the Baptist Mission Press, for the Calcutta Tract and Christian Book Society, 1835). The text contains both Bengali and English (in small print below the Bengali text); *Pilgrim's Progress, Illustrated by a Chinese Artist*, trans. George Piercy in Canton vernacular (1871). The book contains thirty-five black-and-white drawings. All the illustrations set the story in a completely indigenous Chinese setting. There are small Chinese captions on each illustration. The Fiji version is *Ai Tukutuku Kei Vulgai-Lako: A Ya Nai Tukutuku Ni Nona Lako Mai Na Vuravura O Qo Ki Ka Vuravura Ena Muri Mai: Sa Volai Me Vaka Sa Dua Na Tadra. E Vola Taumada*, trans. Ko Misa Joni Puniyani (Sa Laveti Ki Na vosa Vaka-Viti. Sa Tabaki Mai Londoni, E Peritani, 1867).

Bunyan's story.[121] The emerging democracy in Burma is a legacy of the slumbering dissent transmitted by the missionaries.[122]

When missionaries were forced out of Madagascar in 1835, the only legacy they left behind for their converts was boxes of Bibles and copies of *The Pilgrim's Progress*. But because these two books were the only printed volumes in Malagasy, the national language of Madagascar, they were widely read by all people regardless of rank or class. After twenty-six years, the missionaries were allowed to return, not knowing what to expect when they arrived. In her account of the mission history, Helen Barrett Montgomery observed that when the missionaries departed there were fifteen hundred Christians and that when they returned there were seven thousand Christians. In the interim, ten thousand Christians had been sentenced to death, slavery, or exile. Montgomery wondered what could account for such courage. The obvious reason, she answered, was that during the dark years of persecution the new Christians had fed their souls on these books. Stories like these indicate the value of *The Pilgrim's Progress* among Christian missionaries.[123]

One of the most intriguing receptions of Bunyan occurred in China during the Taiping Rebellion of 1851–1864.[124] The story begins

---

[121] Aung San Suu Kyi, "Aung San Suu Kyi in Washington" (September 18, 2012), http://asiasociety.org/video/policy/aung-san-suu-kyi-washington-complete?page=1 (accessed November 11, 2015). For a nuanced and careful examination of Adoniram Judson's preservation and incorporation of Burman culture and manners, see Graham B. Walker Jr., "Building a Christian *Zayat* in the Shade of the Bo Tree," *American Baptist Quarterly* 32, no. 1 (2013): 13–36.

[122] Robert D. Woodberry provides strong empirical evidence for the case that rather than extending colonialism, the work of conversionary Protestant missionaries "heavily influenced the rise and spread of stable democracy around the world." Woodberry, "The Missionary Roots of Liberal Democracy," *American Political Science Review* 106, no. 2 (2012): 244–74. Cf. Andrea Palpant Dilley, "The World the Missionaries Made," *Christianity Today* 58, no. 1 (2014): 34–41. See also Woodberry, "The Shadow of Empire: Christian Missions, Colonial Policy, and Democracy in Postcolonial Societies" (PhD diss., University of North Carolina, Chapel Hill, 2004).

[123] Helen Barrett Montgomery, *The Bible and Missions* (West Medford, Mass.: Central Committee on the United Study of Foreign Missions, 1920), 129–31.

[124] Eugene Powers Boardman, *Christian Influence on the Ideology of the Taiping Rebellion, 1851–1864* (Madison: University of Wisconsin Press, 1952); Margaret Morgan Coughlin, "Strangers in the House: J. Lewis Shuck and Issachar Roberts, First

with the eventual Taiping king, Hong Xiuquan, studying tracts published by Christian missionaries. His inquiry into Christianity came after receiving a heavenly vision that included visitations from two men, one old and the other middle aged. Hong became a Christian convert, and in 1847 he briefly came under the influence of an eccentric and independent Baptist missionary from the United States named Issachar Jacox Roberts, who many fellow missionaries regarded as "ill-qualified" and "illiterate." Hong attended daily Bible classes under Roberts' instruction, though there are questions about how much he understood, given that the two men did not speak the same dialect. Roberts initially regarded Hong's faith as genuine, approving him as a candidate for Christian baptism, but the missionary came to suspect the motives of his student, postponing his baptism indefinitely. Hong thus interrupted his catechetical instruction and returned to his home province, where he continued studying the Bible on his own.

Hong's autodidactic investigations led him to believe that the persons who visited him in his earlier vision were God the Father and God the Son, and that he was the second Son of God and the younger brother of Jesus.[125] He later came to see his own son, the young prince, as part of "a sacred quaternion." Hong became convinced that his divine mission was to expel the foreign Manchu (Qing) dynasty and destroy the idol worship of Confucianism. Under Hong's leadership as the Heavenly King and Savior from Disease, the God worshippers set out to establish the kingdom of heaven on earth. The Taipings

American Baptist Missionaries in China" (PhD diss., University of Virginia, 1972); John A. Rapp, "Clashing Dilemmas: Hong Renan, Issachar Roberts, and a Taiping 'Murder' Mystery," *Journal of Historical Biography* 4, no. 4 (2008): 27–58; Yuwu Song, ed., *Encyclopedia of Chinese-American Relations* (Jefferson, N.C.: McFarland, 2009), s.v. "Issachar Jacox Roberts," 238–39; Jonathan D. Spence, *God's Chinese Son: The Taiping Heavenly Kingdom of Hong Xiuquan* (New York: W. W. Norton, 1996), 280–84; and Yuan Chung Teng, "Reverend Issachar Jacob Roberts and the Taiping Rebellion," *Journal of Asian Studies* 23, no. 1 (1963) 55–67; and Teng, *Americans and the Taiping Rebellion: A Study of American-Chinese Relationship, 1847–1864* (Taipei: China Academy, 1982).

[125] This summary is drawn from the theological debate on March 1861 between Hong and Roberts (and later Joseph Edkins of the London Mission Society). Teng, *Americans and the Taiping Rebellion,* 199–213; and Spence, *God's Chinese Son,* 285–97.

built no chapels but instead regarded their government as a church with the Heavenly King as its head and the government offices as its chapels. Their capital was called Nanjing, the New Jerusalem, where the Heavenly King dwelt and led his Heavenly Army against their evil foreign overlords. The Taipings embraced a political theology with the Ten Commandments as guiding principles and water baptism as a national rite. Hong's church had strict prohibitions against smoking opium and tobacco as well as consuming alcohol, adding that "those who disobey shall be decapitated and none will be spared."[126]

The rebellion very nearly succeeded, gaining the support of followers in the hundreds of millions, but it ended tragically with Hong's suicide in 1864 and the deaths of an estimated twenty to thirty million combatants. The story of the movement's failure is a complicated one, involving the eventual withdrawal of Western support, in part through the diplomatic meddling of Hong's old teacher, Issachar Roberts, who openly opposed his former student and the Taiping church as a heterodox form of Christianity.[127] It is significant to note that some time in the mid- to late 1850s, Hong began reading *The Pilgrim's Progress*, which had recently been translated into Chinese by Christian missionaries. It profoundly shaped the imagination of Hong, who apparently regarded it as second only to the Bible.[128] He was particularly drawn to a book whose author, like himself, received

[126] Franz Michael, ed., *The Taiping Rebellion: History and Documents*, 3 vols. (Seattle: University of Washington Press, 1971), 2:577. Almost any violation of the Taiping "Rules of Conduct" was punishable death.

[127] Joseph Edkins of the London Mission Society regarded Hong as a sincere but deluded fanatic, whose fantasies led him to make heretical theological mistakes based on his "anthropomorphism and gross materialism." Teng, *Americans and the Taiping Rebellion*, 205–6. Eugene Boardman states that "the central features of Christian belief were absent in the religious ideology developed by the Taiping rebels" (*Christian Influence on the Ideology of the Taiping Rebellion*, 116).

[128] Spence cites *The North China Herald* (August 11, 1860), in which Hong's cousin describes *The Pilgrim's Progress* as Hong's favorite book, in *God's Chinese Son*, 281–82; and Rudolf Wagner, *Re-enacting the Heavenly Vision: The Role of Religion in the Taiping Rebellion* (Berkeley: University of California Press, 1982), 15. Thomas H. Reilly is surely correct that Wagner exaggerates the level of inspiration and authority that the Taiping ascribed to *The Pilgrim's Progress*, in *The Taiping Heavenly Kingdom: Rebellion and the Blasphemy of Empire* (Seattle: University of Washington Press, 2004), 76.

a heavenly message by way of dreams and visions. And the book's covert social radicalism appealed to the Chinese peasantry. Imagery from Bunyan's allegory suffused Hong's everyday conversation, religious writings, and official edicts. As Christian reaches the end of his arduous journey when he arrives at the Heavenly City, so the Taipings believed that they would subdue the Manchus under the leadership of their Heavenly King Hong Xiuquan from their Heavenly City of Nanjing. Had the rebellion succeeded, as one historian observed, *The Pilgrim's Progress* "might have become China's earlier little red book."[129] Yet, as another declaimed, Hong Xiuquan "was no Chinese Lenin."[130]

By the 1880s, Christian missionaries in Singapore were employing translations of *The Pilgrim's Progress* among the Straits Chinese (descendants of Chinese immigrants in Malaysia and Singapore). Readings were held in congregations accompanied by the projection of images from scenes using magic lantern slides. In 1905 Methodist missionaries produced a new translation in Baba Malay containing twenty-four illustrations that depict episodes with indigenous cultural images.[131] American missionaries translated *The Pilgrim's Progress* into Syriac in 1848, and it continued to be read, retranslated, and

---

[129] Hill, *Turbulent, Seditious, and Factious People*, 375.

[130] In Boardman's judgment, the rebellion was doomed to failure, due in large part to an insufficient ideology and an incompetent leadership. Boardman, *Christian Influence on the Ideology of the Taiping Rebellion*, 126.

[131] Bonny Tan, "A Graphic Tale in Baba Malay: *Chrita Orang Yang Chari Slamat* (1905)," *Biblioasia*, October 2009. John Bunyan, *Chrita Orang Yang Chari Slamat* [*One Who Seeks Salvation*], trans. William G. Shellabear (Singapore: American Missionary Press, 1905); and idem, *Cherita Darihal Orang Yang Menchari Selamat* [*The Story of One Seeking Salvation*], trans. R. A. Blasdell (Singapore: Malaya Publishing House, 1955); in the Archives and History Library of the Methodist Church in Singapore. Special thanks to Malcolm Tan and Jenny Ng in locating these sources. Roger Sharrock expresses distress over the indigenous illustrations in the missionary editions of *The Pilgrim's Progress* that he thought exemplified a platonizing tendency that disregarded history. It might be asked, however, if sometimes these illustrators might sometimes be closer to the original message than the historicized readings. Roger Sharrock, *John Bunyan* (New York: Macmillan, 1968), 155–56.

republished in Neo-Aramaic throughout the twentieth century.[132] *The Pilgrim's Progress* was widely circulated throughout sub-Saharan Africa largely by the work of Baptist and nondenominational missionaries who made translations in most of the major languages.[133] The Religious Tract Society of London reported in 1903 that its society alone had assisted in translating *The Pilgrim's Progress* into 101 languages worldwide.[134] In short, wherever evangelical missionaries went, indigenous translations of *The Pilgrim's Progress* soon appeared.

The rush of critics to dismiss these translations as merely extensions of colonialism may be premature, for the modern missionary movement that utilized Bunyan's text may have been "both a powerful last thrust of Christendom and an important instrument in bringing about [its] dissolution."[135] As indigenous Christians practiced the faith taught by missionaries, Western colonial powers were caught in a contradiction that the expansionist ideology of Christendom could be maintained only by unchristian coercion. The resulting multiplication and diversification of indigenous expressions of the faith on the mission field ultimately made colonialism untenable, and the center of world Christianity dramatically shifted from the West and North to the South and East. The so-called great century then may be understood as a preeminently Free Church effort and not merely a postcolonial footnote about the extension of Christendom. It is important to ask what role *The Pilgrim's Progress* may have played in

[132] Adam H. Becker, *Revival and Awakening: American Evangelical Missionaries in Iran and the Origins of Assyrian Nationalism* (Chicago: University of Chicago Press, 2015), 126.

[133] Hofmeyr, *Portable Bunyan*, 33.

[134] John Bunyan, *The Pilgrim's Progress* (London: Religious Tract Society, 1903), 8; cited by David N. Dixon, "The Second Text: Missionary Publishing and Bunyan's *Pilgrim's Progress,*" *International Bulletin of Missionary Research* 36 no. 2 (2012): 86.

[135] Wilbert R. Shenk, "The 'Great Century' Reconsidered," in *Anabaptism and Mission*, ed. Wilbert R. Shenk (Scottdale, Penn.: Herald, 1984), 158. Shenk was alluding to the claim by the distinguished church historian Kenneth Scott Latourette, who described the nineteenth century as "the greatest thus far in the history of Christianity," devoting three volumes in his monumental *History of the Expansion of Christianity* to the period. Latourette, *History of the Expansion of Christianity*, 7 vols. (New York: Harper & Row, 1937–1945), 6:442.

bringing about the end of empire.[136] Some African novelists discovered in *The Pilgrim's Progress* a means to critique colonialist oppression and disrupt native power structures.[137] Similarly, in the United States, African American slaves drew from its images in their songs and stories to resist the domesticating forces of slavery.[138] But readers from the receiving culture of these translations did not have to subvert the message of Bunyan's text. Instead, they learned with support from missionaries to follow its logic sometimes to radical conclusions.[139]

The story of the evangelical mission in Jamaica is an important case study. John Rowe, a missionary from the British Baptist Missionary Society (BMS), arrived on the island in 1814, where he joined the work begun three decades earlier by George Liele, a former slave and ordained Baptist preacher from the United States. The Baptists and other nonconformists founded churches and were fervently committed to the education of the slave population despite strong opposition from the colonial government and the state-established Anglican church. Baptists had the largest following among the slave population, among whom they trained lay preachers known for their fiery sermons. From the standpoint of the imperial powers that included the colonial government, the established church, and the planter aristocracy,

---

[136] Brian Stanley, "Christianity and the End of Empire," in *Missions, Nationalism, and the End of Empire*, ed. Brian Stanley (Grand Rapids: Eerdmans, 2003), 1–2. See also Stanley, *The Bible and the Flag: Protestant Missions and British Imperialism in the Nineteenth and Twentieth Centuries* (Leicester: Apollos, 1990); Andrew Porter, *Religion versus Empire: British Protestant Missionaries and Overseas Expansion, 1700–1914* (Manchester: Manchester University Press, 2004); and Dana L. Robert, ed., *Converting Colonialism: Visions and Realities in Mission History, 1706–1914* (Grand Rapids: Eerdmans, 2008).

[137] Hofmeyr, "Bunyan: Colonial, Postcolonial," in Dunan-Page, *Cambridge Companion to Bunyan*, 169; and Hofmeyr, *Portable Bunyan*, 24.

[138] Henry Louis Gates suggests that Ukawsaw Gronniosaw drew upon Bunyan in his slave narrative. Gates, *The Signifying Monkey: A Theory of African-American Literary Criticism* (New York: Oxford University Press, 1989), 133–35; and Albert Raboteau, *Slave Religion: The Invisible Institution in the Antebellum South* (Oxford: Oxford University Press, 1978), 290–318.

[139] Dixon, "Second Text," 86. Hofmeyr suggests that indigenous African readers retained Bunyan's symbols but subverted them by emptying them of their original meaning filling them with new content (*Portable Bunyan*, 87).

the economic viability of Jamaica depended on the slave population, which outnumbered the white population on the island thirteen to one and provided a labor force for the sugar plantations.[140]

The epicenter of dissent was Montego Bay, where there was a large Baptist church led by Thomas Burchell and a congregation in nearby Falmouth led by William Knibb, both BMS missionaries.[141] They laid a theological framework for emancipation on biblical grounds that slaves could not serve two masters (Matt 6:24) as well as on other Scriptures, including "If the Son shall make you free, ye shall be free indeed" (John 8:36); "Ye are bought with a price; be not ye the servants of men" (1 Cor 7:23); "There is . . . neither bond nor free" (Gal 3:28); and "Be not entangled with the yoke of bondage" (Gal 5:1). Although the slaves heard the revolutionary message implicit in these sermons, the missionaries never called for direct political action. Instead, they sought a path of political neutrality, preaching and teaching that the gospel was for slave and free alike, yet supporting the inequality of the economic status quo and the maintenance of law and order. Knibb, however, privately denounced the institution of slavery in a particularly Bunyanesque way, referring to it as "one of the most odious monsters that ever disgraced the earth."[142] Like Bunyan, Knibb saw sinister forces at work behind and through political forces and social figures, suggesting that in the opposition of the

---

[140] Horace O. Russell, prologue to *George Liele's Life and Legacy: An Unsung Hero*, ed. David T. Shannon (Macon, Ga.: Mercer University Press, 2012), 6–12; and John Clarke, *Memorials of Baptist Missionaries in Jamaica* (London: Yates & Alexander, 1869).

[141] Mary Turner, *Slaves and Missionaries: The Disintegration of Jamaican Slave Society 1787–1834* (Urbana: University of Illinois, 1982), esp. chap. 6, 148–78; Brian Stanley, *The History of the Baptist Missionary Society 1792–1992* (Edinburgh: T&T Clark, 1992), 70–80; and Peter Abrahams, *Jamaica: An Island Mosaic* (London: Her Majesty's Stationery Office, 1957), 72–73.

[142] William Knibb, in a letter to his mother shortly after his arrival to Jamaica, in John Howard Hinton, *Memoir of William Knibb* (London: Houlston & Stonemen, 1847), 48. After the slave revolt, he used this language more in public. In his speech at the Byrom Street Chapel in Liverpool (July 24, 1832), he enthusiastically inveighed against "the Monster." Hinton, *Memoir of William Knibb*, 155. See also 248, 252, 261, 495, and 521. Bunyan described Apollyon as "the Monster," drawing from the images in Rev 12–13 and Job 41:15. Bunyan, *Pilgrim's Progress*, 47.

colonial government "the devil has come down with great wrath." When the magistrates ordered Knibb to stop preaching, like Bunyan he responded, "I am sent here to preach, and preach I must and shall take the consequences. The magistrates have no power to stop me."[143]

It is quite natural that Knibb would think in such terms. He grew up in Kettering, Northamptonshire, where Andrew Fuller was pastor of the Baptist church for more than three decades and for over twenty years secretary of the BMS until his death in 1815. William Knibb and his brother Thomas became Baptists while working as apprentices in a printing shop run by Fuller's son. It is quite natural, then, that they would have been familiar with Bunyan's writings through their BMS relationships. Andrew Fuller named *Grace Abounding* and *The Pilgrim's Progress* as instrumental in his own evangelical conversion, and he credited Bunyan's practice of offering a free invitation to all as key to breaking the hold of high Calvinism. Within BMS circles, Bunyan's writings were regarded as a major resource of spiritual inspiration and theological insight.[144] James Mursell Phillippo, another one of the early BMS missionaries to Jamaica, described *The Pilgrim's Progress* as a book that would be found in a typical Baptist home.[145] Because the mission schools in Jamaica were as interested in teaching English literacy as communicating the gospel, *The Pilgrim's Progress* was ideal. Its readable language and evangelical message made it a logical text for use in classrooms and churches. It is no surprise, then, that Joseph Jackson Fuller, who was born a slave in Jamaica, completed two translations of *The Pilgrim's Progress* in Cameroon, where he spent much of his life as a missionary. In his preface, Fuller noted "that no book, apart from the Holy Scriptures . . . would help them as much as the present volume can."[146] Such is the legacy of Bunyan.

[143] Letter from William Knibb to his Mother (September 9, 1828), in Angus Library William Knibb Letters, WI/3, II.

[144] Fuller, *Complete Works*, 1:3, 15, 44.

[145] Edward Bean Underhill, *The Life of James Mursell Phillipo, Missionary in Jamaica* (London: Yates & Alexander, 1881), 370; and James M. Phillippo, *Jamaica: Its Past and Present State* (London: John Snow, 1843).

[146] John Bunyan, *Bedangweri Ya Balondo O Mundi Ma Wasi Na O Mu Mu Mapo: The Pilgrim's Progress*, trans. into Dualla by J. J. Fuller (London: Alexander & Shepheard, 1885); and Hofmeyr, *Portable Bunyan*, 87.

In this context, *The Pilgrim's Progress* was being read so that hidden within its evangelical message the slumbering dissent was ready to be awakened, and in December 1831 the sleepy radicalism began to stir.[147] It was the slaves who took the evangelical theology of the missionaries to its logical conclusion. One of the deacons of the Baptist church in Montego Bay was a Creole slave named Sam Sharpe, who was described as "active, intelligent, and subtle, possessing considerable influence."[148] Also known as Daddy, Ruler, or General, he became the leader of the "Ethiopian Baptists" and what the planters called "the Baptist War." Sharpe followed closely the British antislavery movement, and he knew that, although slavery had been legally abolished in England and its colonies, the Jamaican Assembly and planters would never willingly accept it. Sharpe understood from the gospel that "slaves had a right to be free."[149] He admonished his followers that "if they did not stand up for themselves, and take their freedom, the male slaves would all be put out to the muzzles of the planters' guns, and shot like pigeons."[150]

The plan was simple. Slaves would not return to the fields to harvest the ripe sugar cane after the Christmas holiday unless the planters agreed to pay them for their labor. But what began as a nonviolent protest grew into a violent revolt.[151] Houses were burned, the militia was called out, and several missionaries were arrested.

[147] Larry Kreitzer, *Kissing the Book: The Story of Sam Sharpe as Revealed in the Records of the National Archives at Kew* (Oxford: Regent's Park College, 2013); Horace O. Russell, *Samuel Sharpe and the Meaning of Freedom: Reflections on a Baptist National Hero of Jamaica* (Oxford: Regent's Park College, 2012); Mary Reckord, "The Jamaica Slave Rebellion of 1831," *Past & Present* 40, no. 3 (1968): 108–25; C. Sam Reid, *Samuel Sharpe: From Slave to National Hero* (Kingston, Jamaica: Bustamante Institute, 1988), 41–53; and Bernard Martin Senior, *Jamaica: As It Was, as It Is, and as It May Be* (New York: Negro Universities Press, 1969; orig. pub. London: T. Hurst, 1835), 183–84, 196.

[148] Senior, *Jamaica*, 184; Henry Bleby, *Death Struggles of Slavery* (London: Hamilton, Adams, 1853), 103–20; John Clark, W. Dendy, and J. M. Phillippo, *The Voice of Jubilee: A Narrative of the Baptist Mission, Jamaica* (London: John Snow, 1865), 55–66.

[149] Letter of William Annand (January 2, 1832), in Kreitzer, *Kissing the Book*, 47.

[150] Bleby, *Death Struggles of Slavery*, 133.

[151] Although many of the secondary sources describe Sharpe's strategy as nonviolent, several of the eyewitnesses in his trial reported to have seen him carrying a machete and a pistol, though none of them testified to witnessing Sharpe use them,

Outraged planters destroyed fourteen Baptist church buildings and several other nonconformist chapels. The uprising was quickly put down, and several hundred slaves were killed in the conflict or executed in the trials that followed.[152] Sam Sharpe was hanged on the gallows at noon on May 23, 1832, in the central square of Montego Bay. The words that ring from his testimony were simple and clear. All he wanted was to enjoy the liberty that he read in the Bible was the birthright of every human being.[153] Sharpe and the slave revolt exposed political neutrality as yet another form of domestication.

William Knibb was particularly influential in awakening English Christians from their evangelical slumber. He delivered a passionate address at the annual meeting of the BMS at Spa Fields Chapel in London on June 21, 1832, declaiming colonial slavery and evangelical missions to be "inseparably connected." He asserted that British Christians must join the cause "to break the chain with which the African is bound, or leave the work of mercy and the triumphs of the Redeemer unfinished."[154] He further declared that unless and until slavery was abolished, slaves would rightly refuse to receive the gospel, and before the enthralled audience he announced himself to be "an unflinching and undaunted advocate of immediate emancipation."[155] Knibb concluded with an impassioned appeal:

---

and the charges against him did not include murder. See especially the testimony of Joseph Martin and James Clarke. Kreitzer, *Kissing the Book*, 6–7, 31–32.

[152] Reid, *Samuel Sharpe*, 54–95. It is interesting that in his narrative, Kennedy describes Sharpe in prison reading Bunyan's *The Holy War*, given to him by Henry Bleby, Sharpe's friend and Methodist minister. Kennedy describes Sharpe as stealing a copy of the Bible and *The Holy War* earlier from his master. While these narrative accounts are fiction, it is likely that Sharpe would indeed have read Bunyan's writings, including *The Pilgrim's Progress* and *The Holy War*. Fred W. Kennedy, *Daddy Sharpe: A Narrative of the Life and Adventures of Samuel Sharpe* (Kingston, Jamaica: Ian Randle, 2008), 41–42, 175–77.

[153] Letter of William Annand (January 2, 1832), in Kreitzer, *Kissing the Book*, 47. Kennedy quotes a line from Sharpe: "All I wished was to enjoy that liberty which I find in the Bible is the birthright of every man." Kennedy, *Daddy Sharpe*, 371–72; cited from Shirley C. Gordon, *God Almighty Make Me Free: Christianity in Preemancipation Jamaica* (Indianapolis: Indiana University Press, 1996), 97.

[154] Hinton, *Memoir of William Knibb*, 145.

[155] Hinton, *Memoir of William Knibb*, 147.

If I die without beholding the emancipation of my brethren and sisters in Christ, then, if prayer is permitted in heaven, I will fall at the feet of the Eternal, crying, Lord, open the eyes of Christians in England, to see the evil of slavery, and to banish it from the earth.[156]

In August 1832 the BMS *Missionary Herald* published an article that declared that "to defer emancipation a single day longer than is required by due regard to the welfare of the negroes themselves, would be as politically unwise as it is morally unjust."[157] Thus, the Baptists contributed to the conjunction of forces that finally brought an end to slavery in Jamaica two years later, on August 1, 1834.

William Knibb, Sam Sharpe, and other Christians surely found the Bible to be both the source of a vision of liberty and the conviction to dissent, but they undoubtedly also discovered these in *The Pilgrim's Progress*. Its social implications have at times been lost to readers, who having slipped into spiritual slumber no longer think of themselves as a turbulent, seditious, or factious people. But perhaps therein lies the hope that the spirit of undomesticated dissent—though it may be forgotten—is not lost forever but may at any moment be reawakened by disturbing dreams, leading new dreamers like Bunyan of old on their own dangerous journeys.

---

[156] Hinton, *Memoir of William Knibb*, 148.
[157] *Missionary Herald* 164 (August 1832): 59–60.

3

PROSPEROUS DISSENT
Daniel Defoe

Then Christian and Hopeful went till they came at a delicate Plain, called Ease, where they went with much content; but that Plain was narrow, so they were quickly got over it.[1]

After the death of Faithful in Vanity Fair, Christian escapes, and with his new traveling companion, Hopeful, he comes to "a delicate plain, called Ease." There they rest from their journey "with much content." Yet they are not secure for long, because just on the far side of the plain there is a hill called Lucre where there is a silver mine. Other pilgrims had turned aside from their journey to see it, but, going too close to the brink and the ground under their feet being unstable, they fell into the pit and were killed or maimed.[2] The apprehension of dissenters falling to temptations of wealth and power was shared by Bunyan's publisher and fellow Baptist, Francis "Elephant" Smith,

---

[1] John Bunyan, *The Pilgrim's Progress*, ed. N. H. Keeble (New York: Oxford University Press, 1984), 87. Subsequent citations are to this edition. Michael Watts begins his chapter on the toleration of dissent with this episode, in *The Dissenters*, vol. 1: *From the Reformation to the French Revolution* (Oxford: Clarendon, 1978), 263.

[2] Bunyan, *Pilgrim's Progress*, 87.

in his account of the living and dying Christian.[3] The book's frontispiece contains the picture of a godly Christian with his back to the symbols of wealth, position, and power. In his hands he holds an open Bible, and, with his gaze fixed on heaven toward an extended hand with an outstretched crown, he declares, "For me to live is Christ." The caption reads, "Be thou faithfull unto death, and I will give thee a Crowne of life" (Rev 2:10). The dying Christian has his back to heaven's reward, and his eyes on worldly wealth and power. The description states, "Demas hath forsaken me, haveing loved this present world" (2 Tim 4:10).

Though Smith was more politically active than Bunyan, his account of the living and dying Christian is markedly similar to Bunyan's vision of Vanity Fair and the Plain of Ease. The promise of the crown of life offered to the living Christian is the same thing quoted by Evangelist in his instructions to Christian and Faithful.[4] And Smith's life story bore witness to the dissenter conviction that "to reign,'tis necessary to suffer"[5]—for Smith's *Symptoms of Growth and Decay in Godliness*, like Bunyan's allegorical narrative of pilgrimage, drew from his experience. Jailed and fined multiple times for his radical associations, hounded by Tory critics, and prosecuted relentlessly by government officials for publishing and promoting Whig materials that challenged the status quo, Smith faced arrest, imprisonment, and financial ruin with the conviction that this was the path of faithfulness and that his reward awaited. Bunyan died on August 31, 1688, just before the so-called Glorious Revolution of William of Orange, which resulted in toleration for dissenters. Smith outlived his companion in the struggle, dying on December 22, 1691, and he too was buried in Bunhill Fields. The great persecution was over, but the land of ease carried its own dangers, for it

---

[3] Francis Smith, *Symptoms of Growth and Decay in Godliness* (London: Francis Smith, 1673). Bunyan disliked denominational labels, but he claimed the term "Baptist" (or "Anabaptist"), though his Bedford congregation was an Independent and open communion church during his lifetime. Bunyan, *The Heavenly Footman* (1698), in *The Works of John Bunyan*, ed. George Offor, 3 vols. (Glasgow: W. G. Blackie & Son, 1854; repr., Carlisle, Penn.: Banner of Trust, 1991), 3:383.

[4] Bunyan, *Pilgrim's Progress*, 72. See chapter 2, p. 45.

[5] William Penn, *No Cross, No Crown*, 8th ed. (Leeds: James Lister, 1743; orig. pub. 1668).

was not the end of the journey, and the position of dissenters was more insecure than they imagined.

Making Toleration

In March 1661, John Sturgion published a tract addressed to King Charles II in which he made an impassioned plea for toleration on behalf of "the Baptized People" (the Baptists) "that we may serve the Lord without molestation in that Faith and Order which we have Learned in the Holy Scriptures."[6] Two months later, Thomas Monck and six other General Baptists issued a petition entitled *Sions Groans for her Distressed*, which asserted that because God made the conscience free "no Magistrate, although a Christian, hath power to be a Lord over anothers faith, or by outward force to impose any thing in the worship of God."[7] The appeal of the Baptists and other dissenters was simply to be left alone to worship in their own way. Given the declaration by King Charles to allow "liberty to tender consciences" as long as their differences "do not disturb the general peace of the kingdom," it seemed a reasonable request.[8] Yet the Baptists had good reason to be nervous. For whatever sympathy the new king might have expressed for toleration disappeared after the Fifth Monarchist uprising in January 1661 led by Thomas Venner, setting in motion a series of royal measures aimed at crushing dissenting communities. Despite their pledge of loyalty to the crown and their repudiation of revolution, dissenters were jailed by the hundreds.[9] On October 19, 1661,

---

[6] John Sturgion, *A Plea for Tolleration of Opinions and Perswasions in Matters of Religion* (London: S. Dover, 1661), 17, in Edward Bean Underhill, *Tracts on Liberty of Conscience and Persecution, 1614–1661* (New York: Burt Franklin, 1966), 311–41.

[7] Thomas Monck, Joseph Wright, Geo. Hammon, Will. Jeffery, Francis Stanley, Will. Reynolds, and Fran. Smith, *Sions Groans for her Distressed* (London, 1661), 10–11, in Underhill, *Tracts on Liberty of Conscience*, 343–82.

[8] Charles R., The Declaration of Breda (April 4, 1660), in *The Constitutional Documents of the Puritan Revolution 1628–1660*, ed. Samuel Rawson Gardiner (Oxford: Clarendon, 1889), 351–52; and N. H. Keeble, *The Restoration: England in the 1660s* (Oxford: Blackwell, 2002), 68–70.

[9] Underhill, *Tracts on Liberty of Conscience*, 313–17; Edward Rogers, *Some Accounts of the Life and Opinions of a Fifth Monarchy Man* (London: Longmans, 1867), 327–28. On repudiation of the Fifth Monarchy uprising, see William Kiffen, *The Humble*

an alderman accompanied by the head of the borough interrupted a Baptist meeting at Whitechapel in London. They forcibly removed the preacher, John James, from his pulpit and charged him with treason for calling Jesus Christ the King of England. James was executed on November 26, 1661, based on perjured testimony.[10] By the end of the year Newgate Prison was filled, and most of the prisoners were Baptists.

Paranoid fears of another civil war swirled in government circles, fueling support for high church voices determined to restore the ecclesial and political arrangement of the Laudian past. In December of 1661, Parliament passed the Corporation Act, requiring that anyone elected to public office must swear an oath of loyalty to the king and within a year of election receive "the sacrament of the Lords Supper, according to the Rites of the Church of England."[11] Dissenters who refused to obey on the grounds of conscience were removed from office or fined if they declined to serve after being elected. Over the course of the next five years, Parliament passed a series of acts that became known as the Clarendon Code, named for Edward Hyde, first Earl of Clarendon, who was lord chancellor for Charles II and whose duty it was to enforce the laws.[12] The Corporation Act was followed by the Act of Uniformity in 1662 that made the Book of Common Prayer compulsory for all "public" worship, resulting in the ejection of more than two thousand clergy who refused to comply.[13] Parliament subsequently passed the Conventicle Act in 1664 that prohibited "private" meetings of "five persons or more assembled together over and above those of the same household," making virtually all gatherings

---

Apology of Some Commonly Called Anabaptists (London: Henry Hills, 1661). In addition to Kiffen, the apology was signed by thirty Baptist leaders, including Henry Denne, Henry Hills, Francis Smith, Christopher Blackwood, and Joseph Simpson.

[10] *A Narrative of the Apprehending, Commitment, Arraignment, Condemnation, and Execution of John James* (London, 1662); and Barrington Raymond White, *The English Baptists of the Seventeenth Century* (Didcot: Baptist Historical Society, 1996), 101.

[11] "Charles II, 1661: An Act for the Well Governing and Regulating of Corporations," in *Statutes of the Realm*, vol. 5, *1628–80*, ed. John Raithby (London: G. Eyre & A. Strahan, 1819), 321–23; available at British History Online, http://www.british-history.ac.uk/statutes-realm/vol5/pp321-323 (accessed January 20, 2016).

[12] Keeble, *Restoration*, 120–22 and 141–42.

[13] Charles E. Whiting, *Studies in English Puritanism from the Restoration to the Revolution, 1660–1688* (New York: Macmillan, 1931), 1–42.

of dissenters illegal.[14] Nonconformist ministers were further restricted in 1665 from preaching within five miles of their former parishes.[15] In February 1670, Parliament passed the Second Conventicle Act, which contained even more severe limitations on dissenters.[16]

Legal penalties on dissent were undergirded by religious arguments against toleration from voices within the Church of England. Simon Patrick, a parish priest in London, published a popular treatment of the theological issues at stake in *A Friendly Debate between a Conformist and a Non-conformist*, which, though light hearted, nevertheless depicted dissenters as foolish Christians who believed the spiritual life to be opposed to reason.[17] William Assheton, a fellow of Brasenose College in Oxford University, was more pointed in his critique. He suggested that dissenters were not being persecuted for their faith but being justly punished for the unlawful exercise of religion. He declaimed that dissenters were not innocent sufferers but injurious aggressors, as well as heretical and turbulent schismatics.[18] Samuel Parker—who served as chaplain to the Archbishop of Canterbury, Gilbert Sheldon—made the case against the toleration of dissenters, describing them as "zealots," "wild and fanatique rabble," "peevish, ignorant, and malepert preachers," and "brain-sick." Parker warned that liberty of conscience was dangerous, and he cautioned

---

[14] "Charles II, 1664: An Act to Prevent and Suppresse Seditious Conventicles," in Raithby, *Statutes of the Realm*, 5:516–520; available at British History Online, http://www.british-history.ac.uk/statutes-realm/vol5/pp516-520 (accessed January 22, 2016).

[15] "Charles II, 1665: An Act for Restraining Non-conformists from Inhabiting in Corporations," in Raithby, *Statutes of the Realm*, 5:575; available at British History Online, http://www.british-history.ac.uk/statutes-realm/vol5/p575 (accessed January 22, 2016).

[16] "Charles II, 1670: An Act to Prevent and Suppresse Seditious Conventicles," in Raithby, *Statutes of the Realm*, 5:648–51.; available at British History Online, http://www.british-history.ac.uk/statutes-realm/vol5/pp648-651 (accessed January 21, 2016).

[17] Simon Patrick, *A Friendly Debate between a Conformist and a Non-conformist* (London: R. Royston, 1669), 5. Patrick's *Friendly Debate* went through six editions, and he published two subsequent related volumes, *A Continuation of the Friendly Debate* (London: R. Royston, 1669); and idem, *A Further Continuation and Defence; or, A Third Part of the Friendly Debate* (London: E.G. & A.C., 1670).

[18] William Assheton, *Toleration Disapprov'd and Condemn'd* (London: Francis Oxlad Sen., 1670).

that "the Mischiefs that ensue upon the permitting men the Liberty of their consciences are endless."[19] He laid out his grounds for the case of ecclesiastical sovereignty over individual conscience in matters of religion.

The enforcement and effect of parliamentary legislation, however, was mixed. Although high church personalities continued to call for harsh measures, Lord Chancellor Hyde favored a more moderate course. In reality the code was unevenly enforced, and it reflected the attitude of local leadership and relationships. Those Presbyterians who held out hope for comprehension into the national church were the least affected, but others whose ejection marked a break with Anglicans held their own conventicles and often suffered fines and imprisonment. It was not uncommon for Independent ministers to be jailed, sometimes for years at a time.[20] Baptists tended to feel the brunt of the code more severely, especially those with Fifth Monarchy sympathies. When, for example, ten Baptists were arrested in Aylesbury, Buckinghamshire, for holding an unlawful conventicle in 1663, the justices offered them the option of conforming, going into exile, or submitting to a sentence of death. They were saved only after William Kiffin intervened with the lord chancellor, who brought the case to the attention of the king, who granted immediate reprieve.[21] Quakers suffered the most of all among dissenters, in large measure due to their refusal to take an oath of loyalty to the crown. A statement issued in 1670 reported that eight thousand of their members had been imprisoned since the restoration of the monarchy.[22]

Protestant dissenters as well as Catholic recusants received a reprieve with the Declaration of Indulgence in March 1672, which suspended all penal laws against them. The relief was short lived as the

---

[19] Samuel Parker, *A Discourse of Ecclesiastical Politie*, 3rd ed. (London: John Martyn, 1671), i–ii, 2.

[20] Whiting, *Studies in English Puritanism*, 43–81; and Watts, *Dissenters*, 1:227–38.

[21] Joseph Ivimy, *A History of the English Baptists*, 4 vols. (London: Isaac Taylor Hinton, Warwick Square, and Holdsworth & Ball, St Paul's Church-Yard, 1811–1830), 1:335–38; and White, *English Baptists of the Seventeenth Century*, 106.

[22] *A Short Relation of Some Part of the Sad Sufferings and Cruel Havock and Spoil, Inflicted on the Persons and Estates of the People of God, in Scorn Called Quakers* (London, 1670).

declaration was withdrawn the following year, but other matters pre-occupied the government, taking heat off dissenters in the late 1670s. Growing concerns about the prospect that the king's brother, a Roman Catholic, might succeed him were amplified by rumors of a "Popish Plot" in 1678, which purported that a group of Catholics were planning to murder Charles and to put James on the throne. It was believed that the end result of having a Catholic king would be a return to Catholicism as the established Church of England. The story was eventually discovered to be a fabrication, but it succeeded in lighting the fires of anti-Catholic hysteria that swept the nation. Parliament finally got involved, considering a bill that would have excluded James from the throne. Though the bill never passed, the exclusionary controversy contributed to the formation of the two parties that dominated the political landscape over the next century. Whigs supported the bill, and Tories opposed it.[23] The political downside for Protestant dissenters was that the sentiments of King Charles II turned against them, but, on the upside, moderate Anglicans began to look to dissenters for common cause in opposing a Roman Catholic succession, resulting in a fragile Whig-dissenter coalition.

As Parliament deliberated in March 1681, dissenting publisher Francis "Elephant" Smith disseminated antigovernment news and information by distributing his pamphlet *Vox Populi* to members of Parliament and communicating to the wider public through his broadsheets *Democritus Ridens* and *Smith's Protestant Intelligence*.[24] In April the government arrested and imprisoned him on charges of treason.

[23] Richard L. Greaves, *Secrets of the Kingdom: British Radicals from the Popish Plot to the Revolution of 1688–1689* (Stanford: Stanford University Press, 1992), 5–52.

[24] Francis Smith propagated the rumor of the Popish Plot, attesting to its "undeniable confirmation," in *Vox Populi; or, The Peoples Claim to Their Parliaments Sitting, to Redress Grievances, and Provide for the Common Safety, by the Known Laws and Constitutions of the Nation Humbly Recommended to the King and Parliament at their Meeting at Oxford, the 21st of March* (London: Francis Smith, 1681), 1. The word "Protestant" in the newspaper title like *Smith's Protestant Intelligence* was a sign that it was a Whig publication and thus against Catholic succession to the throne. James Sutherland, *The Restoration Newspaper and Its Development* (Cambridge: Cambridge University Press, 1986), 14–16; and C. John Sommerville, *The News Revolution in England* (New York: Oxford, 1996), 92 and 137.

Although he was released in June for lack of evidence, it effectively silenced his press for the short term. Smith remained a thorn in the side of Tory politicians. On one notorious occasion in September 1680, he was brought before a grand jury in London for printing "mischievous, malicious, scandalous, and seditious" materials. As it turns out, he had simply reprinted a report of the extravagant spending by public officials on food and wine. When the jury returned a verdict of *ignoramus*, the enraged and embarrassed judge, Sir George Jeffreys (later lord chancellor), turned his wrath against members of the jury.[25] Smith's political printing was so effective and regarded as so dangerous that Roger L'Estrange, surveyor of the presses, launched a vicious publicity campaign in order to discredit him. A salacious broadside ballad entitled *The Leacherous Anabaptist; or, The Dipper Dipt'* lampooned Smith, suggesting that he attempted to seduce a woman with the offer of twelve Geneva Bibles.[26] But Smith suffered more than a damaged reputation. He estimated that between 1660 and 1680 his losses in fines, seizures, and other damages due to government prosecutions amounted to £1,400.[27] In 1684 he was pilloried and fined £500 for his part in publishing the antimonarchical poem *A Ra-Ree Show*.[28] Unable to raise money for his release, Smith remained in prison until January 1688, when he was given royal pardon.

Another dissenter concerned about the danger of a Catholic monarchy was a young London merchant and Presbyterian dissenter named Daniel Defoe. With the death of Charles on February 6, 1685, the crown passed to his brother, James II. When fears about what an

---

[25] Francis Smith, *An Account of the Injurious Proceedings of Sir George Jeffreys, Knt., Late Recorder of London, Against Francis Smith, Bookseller with His Arbitrary Carriage Towards the Grand-Jury at Guild-Hall, Sept. 16, 1680, Upon an Indictment Then Exhibited Against the Said Francis Smith, for Publishing a Pretended Libel, Entituled, An Act of Common-Council for Retrenching the Expences of the Lord Mayor and Sheriffs of the City of London, &c.* (London: Francis Smith, 1681). Smith addressed his pamphlet to Anthony Ashley Cooper, Earl of Shaftesbury, a leading politician and a founder of the Whig Party.

[26] *The Leacherous Anabaptist; or, The Dipper Dipt'* (London, 1681).

[27] Smith, *Account of the Injurious Proceedings*, 19.

[28] *A Ra-Ree Show* (London: For B.T., 1681). The authorship of the poem was never fully determined, though, because it was performed by Stephen College, it was attributed to him. He was executed for treason.

openly Catholic sovereign might do contributed to the ill-fated rebellion led by the illegitimate son of Charles II (James Scott, Duke of Monmouth), Defoe joined the insurgence.[29] He managed to escape after defeat at the Battle of Sedgemoor on July 6, 1685, and he eluded the Bloody Assizes that followed. Though he was eventually pardoned, Defoe's early experience deeply influenced his lifelong resistance as an undomesticated dissenter, albeit one chastened by political reality.[30] As it turns out, concerns about the new king's policies proved overblown, or at least misdirected, for Protestant dissenters were treated surprisingly well by James II. In April 1687 James issued his *Declaration for Liberty of Conscience*, which would repeal the laws and Test Acts that had penalized religious dissent since the restoration of the monarchy. The declaration, if approved by Parliament, would mean political participation and freedom of worship for Protestant nonconformists and Catholic recusants. When it became clear that Parliament would not approve his declaration, James used his powers of dismissal to purge parliamentary boroughs and seek to replace the displaced members with Catholics, nonconformists, and Anglicans who would support the declaration and the repeal of the Test Acts and Penal Laws. He sent agents, known as regulators, throughout England to advocate for repeal, most of whom were Baptist ministers.[31] On August 24, 1688, James called for a general election, which he withdrew when he learned

[29] Robert Dunning, *The Monmouth Rebellion: A Guide to the Rebellion and Bloody Assizes* (Wimborne: Dovecote, 1984), 61–64; and William Richard Emerson, *Monmouth's Rebellion* (New Haven: Yale University Press, 1951), 48–64.

[30] Paula R. Backscheider, *Daniel Defoe: His Life* (Baltimore: Johns Hopkins University Press, 1989), 35–40. Dissenters had a vital presence in the West Country with meeting houses in the towns where many of Monmouth's militia originated. Dunning, *Monmouth Rebellion*, 21–22. But Christopher L. Scott has shown that, though certain parts of the West Country were dissenter strongholds, it is unlikely that the militia supporting the rebellion were comprised largely of nonconformists, who accounted for less than 4 percent of the population in the western counties. Scott, *The Maligned Militia: The West Country Militia of the Monmouth Rebellion, 1685* (Burlington, Vt.: Ashgate, 2015), 256–61.

[31] Scott Sowerby, *Making Toleration: The Repealers and the Glorious Revolution* (Cambridge, Mass.: Harvard University Press, 2013), 1–22. Sowerby suggests that there were probably fewer than fifteen regulators, of which thirteen are known. Ten were known to be Baptist. Sowerby, *Making Toleration*, 38, 136, and 316n62.

about the coming invasion by William of Orange. Soon after William landed in England on November 5, 1688, James II fled to France, abdicating his rule. Parliament offered the crown jointly to William and his wife, Mary, ensuring a Protestant succession. Parliament approved the Act of Toleration, granting freedom of worship to Protestant nonconformists, which was given royal assent on May 24, 1689.[32] The great persecution of dissenters was over, and although full statutory freedom of religion was not granted to dissenters in England until the late nineteenth century, they did nevertheless enter into a land of ease.[33]

The Toleration Act ensured that the Anglican Church would remain the established religion of England. One of the characters in Henry Fielding's novel *Tom Jones* puts this establishment in simple terms, as he intoned, "When I mention religion, I mean the Christian religion; and not only the Christian religion, but the Protestant religion; and not only the Protestant religion, but the Church of England."[34] Given this privileged position, nonconformists were to be granted limited freedoms, even allowing those who "scruple the baptizing of infants" to take exception to the articles that touch on infant baptism in their subscription to the Thirty-Nine Articles.[35] Yet this new settlement regarded liberty as a political gift, not as a natural right. Full liberty of conscience did not extend to Protestant dissenters. They were tolerated but not free. Though they could worship without interference from church or state authorities, nonconformists still could not hold public office, attend university, or serve in the military. Catholics were not included in the limited freedoms under the terms of the Toleration Act. They had to wait until 1829 for that to change. The new church-state settlement allowed ample room for Tories in Parliament and the high church clergy to continue conspiring against religious dissenters. Still, the Toleration Act provided new opportunities that resulted in rising economic prosperity among nonconformists. No longer were

---

[32] The Toleration Act of 1689, in *The Eighteenth Century Constitution, 1688–1815*, ed. E. Neville Williams (Cambridge: Cambridge University Press, 1960), 42–46.

[33] Russell Sandberg, *Law and Religion* (Cambridge: Cambridge University Press, 2011), 26–28.

[34] Henry Fielding, *The History of Tom Jones, a Foundling*, 4 vols. (London: C. Cooke, 1792), 1:115–16.

[35] Toleration Act, X, in Williams, *Eighteenth Century Constitution*, 44.

they tinkers and poor people. Their new social standing led to upward mobility. A growing number became merchants, skilled trade workers, or self-employed artisans. As a rule, Presbyterians were more prosperous than Congregationalists, and both were better off than Baptists or Quakers.[36] Yet this newfound ease further removed them from the struggles and suffering that earlier generations of dissenters had experienced. With the support of William and Mary, the Whigs in Parliament advocated for continued liberty of nonconformists—although, with one hand, Whig politicians worked to secure support from dissenters, and, with the other, they carefully held them at a safe distance.

The struggle has always been to explain how England came to reverse its policy of state-sponsored persecution in favor of civil toleration. In the opening chapter of the first volume of his immensely popular *The History of England*, Thomas Babington Macaulay stated his intention to show how from the settlement of 1689, England rose "from a state of ignominious vassalage . . . to the place of umpire among European powers."[37] This viewpoint of narrating the shift from medieval to modern as a story from cruelty to civility became known as Whig history. Following this line of thought, Herbert Butterfield described the history of Protestant England as a process of gradual toleration that eventually reached its climax in expressions of liberal democracy and constitutional republicanism.[38] Revisionists rightly argue that this approach oversimplifies events as a teleological narrative with a predetermined end, and just as problematic is the fact that it transforms the voices of religious dissenters by treating them as if they were secular liberals.[39] But the story is neither as easy as the

[36] Watts, *Dissenters*, 1:346–66.

[37] Lord Thomas Babington Macaulay, *The History of England from the Accession of James II*, ed. Charles Harding Firth (London: Macmillan, 1913; originally published in 1848), 1. Macaulay described Defoe as "an unprincipled hack, ready to take any side of a question." Macaulay concluded, "Altogether I do not like him." George Otto Trevelyan, *The Life and Letters of Lord Macaulay*, 8 vols. (New York: Harper & Brothers, 1876), 2:383–84.

[38] Herbert Butterfield, *The Whig Interpretation of History* (New York: Scribner, 1951).

[39] Alexandra Walsham, *Charitable Hatred: Tolerance and Intolerance in England 1500–1700* (Manchester, U.K.: Palgrave, 2006). Revisionists attempt to recapture the

liberals assume nor as inconclusive as the revisionists assert. The history of the liberty of conscience is a muddled and complex story.[40] It reveals that modern political toleration was not the product of secular liberals alone but rather also involved dogmatic sectarians who, even under the state policy of persecution, refused to conform. The result was not the appeal to religious liberty merely as a "loser's creed" but rather a robust pluralism of Presbyterians, Baptists, Independents, and Quakers, as well as more obscure and eccentric dissenting groups that included Levellers, Diggers, Ranters, Seekers, Familists, Socinians, Muggletonians, and finally even Catholics, which unflaggingly challenged the established church that preached religious uniformity and the civil powers that enforced it.

In many ways Daniel Defoe epitomized the new class of prosperous and respectable dissenters that illustrates this complicated history. He was educated in a dissenting academy and initially intended to enter the ministry as a Presbyterian, but instead he chose to follow his father in a life of trade and politics. His career in business was marked by a series of financial successes and setbacks, but it was as an essayist that he gained public notoriety. In matters of politics, Defoe's sentiments were with the Whigs, though his political associations included Tories. He recognized that over time party names had changed from "Cavalier and Roundhead" to "Royalists and Rebels" to "Tories and Whigs." Yet these descriptions concealed the real division, which, he argued, "has always been barely *the Church and the Dissenter.*"[41]

Though the names may change, the binary reality remained constant. Here, there was no question where Defoe's loyalties lay. When it came to matters of conscience, he was a stickler. At a time when many

strangeness of early modern England by stressing the religious intolerance of the established church toward Catholics and radical puritan sects. Revisionist critiques have debunked liberal myths of medieval Europe as a benighted and violent society, the notion of the Enlightenment as a benevolent and tolerant movement, and the caricature of John Locke as a lone intellectual who single-handedly rescued England from the theory and policy of state-sponsored persecution.

[40] John Coffey, *Persecution and Toleration in Protestant England, 1558–1689* (New York: Longman, 2000), 1–20.

[41] Daniel Defoe, *A New Test of the Church of England's Loyalty* (London, 1702), 3; emphasis in original.

of his fellow dissenters were supporting the declaration of James II with the repeal of the Test Acts and Penal Laws, Defoe cautioned them to be suspicious of a more sinister hidden motive behind. For the king, Defoe argued, "Liberty of Conscience is not the *last End*, but only a *Means* in order to some *further* End," and, he continued, "the *Means* is seldom valued when the *End* is obtained." The final end of the king's declaration, Defoe warned, is nothing more than "to promote popery." He concluded that it was better to keep the penal laws and live under the authority of the Church of England "than fall under the lash of a *Popish Supremacy*."[42] For Defoe, dissent was not disposable. It was a matter of conscience. This is the conviction of undomesticated dissent.

But Defoe saved his sharpest criticism for dissenters who communed in the Church of England in order to qualify for the privilege of employment or public office, accusing them of mortgaging their consciences and playing a game of bopeep with the Almighty. Anyone capable of acting contrary to the light of the conscience, he declaimed, is capable of anything. For Defoe, there was no room for the compromise of occasional conformity. He maintained that it was permissible to conform until God gave the conscience "light enough to chuse by" and "Grace to be Obedient to the Convictions of [one's] own Heart," "whether that be to Conform or Dissent," but each one must "judge for him [or her] self."[43] In 1701, Defoe republished his tract *The Occasional Conformity of Dissenters* with an added preface addressed to the prominent London Presbyterian minister John Howe. One of Howe's congregants, Sir Thomas Abney, had been elected lord mayor, and, in compliance with the Test Acts, he had received communion in the Church of England in the morning and attended his Presbyterian chapel later on the same day. Defoe demanded that Howe either publically defend or oppose occasional conformity in principle. Howe deeply resented Defoe's suggestion

[42] Daniel Defoe, *A Letter to a Dissenter from His Friend at the Hague Concerning the Penal Laws and the Test, Shewing that the Popular Plea for Liberty of Conscience is not Concerned in that Question* (Tot de Hague: Gedrunckt door Hans Verdraeght, 1688), 1–4; emphasis in original.

[43] Daniel Defoe, *An Enquiry into Occasional Conformity* (London, 1698), 29.

that the occasional conformity was rooted in self-interest, hypocrisy, or inconsistency. He responded to Defoe's anonymous tract, derisively referring to him throughout as "Mr. Prefacer," reminding him of the deep conviction of nonconformity respecting the individual conscience and admonishing him that no one set him up as "the conscience-general to [hu]mankind!"[44]

When William died in 1702, the new Queen Anne and her Tory government grew intolerant of nonconformists. By calling attention to occasional conformity, Defoe had intended to strengthen dissent, but his pamphlet on the subject had the opposite effect. The House of Commons proposed a bill on occasional conformity, which would have closed the loopholes in the Test Acts and excluded dissenters entirely from public office. Defoe again rose to the occasion to fight with his pen on behalf of dissenters, composing an anonymous tract entitled *The Shortest-Way with the Dissenters* in which he assumed a Tory voice criticizing dissenters. He adapted the most inflammatory language of high church sermons, which demanded repeal of toleration for dissenters, issuing a call "to root out this cursed race from the World." He urged that nonconformists be shown no mercy, lest like Israel's sparing of the Amalekites they become grounds for God's judgment on the church.[45] Defoe intended his message ironically, but his readers (at

---

[44] Daniel Defoe, *A Letter to Mr. How By Way of His Considerations to the Preface to "An Enquiry in to the Occasional Conformity of Dissenters"* (London, 1701). Backscheider, *Daniel Defoe*, 89. Howe, "Some Considerations of a Preface to an Inquiry Concerning the Occasional Conformity of Dissenters," in *The Works of the Rev. John Howe*, ed. J. P. Hewlett, 3 vols. (London: William Tegg, 1848; repr., Ligonier, Penn.: Soli Deo Gloria, 1990), 3:543. Howe's language is serious and formal, but his tone is mocking and sarcastic. Beginning with the opening sentence, Howe expresses frustration that Defoe hid his own name (publishing his tract anonymously) while exposing Howe publicly by name. Howe concludes with a scolding rebuke that if Defoe's judgment is true about occasional conformists, then "that truth, accompanied with your temper and spirit, is much worse than their error." Howe, *Works*, 3:536–52.

[45] Daniel Defoe, *The Shortest-Way with the Dissenters; or, Proposals for the Establishment of the Church* (London, 1702), 19. See Wayne C. Booth, *The Rhetoric of Fiction*, 2nd ed. (Chicago: University of Chicago Press, 1983), 318–20. Not only did Defoe borrow language from his contemporaries. As Ellen F. Davis points out, Defoe's description of the slaying of the Israelites after the incident with the golden calf is almost

least initially) took it literally.[46] His satire was more subtle than that of his contemporary Jonathan Swift, whose "modest proposal" that poor Irish parents sell their children to the wealthy to be eaten as food could hardly have been misunderstood.[47] When Defoe was finally discovered to be the author of *The Shortest-Way*, the reaction was overwhelmingly negative from dissenters, Tories, and most of all the queen. His best intentions again backfired. He was charged with seditious libel and sentenced to the pillory for three days and served five months in Newgate Prison.

There on the scaffold, Defoe would be publicly exposed as a criminal, his body ritually subjected to torture, performed on the stage of punitive theater and manifesting the sovereign will of empire. It was expected that the crowd, which would gather for this spectacle, would not be mere spectators but be part of the machinery of torture, joining as participants in the drama of punishment, approving the penalty and becoming instruments of torment, hurling not only insults and abuse but also rotten vegetables, dead animals, and brickbats. Yet Defoe subverted the powers, distributing copies of his poem *A Hymn to the Pillory*, thus transforming the scaffold into a stage of his own performance, where the crowd saw the lines of his poem enacted before their eyes. The state claimed his punishment served the interest of justice. "But," Defoe's hymn intoned:

---

identical to Anglican bishop Joseph Hall's language in his *Contemplations Upon the Principal Passages of the Holy Story*, vol. 2 (London: H. L[ownes], 1614). Davis, *Imagination Shaped: Old Testament Preaching in the Anglican Tradition* (Valley Forge, Penn.: Trinity International, 1995), 129.

[46] Robert C. Rathburn observed that Defoe's satire was "doubly ironic in that the persons satirized took him seriously." "The Makers of the British Novel," in *From Jane Austen to Joseph Conrad*, ed. Robert C. Rathburn and Martin Steinmann Jr. (Minneapolis: University of Minnesota Press, 1958), 5; cited by Booth, *Rhetoric of Fiction*, 320n16.

[47] Jonathan Swift, *A Modest Proposal for Preventing the Children of Poor People in Ireland from Being a Burthen to Their Parents or the Country* (London, 1729); available at Project Gutenberg, http://www.gutenberg.org/files/1080/1080-h/1080-h.htm (accessed February 22, 2016).

Justice is Inverted when
Those Engines of the Law,
Instead of pinching Vicious Men,
Keep honest ones in awe.[48]

What the powers that be intended as a display of state sovereignty was turned against them as a means of public shame and a manifestation of moral defeat. It was Defoe's finest hour, for, in being a pilloried man, he joined the cloud of witnesses who suffered unjustly for the sake of justice. And thus he bore in his body what he had failed to gain in his print.

Defoe continued to support the cause of dissent, though he observed their declining numbers and waning strength as a result of the domesticating strategies to punish nonconformity and reward conformity. He persistently opposed the imposition of religious tests, which he argued "are a Bait to People to Banter their Consciences,"[49] and he consistently supported dissenters and their cause, portraying Anglicans as the true "turbulent and factious spirits" in matters of religion.[50] He considered dissenters to be quiet and peaceable, zealous in matters of religion and differing only in principles of conscience. But despite his advocacy for the religious convictions of dissent, Defoe had reservations about the social conventions of dissenters. He shared their basic vision but not their way of life. He saw them as "narrow, mean-spirited, short-sighted, self-preserving, friend-betraying, poor-neglecting people."[51] He regarded them to be fussy and fissiparous, inclined to separation and division, holding firm to what they believed to be true and having no charity toward those who differ. The relationship was complex. Though the dissenting tradition was deeply rooted in his experience, and though he remained committed to its basic

[48] Daniel Defoe, *A Hymn to the Pillory* (London, 1703), in *The Shortest Way with the Dissenters and Other Pamphlets* (Oxford: Basil Blackwell, 1974), 150.

[49] Daniel Defoe, *A Dialogue Between a Dissenter and the Observator, Concerning "The Shortest Way with the Dissenters"* (London, 1703), 17.

[50] Daniel Defoe, *A Second Volume of the Writings of the Author of The True-Born Englishman* (London, 1705).

[51] Daniel Defoe, *The Consolidator* (London, 1705), in *The Novels and Miscellaneous Works of Daniel De Foe*, Bohn's Standard Library (Oxford: D. A. Talboys, 1840), 9:365.

convictions, over time Defoe grew alienated from dissenters, preferring to go his way alone on his own island.

SEEKING VOCATION

When Queen Anne died and George I assumed the English throne in 1714, the Whigs, who were more favorable to the dissenters, regained power. Five years later, Defoe published *The Life and Strange Surprising Adventures of Robinson Crusoe*, which became immediately popular and is still widely regarded as his greatest work. *Robinson Crusoe* was not only Defoe's first novel; it is considered the first modern novel by any author. He described it as an "allegoric history,"[52] although it was a more a work of allegorical autobiography since he drew from his own experience, not unlike Bunyan did in *The Pilgrim's Progress*. Yet Defoe's description indicates a deep suspicion of the hermeneutical inclination to slide from allegory to allegorization, which views the text and the world as mere extensions of meaning to be found in another reality of a mythic world.[53] The move to otherworldliness is made easier by Bunyan's strategy to resist the domestication of empire by turning inward to the interior realm of the soul.

But this temptation is exhibited not so much in Bunyan himself as it is in the history of interpretation of his allegory, when in search of "other meanings" readers recoil from the social and material world to a mythical and spiritual reality. Such a move sees salvation as entirely about an otherworldly journey. Defoe's account of Christian pilgrimage in *Robinson Crusoe* as "allegoric history" explicitly rejects this flight from materiality present in certain pietistic allegorizations of works like *The Pilgrim's Progress* and subverts the deep tendency toward otherworldliness. This interpretive shift thus arises from Defoe's reception of the allegorical tradition, but his hermeneutical swerve from it also

---

[52] Daniel Defoe, preface to *The Farther Adventures of Robinson Crusoe* and Preface to *Serious Reflections during the Life and Surprising Adventures of Robinson Crusoe*, in *Robinson Crusoe*, Norton Critical Edition, ed. Michael Shinagel (New York: W.W. Norton, 1994), 239–43. Subsequent references are to the Norton Critical Edition.

[53] Jordan Rowan Fannin, "The Promise and Temptation of Allegory: Reading the Possibility of Pilgrimage in (Baptist) Bunyan and (Catholic) O'Connor," *American Baptist Quarterly* 33, nos. 3–4 (2014): 267–89.

indicates the correction of the received understanding.[54] Crusoe's story may be seen, then, as a political and economic renarration—indeed, a kind of Whig history of the Christian life that takes account of the new social and religious realities in which dissenters found themselves in the eighteenth century. For as Defoe shows, the choice is not (pace Francis Smith) whether to be worldly or godly but how the vocation of a godly Christian entails worldly responsibilities.

The story of Crusoe is set in the year 1651 during the Cromwellian era when Protestants were in charge of the reform of church and state, but the narrative world resembles an England where Presbyterians were out of power. The plot of Defoe's narrative begins with conflict as the opening scene describes an argument between Crusoe (representing the new world of economic opportunity) and his father (signifying the way of old dissent). The impatient young Crusoe, longing for adventure, desires to go to sea. His father advises him that a calling in law is more fitting for a young man of life's middle station, warning that God would not bless him if he ventures off foolishly. It was typical advice for middling Christians of puritan stock, as William Perkins argued in his *A Treatise of the Vocations* that "every particular calling must be practiced in and with the general calling of a Christian."[55] What this meant vocationally was that Christians were to show themselves to be Christians not only in their congregation and in their conversation but also in whatever worldly calling they might pursue. The hope of Crusoe's father, then, is not simply that his son might prosper as a lawyer but that he might show himself to be a Christian in the practice of law.

At first, Crusoe complies, but the lure of the high seas is too much. Against the advice of his father and the tears of his mother, Crusoe resolves to run away, and so with a friend he boards a ship bound for London. When a storm nearly takes both of their lives, his companion returns home. Struck by parental and providential warnings

[54] Harold Bloom calls this "creative correction" a "misprision," in *The Anxiety of Influence: A Theory of Poetry*, 2nd ed. (New York: Oxford University Press, 1997), 30. This poetic influence will be explored more fully in the next chapter.

[55] William Perkins, *A Treatise of the Vocations*, in *The Work of William Perkins*, ed. Ian Breward (Appleford, Abingdon: Sutton Courtenay, 1970), 456.

of catastrophe ahead, but also with the voice of his conscience, which continues to reproach him for his disobedience, Crusoe briefly contemplates turning back as well.[56] He imagines that his own father like the father in Jesus' parable might also kill the fatted calf and celebrate his homecoming (Luke 15:23). Echoing his father's earlier admonition, the ship captain also issues a warning, urging him to take the storm as a sign that, like Jonah, seafaring is not his calling. But even though the captain exhorts him that, if he tempts providence, he will surely see the hand of heaven against him, Crusoe follows the path of the Prodigal Son, determined to continue his rebellious journey, knowing full well it leads to the far country. Then, reflecting on the nature of repentance, he adds:

> As to going Home, Shame opposed the best Motions that offered to my Thoughts; and it immediately occurr'd to me how I should be laughed at among the Neighbours, and should be asham'd to see, not my Father and Mother only, but even every Body else; from whence I have since often observed, how incongruous and irrational the common Temper of [Hu]Mankind is, especially of Youth, to that Reason which ought to guide them in such cases, *viz.* that they are not asham'd to sin, and yet are asham'd to repent; not asham'd of the Action for which they ought justly to be esteemed Fools, but are asham'd of the returning, which only can make them be esteem'd wise Men.[57]

Crusoe recognizes the irony of being driven not by shame of sinning (which he knows to be foolishness) but by shame of returning, which he knows to be wisdom. Yet the thought of being humiliated by family and friends outweighs the reward of repentance. So he boards a ship in London bound for Africa in search of worldly fortune rather than pursuing an acceptable Christian calling in the law. Here, Defoe's understanding of the operations of the conscience follows the standard puritan account offered by William Ames, who described the conscience as "man's judgement of himself, according to Gods judgement

---

[56] Defoe, *Robinson Crusoe*, 7.
[57] Defoe, *Robinson Crusoe*, 13.

of him."[58] According to this view, the conscience is not the natural law of God written on the heart but rather the apprehension of that law. And because of the effect and power of sin, the conscience can go astray.

Following a successful voyage, Crusoe embraces his questionable calling as "a sailor and a merchant," though his prosperity is cut short when his friend and captain dies unexpectedly. As he embarks on another journey, his ship is seized by pirates, and he is taken to Morocco as prisoner with the crew. After two years he breaks free from his captors and is rescued by a Portuguese vessel, which brings him safely to Brazil, where he establishes a prosperous plantation. But once again the call of the sea is too strong, and, eight years to the day from when he left his father's home in England, Crusoe joins an expedition bound for Africa to bring back slaves for a group of Brazilian planters and merchants. The expedition soon goes terribly bad as the ship is caught in a violent storm and founders at sea. Robinson Crusoe alone among all the crew survives, as he is washed up on a deserted island, where he remains for twenty-eight years.

Crusoe soon begins salvaging cargo from the wreckage of the ship, which he laboriously brings to shore, as, in good puritan fashion, he lets nothing go to waste that might be put to good use. Dissenters like Defoe were schooled in the virtues of thrift and hard work, which served them well in business. Yet Crusoe's experiment is about more than economic prosperity. It is his struggle to come to terms with his vocation. Defoe knew firsthand the failure of ministry, business, and politics. Crusoe's life had been shipwrecked. He is washed up on the shore in a place not of his choosing. Now he must imagine life starting anew. He must answer the question about what his true calling is. The entry in Crusoe's journal just after his arrival on the island describes coming through "a dreadful Storm" and washing up alone on a dismal place that he calls "the Island of Despair."[59] Like Bunyan's pilgrim, Defoe's castaway leaves home, fleeing not "the wrath to come" but the storms of life, seeking not personal salvation but economic security.

---

[58] William Ames, *Conscience, with the Power and Cases Thereof* (London, 1639), I.2, 40.

[59] Defoe, *Robinson Crusoe*, 52.

His Slough of Despond is an entire island, though there is no Help offering an outstretched hand. He is all alone. Yet he soon finds the prosperity he desires. But the more he prospers, the more he senses that he is running from his true calling.[60]

There, in the far country, he discovers something that has eluded him in his restless journey—freedom. This new liberty of soul comes through an experience of grace one day in June of his first year on the island when he is seized by fever. Afraid and alone, he begins to pray: "Lord look upon me, Lord pity me, Lord have Mercy upon me."[61] His anguished prayers are followed by sleep, but his rest is interrupted by a terrible dream in which he sees a figure who looks like the Grim Reaper descending from a black cloud filled with fire. The earth shakes as this creature touches down, and, as he approaches Crusoe with a long spear, the ominous personage speaks with a most terrible voice: "Seeing all these Things have not brought thee to Repentance, now thou shalt die."[62] Defoe noted that "Spectre and Apparition make great Noise in the World." Yet he observed that it would be a mistake to "allow no Apparition at all" or to assume that "every Apparition be the Devil."[63] The notion that God speaks directly through dreams was a common feature of puritan religion, as of course it is also a common feature of the Bible. Bunyan's conversion experience likewise began with a vision in which he saw a high sunlit mountain and himself shivering in the cold with a wall separating him from the mountain and the sun's warmth.[64] And one need not look further than any puri-

---

[60] J. Paul Hunter stresses the similarity between *The Pilgrim's Progress* and *Robinson Crusoe*, showing that they share similar patterns of spiritual autobiography. Hunter, *The Reluctant Pilgrim: Defoe's Emblematic Method and Quest for Form in "Robinson Crusoe"* (Baltimore: Johns Hopkins Press, 1966), 89.

[61] Defoe, *Robinson Crusoe*, 64.

[62] Defoe, *Robinson Crusoe*, 65.

[63] Daniel Defoe, preface to *An Essay on the History and Reality of Apparitions* (London: J. Roberts, 1727).

[64] John Bunyan, *Grace Abounding to the Chief of Sinners*, ed. W. R. Owens (London: Penguin, 1987), §53, 18. Bunyan states that his book *The Pilgrim's Progress* was delivered to him "under the similitude of a dream," to which the final line attests: "So I awoke, and behold it was a Dream." *Pilgrim's Progress*, 133.

tan grave from the period to see how deeply that the angel of death permeated the religious imagination.

Crusoe awakens from his dream still sick with fever, yet the memory of his disturbing vision lingers long after it passed. Wondering why he is so afflicted, he takes a Bible that he recovered from the ship. He opens it, and the first words that catch his eyes are these: "Call on me in the Day of Trouble, and I will deliver, and thou shalt glorify Me" (Ps 50:15).[65] He thinks to himself, "Can God deliver me from this Place?"[66] Days later, after the fever had passed, he finds himself still thinking about God's promise of deliverance. It occurs to him that God has delivered him, but he has not glorified God by being thankful for his deliverance. So he kneels down and gives thanks to God for his recovery from the sickness that brought him near death. What may have begun for Crusoe as a kind of bibliomancy seeking to divine an oracular voice through the random reading of a biblical text becomes for him the discipline of *lectio continua* in which he resolves from that day forward to demonstrate his gratitude by reading the Bible every day.

Over the course of his study, it strikes Crusoe that all his searching has not brought him the one thing that would make him wise. Reading in Acts 5:31, he comes across these words: "He is exalted a Prince and a Saviour, to give Repentance, and to give Remission." Crusoe calls out to the Lord, and again his prayer is answered. But whereas the first time he asked for deliverance from sickness, in his second request he construes his need for deliverance in a very different sense. For it now occurs to him that being a castaway from God is far worse than being a castaway from civilization. He cries out, "Jesus, thou Son of David, Jesus, thou exalted Prince and Saviour, give me Repentance!"[67] Yet his conversion is not so much an instantaneous event as it is a process with discernable stages. As John Newton later noted in his famous

---

[65] Defoe, *Robinson Crusoe*, 69. Defoe cites Ps 50:15 in the footnote. Like Bunyan, Defoe's Scripture quotations are most often from the King James Version rather than the Geneva Bible. Valentine Cunningham, "Daniel Defoe," in *The Blackwell Companion to the Bible in English Literature*, ed. Rebecca Lemon, Emma Mason, Jonathan Roberts, and Christopher Rowland (Malden, Mass.: Wiley-Blackwell, 2009), 345–58.

[66] Defoe, *Robinson Crusoe*, 69.

[67] Defoe, *Robinson Crusoe*, 71.

hymn, God's "Amazing Grace" first teaches the heart to fear (stage 1) before those fears can be relieved (stage 2) or finally celebrated in the hour of first belief (stage 3).[68] And so the Christian journey continued beyond conversion, for, if everything is conversion, then "the Christian story ceases to be a story."[69]

Eleven years later, a third memorable event marks Crusoe's experience of grace. While walking on the beach one day about noon, he comes upon a human footprint. For a moment he stands "thunderstruck," as if he has seen a ghost. Sensing imminent danger, he retreats to his fortress. A single footprint transforms him from a man of solitude seeking community into a person in isolation living in terror of other human beings. His greatest desire, companionship, has now become his greatest anxiety. Terrified by thoughts of a cannibal invasion or, worse yet, of a satanic onslaught, he is unable to sleep. For months he is held captive to his fears. Then one morning, while lying in his bed, the familiar words of Scripture come into his thoughts: "Call on me in the Day of Trouble, and I will deliver, and thou shalt glorify Me."[70] Again he prays for deliverance. Seeking a word, he picks up the Bible. This time it falls open to Psalm 27:14: "Wait on the Lord, and be of good Cheer, and he shall strengthen thy Heart; wait, I say,

---

[68] "Amazing Grace," verse 2, in John Newton and William Cowper, *The Olney Hymns* (Bucks, U.K.: Arthur Gordon Hugh Osborn for the Cowper & Newton Museum, 1979; facsimile from the 1st ed. at Cowper & Newton Museum, published in 1779). Although there was wide agreement among puritans about the *ordo salutis*, which held that conversion was an arduous process preceded by preparatory stages, there was no consensus on the morphology of conversion; see W. R. Owens, introduction to Bunyan, *Grace Abounding*, xxiii. For discussions of divergent morphological accounts, see Jerald C. Brauer, "Conversion: From Puritanism to Revivalism," *Journal of Religion* 58, no. 3 (1978): 233; Edmund S. Morgan, *Visible Saints* (New York: New York University Press, 1963), 90–91; Elizabeth Reis, "Seventeenth-Century Puritan Conversion Narratives," in *Religions of the United States in Practice*, ed. Colleen McDannell (Princeton, N.J.: Princeton University Press, 2001), 1:22–26; Patricia Caldwell, *The Puritan Conversion Narrative: The Beginnings of American Expression* (Cambridge: Cambridge University Press, 1983). On the process of conversion, see chap. 2, "Interpreters of the Dream."

[69] James Wm. McClendon Jr., *Doctrine: Systematic Theology*, vol. 2 (Waco, Tex.: Baylor University Press, 2012), 141.

[70] Defoe, *Robinson Crusoe*, 114.

on the Lord."[71] A wave of inexpressible comfort washes over him, and he finds himself able to trust in God's providential care.[72]

Crusoe's father had in fact warned him that, if he did not repent at home when he had leisure, he would be left alone with none to assist him.[73] Indeed, it might be argued that he does make his way alone and without assistance, and thus it might seem he encourages others to do the same. For unlike Bunyan's Christian, who always travels with fellow pilgrims, Defoe's modern journey is a lonely one. Friends come and go, but most of the time Crusoe walks alone. Yet such a reading fails to consider the striking way in which Defoe's fictional experiment was cast in the form of an autobiographical narrative that gave voice to other travelers journeying into the capitalist and individualist social world that was emerging.[74] As such the novel is an inherently social document set forth as a paradigm for other castaways in the modern world to discern the experience of grace.

"The Story is told," as Defoe stated in the preface, "to justify and honour the Wisdom of Providence," but noticeably absent is the struggle over the convert's status as elect or damned that so permeates earlier conversion narratives in the seventeenth century.[75] This is not to suggest that Crusoe's Christian journey is anxiety free, but it is a struggle arising from the *shame* induced by the knowledge that he deliberately and willfully disobeyed his father's advice rather than a fear rooted in the certainty of his *guilt* because he is not one of God's elect. The autobiographical elements are surely a reflection of Defoe's own mental states as he made his spiritual and theological journey beyond the old puritanism. But even though Defoe surely drew from

---

[71] Defoe, *Robinson Crusoe*, 114.

[72] The great English and Australian Baptist preacher Frank W. Boreham saw the threefold deliverance of Crusoe to be paradigmatic of Christian experience. For Boreham concluded that "whosoever shall call on the Name of the Lord, the same shall be saved" (Rom 10:13). Boreham, *A Handful of Stars* (New York: Abingdon, 1922), 32.

[73] Defoe, *Robinson Crusoe*, 6.

[74] So Charles Taylor argues more generally about puritanism as a source of selfhood, in *Sources of the Self: The Making of Modern Identity* (Cambridge, Mass.: Harvard University Press, 1989), 184.

[75] Defoe, *Robinson Crusoe*, 3; and John Stachniewski, *The Persecutory Imagination: English Puritanism and the Literature of Despair* (Oxford: Clarendon, 1991), 7, 12, 40–42.

his own experience in writing an allegorical autobiography, the overall narrative structure follows the arc of the biblical story, drawn from the parable of the Prodigal Son, the book of Job, and to some extent the book of Jonah. This emphasis on personal faith, however, should not be taken as a suggestion that doctrinal theology is unimportant. Indeed, *Robinson Crusoe* is more than just a modern catechetical instrument. It is an attempt at a narrative theology for the coming faith amidst modernity just as *The Pilgrim's Progress* was a kind of prose epic for an earlier era when modern individualism was first coming to the fore. Yet, as it turned out, the theological vector of this emergent faith of the Christian as a new social being was more problematic than Defoe could have imagined.[76]

Before prospective church members were admitted into the church, they were required to give an account of their experience, which required catechetical instruction. Defoe offered a description of Christian instruction. Twenty-four years of solitude are broken with the arrival of another human being whom Crusoe rescues from being killed by neighboring islanders. He gives his companion the name "Friday" for the day of the week on which he arrives, and soon Crusoe makes it his business to teach his new understudy "every Thing, that was proper to make him useful, handy, and helpful."[77] Of first importance is language, including the grammar of the faith. Although he readily admits that he is ill equipped in the art of casuistry, Crusoe prays that God would enable him to bring his student "to the true Knowledge of Religion, and of the Christian Doctrine, that he might know Christ Jesus, *to know whom is Life eternal*."[78] Crusoe reluctantly takes up the role of catechist by asking Friday a series of questions about basic doctrines and engages him in reflecting on the bearing of each query for his own faith.

---

[76] I am using phrase "the coming faith" to denote the approach of theological liberalism, which I describe as "mainly about adjustment and accommodation to the modern world," in Gary Dorrien, *The Making of American Liberal Theology: Idealism, Realism, and Modernity, 1900–1950* (Louisville: Westminster John Knox, 2003), 389.

[77] Defoe, *Robinson Crusoe*, 152.

[78] Defoe, *Robinson Crusoe*, 159; emphasis in original.

Crusoe's account of Christian doctrine has the familiar ring of Presbyterianism, yet he makes no appeal to the conventional language of the Westminster Confession or to its shorter or longer catechisms.[79] Instead, his catechetical instruction is based on a strict biblicism without the aid of any creed or confession. Reflecting on his theological task, Crusoe appeals to the perspicuity of Scripture on matters, which make one "wise unto salvation" because, he contends, the meaning is "so plainly laid down in the Word of God; so easy to be receiv'd and understood." He says that he learned this hermeneutical principle from his own experience, as he expresses, "[T]he bare reading . . . [of] the Scripture made me capable of understanding enough of my Duty, to carry me directly on to the great Work of sincere Repentance for my Sins, and laying hold of a Saviour for Life and Salvation."[80] But in this approach to Christian doctrine, Crusoe was far from alone. He was simply stating a widely shared belief among Protestants in the seventeenth century.

The Particular Baptists, for example, contended that the meaning of the Bible is sufficiently plain to be understood by anyone and everyone, affirming that "in this written Word God hath plainly revealed whatsoever he hath thought needful for us to know, beleeve and acknowledge, touching the Nature and Office of Christ, in whom all the promises are Yea and Amen."[81] Most dissenters held to this plain sense understanding of Scripture, believing that "not only the learned, but the unlearned, in a due use of ordinary means, may attain to a sufficient understanding of them." Yet not everyone agreed that this clarity extended to the whole of the Scriptures. As the Westminster Confession attested, "all things in Scripture are *not alike plain* in themselves, *nor alike clear* unto all."[82] In contrast to Crusoe—who understands the Bible through and through as the plainly revealed Word of God and thus accessible to anyone and everyone—other Christians

---

[79] The Westminster Confession of Faith and Westminster Catechism (published in 1647), in *Creeds of the Churches*, ed. John H. Leith (New York: Anchor Books, 1963).

[80] Defoe, *Robinson Crusoe*, 160.

[81] First London Confession, VIII, in William Latane Lumpkin, *Baptist Confessions of Faith* (Valley Forge, Penn.: Judson, 1959), 158.

[82] Westminster Confession, I.7, in *Creeds of the Churches*, 3rd ed., ed. John H. Leith (Louisville, Ky.: Westminster John Knox, 1982), 196; emphasis added.

held the Bible to be "both clear *and* obscure, not merely clear *or* obscure."[83] Reading for the knowledge of "the Christian doctrine" therefore required some hermeneutical assistance, as Scripture alone would not suffice, since creeds and confessions are necessary, they argued, to interpret it aright.

Crusoe's assertion that the "bare reading" of Scripture is sufficient for determining "the Christian doctrine," though set in the context of the mid-seventeenth century, actually reflects later events. During the time that Defoe was completing his novel, which was published in April 1719, the dissenting ministers of London were embroiled in a bitter controversy. In February they assembled at Salters' Hall to debate the question of whether doctrinal orthodoxy with respect to the Trinity should be determined by *the Scriptures and* a confession of faith or whether *the Scriptures alone* were sufficient. Those who called for subscription to a confession in addition to the Bible became known as "subscribers." The other side that insisted that "the Bible is the only perfect rule of faith" were called "nonsubscribers." When a vote was taken, the nonsubscribers won by a narrow majority of fifty-seven to fifty-three, leading one contemporary commentator to remark that "the Bible carried it by four."[84] But the issue was far from resolved, as the effects lingered for decades. In a pamphlet written in the same year as the Salters' Hall controversy, Defoe dismissed the dispute as frivolous, producing more heat than light. But, more problematic, he suggested that the controversy would result in more harm than good, exclaiming:

> What dreadful Work is this, that the *Dissenters* should be throw-
> ing Dirt at one another, and the Ministers should be Inveighing

---

[83] James Patrick Callahan, "*Claritas Scripturae*: The Role of Perspecuity in Protestant Hermeneutics," *Journal of the Evangelical Theological Society* 39, no. 3 (1996): 357; emphasis added.

[84] Alexander Gordon, *Heads of English Unitarian History* (London: Philip Green, 1895), 33–34; Alexander Gordon, "The Story of Salters' Hall," in *Addresses Biographical and Historical* (London: Lindsey Press, 1922); and John Shute Barrington, *An Account of the Late Proceedings of the Dissenting Ministers at Salters-Hall* (London: J. Roberts, 1719). Shute, later Viscount, Barrington was a Congregationalist and leader of the nonsubscribers.

against, and Exposing one another, when their Enemies are so ear-
nestly struggling to throw Dirt at both Sides![85]

Defoe believed that the division between subscribers and nonsubscribers would aid the established church and result in a loss of liberty
for all dissenters.[86] He urged both sides to lay aside their differences,
forgiving and forbearing one another in love. Crusoe's dismissive reference to religious "Disputes, Wranglings, Strife and Contention" as
"all perfectly useless" reflects the state of dissent at the Salters' Hall
controversy, but his affirmation of "The Word of God" as "the sure
Guide to Heaven" clearly indicates that his sympathy is with the
nonsubscribers.[87]

To his credit, Crusoe recognizes that when it comes to matters of
Christian doctrine he possesses more sincerity than knowledge, and
that in large measure he is actually instructing himself as much as
his catechumen. When he reluctantly begins laying a foundation of
religious knowledge, he starts by asking questions about God's creation and providential care and, from there, moves on to the theme of
Christ's redemptive work. On these subjects he finds Friday remarkably receptive, but, when their conversation turns to the Devil, Crusoe
comments, "I found that it was not so easie to imprint right Notions
in his Mind."[88] Friday wants to know why, if God is all-powerful, he
does not simply kill the devil, or, if he is all merciful, why not just save
everyone, including the devil. Realizing they are headed down a path
leading nowhere, Crusoe breaks off the discussion. And he concludes
his theological instruction with this observation: "I cannot see the least
Use that the greatest Knowledge of the disputed Points in Religion,
which have made such Confusions in the World, would have been to
us if we could have obtained it."[89]

Disputed questions about the devil, though placed on the lips of
this aboriginal islander, undoubtedly represent the skeptical foolishness

[85] Daniel Defoe, *A Letter to the Dissenters* (London: J. Wright, 1719), 12.
[86] Defoe, *Letter to the Dissenters*, 14.
[87] Defoe, *Robinson Crusoe*, 160.
[88] Defoe, *Robinson Crusoe*, 156.
[89] Defoe, *Robinson Crusoe*, 160.

of the sort that dissenters like Defoe held in contempt.[90] As he contended in his *The History of the Devil*, the reality of Satan is no excuse for human responsibility, for

> Bad as he is, the Devil may be abus'd
> Be falsly charg'd, and causelesly accus'd,
> When Men, unwilling to be blam'd alone,
> Shift off these Crimes on Him which are their Own.[91]

Yet Defoe recognized that the power of Satan's work was subtle and persuasive, as he explained in his satirical poem *The True-Born Englishman*:

> He needs no Standing-Army Government;
> He always rules us by our own Consent:
> His Laws are easy, and his gentle Sway
> Makes it exceeding pleasant to obey. [92]

Nor could the questions of doubters guided by skeptics lead to any good end either, as the father in Defoe's *New Family Instructor* explains to his children, saying, "And all the poor doubting Souls who are bewildered by Uncertainties, and bemused by the Learned Perplexities of these Men, must live, nay, which is worse, must die, in the same Uncertainty; not knowing *in whom they have believed*."[93] Indeed, Crusoe's theology reflects Defoe's aversion to speculative abstraction,

---

[90] The father conversing with his children in *New Family Instructor* heaps scorn on "Deists and Hereticks" who question the plain and clear Scripture evidence for the deity of Christ. The father concludes, "[W]e do not need these disputing Gentlemens determining of these Things so much as they imagine we do; let us search the Scripture, and seek the Guidance of the Spirit to interpret that Scripture, and to guide us to the knowledge of Christ, and he will guide us." Daniel Defoe, *New Family Instructor* (London: T. Warner, 1727), 351.

[91] Daniel Defoe, *The History of the Devil*, 2nd ed. (London: T. Warner, 1727), title page. Although Defoe himself accepted the reality of both "*God* and *the Devil*" (because, as he argued, whoever "denies one, generally denies both"), he nevertheless believed that deists thought too little of the devil while Milton thought too much of him. Defoe, *History of the Devil*, 22–23. Nevertheless, Defoe never clearly explained his views on the nature and extent of evil personified.

[92] Daniel Defoe, *The True-Born Englishman: A Satyr* (London, 1701), I.5.

[93] Defoe, *New Family Instructor*, 367; emphasis in original.

as when he asked in his poem on the divinity of Christ, "How shall a Mortal Thought describe thy Being?" To which he answered that such conjecture is "Far above Nature's Reach, above her Sight."[94] Crusoe the catechist thus commends a theology of plain truths, similar to that described by John Dryden, who observed:

> Faith is not built on disquisitions vain;
> The things we *must* believe, are *few*, and *plain*.[95]

Toward the end of his narrative, when he has been joined by two more inhabitants, Crusoe reflects on the place of religion in society. He observes that in his island kingdom there are subjects of three religions: Protestant, Catholic, and Pagan. Yet unlike his homeland in which there is an established church that grudgingly tolerates dissenters, Crusoe notes, "I allow'd Liberty of Conscience throughout my Dominion."[96] It was a theme about which Defoe had given much thought, especially in his poem *Jure Divino*, where he satirized the notion of divine right rule and defended revolutionary principles of freedom, arguing that resisting oppression is as natural as fire ascending or water flowing downward.[97] His account of justice is demonstrably Lockean, though Locke is noticeably absent from the discussion.[98] But, in *Robinson Crusoe*, Defoe imagines the extension of religious liberty from Protestant dissenters to Catholics and unbelievers. Such a society was unimaginable to Locke, who argued that toleration should not apply to Catholics, because they "deliver themselves up to the Protection and Service of another prince."[99] But the same was true of Catholic theorists who assumed that non-Catholics could not be loyal

---

[94] Daniel Defoe, "Trinity: Or, the Divinity of the Son," in the *New Family Instructor*, 369 and 384.

[95] Dryden, *Religio Laica*, 431–32, in *The Poetical Works of John Dryden*, ed. George Gilfillan (New York: D. Appleton, 1857), 194; emphasis in original.

[96] Defoe, *Robinson Crusoe*, 174.

[97] Daniel Defoe, *Jure Divino: A Satire in Twelve Books* (London, 1706), 8:30.

[98] Backscheider, *Daniel Defoe*, 169–72; and also Martyn P. Thompson, "The Reception of Locke's Two Treatises," *Political Studies* 24, no. 2 (1976): 184–91.

[99] John Locke, *A Letter concerning Toleration* (Indianapolis: Liberty Fund, 2010), 52; also in *The Works of John Locke*, 10 vols. (London: Thomas Tegg, 1823), 5:1–58. William Petty, a contemporary of Locke, promoted "Liberty of Conscience as the inherent

citizens.[100] It was dissenters who thought about a multifaith world as possible. Defoe echoed the claim of the Baptist Thomas Helwys, that religious liberty applied to "heretics, Turks, Jews, or whatsoever," as well as to his own community of dissenters[101]—or Roger Williams, who established the colony of Providence Plantation as "a shelter for persons distressed of conscience" where Baptists, Congregationalists, Quakers, and other religious dissenters lived at peace with one another alongside the indigenous Indian people.[102]

Here, the reader gets a glimpse of the practical value inherent in the politics of dissent. In many respects, *Robinson Crusoe* anticipated the emergence of modern religious freedom, which over time came to reverse the policies of state-sponsored persecution in favor of civil liberty. The experiential faith of Robinson Crusoe would contribute to the common good of many who were not Defoe's fellow dissenters. The Whig Party championed principles that came to be embodied in liberal democracy and in constitutional republicanism, both of which continued to provide ease for dissenters. Religious liberty, as Crusoe's short-lived island experiment suggests, was not merely a "loser's creed" but rather put forth as a political good for all, as Roger Williams, John Locke, and Thomas Jefferson argued more forcefully.[103] And moder-

---

and Indealable Right of Mandkind." For Petty, unlike Locke, full liberty extended to all people, including Catholics. Quoted in Sowerby, *Making Toleration*, 258.

[100] Pope Clement VIII, on March 21, 1592, exhorted the conquered subjects to be fully loyal "to our very dear son in Christ, Felipe the Catholic king of Spain and the Indie," assuming that non-Catholics could not be loyal subjects. Luis N. Rivera, *A Violent Evangelism: The Political and Religious Conquest of the Americas* (Louisville, Ky.: Westminster John Knox, 1992), 216.

[101] Thomas Helwys, *A Short Declaration of the Mystery of Iniquity* (1611/1612), ed. Richard Groves (Macon, Ga.: Mercer University Press, 1998), 53. See also Ernest A. Payne, *Thomas Helwys and the First Baptist Church in England*, 2nd ed. (London: Baptist Union of Great Britain, 1966), 18.

[102] "Confirmatory Deed of Roger Williams and his wife, of the lands transferred by him to his associates in the year 1638," in *Records of the Colony of Rhode Island and Providence Plantations* (Providence, R.I.: A. Crawford Greene and Brother, 1856–1865), 1:22–25 (a.k.a. *Records of Rhode Island*).

[103] Williams, *The Bloudy Tenent of Persecution*, in *The Complete Writings of Roger Williams*, vol. 3 (New York: Russell and Russell, 1963; repr., Paris, Ark.: Baptist Standard Bearer, 2005); Locke, *A Letter concerning Toleration*, in *Works* (London: Thomas Tegg, 1823), 5:1–58; and Jefferson, A Bill for Establishing Religious Freedom (published

nity received the complementary gift of religious pluralism at no extra charge. It was precisely this sort of vision of "true religion" that made it possible for Catholics, Protestants, Jews, and other people of faith to live together in a social space where *none* is established and *all* are free.

Yet *Robinson Crusoe* is not simply political theory or partisan politics thinly disguised as an adventure tale.[104] Instead, it imagines what a world might look like if dissenters were in a position of power and influence. But, in the real world, the influence of dissenters was limited and dependent on political power brokers. Even then, the close and complicated relationship between dissenting religion and republican politics did not come without a price. English Presbyterianism and other dissenters, chiefly the General Baptists, continued down the road laid out by revisions of "the Christian doctrine" that began at Salters' Hall, as the theology of nonsubscription tended toward heterodoxy.[105] And as the theology of liberty became more deeply connected with Whig republicanism, the old doctrinal orthodoxy faded as well.[106] These connections did not escape the perceptive notice of John Henry Newman, who saw in modern liberalism simply a revival of the ancient heresy of Arianism and its later iteration of Socinianism.[107]

---

in 1777 but not approved by the Virginia legislature until 1786), in *The Papers of Thomas Jefferson* (Princeton, N.J.: Princeton University Press, 1950), 2:545–47.

[104] Philip Nicholas Furbank and W. R. Owens, *A Political Biography of Daniel Defoe* (London: Pickering & Chatto, 2006), 174–77.

[105] For a list of the publications by the subscribers and nonsubscribers at Salters' Hall, see Hilarius de Synodis, *An Account of the Pamphlets Writ This Last Year Each Side by the Dissenters* (London: James Knapton, 1720), 25–36. Among the Presbyterians there were forty-eight nonsubscribers and thirty subscribers at Salters' Hall. For a history of the theological devolution of Presbyterianism in England, see Charles Gordon Bolam, Jeremy Goring, H. L. Short, and Roger Thomas, *The English Presbyterians* (London: Allen & Unwin, 1968), 151–74; and Alexander Hutton Drysdale, *History of the Presbyterians in England: Their Rise, Decline, and Revival* (London: Presbyterian Church of England, 1889), 489–515.

[106] Tim Harris, *Restoration: Charles II and His Kingdoms, 1660–1685* (London: Penguin, 2005), 300–309.

[107] John Henry Newman defines theological liberalism as a heresy because, he argues, "[t]here is no existing authority on earth competent to interfere with the liberty of individuals in reasoning and judging for themselves." Newman, *Apologia Pro Vita Sua*, ed. David J. DeLaura (New York: W.W. Norton, 1968), 223. See also Robert

Yet for Crusoe, as for the father in Defoe's *Family Instructor*, the child of God must stand firm in faith and gaze not by foolish reason, seeking that which lies beyond the limits of human understanding:

> Believe and wonder, wonder and believe;
> Bring down our reasoning Follies to our Faith,
> To what we cannot comprehend, resign,
> And wait the glorious state where all our Eyes
> Illuminated from himself, shall see
> God as he is, and all be Gods like him.[108]

But perhaps the theology of Scripture evidence and plain truth was not to blame so much for what it said as for what it left unsaid, making space for theological revisionism to redefine the nature of Christian doctrine.[109] This mixed legacy, however, does not diminish the fact that what Defoe produced in *Robinson Crusoe* was not simply the first modern novel but a new and revised account of prospering dissent. Yet it marks a change. Whereas, in the old dissent, Christian pilgrims like Bunyan and Crusoe's father walked together, in the new dissent, travelers like Crusoe and Defoe himself must for the most part walk alone.

Pattison, *The Great Dissent: John Henry Newman and the Liberal Heresy* (New York: Oxford University Press, 1991), 100–104.

[108] Defoe, "Trinity," in the *New Family Instructor*, 371. Defoe's free verse poem is read by the father as a conclusion to his long conversation with his daughter and son in which he leads them through Scripture teaching to affirm the full divinity and humanity of Christ.

[109] Matthew Kadane, "Anti-Trinitarianism and the Republican Tradition in Enlightenment Britain," *Republics of Letters* 2, no. 1 (2010): 38–54. Calvinists like John Edwards especially blamed John Locke's *Reasonableness of Christianity* for being "all over Socianized" and for creating an intellectual culture of unitarianism. Edwards, *Some Thoughts concerning the Several Causes and Occasions of Atheism* (London: J. Robinson, 1695), 113. On Locke and unitarianism, see John Marshall, "Locke, Socianism, 'Socinianism,' and Unitarianism," in *English Philosophy in the Age of Locke*, ed. M. A. Stewart (Oxford: Clarendon, 2000), 111–82.

Politicizing Dissent

Robinson Crusoe is the most widely read, published, translated, adapted, and imitated novel ever written in the English language.[110] Since April of 1719, when one thousand copies of the first edition appeared, it has never been out of print. By the end of the year, it went through eight editions, and translations had been published in French, German, and Dutch. It was a runaway success. Defoe sought to capitalize on the popular reception with a sequel (*The Farther Adventures of Robinson Crusoe*) as well as several other seagoing stories.[111] Pirated and abridged versions soon appeared, taking advantage of the public interest. By the end of the eighteenth century, there were already 130 editions in English alone, and, by the end of the nineteenth century, the number of editions, variations, and translations rose to more than seven hundred. Now there are well over one thousand.[112] Its initial popularity was due to the story itself. Samuel Johnson praised it, exclaiming, "Was there ever yet anything written by mere [hu]man that was wished longer by its readers, excepting *Don Quixote*, *Robinson Crusoe*, and the *Pilgrim's Progress?*"[113] The reasons for its reception are worth pondering.

The fascination with *Robinson Crusoe* was in full swing in the mid-nineteenth century, when Wilkie Collins wrote his novel *The Moonstone*, in which one of the narrators, Gabriel Betteredge, is obsessed with *Robinson Crusoe*, even to the point of considering it his "Bible." Throughout the story, Betteredge continues to refer to the book, declaring that he is drawn to the story because of its transcendent quality. He explains,

[110] Clarence S. Brigham, "Bibliography of American Editions of *Robinson Crusoe* to 1830," *American Antiquarian Society* (October 1957): 137.

[111] Daniel Defoe, *The Farther Adventures of Robinson Crusoe* (London: W. Taylor, 1719); *The King of Pirates* (1720); *The Life, Adventures and Pyracies of the Famous Captain Singleton* (1720); *Colonel Jack* (1723). His sequel of moral essays was successful in riding the wave of interest in Crusoe stories: *Serious Reflections during the Life and Surprising Adventures of Robinson Crusoe* (London: W. Taylor 1720).

[112] Richard West, *The Life and Strange Surprising Adventures of Daniel Defoe* (New York: HarperCollins, 1997), 248.

[113] James Boswell, *Life of Johnson*, ed. George Birkbeck Hill, 6 vols. (New York: Harper, 1891), 3:267–68.

Such a book as *Robinson Crusoe* never was written, and never will be written again. I have tried that book for years—generally in combination with a pipe of tobacco—and I have found that it is my friend in need in all the necessities of this mortal life. When my spirits are bad—*Robinson Crusoe*. When I want advice—*Robinson Crusoe*. In past times when my wife plagued me; in present times when I have had a drop too much—*Robinson Crusoe*. I have worn out six stout *Robinson Crusoes* with hard work in my service. On my lady's last birthday she gave me a seventh. I took a drop too much on the strength of it; and *Robinson Crusoe* put me right again. Price four shillings and sixpence, bound in blue, with a picture into the bargain.[114]

Throughout the story Betteredge turns to the book, opening pages, sometimes randomly, to see what words of wisdom will be revealed to him. It is a highly eccentric usage of Defoe's novel, to be sure. Yet it illustrates the level to which *Robinson Crusoe* penetrated popular audiences, being elevated to the status of a classic text within the canon of English literature.[115]

The inclusion of *Robinson Crusoe* on the list of great books came quickly because it tells a compelling story. Its plot set the template for future adventure tales, and there was the added attraction of shipwrecks, pirates, and cannibals, but most of all human survival. George Chalmers, though a Tory in his political views, wrote the first biography of Defoe, in which he declaimed of *Robinson Crusoe* that "few books have ever so naturally mingled amusement with instruction." Chalmers explained that "the attention is fixed, either by the simplicity of the narration, or by the variety of the incident; the heart is amended by a vindication of the ways of God to [hu]man[ity]: and the

---

[114] Wilkie Collins, *The Moonstone: A Romance* (New York: Harper, 1874), 18–19. Collins is acknowledging the widespread reading of *Robinson Crusoe* while at the same time critiquing it. Thanks to Judith Heyhoe for calling Collins' novel to my attention.

[115] On the history of interpretation of Defoe and *Robinson Crusoe*, see Philip Nicholas Furbank and W. R. Owens, *The Canonization of Daniel Defoe* (New Haven: Yale University Press, 1988); Pat Rogers, ed., *Defoe: The Critical Heritage* (London: Routledge & Kegan Paul, 1972); and Defoe, *Robinson Crusoe*, 227–432.

understanding is informed by various examples."[116] The basic narrative became so popular that it even created its own genre, which continually recurs in literature, film, and popular media.[117] Yet *Robinson Crusoe* is remembered not primarily for its adventurous plot but for its main character, Robinson Crusoe, who is a hero of mythic proportions. Precisely what sort of myth it is, though, is not immediately apparent.[118]

Crusoe has often been portrayed as the industrious capitalist whose success is largely dependent on his prudent and thrifty puritan values embodying the myth of economic self-fulfillment. This is precisely the image that Karl Marx focused on, attacking *Robinson Crusoe* as a capitalist manifesto that simply underwrote the individualism of bourgeois society.[119] But whereas Marx portrayed Crusoe's religion as mere entertainment, Max Weber saw Crusoe as an important symbol of the transformation from a religious to a worldly asceticism that embodied the spirit of Western capitalistic societies.[120] According to this version of the myth, Crusoe is a venture capitalist who exemplifies the Protestant work ethic. And yet, as Weber observed, inhabitants of the modern world, who live into the economic existence of a secular vocation derived from an earlier Protestantism, are entirely unable to understand or even imagine the religious inheritance that has been passed on to them in this vocation.[121]

No one has emulated this capitalist myth embodied in *Robinson Crusoe* better than Benjamin Franklin (1706–1790). He is the quintessential American—heroic not because of his military exploits but because of his popular appeal as a person of the working class who became financially successful, the archetype of a "self-made man," who symbolized the American dream of social mobility. Franklin embodies

[116] George Chalmers, *The Life of Daniel De Foe* (London, 1790; repr., Oxford: D. A. Talboys, 1841), 74.

[117] The term "Robinsonade" to describe the Crusoe genre was coined by Johann Gottfried Schnabel in his novel *Die Insel Felsenburg* (*The Island Stronghold*, 1731).

[118] Ian Watt, "Robinson Crusoe as a Myth," in Defoe, *Robinson Crusoe*, 289.

[119] Karl Marx, *Capital*, trans. Samuel Moore and Edward Aveling, Great Books of the Western World (Chicago: Encyclopaedia Britannica, 1952), 50:33–35.

[120] Max Weber, *The Protestant Ethic and the Spirit of Capitalism*, trans. Talcott Parsons (New York: Charles Scribner's Sons, 1958), 176.

[121] Weber, *Protestant Ethic*, 155.

the narrative of how ordinary people can acquire wealth and prosperity through frugality and industry.[122] In his *Autobiography* Franklin tells about his love for literature and book collecting, which began early in life. He was so moved after reading *The Pilgrim's Progress* that his first collection of books was of Bunyan's works. But Franklin's interest in Bunyan seems to have been more about literary style than theological ideas, for, as he explains, he had "become a real doubter in many points of our religious doctrine."[123] Over time the homely puritan prose wore thin, and, as a young man, he traded his copies of Bunyan's works for Burton's *Historical Collections*.[124] Though Franklin fondly referred to Bunyan as his "old favorite author," his search for more elegant language led to the broadening of his literary interests. At some point Franklin encountered Defoe's *Essay on Projects*, which he says occasioned a "turn of thinking that had an influence on some of the principal future events of [his] life."[125]

Franklin was thoroughly familiar with *Robinson Crusoe*. On May 4, 1738, he advertised an edition for sale in the *Pennsylvania Gazette*.[126] It was, after all, the most popular book sold in the American colonies

[122] Gordon Wood, *The Americanization of Benjamin Franklin* (New York: Penguin, 2005), 1–16.

[123] Benjamin Franklin, *Autobiography: An Authoritative Text, Contexts, Criticism*, ed. Joyce E. Chaplin (New York: W.W. Norton, 2012), 21.

[124] Franklin, *Autobiography*, 17. Also see Edwin Wolf II and Kevin J. Hayes, *The Library of Benjamin Franklin* (Philadelphia: American Philosophical Society, 2006), 4–6.

[125] Franklin, *Autobiography*, 17–18.

[126] "Extracts from the *Gazette*, 1738" (May 4, 1738), in Franklin, *The Papers of Benjamin Franklin*, vol. 2, *January 1, 1735, through December 31, 1744*, ed. Leonard W. Labaree (New Haven: Yale University Press, 1960), 209–17. One copy of a French translation of *Robinson Crusoe* was in Franklin's personal library. "List of Books, [before 31 December 1781?]," in Franklin, *Papers*, vol. 36, *November 1, 1781, through March 15, 1782*, ed. Ellen R. Cohn (New Haven: Yale University Press, 2002), 330–38. On Franklin's personal library, see Edwin Wolf II, "The Reconstruction of Benjamin Franklin's Library: An Unorthodox Jigsaw Puzzle," *Papers of the Bibliographical Society of America* 56, no. 1 (1962): 1–16; and Wolf and Hayes, *Library of Benjamin Franklin*, 241–42. *The Franklin Papers* are available online in searchable texts at Founders Online, National Archives, http://founders.archives.gov/.

from the time of its first publication.[127] Perry Miller went so far as to suggest that in the 1730s "few in America were aware of Pope and none of Swift," but all were "adoring of *Robinson Crusoe*."[128] Though Franklin talked only briefly about his understanding of Crusoe, he frequently alluded to the story, especially to Friday's skepticism about the devil.[129]

[127] Brigham lists 125 editions and versions published in America before 1830, in "Bibliography of American Editions of *Robinson Crusoe* to 1830," 145. It is possible that Franklin could have come across one of the early American editions, though it is more likely that he acquired one published in England. The first printing of *Robinson Crusoe* in America was published by Samuel Keimer in Philadelphia in 1725. It was entitled *Serious Reflections during the Life and Surprising Adventures of Robinson Crusoe*. There was an edition published in Boston in 1757 entitled *The Life of Robinson Crusoe, of York, Written by Himself*. One of the most popular editions was published by Hugh Gaine at New York in 1774 under the title *The Wonderful Life and Surprising Adventures of the Renowned Hero, Robinson Crusoe*. Several more editions were printed in America: one by Nathaniel Coverly in Boston in 1779 and an abridged version by Isaiah Thomas in 1786. Several more American editions were published in the 1790s. Brigham, "Bibliography of American Editions of *Robinson Crusoe* to 1830," 137–40. Digital images of these are available in the database Early American Imprints, Series I (1639–1800) and II (1801–1819). Catalogues of colonial booksellers and bookstores from the period show that editions of *Robinson Crusoe* were readily available—e.g., *A Catalogue of Novels and Romances, for Sale by John Conrad & Co. No. 30, Chesnut-Street* (Philadelphia: M. & J. Conrad, 1804); *Catalogue of Books Imported from London in the Ships Sterling, Jane, and Cornplanter, and for Sale by C. and A. Conrad & Co.* (Pennsylvania: C. & A. Conrad, 1807); *General Catalogue, of the Theological and Literary Book-store, Kept by William W. Woodward, No. 52, South Second Street* (Philadelphia: William W. Woodward, 1812); and *Catalogue of Novels and Romances, Being Part of an Extensive Collection for Sale by M. Carey and Son, Corner of Chesnut and Fourth Streets* (Philadelphia: M. Carey & Son, 1817).

[128] Perry Miller, *Jonathan Edwards* (New York: William Sloan, 1949; repr., Lincoln: University of Nebraska Press, 2005), 109.

[129] Franklin, *Autobiography*, 26. Franklin alludes to Crusoe in his letters: "From Benjamin Franklin to John Whitehurst, 27 June 1763," in Franklin, *Papers*, vol. 10, *January 1, 1762, through December 31, 1763*, ed. Leonard W. Labaree (New Haven: Yale University Press, 1966), 300–303; and "A Letter from a Gentleman in Crusoe's Island [April? 1764]," in Franklin, *Papers*, vol. 11, *January 1, through December 31, 1764*, ed. Leonard W. Labaree (New Haven: Yale University Press, 1967), 184. Letters written to Franklin also referenced Crusoe, suggesting that it was a common narrative: "To Benjamin Franklin from Feutry [April 9, 1777]," in Franklin, *Papers*, vol. 25, *October 1, 1777, through February 28, 1778*, ed. William B. Willcox (New Haven: Yale University Press, 1986), 363–65; "To Benjamin Franklin from William Alexander, 28 December 1777," in Franklin, *Papers*, vol. 30, *July 1 through October 31, 1779*, ed. Barbara B. Oberg

There are hints of influence in Franklin's experience. He tells about seeking his fortune at sea, like Crusoe, and his *Poor Richard's Almanack*, published annually from 1732 to 1758, imitated Defoe's wit and style. Franklin also wrestled with many of the same issues as Defoe, as a tradesman turned gentleman, as both described the life of the emerging middle class coming from the common working folk.[130] But, more importantly, Franklin embodied the Crusoe myth in his reenactment of it anew. Seen in this way, *Robinson Crusoe* displays the germ of Protestant religion as it grew into an understanding of Christians as having a secular vocation. Yet it is important to note that the inner and outer worlds of Defoe's fictional character are as close to Bunyan's *Grace Abounding to the Chief of Sinners*[131] as to Franklin's *The Way of Wealth*.[132] And, as such, Crusoe stands as a transitional figure between the God-drenched world of English puritanism and the lonely existence of capitalistic and materialistic modernity. For the old dissent, faith had its roots in "the experience of grace," and yet the emerging new world demanded a revised account of Christian experience.

Franklin Americanized the heroic myth of economic self-sufficiency, showing what Crusoe might look like had he washed up in Boston Harbor or in New York City. He became a pattern for understanding the story in successive generations.[133] It was common for a typical American home library to contain a copy of *Robinson Crusoe*, for this was precisely the sort of literature that young people were encouraged to read.[134] One reviewer of an 1844 illustrated version declared that such a fine edition should have appeared much earlier

---

(New Haven: Yale University Press, 1994), 434–35; and "To Benjamin Franklin from Dumas, 2 October 1779," in Franklin, *Papers*, vol. 23, *October 27, 1776, through April 30, 1777*, ed. William B. Willcox (New Haven: Yale University Press, 1983), 574.

[130] Wood, *Americanization of Benjamin Franklin*, 41 and 51.

[131] Bunyan, *Grace Abounding*.

[132] Benjamin Franklin, *The Way of Wealth* (New York: Random House, 1930).

[133] A popular abridged version of Joachim Heinrich Campe's adaption, *The New Robinson Crusoe*, was published by Thomas Powers in New York in 1810. It went through multiple printings over the next fifteen years. It described Crusoe as an American and New York as "his native city." Brigham, "Bibliography of American Editions of *Robinson Crusoe* to 1830," 142–43.

[134] On December 25, 1912, when my grandfather was ten years old, his father gave him a copy of Daniel Defoe's *The Life and Strange Surprising Adventures of Robinson*

because "[t]his work is always in great demand," adding, "every body reads *Robinson Crusoe*."[135] An article from the *New York Evangelist* at the turn of the twentieth century began with the statement that "no book has been more popular with boys and girls than the story of *Robinson Crusoe*."[136] It made sense that parents would want to introduce their adolescent children to the world of adventure.[137] At first blush such a phenomenon may seem to suggest that *Robinson Crusoe* was a kind of civic primer in the moral education, but something much more archetypal was at play. It was assumed that by following the example of Crusoe, after a time of restless exploration, young people would complete their education, seek respectable employment, settle down and raise a family, and join a church in the community. Yet even the choice of which church was a signal of social standing, following the generalization that Baptists became Methodists when they learned to read; Methodists became Presbyterians when they made money; and Presbyterians became Episcopalians when they inherited the family business. It is understandable, then, that the story of a castaway merchant-adventurer became a kind of prose epic of economic self-sufficiency for middle-class America.

Yet such a reading of *Robinson Crusoe* seems more shallow than false. It refracted the narrative through the lens of economic self-sufficiency and the later cultural assumptions of moral self-reliance resulting in not only a peculiarly American perspective but also a strangely secular one that wiped the narrative clean, leaving no residual traces of its puritan lineage.[138] The result was a story that often

---

Crusoe, of York, Mariner (New York: R. H. Russell, 1900), with original sketches by Louis and Frederick Rhead.

[135] *Robinson Crusoe*: Illustrated with 200 Engravings, Published by D. Appleton & Co., No. 200 Broadway, New York. *The Rural Repository Devoted to Polite Literature, Such as Moral and Sentimental Tales* (May 4, 1844), 151.

[136] "Robinson Crusoe," *New York Evangelist*, April 1, 1897, 18.

[137] Some commentators pointed out that reading Defoe's novel as adolescent adventure literature obscured its deeper religious content. See, e.g., "The Religion of Robinson Crusoe: Belief in Providence Was Its Outstanding Feature," *Current Opinion* 67, no. 3 (1919): 177.

[138] Emerson, "Self-Reliance," in *The Complete Writings of Ralph Waldo Emerson* (New York: Wm. H. Wise, 1929), 1:138–52. For an account of how individual liberty became the animating principle of American culture, see Barry Alan Shain, *The*

came to resemble the formulaic Horatio Alger "rags-to-riches" myth more than the complicated narratives of earlier dissenters, which scrupulously combed through their experience in search of signs of grace.[139] The puritan attention to the inner life found expression at a deeper level in Defoe's novel, not only in its religious themes, but in the psychological forces that drive its characters and plot. In this sense it can be explained as simply telling the universal story of the adolescent male desiring independence, which appears in the opening scene in the conflict between Crusoe and his father. This tension between characters intensifies as Crusoe's mother supports her husband over her son. Desire and betrayal compounded with guilt and shame propel the story, and the energy of these psychodynamic forces moves the narrative along, pushing Crusoe like Oedipus away from home on his quest for personal autonomy.[140] Defoe then inserts this human story within the biblical narrative of the Prodigal Son, making it an account not only of adolescent independence but of human agency struggling against divine providence. And, in doing so, he provides additional energy to drive the plot toward resolution of the conflict. But the sense of the self in Defoe's novel is shaped by more than inner urges and desires. Crusoe's story is not merely an adventure tale of a castaway motivated by erotic forces but a tale of a man imprisoned by nature, isolated from society, and subjected to the panoptic gaze of providence. It anticipates the ways the modern state would deploy

---

Myth of American Individualism: The Protestant Origins of American Political Thought (Princeton, N.J.: Princeton University Press, 1994), 10–11; and Robert N. Bellah et al., eds., *Habits of the Heart: Individualism and Commitment in American Life*, updated ed. (Berkeley: University of California Press, 1996), 142–63.

[139] Horatio Alger Jr. popularized the American rags-to-riches story, beginning with his novel *Ragged Dick* (Philadelphia: John C. Winston, 1868). See Carol Nackenoff, "The Horatio Alger Myth," in *Myth America: A Historical Anthology*, 2nd ed., ed. Patrick Gerster and Nicholas Cords (St. James, N.Y.: Brandywine, 2006), 2:72–76.

[140] Although he does not discuss *Robinson Crusoe*, this psychological explanation of its plot is consistent with the sort of theoretical account offered by Peter Brooks in his *Reading for the Plot: Design and Intention in Narrative* (Cambridge, Mass.: Harvard University Press, 1984); see esp. chap. 2, "Narrative Desire," 37–61, and chap. 4, "Freud's Masterplot," 90–112. A more detailed, even allegorical, Freudian interpretation may be found in Eric Berne's "The Psychological Structure of Space with Some Remarks on *Robinson Crusoe*," *Psychoanalytic Quarterly* 25, no. 4 (1956): 549–67.

punitive interventions to domesticate incorrigible dissenters through surveillance rather than the old ways of staging events for public spectacle, producing not mere external conformity to its laws but a society shaped by the interiorizing of discipline.[141] Psychosocial theories surely contribute to a deeper understanding of the forces at work in *Robinson Crusoe*, but they fail to account for other aspects of its narrative.

More recently, some readers have suggested that *Robinson Crusoe* is an allegory of Western colonialism. They describe it as the "prototype of literary imperialism," whose "protagonist is the founder of a new world, which he rules and reclaims for Christianity and England."[142] Postcolonial critics like Edward Said see Crusoe as the embodiment of the "Occidental gaze" that construes the Other in romanticized and exoticized characterizations.[143] The depiction of the exotic inhabitants in the new world as "savages" and "cannibals" forces Crusoe to maintain social distance between himself and them. Yet his concern is not alterity but similarity, or even identity. He is not afraid that the Other may be unlike him; he is afraid that the Other may be too much like him or, worse yet, that the Other may be him.[144] Crusoe's relationship with Friday in particular complicates his attempts to maintain a sharp distinction of otherness. But a deeper complication arises from the fact that *Robinson Crusoe* is not simply a colonial novel. It is a religious one as well. The dual plots tell the story of Crusoe's mastery of nature, the wilderness of his island, and his mastery of his own sinful nature, the wilderness of his soul.[145] When, for example, Crusoe becomes aware of the cannibals on his island, he struggles to come to terms with his own

---

[141] John Bender, *Imagining the Penitentiary: Fiction and the Architecture of Mind in Eighteenth-Century England* (Chicago: University of Chicago Press, 1987), 43–62. Bender's description broadly follows the account of Michel Foucault's *Discipline and Punish* (New York: Vintage Books, 1977), esp. 195–256.

[142] Martin Burgess Green, *Dreams of Adventure, Deeds of Empire* (New York: Basic Books, 1979), 11; and Edward W. Said, *Culture and Imperialism* (New York: Knopf, 1993), 70.

[143] Edward Said, *Orientalism* (New York: Vintage Books, 1979), 59.

[144] Jonathan Z. Smith, "What a Difference a Difference Makes," in *"To See Ourselves as Others See Us": Christians, Jews, and "Others" in Late Antiquity*, ed. Jacob Neusner and Ernest S. Frerichs (Chico, Calif.: Scholars Press, 1985), 47.

[145] Dennis Todd, *Defoe's America* (Cambridge: Cambridge University Press, 2010), 32.

savage impulses of revenge. Yet Defoe returns to the distinction by showing that Friday *is* a cannibal while Crusoe is only *like* a cannibal.[146]

That *Robinson Crusoe* continues to generate such a surplus of meanings is evidence that it is a classic text.[147] It invites deeper and closer readings. Yet these interpretations, as powerful as they are, stand in danger of reducing it to a narrative of economic self-sufficiency, or a psychological account of human struggle, or a manifesto for global domination, with little interest in its religious and theological outlook. Any reader of *Robinson Crusoe* that fails to attend to its location within the tradition of Protestant dissent thins out its narrative and risks turning the text into a mere cipher for the latest and most fashionable theory. When Walter Wilson published his *Memoirs of the Life and Times of Daniel Defoe*, he noted that anyone who is not a "friend to civil and religious liberty" would find little sympathy for Defoe's writings.[148] Wilson made no attempt to conceal that his interest in Defoe was religious and that his intent was "to awaken Dissenters to the study of their own principles."[149] Chief among these was the conviction that the establishment of religion turned the church into a political institution, which was at war with the essential beliefs it professes to uphold.[150] And for Wilson there was no greater champion of religious liberty than Defoe, who once cleverly opined:

Of all the Plagues with which Mankind are curst,
Ecclesiastic Tyranny's the worst.[151]

It is no surprise, then, that Frank Boreham (1871–1959), one of the most popular English and Australian evangelical preachers of his

---

[146] Todd, *Defoe's America*, 168.

[147] David Tracy, *Analogical Imagination: Christian Theology and the Culture of Pluralism* (New York: Crossroad, 1981), 108–9.

[148] Walter Wilson, *Memoirs of the Life and Times of Daniel Defoe*, 3 vols. (London: Hurst, Chance, 1830), 1:xvii–xviii. See also 3:210, 387, 630.

[149] Walter Wilson, *The History and Antiquities of Dissenting Churches and Meeting Houses in London, Westminster, and Southwark*, 4 vols. (London: Printed for the Author, 1808–1814), 4:435.

[150] Wilson, *History and Antiquities*, 4:448.

[151] Defoe, *The True-Born Englishman: A Satyr* (1701), in *The Novels and Miscellaneous Works of Daniel De Foe*, Bohn's Standard Library (London: George Bell, 1894–1899), 5:451.

generation, read *Robinson Crusoe* as a classic text of Free Church dissent or that William Carey (1761–1834), the founder of the modern missionary movement, was first inspired to imagine a global mission by reading about Crusoe's adventure.[152] For, among English nonconformists, Defoe continued to be read as an outstanding voice for the principles of their tradition.

The revolutionary principles of liberty that dissenters defined and that Defoe defended were really never settled. They have always been contested. The lines of disagreement were sharply drawn at Putney on October 28–30, 1647, as the Council of the Army debated what sort of government to set up after the monarchy was abolished. There, radicals like Thomas Rainsborough insisted on universal suffrage as a natural right, and moderates like Oliver Cromwell argued that voting must be strictly limited to landowners.[153] Though these principles found expression during the brief interlude of the Commonwealth and were kept alive among dissenters after the restoration of the monarchy, they never became dominant in English politics. Yet these radical notions of liberty that dissenters lived out and Defoe lined out played a crucial role in the lively experiment that became the United States of America. Against the theocrats at Massachusetts Bay, Roger Williams, a dissenting minister and the founder of the Rhode Island colony, argued that "enforced uniformity of religion throughout a nation or civil state, confounds the civil and religious" and "denies the principles of Christianity and civility," and, he added, "that Jesus Christ has come in the flesh."[154]

[152] Boreham, *Handful of Stars*, chap. 2; James Culross, *William Carey* (London: Hodder & Stoughton, 1881), 28; and S. Pearce Carey, *William Carey* (London: Hodder & Stoughton, 1926), 20.

[153] William Clarke, *The Clarke Papers*, vol. 1, ed. Charles Harding Firth (London: Camden Society, 1891).

[154] Williams, *Bloudy Tenent of Persecution*, in *Complete Writings*, 3:4. John M. Barry surely overstates the influence and exaggerates the evidence by claiming that Williams was the creator of the American soul; see Barry's important book *Roger Williams and the Creation of the American Soul: Church, State, and the Birth of Liberty* (New York: Viking, 2012). William G. McLoughlin and Perry Miller offer a more historically nuanced view in concluding that Williams had no *direct* influence on the shaping of religious liberty in American democracy. McLoughlin, *New England Dissent, 1630–1833*, 2 vols. (Cambridge, Mass.: Harvard University Press, 1971), 1:8; and

It was surely the influence of these principles of liberty that resulted in Article VI of the United States Constitution, which declares in the strongest possible language that "no religious test *shall ever be required* as a qualification to any office or public trust under the United States."[155] This was to be the only reference to religion in the entire document, but an important one. It reflected the fact that the conviction of religious liberty in England was forged in the fires of one religious test after another, but even this legal provision against religious tests was not sufficient for John Leland and the Baptists of Virginia. Leland laid out his objections to the Constitution on the grounds that religious liberty "is not sufficiently secured" because a majority of Congress and the president "may oblige all others to pay to the support of their System as much as they please."[156] For Leland, true liberty was more than toleration, which presupposes preeminence of one and indulgence of others. Genuine liberty, he argued, must apply equally to "Jews, Turks, Pagans and Christians."[157] Liberty must be *for all*, or it is not liberty *at all*. To secure this liberty, Leland met with James Madison, who was preparing to run for the Constitutional Congress of 1788 as a representative of Orange County, Virginia. Leland protested that the Constitution had no provision for religious liberty. Madison agreed, but he reminded Leland of his efforts to secure religious liberty

---

Miller, "Roger Williams: An Essay in Interpretation," in Williams, *Complete Writings*, 7:10. See also Curtis W. Freeman, "Roger Williams, American Democracy, and the Baptists," *Perspectives in Religious Studies* 34, no. 3 (2007): 267–86; and LeRoy Moore Jr., "Roger Williams and the Historians," *Church History* 32 (December 1963): 432–51.

[155] Constitution of the United States of America, Article 6; emphasis added.

[156] "John Leland's Objections to the Constitution without a Bill of Right," sent to James Madison by Joseph Spencer (February 28, 1788), in *Documentary History of the Constitution* (Washington, D.C.: Department of State, 1905), 4:526–29; and L. H. Butterfield, "Elder John Leland," *Proceedings of the American Antiquarian Society* 62 (1952): 187–88. The Virginia Baptist General Committee discussed the Constitution on March 7, 1788, and agreed unanimously that it did not make "sufficient provision for the secure enjoyment of religious liberty." Robert B. Semple, *A History of the Rise and Progress of the Baptists in Virginia*, rev. ed. (Richmond, Va.: Pitt & Dickinson, 1894), 102.

[157] John Leland, "The Virginia Chronicle," in *The Writings of the Late Elder John Leland*, ed. L. F. Greene (New York: G. W. Wood, 1845; repr., New York: Arno, 1969), 118.

in the Virginia Legislature and assured him he would do the same if elected to the Constitutional Convention. At the end of their conversation, Leland and the Baptists agreed to support Madison, who was elected by a large margin. Virginia passed the Constitution, and Madison wrote the Bill of Rights, which was approved in 1791. The First Amendment made good on his promise to religious dissenters, leaving no room for a nationally established church, for it declared that "Congress shall make no law respecting an establishment of religion, or prohibiting the free exercise thereof."[158]

Although Crusoe may be missing from these revolutionary conversations in America, it was the same basic principles that animated their desires and a familiar political-religious coalition that dissenters like Defoe negotiated in England.[159] These were radical ideas that often blurred the boundary between civil and religious, as conceptions about how they got worked out were almost entirely political.[160] Religious dissenters sought to express their beliefs in political ways while resisting partisan attempts to domesticate their dissent. It was a fragile alliance but one that proved it could be mutually beneficial. Yet the politicizing of dissent required coming to terms with the emerging modern world and its new social arrangements. Though the old ship of religious dissent had run aground on the shoals of modernity, Defoe gestured in a direction for prospering dissenters like himself to start again. As G. K. Chesterton once noted, the greatest part of the story may be Crusoe's simple inventory of things saved from the wreckage of his ship. For it suggests that the future for Christians living in the

---

[158] Amendments to the Constitution of the United States of America, Amendment 1. The meeting between Leland and Madison occurred somewhere between Fredericksburg and Orange, Virginia, in March 1788. Although there is no historical record of the encounter, it certainly must have taken place. Butterfield, "Elder John Leland," 188–90. A very embellished account is related by William Pope Dabney, "President Madison and the Baptist Preacher," *Harper's New Monthly Magazine*, August 1881, 446–48.

[159] Dissenters in America drew from Locke's Second Letter on Toleration. See John Leland, "The Rights of Conscience Inalienable," in *Writings*, 179–92. John Locke, *Letter concerning Toleration*, in *Works*, 48.

[160] Gordon S. Wood, *The Radicalism of the American Revolution* (New York: Vintage Books, 1993), 5.

wilderness of the modern world depends not on inventing the faith anew but on retrieving the faith from the church and its earlier traditions to adapt to the new situation.[161] And, perhaps in doing so, Crusoe points a way for other castaways whose ecclesial ships have sunk as they seek to make a life on the desert island of modernity.

[161] Gilbert K. Chesterton, *Orthodoxy* (New York: Image/Doubleday, 1959), 64.

4

APOCALYPTIC DISSENT
William Blake

*Let every Christian, as much as in him lies, engage himself openly &
publicly before all the World in some Mental pursuit for the Building up
of Jerusalem.*[1]

Albion Mills was the first great factory in London. The towering
five-story structure located on Blackfriars Road rose up like a
modern colossus from the south bank of the River Thames. Its machinery featured massive iron wheels turned by huge metal cogs and shafts,
complete with twenty pairs of gigantic millstones. Two of the world's
largest double-acting rotary steam engines, newly designed by the
Scottish engineer and inventor James Watt, powered the works.[2] It
was widely regarded as a mechanical wonder of the world, transforming ancient Albion into modern England as the undisputed leader of
the industrialized world. The scale of operation enabled Albion Mills
to gain a virtual monopoly on flour production in London, forcing
small wind-powered operations out of business and replacing a skilled
work force with machines. On the evening of March 2, 1791, Albion

---

[1] William Blake, *Jerusalem*, 77.pref., in *Blake Complete Writings*, ed. Geoffrey
Keynes (London: Oxford University Press, 1969), 717. Subsequent citations are to this
edition, noting also the book divisions and line numbers in the original.
[2] Lionel Thomas Caswell Rolt, *James Watt* (New York: Arco, 1963), 97–99.

Mills burned to the ground. Arson was suspected but never proved. The crowd that gathered to watch as an inferno of flames engulfed the structure made no attempt to help save the building. Robert Southey, the poet, reported that "before the engines had ceased to play upon the smoking ruins, ballads of rejoicing were printed and sung on the spot."[3] One song celebrated the fiery destruction, imploring:

> Now God bless us one and all,
> And send the price of bread may fall.
> That the poor with plenty may abound,
> Tho' the Albion Mills burnt to the ground.[4]

Albion's proprietors adamantly disputed claims that they were responsible for the rising cost of flour, attesting that they had "lowered the Price of Flour and regulated the Market," resulting in "a very considerable Saving to the Public."[5] But the working class, who lived largely on a diet of bread, thought otherwise. Social and economic instability exacerbated by the soaring price of bread had already set off political revolution in France, and similar risings of the poor were coming to England. It was a sign of the turbulent transition from the old moral economy of a fair price to the new political economy of a free market.[6] Yet, beneath the surface of such fundamental change, there was an underlying constancy. As the gentry had endeavored to keep their laborers hand tamed, so it was thought that market forces would keep the working class domesticated. But there were destabilizing factors at play that were beyond the control of the powers that be. The establishment always feared the dangerous influence of apocalyptic visions bubbling up among undomesticated dissenters. Theirs was a vision that might, if believed, "turn the world upside down."[7]

---

[3] Robert Southey [Don Manuel Alvarez Espriella], Letter 66, in *Letters from England*, 3 vols. (London: Longman, Hurst, Rees & Orme, 1814), 3:180–81.

[4] "The Albion Mills on Fire" (London: C. Sheppard, March 10, 1791), verse 8.

[5] *Albion Mill: State of Facts* (London, 1791), 1.

[6] Edward Palmer Thompson, "The Moral Economy of the English Crowd in the Eighteenth Century," *Past and Present* 50 (1971): 76–136. See also Thompson, *Customs in Common* (New York: New Press, 1991).

[7] The phrase about turning the world upside down comes from Acts 17:6, but its use may be attributed William Dell, *Several Sermons and Discourses* (London: J. Sowle,

The dreams of enthusiasts inspired by extreme notions threatened to destroy the emerging modern world built on capital and technology. It was reason enough to suspect that a dangerous apocalyptic enthusiasm lay hidden beneath the smoldering ashes of Albion Mills.

William and Catherine Blake moved to their home in the neighboring parish of Lambeth just before the fire. Unlike Erasmus Darwin, a friend of Watt and public intellectual who praised Albion Mills as "a grand and successful effort of human art,"[8] William Blake was not enamored with such monuments of industry. Instead, he envisioned an ominous shadow enveloping "England's green & pleasant land" and saw the great factories not as instruments of social progress but as "dark Satanic mills."[9] The burned and blackened shell that once was Albion Mills stood almost twenty years after the fire, its gates shut and "Thou shalt not" written over the door.[10] The image of the once grand structure's ruined and crumbling skeleton stuck with Blake over the years as he reflected on how the crushing wheels of industry driven by the whirring spindles of logic dehumanized human beings. But it was not just these chapels of the Industrial Revolution against which he registered his dissent. He perceived the entire materialistic and mechanistic universe to be connected to something far more sinister through an intricate web of relations among rationality, religion, culture, and commerce. The fabric of modern society in which the woof of reason was woven through the warp of science enslaved the mind

---

1709), 6, 109, 144, and 481; cited in Christopher Hill, *The World Turned Upside Down* (London: Penguin, 1972), 94. It became a watchword for the Digger leader Gerrard Winstanley, who declaimed that "freedom is the man that will turn the world upside downe," in "A Watch-Word to the City of London and the Armie," in *The Works of Gerrard Winstanley*, ed. George H. Sabine (Ithaca, N.Y.: Cornell University Press, 1941), 316.

[8] Darwin, Letter to Matthew Boulton (May 9, 1791), *The Collected Letters of Erasmus Darwin*, ed. Desmond King-Hele (Cambridge: Cambridge University Press, 2007), Letter 91–6; 380–81. Darwin was a close personal friend of Boulton, the manufacturer who built Albion Mills, and wrote to express his sincere grief for "the conflagration of the Albion Mills."

[9] Blake, *Milton*, 1.8, 16, in *Blake Complete Writings*, 481.

[10] William Blake, *The Garden of Love*, in *Blake Complete Writings*, 215. Peter Ackroyd connects the Albion Mill with the chapel in Blake's *Garden of Love* and the "dark Satanic Mills," in *Blake* (New York: Ballantine Books, 1995), 129–30.

into habits of thought that reduced human beings to mere sensations and nature to simple laws.[11]

BIBLE-SOAKED ENTHUSIASM

In the twenty-first chapter of his Apocalypse, the apostle John sees a vision of the New Jerusalem, descending from heaven "as a bride adorned for her husband" (Rev 21:2). And he hears a loud voice announcing:

> See, the home of God is among mortals.
> He will dwell with them;
> they will be his peoples,
> and God himself will be with them;
> he will wipe every tear from their eyes.
> Death will be no more;
> mourning and crying and pain will be no more,
> for the first things have passed away. (Rev 21:3-4, NRSV)

Then, John heard the voice of the One seated on the throne, saying, "See, I am making all things new" (Rev 21:5, NRSV). It is a vision that inspired dissenters for generations to persevere with patience. They saw themselves, like Abraham, as looking ahead in their earthly journey "to the city that has foundations, whose architect and builder is God" (Heb 11:10, NRSV). They lived in hope that God was preparing a city for them (Heb 11:16). But to reach Jerusalem would require a drastic transformation of their eschatological thinking. Earlier dissenters had made similar moves. Bunyan converted millenarianism into an apocalypse of the soul that connected with the earlier theology of conversion. Daniel Defoe saw signs of the eschatological hope being worked out in the economic and social spheres of emerging political liberalism. Both still believed that the civil and ecclesiastical structures, though corrupt, could be part of bringing down Antichrist. In Blake's vision, church and state were no longer instruments of God's justice but servants of the beast "among these dark Satanic mills," and Jerusalem would have to be built anew "in England's green & pleasant Land."[12]

---

[11] Blake, *Milton*, 1.6–14, in *Blake Complete Writings*, 483.

[12] Blake, *Milton*, 1.8, 16, in *Blake Complete Writings*, 481.

The denominations of old-line dissent underwent significant changes in the eighteenth century. After the Salters' Hall controversy of 1719, the Presbyterians and General Baptists went into steep decline.[13] During the same time, Quakers quietly changed, losing much of their earlier evangelistic energy. By the end of the century, the largest numbers of Protestant nonconformists were aligned with the three evangelical movements: Congregationalists, (Particular) Baptists, and Methodists.[14] The puritan theology shared by all Protestant dissenters served as both a repressive and a revolutionary force. Its apocalyptic vision of a coming new world inspired hopes of social change, but its work ethic sought to maintain a disciplined labor force and an orderly society.[15] By the late eighteenth century, this tension began to collapse, and dissenters split into two groups: evangelicals and radicals. One drew its energy from the new evangelical revival and emerging missionary movement that tended toward a moderate Tory support or neutrality toward government, and the other republican group welcomed revolution in France and America as a powerful force of ecclesiastical disestablishment. But, whereas evangelicals tended to demonstrate the love of God and neighbor outside the structures of political reform, radicals were increasingly ostracized and disenfranchised from participation in social and political life.

William Blake was raised in a nonconformist home. His mother was a Moravian.[16] His connection to dissenting churches, however,

[13] See chap. 3, pages 111–12.

[14] Charles Gordon Bolam, Jeremy Goring, H. L. Short, and Roger Thomas, *The English Presbyterians* (London: Allen & Unwin, 1968), 151–74; Alexander Hutton Drysdale, *History of the Presbyterians in England: Their Rise, Decline, and Revival* (London: Presbyterian Church of England, 1889), 489–515; Raymond Brown, *The English Baptists of the Eighteenth Century* (London: Baptist Historical Society, 1986), 56–67; A. C. Underwood, *A History of the English Baptists* (London: Carey Kingsgate, 1956), 126–27; Hugh Barbour, *The Quakers of Puritan England* (New Haven: Yale University Press, 1964), 241; and Michael Watts, *The Dissenters*, vol. 2, *The Expansion of Evangelical Nonconformity* (Oxford: Clarendon, 1995), 2–3.

[15] Christopher Hill describes the tensions between the seditious and industrious dimensions of puritanism, in *Society and Puritanism in Pre-revolutionary England*, 2nd ed. (New York: Schocken Books, 1967), 30–144.

[16] Marsha Keith Schuchard and Keri Davis, "Recovering the Lost Moravian History of William Blake's Family," *Blake: An Illustrated Quarterly* 37 (2004): 36–43.

is complicated. During his adult life, he was never formally associated with any church or chapel.[17] He was buried in Bunhill Fields, the dissenter burial grounds, with his wife, parents, and other family members. Several of the poet's close friends and relatives were members of a Baptist congregation that met in central London. It is likely that the Blakes attended meetings there too. John Martin, the pastor of the church, apparently knew him well enough. When "asked if he did not think Blake was 'cracked,'" he answered, "Yes, but his is a crack that lets in the light." Even Blake's association with the teaching of the mystical theology of Emanuel Swedenborg (1688–1772) has a strange Baptist connection. Joseph Proud, the defrocked General Baptist minister turned Swedenborgian, invited Blake to join the New Jerusalem Church in London.[18] Though he declined to become a member, Blake

---

Schuchard and Davis amended and extended this earlier essay: Keri Davies, "William Blake's Mother," *Blake: An Illustrated Quarterly* 33 (1999): 36–50. They have established that Blake's mother, Catherine Wright, was raised in a Moravian home in the Nottinghamshire village of Walkeringham. She was married to Thomas Armitage (1746–1751). They were members of the Fetters Lane Moravian Chapel in London until the death of her husband. She married James Blake in 1752.

[17] In his remembrance, John Thomas Smith states emphatically that Blake "did not for the last forty years attend any place of Divine Worship," though Smith adds, "he was not a Free-thinker, as some invidious detractors have though proper to assert, nor was he ever in any degree irreligious." Smith, *Nollekens and His Times* (London: Richard Bentley & Sons, 1895 [1828]), cited in Gerald Eades Bentley Jr., *Blake Records*, 2nd ed. (New Haven: Yale University Press, 2004), 607. Henry Crabb Robinson states that Blake belonged not to the Church of England "but to a dissenting community," although he added that Blake did not regularly attend any Christian church. Robinson, "Künstler, Dichter, und Religiöser Schwärmer (from *Vaterländisches Museum*, 1811), in Bentley, *Blake Records*, 599.

[18] Bentley, *Blake Records*, xxv, 68, 599. The church first met at Glasshouse Street very near the home where the poet's father (James Blake) and uncle (John Blake) lived (1744–1753). The poet's uncle John Blake is likely the "—— Blake" who joined the congregation on June 28, 1769, when the poet was eleven years old. The congregation moved to a meeting house on Grafton Street in 1750. John Martin was the minister from 1774 until 1815. William Thomas Whitley, *The Baptists of London, 1612–1928* (London: Kingsgate, 1928), 127–28. John Linnell, artist and friend of William Blake, was a member of the congregation when it met on Keppel Street in central London. He made portraits of a number of Baptists of the day, including William Newman (first principal of the Stepney Academy) and John Martin (pastor at Keppel Street). Later, the church withdrew from Linnell and his wife. Ernest Payne, "John Linnell,

remained associated with those who were connected to the church and its ideas, and his circle of friendships included Swedenborgians and others within the fringe of deists and mystics. If Blake ever was part of the Baptists, the hyper-Calvinism and antirepublicanism of their minister John Martin would have been reason enough to drive him away.[19] Though the details of Blake's church membership may be sketchy, his roots in nonconformist Christianity and particularly in the historic dissenting tradition are significant, for it suggests that his work did not emerge spontaneously from the untutored imagination of an eclectic and eccentric genius.

Baptists and other old-line dissenting groups were historically committed to the repeal of the Test and Corporation Acts, which restricted government offices to members of the Church of England. Their efforts were ultimately successful in 1828, followed by the disestablishment of the Church of England in 1830. Not surprisingly, John Martin offended nonconformists of all sorts when he published a letter in 1790 opposing the repeal of the Test and Corporation Acts. Although Martin began his ministry among progressives, over time he became increasingly conservative theologically and politically, regressing to the high Calvinism of his youth and the new Toryism of the emerging evangelicals. Ordained by the Particular Baptists in the Northamptonshire Association, before coming to London, he had supported the evangelical theology of Jonathan Edwards, but Martin gradually became an outspoken opponent of this new theology and his former Northampton colleague Andrew Fuller.[20] He further offended his fellow nonconformists by declaring in a sermon on January 14, 1798,

---

the World of Artists and the Baptists," ed. Roger Hayden, *Baptist Quarterly* 40, no. 1 (2003): 22–35. *Oxford Dictionary of National Biography* (Oxford: Oxford University Press, 2004–2014), s.v. "Proud, Joseph," by Peter J. Lineham; and Robert Hindmarsh, *Rise and Progress of the New Jerusalem Church*, ed. Rev. Edward Madeley (London: Hodson & Sons, 1861), 128.

[19] *Oxford Dictionary of National Biography*, s.v. "Martin, John," by John H. Y. Briggs; and Joseph Ivimey, *A History of the English Baptists*, 4 vols. (London: Isaac Taylor Hinton, 1830), 4:342–50 and 4:77–82. The hyper-Calvinism and antirepublicanism of Martin undoubtedly would have been very uncongenial to Blake, whose revolutionary politics were no secret.

[20] Brown, *English Baptists of the Eighteenth Century*, 90.

at Broad Street Chapel that, if the French were to invade England, many dissenters would join them. Martin afterward defended his remarks, suggesting that many of them "have wished to plant what they call the Tree of Liberty in Great Britain," alluding to the famous image by Thomas Jefferson, who declaimed that the tree must be "refreshed from time to time with the blood of patriots and tyrants."[21] The nonconformist managers of the Broad Street lectures excluded Martin as unfit to provide further instruction.

The Baptists were somewhat more conflicted given that, though they welcomed the revolutionary disestablishment of the Catholic church in France and supported the repeal of laws that privileged the Church of England, they did not want to appear supportive of extending revolution to England. When it was all said and done, they excluded Martin from membership for his "highly calumnious" remarks.[22] But suspicion of the Baptists continued. Though he was a tireless advocate of civil and religious liberty, Robert Hall, the influential minister of the Baptist church in Cambridge, published a sermon in which he categorically denounced the principles of the French Revolution as a gross expression of "modern infidelity," suggesting that such "barbarities" were not the expression of Christian liberty but might rather be the inevitable result of atheism.[23] Yet the censure of John Martin illustrates the tension that existed in the wider community of dissenters on matters of reform, revolution, and republicanism. On the one hand was an evangelical theology that avoided challenging the state establishment of the church, and on the other was a tradition of radical dissent that had become so weakened by political repression that it lacked the capacity to mount a vigorous campaign of resistance. The churches of old-line nonconformity were caught betwixt and between.

---

[21] Thomas Jefferson to William Stephens Smith (November 13, 1787), in *The Papers of Thomas Jefferson* (Princeton, N.J.: Princeton University Press, 1950), 12:356–57.

[22] *Oxford Dictionary of National Biography*, s.v. "Martin, John," by John Briggs; and Ivimey, *History of the English Baptists*, 4:77–82.

[23] Robert Hall [Jr.], "Modern Infidelity Considered," in *The Works of Robert Hall*, 6 vols. (London: Henry G. Bohn, 1851), 2:13–60.

Even if William Blake had wished to do so, there was not a strong enough dissenting community for him to have turned to that was capable of imagining the storming of Antichrist and possessing the will and resources to build Jerusalem. In any event Blake did not see evangelical quietism or political activism as offering a viable strategy for the ongoing reformation of Christianity and society—for, in his view, the corruption of religion went too deep. It was so rooted in the structures of human consciousness that nothing less than an apocalyptic transformation of the mind could redeem the imagination. Ultimately, his was a dissenting theology without a community of dissent to sustain it. It is true that Blake viewed Methodism in a positive light, especially when it came to resisting the distortion of deism and seeking the religion of Jesus, which in his view was about forgiveness and friendship.[24] The influence of his Moravian mother no doubt inclined him favorably toward Methodist piety. There are signs that suggest Blake was closer to the evangelical vision of Methodism than might be expected. Even in correcting Wesley's Lockean empiricism, by urging an affirmation of the innate status of the poetic imagination, Blake was moving in the same general direction as the "reasonable enthusiasm" of the Methodists.[25]

Yet Blake was too eclectic to be identified with the religion of Mr. Wesley.[26] Blake was political. Wesley was pietistic. But the key difference between them was that Blake was an unambiguous and unrepentant dissenter, a label Wesley steadfastly and adamantly resisted throughout his lifetime. "We are not *Dissenters*," Wesley declaimed in 1766, continuing, "We will not, dare not separate from the Church."[27]

[24] Blake, *Jerusalem* 52.pref., in *Blake Complete Writings*, 682.

[25] Jennifer G. Jesse, *William Blake's Religious Vision: There's a Methodism in His Madness* (Plymouth, U.K.: Lexington Books, 2013), 209. The phrase "reasonable enthusiasm" was coined by Henry D. Rack in his magisterial study *Reasonable Enthusiast: John Wesley and the Rise of Methodism*, 3rd ed. (London: Epworth, 2002).

[26] Michael Farrell argues that Methodism was only "one component" of a more "eclectic theology," in *Blake and the Methodists* (New York: Palgrave Macmillan, 2014), 29.

[27] Wesley, Annual Minutes, 1766, in *The Methodist Societies: The Minutes of Conference*, in *The Works of John Wesley* (Nashville: Abingdon, 2011), 10:325; emphasis in original. In the Large Minutes 1780–1789, the question is answered slightly differently.

Blake believed in the church universal, but, in contrast to Wesley, he openly renounced the Church of England with loathing words only a separatist could utter. In language that echoed his identification of the industrial factories as satanic, Blake exclaimed, "Every black'ning Church appalls."[28] And he repeated an ancient proverb:

> Remove away that black'ning church:
> Remove away that marriage hearse:
> Remove away that man of blood:
> You'll quite remove the ancient curse.[29]

Blake's quarrel was not with the pure religion of the Lamb of God, which "in ancient time," he believed, did "walk upon England's mountain green."[30] He opposed the corruption of the everlasting gospel, and he resisted the domestication strategies of empire.

Like Defoe's, his dissent was a lonely journey, without church or chapel. He stirred from his sleep, as Crusoe does, to find a darkness descending on his island of Albion. Yet the ominous vision was not of the Angel of Death. Instead, when Blake, like Bunyan, awakened from his dogmatic slumber, he envisioned a beastly figure rising out of the sea while the great dragon Satan watched from afar and another beast rising from the earth with a hissing serpentine voice that sounded like the dragon (Rev 13:1-18). He saw a vision of empire, where state and church were united as one and where the evil powers of king and priest ruled society.[31] He refused to abide a religion where the pious "praise God & his Priest & King" while poor children are clothed "in the clothes of death."[32] Blake was no Methodist. He emphatically and unequivocally renounced the service of the established church. For Blake, the Church of England was not the bride of Christ. It was the synagogue of Satan, the whore of Babylon, the second beast of the

---

Instead of describing dissent in terms of separation, the answer is cast in terms of renouncing "the service of the church." *Works of John Wesley*, 10:922.

[28] William Blake, "London," in *Blake Complete Writings*, 216.

[29] William Blake, "An Ancient Proverb," in *Blake Complete Writings*, 176.

[30] Blake, *Milton*, 1.1–4, in *Blake Complete Writings*, 480.

[31] Blake, "London," in *Blake Complete Writings*, 216.

[32] William Blake, "The Chimney Sweeper," in *Blake Complete Writings*, 212.

apocalypse.[33] His was a prophecy against empire. His was a hope for a Christianity after Christendom. His was an undomesticated dissent.

Blake had radical associations, especially during the period he was writing his revolutionary prophecies, *The French Revolution* (1791) and *America* (1793). It is even possible that he may have attended some of the weekly Jacobin gatherings in the home of his printer, Joseph Johnson, which included such notable persons as Joseph Priestley and Thomas Paine.[34] But the strongest suggestion of Blake's subversive sentiments are in his admiring references to them as defenders of liberty.[35] Yet, after the French Revolution, any support for seditious politics became dangerous. When Edmund Burke published his famous attack on the French Revolution, Thomas Paine answered it with his immensely popular tract the *Rights of Man* that defended the right of the people to overthrow any government that does not protect their natural rights. Paine called for the abolition of monarchy and the establishment of republican government.[36] King George III responded on May 21, 1792, by issuing a *Royal Proclamation against Seditious Writings and Publications*, but by then Paine had already fled to safety in France. Yet suspected revolutionaries were surveilled by a national network of informants and spies.

The danger of harboring such seditious ideas is evident in the July 14, 1791, riots of "church and king," which erupted from the popular hostility toward dissenters, who at the time were waging a campaign to repeal the Test and Corporation Acts. The home and library of Joseph Priestley, the leading intellectual dissenter, was destroyed

---

[33] Blake, *Milton*, 38.37 and 39.61, in *Blake Complete Writings*, 530 and 532.

[34] Earlier biographers exaggerated the intimacy of Blake's relationship with Paine. Alexander Gilchrist, *The Life of William Blake*, "*Pictor Ignotus*" (London: Macmillan, 1863), 92–97. David V. Erdman rightly notes that "Blake's association with 'the Paine set' and the Johnson 'coterie' are based on circumstantial details and anecdotes." *Blake: Prophet against Empire; A Poet's Interpretation of the History of His Own Times*, 3rd ed. (Princeton, N.J.: Princeton University Press, 1977), 154.

[35] Paine is named four times in Blake, *America*: 3:4, 9:11, 12:7, and 14:2, in *Blake Complete Writings*, 197, 199, 200, and 201. Blake addresses his annotations to *An Apology for the Bible* by Bishop R. Watson (1797) to Thomas Paine, and he furiously defends Paine throughout the text. *Blake Complete Writings*, 383–96.

[36] Edmund Burke, *Reflections of the Revolution of France* (London: James Dodsley, 1790); Thomas Paine, *Rights of Man* (London: J. S. Jordan, 1791).

by a pro-church and pro-king mob with the approval and support of King George III.[37] Even more moderate dissenters felt the brunt of the antirevolutionary backlash, like the Baptist minister William Winterbotham, who was jailed for preaching a sermon on November 5, 1792, in which he referred to the struggle for liberty in France, saying,

> Look to the events of the campaign, the Lord has brought the counsel of their enemies to naught, put his hook in their nostrils, and his bit in their mouths, and turned them back by the way they came—Oh! that men would praise the Lord for his goodness and for his wonderful works to the children of men.

Winterbotham admonished his listeners to "labor to spread the rays of divine truth abroad" and to "pray for and strive to propagate the glorious Gospel of peace." He reminded them that, as Christians, "We want neither Revolution nor Blood," but he urged them to attend to their duty to seek "reform in the representative system" and to instill in the next generation "proper principles of civil and religious liberty." His remarks were taken as seditious, and he was sentenced to four years in prison and fined £200.[38]

The contrast between the politics of Methodism and old-line dissent is nowhere more visible than in John Wesley's *A Calm Address to Our American Colonies*, which rebuked British dissenters and defended the right of Parliament to tax the American colonies, urging them to "fear God and honour the king."[39] Wesley's *Calm Address* went through nineteen editions, amounting to one hundred thousand copies being circulated within a year. It evoked an intense storm of reactions. Supporters of the American cause, especially other nonconformists, reacted quickly and strongly, overwhelming him in an avalanche of

---

[37] Michael Watts, *The Dissenters*, vol. 1: *From the Reformation to the French Revolution* (Oxford: Clarendon, 1978), 486–87.

[38] William Winterbotham, *The Trial of Wm. Winterbotham . . . for seditious words*, 2nd ed. (London: William Winterbotham, 1794); and Winterbotham, *The Commemoration of National Deliverance and the Dawning Day: Two Sermons, Preached November 5th and 18th, 1792* (London: William Winterbotham, 1794), 34–38.

[39] John Wesley, *A Calm Address to Our American Colonies* (Bristol: Bonner & Middleton, 1775), 19.

criticism.[40] One of his most popular detractors was Caleb Evans, pastor of Broadmead Baptist Church (one of the most influential congregations of old-line dissent) and tutor at Bristol Academy (the oldest theological school among the Baptists). For Evans, the "great *American question*" was intricately interwoven with "the British constitution and British liberty," and he contended that the American Revolution was "one of the best causes in the world."[41] Evans defended the American claim that taxation without consent—that is, without parliamentary representation—is slavery, and he accused Wesley of seeking "to inflame the minds of [the English] people against their American brethren."[42] Evans was an advocate of political reform, but he rejected republican ideals. He advocated for the historic Free Church conviction of religious liberty, which he defined as "the liberty of worshipping God and attending religious instruction according to the dictates of our own conscience."[43] Yet he held more firmly to the true source and expression of liberty, as he explained,

> I cannot take my leave of you, Brethren, without reminding you of that highest of all liberty to which you are called as Christians, even *the glorious liberty of the children of God*. . . . If the Son make you free, the Son of God by his word and spirit and grace, then and not till then shall you be *free indeed*: free from condemnation, sin and ruin, free denizens of the new Jerusalem. [44]

The political outlook of Evans invoked the familiar imagery of apocalyptic employed by old-line dissenters like Vavasor Powell and Francis

---

[40] Glen O'Brien, "John Wesley's Rebuke to the Rebels of British America: Revisiting the *Calm Address*," *Methodist Review* 4 (2012): 31–55.

[41] Caleb Evans, *Political Sophistry Detected; or, Reflections on the Rev. Mr. Fletcher's Late Tract Entitled "American Patriotism"* (Bristol: William Pine, 1776), 14 and 35; emphasis in original.

[42] Caleb Evans, *Letter to the Rev. Mr. John Wesley*, new ed. (Bristol: William Pine, 1775), 24.

[43] Caleb Evans, *British Constitutional Liberty* (Bristol: William Pine, 1775), 15. Evans preached this sermon on November 5, 1775, taking as his text: "Brethren, ye have been called to liberty: only use not liberty as an occasion to the flesh, but by love serve one another" (Gal 5:13).

[44] Evans, *British Constitutional Liberty*, 31–32; emphasis in original.

"Elephant" Smith, but it was recast in the emerging new political theory of Whiggism, championed by John Locke.[45]

Methodism occupied a political middle ground between the Church of England and the historic groups of nonconformity. This hybridity has been described as a kind of "high church nonconformity." In broad terms, Methodists tended to be soft Tories and opposed to social revolution, whereas the old-line dissenters were inclined toward Whiggish reform and sometimes sympathetic with the politics of republicanism. Yet England did not follow the revolutions in America or France. It has been suggested that the reason is due to the moderating effects of Methodism, which brought about a new work-discipline that provided a stabilizing influence.[46] It is not an overstatement of

[45] The terms "Whig" and "Tory" had been in use since the late seventeenth century to describe the two opposing political parties. Tories were associated with the issues and interests of high church Anglicanism and the landed gentry. Whigs were also often from the gentry but also increasingly connected to the emerging middle class and claims of political liberty that were sympathetic to religious dissenters. Adapting the imagery of old-line dissent to political Whiggism was done even more effectively by John Leland (1754–1841), a pivotal figure among Baptists in colonial America. Leland staunchly defended the historic convictions of the liberty of conscience and the disestablishment of the church from the state, but he reframed these using Lockean and Madisonian language with its theories of natural rights and voluntary associations. Leland, like Evans, defined the liberty of conscience as "the inalienable right that each individual has, of worshipping his God according to the dictates of his conscience, without being prohibited, directed, or controlled therein by human law, either in time, place, or manner." Leland, *A Blow at the Root*, in *The Writings of the Late Elder John Leland*, ed. L. F. Greene (New York: G. W. Wood, 1845; repr., New York: Arno, 1969), 239. See also idem, "The Rights of Conscience Inalienable," in *Writings*, 179–92. Nathan Hatch observes that Leland "turned a quest for self-reliance into a godly crusade" as his populist version of liberal individualism "combined ideological leverage of evangelical urgency and Jeffersonian promise." Hatch, *The Democratization of American Christianity* (New Haven: Yale University Press, 1989), 101. Hatch shows how Methodists like Francis Asbury and Mormons like Joseph Smith and Brigham Young similarly democratized their versions of Christianity in America during the transitional period between 1780 and 1830.

[46] Elie Halévy, *A History of the English People in the Nineteenth Century*, trans. E. I. Watkin and D. A. Barker (London: Ernest Benn Limited, 1912), 1:514. See also Halévy, *The Birth of Methodism in England*, trans. Bernard Semmel (Chicago: University of Chicago Press, 1971). His conclusion was that the Evangelical movement imbued the working class with a conservative and antirevolutionary spirit "from which

the social influence of Methodism to suggest that there can be little question that the Wesleyan revival resulted in the emergence of a religiously inclusive and socially powerful evangelical movement, which was predominantly made up of Methodists but incorporated a broad spectrum of Independents and Baptists, as well as members of the Church of England.[47] And though evangelicals were drawn together to exert pressure on government, especially in their united efforts in opposition to slavery and laws restricting religious freedom among nonconformists, as a general rule they discouraged involvement in politics. Consequently, the political quietism and loyalism of Methodism gradually spread to the wider evangelical community.[48] As the old dissenting groups gradually embraced the evangelical revival, they became less politically involved.[49] Andrew Fuller, the secretary of the Baptist Mission Society, is fairly typical. Though he confessed that his own political predilections were on the side of Whiggism, he advised

---

the established order had nothing to fear." Halévy, *History of the English People*, 1:371. For Halévy, the words "Evangelical" and "Methodist" were almost interchangeable, as he explained, "Evangelicalism was . . . but a variety of Methodism." *History of the English People*, 1:399. In short, Halévy stated that "Methodism was the antidote to Jacobinism." For an evaluation of Halévy's thesis, see Elissa S. Itzkin, "The Halévy Thesis: A Working Hypothesis? English Revivalism: Antidote for Revolution and Radicalism 1789–1815," *Church History* 44, no. 1 (1975): 47–56; J. D. Walsh, "Elie Halévy and the Birth of Methodism," *Transactions of the Royal Historical Society*, 5th ser., 25 (1975): 1–20; and Semmel, "Elie Halévy, Methodism, and Revolution," in Halévy, *Birth of Methodism in England*, 1–29. The argument that the Wesleyan revival shifted the political energy in England away from more subversive social reform was more forcefully made by Edward Palmer Thompson in his magisterial work of social history: *The Making of the English Working Class* (Middlesex: Penguin, 1970). In Thompson's account, the Wesleyan revival was a "high church nonconformity" that occupied a middle position between dissent and establishment. He showed how Methodism and evangelicalism more generally played a significant social role by bringing about a new work-discipline that provided a socially stabilizing influence and prevented revolution in England in the 1790s.

[47] David Bebbington, *Evangelicalism in Modern Britain: A History From the 1730s to the 1980s* (Grand Rapids: Baker, 1992), 20–34.

[48] Wesley advised those within the Methodist connection to avoid politics. David Hempton, *Methodism and Politics in British Society, 1750–1850* (Stanford: Stanford University Press, 1984), 47.

[49] Bebbington, *Evangelicalism in Modern Britain*, 72–73.

that "it is not for the wise and the good to enlist themselves under their respective standards" of Whig or Tory or, he added, "to believe half what they say."[50] After the French Revolution, evangelicals were overwhelmingly Tory in their politics, and this conservatism surely had a stabilizing effect on the social conditions in England.[51]

Blake's religious outlook was less akin to the new evangelical non-conformity of Methodism than the old ways of dissent, and his politics leaned in a more subversive direction rather than the middle way of the Baptists and Independents. That Blake's vision looked back to the inspiration of old dissent is suggested by those who knew him well. Henry Francis Cary, the respectable translator of Dante, once remarked to John Flaxman, the sculptor (and long-time friend of Blake), "Blake is a wild enthusiast, isn't he?" Ever loyal to his friendship, Flaxman stiffly replied, "Some think me an enthusiast."[52] But the suspicion was not misplaced. There was a wild enthusiasm about Blake that stood in the antinomian stream of dissent, which has been described as "Calvinism's lower-class alter ego."[53] This perspective was fostered among ordinary people in congregations free from clerical control. It laid stress on the love and forgiveness of Christ and taught them to be suspicious of the kingdom of the beast. Antinomianism was grounded in a peculiar debate about the moral directives of the law in relation to justification by faith.[54] In his work *The Marrow of Mod-*

---

[50] Fuller, "Thoughts on Civil Polity," in *The Complete Works of Rev. Andrew Fuller*, ed. Joseph Belcher, 3 vols. (Philadelphia: American Baptist Publication Society, 1845; repr., Harrisonburg, Va.: Sprinkle, 1988), 3:671.

[51] Bebbington, *Evangelicalism in Modern Britain*, 73.

[52] Bentley, *Blake Records*, 317.

[53] Hill, *World Turned Upside Down*, 162.

[54] David R. Como distinguishes between two types of antinomianism, which he describes as "perfectionist" and "imputative." The perfectionist strain had its roots in Familism and presupposed that believers were free from the Law and sin derived from an inherent perfection that rendered them pure in this life. The imputative type thought that believers remained sinful but were regarded as perfect, just, and sin-less before God. In reality, as Como observes, most antinomians were somewhere in between. Como, *Blown by the Spirit: Puritanism and the Emergence of an Antinomian Underground in Pre-Civil-War England* (Stanford: Stanford University Press, 2004), 38–41.

ern Divinity (1645), Edward Fisher, the barber-surgeon and amateur divine, offered a classic description of those called antinomians:

> They are by Christ freely justified from the guilt of sin, though still they retain the filth of sin; these are they that content themselves (with Gospel knowledge) with meer notions in the head, but not in the heart, glorifying and rejoicing in free grace, and justification by faith alone, professing faith in Christ, and yet are not possessed of Christ; these are they that can talk like Believers, and yet do not walk like Believers; these are they that have language like Saints, and yet have conversation like devils; these are they that are not obedient to the Law of Christ, and therefore are justly called *Antinomians*.[55]

For "Marrow Men" like Fisher, true faith was to be found in the middle way between antinomianism and legalism.[56]

Yet Blake was no middle-walker. His moral, theological, and political vision was subversive. The deep antihegemonic influences of early dissent on Blake are nowhere more evident than in his sustained attack on legalism and morality masquerading as true religion, marking his affinity with the stream of puritanism from Ranters like Abiezer Coppe to Antinomians like Tobias Crisp.[57] The antinomian impulse was by no means limited to the most extreme voices. It could also be found among moderates like John Bunyan, who depicted the pathological danger of legalism in *The Pilgrim's Progress* when, on the

---

[55] Edward Fisher, *The Marrow of Modern Divinity* (London: J. S., 1658), "To the Reader"; emphasis in original. Fisher's book went through multiple printings and revisions, beginning with the first edition in 1645. Fisher's book is set up as a dialogue between *Evangelista* (a minister of the gospel), *Nomista* (a legalist), *Antinomista* (an antinomian), and *Neophtes* (a young Christian).

[56] For a full account of the conflict, see David C. Lachman, *The Marrow Controversy* (Edinburgh: Rutherford House, 1988). A controversy erupted somewhat earlier along the same lines in New England, resulting in the trial of Anne Hutchinson. David D. Hall, *The Antinomian Controversy, 1636–1638: A Documentary History*, 2nd ed. (Durham, N.C.: Duke University Press, 1990).

[57] Abiezer Coppe, *A Fiery Flying Roll* (London, 1649); and Tobias Crispe, *Christ Alone Exalted in the Perfection and Encouragement of the Saints*, 2nd ed. (London: M. S., 1646). Arthur L. Morton, *The Everlasting Gospel: A Study in the Sources of William Blake* (New York: Haskell House, 1966), 41–55.

advice of Mr. Worldly Wiseman, Christian turns out of the way to visit Mr. Legality from the village of Morality in hope of lightening his burden. But as he comes near the house, the high hill called Sinai hangs out so far that he can go no further for fear that that it will fall on his head; and the more he lingers, the heavier his burden seems to grow. He is rescued only by the appearance of Evangelist, who directs him back to the path, admonishes him that "the just shall live by faith," and warns him that "as many as are of the works of the Law, are under the curse."[58] Yet unlike Bunyan, who like Fisher and the "Marrow Men" sought a mean between antinomianism and legalism that found the law of some use to true religion, Blake was more extreme. For him, the religion of Jesus is diametrically opposed to the religion of rules. In his apocalyptic account, the law is a power that is animated by the Satanic. In the final scene of *The Marriage of Heaven and Hell*, Blake puts the words of legalism in the mouth of the angel and the gospel message in the voice of the devil, who protests that "no virtue can exist without breaking these ten commandments," adding that "Jesus was all virtue, and acted from impulse, not from rules."[59]

Antinomianism does not so much provide the interpretive key to understanding Blake, but rather it suggests a basic framework of his thought. In his understanding, the religion of Jesus replaced a religion of law with the visionary religion of love. Blake's prophetic imagination was shaped by mystical currents that flowed through the

---

[58] John Bunyan, *The Pilgrim's Progress*, ed. N. H. Keeble (New York: Oxford University Press, 1984), 16–20. Subsequent references are to this edition. Bunyan tended to ascribe a purely negative effect to the law, which can only condemn a sinner. For example, he declared, "When God brings sinners into the covenant of grace, he doth first kill them with the covenant of works, the moral law, or Ten Commandments." Bunyan, *The Doctrine of the Law and Grace Unfolded* (1659), in *The Works of John Bunyan*, ed. George Offor, 3 vols. (Glasgow: W. G. Blackie and Son, 1854; repr., Carlisle, Penn.: Banner of Trust, 1991), 1:541. Richard L. Greaves comments that Richard Baxter called Bunyan an antinomian, and not without merit. Greaves, *Glimpses of Glory: John Bunyan and English Dissent* (Stanford: Stanford University Press, 2002), 109. Yet Bunyan was not always consistent, sometimes pointing to a positive view of the law, suggesting, for example, that "obedience to the law is a fruit of our believing." Bunyan, *A Vindication of Gospel Truths Opened* (1657), in *Works of John Bunyan*, 2:190.

[59] William Blake, *The Marriage of Heaven and Hell*, 24, in *Blake Complete Writings*, 158.

dissenting tradition. Though his antinomianism had its roots in an earlier Calvinistic-puritan theology—like John Everard (1584?–1640), who incorporated ideas from a wide range of mystical and hermetic texts, including the writings of Familists and *Theologia Germanica*— Blake's eclectic borrowing from an extensive canon of spiritual literature arose from the hermeneutical assumption that the letter of the Scriptures cannot be understood until the reader allows the mystery of the Spirit to discern the meaning behind the letter.[60] Critics have been quick to point to Swedenborgian and Neoplatonic sources of influence,[61] but until fairly recently they have not seriously explored the possibility of a vector to old-line dissent through the Muggletonians, a mysterious seventeenth-century sect.[62] The emergence of the Muggletonian archives in the 1970s confirmed that they had a continuous existence through Blake's time and into the twentieth century. Followers of Lodowick Muggleton (1609–1698), an obscure and enigmatic London tailor, believed that he was one of the two witnesses mentioned in Revelation 11:3 who had been sent to prophesy in the last days.[63]

Muggletonians were fiercely antinomian, antirationalistic, antiauthoritarian, and anti-Trinitarian, all of which were core themes for

[60] Nigel Smith, *Perfection Proclaimed: Language and Literature in English Radical Religion 1640–1660* (Oxford: Clarendon, 1989), 115.

[61] Morton D. Paley has demonstrated the continuing influence of Swedenborg on Blake. Paley, *William Blake* (New York: E. P. Dutton, 1978), 20–23. Kathleen Raine does not explore the noncomformist influences of Blake's Christianity but rather looks to hermetic sources. Raine, *Blake and the New Age* (London: George Allen, 1979), 32–50.

[62] Edward Palmer Thompson argues that the Muggletonian "church" is the historical vector that connects Blake with the tradition of old dissent. Thompson, *Witness against the Beast: William Blake and the Moral Law* (Cambridge: Cambridge University Press, 1993), 65–105. Christopher Hill has echoed Thompson's argument about the Muggletonian connection in Blake. Hill, *A Turbulent, Seditious, and Factious People: John Bunyan and His Church, 1628–1688* (Oxford: Oxford University Press, 1998), 345; and Hill with Barry Reay and William Lamont, *The World of the Muggletonians* (London: Temple Smith, 1983).

[63] John Reeve and Lodowick Muggleton, *A Transcendent Spiritual Treatise* (1652), I, and John Saddington, *The Articles of True Faith* (1675), XLIIII–XLV, in *The Acts of the Witnesses: The Autobiography of Lodowick Muggleton and Other Early Muggletonian Writings*, ed. Ted Leroy Underwood (Oxford: Oxford University Press, 1999), 142 and 174.

Blake as well. Their antirationalism was grounded in the doctrine that there were two seeds in every person—seeds of the woman and of the serpent. One promoted faith; the other, reason.[64] Their antiauthoritarianism, like Blake's, was rooted in an apocalyptic vision in which the beast was embodied in the civil magistrates and his false prophet in the serpent ministers of the established church.[65] Their anti-trinitarianism arose from a peculiar form of unitarianism that conceived of God the Father as existing from eternity as a spiritual human and entering the womb of the Virgin Mary to become a mortal human in Jesus.[66] After the crucifixion, the Father and Son as one united person ascended into heaven (about six miles above the earth according to their account), where he continued to reign in human form.[67] As one critic has put it, "There was quite simply no one else like them."[68] Although Muggletonian themes appear prominently in Blake's works, and circumstantial evidence suggests that he may have been acquainted with their writings and possibly even incorporated some of their ideas into his own prophetic vision, there is no proof that Blake was actually associated

[64] John Reeve and Lodowick Muggleton, *The Acts of the Witnesses*, 1.14.15–29, in Underwood, *Acts of the Witnesses*, 50–51.

[65] Reeve and Muggleton, *Transcendent Spiritual Treatise*, X, in Underwood, *Acts of the Witnesses*, 163–64.

[66] Reeve and Muggleton, *Transcendent Spiritual Treatise*, VI, in Underwood, *Acts of the Witnesses*, 153–54. Their interpretation of the Johannine Comma—that "there are three that bear record in heaven, the Father, the Word, and the Holy Ghost: and these three are one" (1 John 5:7)—is instructive. They read this verse not as a reference to the three persons of the godhead but as a description of three ages: the water as denoting the commission of Moses and the prophets under the Law, the blood as the commission of the apostles under the appointment of the Lord Jesus, and the Spirit as the commission to the two witnesses (viz., Reeve and Muggleton) prophesied in Rev 11:3, who were to come in the last age. Reeve and Muggleton, *Transcendent Spiritual Treatise*, IX, in Underwood, *Acts of the Witnesses*, 161.

[67] Ted Leroy Underwood, editor's introduction to *Acts of the Witnesses*, 15. Underwood cites Muggleton's *A Discourse between John Reeve and Richard Leader* (1682), which describes heaven to be six miles above the earth.

[68] Ted Vallance, review of *The Acts of the Witnesses: The Autobiography of Lodowick Muggleton and Other Early Muggletonian Writings*, ed. Ted L. Underwood, *H–Albion*, November 2001, https://networks.h-net.org/node/16749/reviews/17647/vallance-underwood-acts-witnesses-autobiography-lodowick-muggleton-and.

with Muggletonianism.[69] His theological outlook was to be sure eclectic, and it lacked ecclesial expression.

These ecstatic experiences inspired his poetic imagination and enabled him to write (as he described it) by "immediate dictation." And it is this awareness that dreams and visions are pathways for the immediate consciousness of God that links Blake with the prophetic tradition of earlier dissenters, like Anna Trapnel (fl. 1642–1660), whose poetic and prophetic utterances were also given by immediate dictation.[70] But, in other ways, Blake was closer to his prophetic contemporaries like Richard Brothers, the self-declared apostle of Anglo-Israelism, who predicted that the lost tribes of Israel would gather in 1795 when King George III would relinquish the throne to Brothers, resulting in a new exodus to Palestine, the rebuilding of Jerusalem, and the inauguration of the millennial kingdom.[71] The apocalyptic visions of Brothers appealed to the sense of collective hysteria in England at the time heightened by the horrors of the French Revolution. But such speech could not be tolerated by the powers. Brothers was convicted of treason and incarcerated with the criminally insane. Upon his release Brothers continued his prophetic ministry in a more circumspect manner, publishing *A Description of Jerusalem*, which envisioned the building of the New Jerusalem upon the ruins of London.[72] Two years later, Blake began working on his poem *Jerusalem*, which

[69] William Lamont is more emphatic, concluding that Thompson's argument for a Muggletonian connection to Blake is based on a series of "pleasant fictions," lacking "ordinary, documented facts." Lamont, *Last Witnesses: The Muggletonian History, 1652–1979* (Burlington, Vt.: Ashgate, 2006), 142.

[70] See especially Anna Trapnel, *Poetical Addresses or Discourses Delivered to a Gathering of "Companions" in 1657 and 1658* (London?, 1659?), 76. Folio Volume, 990 pages in the Bodleian Library, Oxford University. Shelf number S.1.42. Katherine Sutton (fl. 1630–1663) and Anne Wentworth (1629/30–1693?) made similar claims. See also Curtis W. Freeman, ed., *A Company of Women Preachers: Baptist Prophetesses in Seventeenth-Century England* (Waco, Tex.: Baylor University Press, 2011). See also Smith, *Perfection Proclaimed*, 73–103.

[71] Richard Brothers, *A Revealed Knowledge of the Prophecies and Times* (London, 1794).

[72] Richard Brothers, *A Description of Jerusalem: Its Houses and Streets, Squares, Colleges, Markets, and Cathedrals* (London: George Diebau, 1801).

in contrast to the literalism described by Brothers offered a spiritual vision of the city.

Blake was connected to his fellow London engraver and religious enthusiast William Sharp, who was a disciple of Brothers and Joanna Southcott, the prophetess of Devon. Southcott acquired a huge popular following after the appearance of her first booklet, *The Strange Effects of Faith*, published in 1801, the same year that Brothers' book on Jerusalem appeared. But unlike Brothers, who was widely dismissed as an addle-brained crank, Southcott emerged as a national celebrity from the epicenter of the radical underworld.[73] Like earlier prophetesses of the seventeenth century, Southcott dictated her oracles from a trancelike state, which predicted auguries of coming catastrophe and depicted the Church of England as the whore of Babylon and the clergy as spiritual fornicators. Her followers spanned the countryside, numbering by some estimates over a hundred thousand, but like many apocalyptic movements the Southcottians were dealt a devastating blow when she died in great fanfare without giving birth to the Messiah at age sixty-four as she had predicted.[74] Blake somewhat sympathetically satirized the "virginity" and vacuity of Southcott, saying,

Whate'er is done to her she cannot know,
And if you'll ask her she will swear it so.
Whether 'tis good or evil none's to blame:
No one can take the pride, no one the shame.[75]

Yet Blake's prophetic imagination was less like his contemporaries (whose apocalyptic visions were the "phantom of the over heated

[73] Iain McCalman, *Radical Underworld: Prophets, Revolutionaries and Pornographers in London, 1795–1840* (Cambridge: Cambridge University Press, 1988), 61–62.

[74] James K. Hopkins, *A Woman to Deliver Her People: Joanna Southcot and English Millenarianism in an Era of Revolution* (Austin: University of Texas Press, 1982); Susan Juster, "Mystical Pregnancy and Holy Bleeding: Visionary Experience in Early Modern Britain and America," *William and Mary Quarterly* 57, no. 2 (2000): 249–88; and E. P. Thompson, *Making of the English Working Class*, 420–28.

[75] William Blake, "On the Virginity of the Virgin Mary & Johanna Southcott," in *Blake Complete Writings*, 418.

brain")[76] and more like Bunyan in the conviction that dreams and visions are a liminal space between time and eternity—a spiritual world. And because Blake's *Jerusalem* is a vision, it is first and foremost an image to be seen through the eye of the mind more than a poem whose meaning emerges by being studiously analyzed. It is impossible, then, to appreciate what Blake says without seeking to see what he saw, for he sees the world not as others see it but as he imagines it through the eyes of prophetic vision.

The principal source of inspiration for Blake's writing, however, can be traced not to middling and radical sects of old dissent or the emergent groups of new nonconformity but to his reading of the Bible, which he described as "fill'd with Imagination & Visions from End to End."[77] It has been suggested that everything in Blake's work may be found in the Bible.[78] His poems and paintings are saturated with biblical imagery, especially the books of the prophets in the Old Testament. Scripture was the generative source of Blake's poetic imagination and prophetic vision. It provided images that enabled him to think outside the dominant ideological structures of his day.[79] Yet the way he read the Bible had more in common with the spiritual exegesis of rabbinic, patristic, and medieval communities than the emerging modern critical scholarship of his own time.[80] Following St. Paul's hermeneutical dictum that "the letter killeth, but the spirit giveth life" (2 Cor 3:6), Blake left behind an obsession with the letter of the text, believing that deep meanings are "spiritually discerned" (1 Cor 2:14).[81] What made

[76] Blake, *Jerusalem*, 4.24, in *Blake Complete Writings*, 622.

[77] William Blake, "Annotations to Berkeley's 'Siris,'" in *Blake Complete Writings*, 774. Harold Bloom, *The Complete Poetry and Prose of William Blake*, by William Blake, ed. David V. Erdman (Berkeley: University of California Press, 2008), 934–35.

[78] Ackroyd, *Blake* 25.

[79] Walter Brueggemann, *The Prophetic Imagination* (Philadelphia: Fortress, 1978).

[80] Christopher Rowland, *Blake and the Bible* (New Haven: Yale University Press, 2010), 9.

[81] Rowland, *Blake and the Bible*, 20–23; and Christopher Rowland, "Blake and the Bible: Biblical Exegesis in the Work of William Blake," in *Biblical Interpretation: The Meanings of Scripture—Past and Present*, ed. John M. Court (London: T&T Clark, 2003), 168–84; and Jonathan Roberts and Christopher Rowland, "William Blake," in *The Blackwell Companion to the Bible in English Literature*, ed. Rebecca Lemon et al. (Malden, Mass.: Wiley-Blackwell, 2009), 373–82. Blake cites both of these Pauline

the Bible interesting for Blake is that it has the capacity to speak afresh each time it is read. Here, he stood in line with the pilgrim dissenter John Robinson, who declaimed that "the Lord has more truth and light yet to break forth out of his holy word."[82]

Blake's move away from the puritan emphasis on the perspicuity of the literal sense and toward an exploration of the ambiguity of the spiritual sense had antecedents among spiritualists like Sebastian Franck (1499–1543) and Caspar von Schwenckfeld (1489–1561), Familists like Henrik Niclaes (1502–1580), and mystics like Jacob Boehme (1575–1624) and John Pordage (1607–1681).[83] But though Blake traveled in similar hermeneutical directions, his outlook was more eclectic. Nor did Blake's reading stop with the biblical canon. He read widely in the classical and popular literature of the hermetic tradition from which he drew liberally in constructing an elaborate mythology.[84] Yet Blake was no antiquarian, mystic, occultist, or theosophist. His deep interest

---

texts on his second plate in *Illustrations of the Book of Job* (1825). Blake ironically stated that he read the Bible "in its infernal or diabolical sense." Blake, *Marriage of Heaven and Hell*, 24, in *Blake Complete Writings*, 158.

[82] Edward Winslow, *Hypocrisie Unmasked: A True Relation of the Proceedings of the Governor and Company of the Massachusetts against Samuel Gorton of Rhode Island* (London: Rich. Cotes, 1646; repr., New York: Burt Franklin, 1968), 97; and William Bradford, *Bradford's History "Of Plimouth Plantation" from the Original Manuscript with a Report of the Proceedings Incident to the Return of the Manuscript to Massachusetts* (Boston: Wright and Potter, 1899), 71–83. See also Walter H. Burgess, *John Robinson, Pastor of the Pilgrim Fathers: A Study of His Life and Times* (New York: Harcourt, Brace & Howe, 1920), 239–40; Robert Ashton, ed., *The Works of John Robinson: Pastor of the Pilgrim Fathers* (London: John Snow, 1851), 1:xliv–xlv.

[83] Blake played a role in the English reception of Boehme. As Nigel Smith argues, the opacity of Boehme's writings convinced Blake of their status as genuine prophecy and inspired him to pursue a mystical direction of prophecy and poetry. Smith, "Did Anyone Understand Boehme?" in *An Introduction to Jacob Boehme: Four Centuries of Thought and Reception*, ed. Ariel Hessayon and Sarah Apetrei (New York: Routledge, 2014), 98–119. Susanne Sklar shows how Blake borrowed and adapted from Boehme in the cosmology and other allusive imagery of *Jerusalem*. Sklar, *Blake's "Jerusalem" as Visionary Theatre: Entering the Divine Body* (New York: Oxford University Press, 2011), 28–35.

[84] Kathleen Raine, *Blake and Tradition*, 2 vols. (Princeton, N.J.: Princeton University Press, 1968); and George Mills Harper, *The Neoplatonism of William Blake* (Chapel Hill: University of North Carolina Press, 1961).

was in the Bible and poetry that resembled it.[85] But it would be a mistake to downplay the formative influence of the dissenting tradition on him. For Blake's ties to nonconformist ideas went far beyond his church affiliations, such as they were. Though he borrowed freely from Neoplatonic, gnostic, and alchemic sources, his prophetic imagination was birthed and nurtured by the spirituality of old-line dissent.[86] He has been described as "a Bible-soaked English Protestant," whose sense of poetic vision was derived from his reading of the Scriptures, which he adapted and reshaped.[87] Yet, for Blake, the hermeneutical issue was a matter not of perspicuity but of ocularity, and the Bible was not an encyclopedia of religious information but more like a set of lenses to envision the world prophetically.

The influence of Bunyan on Blake is readily apparent, providing a definite historical vector to earlier dissenters. His twenty-eight water color illustrations of *The Pilgrim's Progress* as well as his allusions to Bunyan's allegory offer insight into why and how this story impressed him.[88] That he identified with Bunyan's Christian is evident, as he wrote in a letter to his patron William Hayley, "I shall travel on the strength

[85] Bloom, *Complete Poetry and Prose of William Blake*, 934–35.

[86] Rowland shows the hermeneutical affinities of Blake with dissenters, including Gerrard Winstanley, Hans Denck, Ralph Cudworth, and Abiezer Coppe. Rowland, *Blake and the Bible*, 157–80.

[87] Northrop Frye, "William Blake," in *The English Romantic Poets and Essayists*, ed. Lawrence Houtchens and Carolyn Houtchens (New York: Modern Language Association, 1957), 18. Frye stated that "what united Blake and Milton, for all their differences . . . was their common dependence on the Bible and the fact that the Bible had a framework of mythology that both Milton and Blake had entered into." Frye, *Northrop Frye in Conversation*, ed. David Cayley (Concord, Ont.: Anansi, 1992), 48; cited by Ian Singer, introduction to *Fearful Symmetry*, ed. Nicholas Halmi, in *The Collected Works of Northrop Frye*, by Frye, ed. Alvin A. Lee, 30 vols. (Toronto: University of Toronto Press, 1996), 14:xxxii. Similarly, Morton D. Paley argues that "Blake's adaptation of biblical style is the single most important contributing factor to the poetry of Jerusalem." Paley, *The Continuing City: William Blake's Jerusalem* (Oxford: Oxford University Press, 1983), 44.

[88] Gerda S. Norvig, *Dark Figures in the Desired Country: Blake's Illustrations to "The Pilgrim's Progress"* (Berkeley: University of California Press, 1993). Norvig resists the temptation to offer a reductionist reading that explains Bunyan's narrative and Blake's images in Freudian or Jungian categories. Rather, she seeks to draw out Blake's symbolic meanings through psycho-aesthetic analysis.

of the Lord God as a Poor Pilgrim."[89] Though Blake regarded allegory to be inferior to symbolism, he admitted that "allegory is seldom without some vision" and that Bunyan's tale "is full of it."[90] Blake's illustrations attend to the text with great detail, finding even deeper symbols in Bunyan's dreams than did the dreamer himself. Among the circle of young painters in London with whom he associated, Blake was known as "the Interpreter" and his home as "the House of the Interpreter," an obvious allusion to Christian's spiritual guide in Bunyan's story. Yet, in his interpretive role, Blake did not simply hand on the spiritual tradition as he received it. Instead, he swerved from it in an act of "creative correction" or "misprision."[91] And this misreading, rather than simply denoting difference, is actually a crucial indicator of poetic influence. This interpretive shift breaks through in Blake's earlier engraving of the man sweeping Interpreter's parlor. Bunyan explains the simple allegorical meaning of his vision:

> This Parlor, is the heart of a Man that was never sanctified by the sweet Grace of the Gospel: The dust, is his Original Sin, and inward Corruptions that have defiled the whole Man. He that began to sweep at first, is the Law; but She that brought water, and did sprinkle it, is the Gospel.[92]

Blake subverts these symbols, transforming the dust-sweeping man into a sinister bat-winged devil surrounded by demons hovering round a swirling black cloud of dust, and transforming the woman who sprinkles water from a domestic servant into an angel of light. It displays his

[89] William Blake, Letter to William Hayley (December 4, 1804), in *Blake Complete Writings*, 853.

[90] William Blake, *A Vision of Last Judgment*, in *Blake Complete Writings*, 604. Blake's concern about allegory was that it turned the symbol into a cipher to be decoded in search of another meaning that was an abstraction, whereas what he called "vision" or "imagination" opened up a higher sense of meaning without rendering the symbol merely instrumental. Rowland, *Blake and the Bible*, 9–11.

[91] Harold Bloom, *The Anxiety of Influence: A Theory of Poetry*, 2nd ed. (New York: Oxford University Press, 1997), 30. Blake's greatest poetic anxiety is personified in the specter of Milton's influence, which he seeks to overcome in the poem *Milton*. Bloom, "Jerusalem: The Bard of Sensibility and the Form of Prophecy," in *William Blake*, ed. Harold Bloom (New York: Chelsea House, 1985), 92–93.

[92] Bunyan, *Pilgrim's Progress*, 25.

rejection of the first use of the law, as defined by Calvin and followed by Bunyan, and it reveals Blake's deep conviction of the law as an end in itself as a destructive force opposed to the redemptive process.[93]

Blake's anxiety over Bunyan's influence can be seen in his vision of the New Jerusalem from "Beulah Land." The image is found in an obscure prophecy in Isaiah 62:4, in which God promises the Jews who return from exile to Jerusalem that the land of Judah will be no longer called Desolate (*Shemamah*) but called Married (*Beulah*). Bunyan extends the image of Beulah to become a trope for the land "next door to heaven," where just before death the saints can see the city of God, and where the love of bride and bridegroom are renewed, so that the desire for heaven becomes erotically awakened as Christian and Hopeful fall sick like lovers, "sick of love" (Song 5:8).[94] Bunyan's image of Beulah land as the place for visions of heaven prior to death survived in the evangelical tradition through preaching and hymnody, like the chorus of the gospel song by Edgar Page Stites, which exclaims:

> O Beulah land, sweet Beulah land!
> As on thy highest mount I stand,
> I look away across the sea
> Where mansions are prepared for me
> And view the shining glory shore
> My heaven, my home forever more.[95]

Though Stites' song was written after Blake's death, it voices an account of hope rooted in the reception of Bunyan by popular

[93] John Calvin, *Institutes of the Christian Religion*, II.1.6–9, ed. John T. McNeill, trans. Ford Lewis Battles (Philadelphia: Westminster, 1960), 354–58.

[94] Bunyan, *Pilgrim's Progress*, 44 and 126–27. Christiana and her fellow pilgrims arrive at Beulah to rest before crossing the River of Death in *Pilgrim's Progress*, part 2, 254–55. The pilgrims who dwell in Beulah hear heavenly voices and see celestial visions. The image of Beulah may also reflect the change in Bunyan's eschatological outlook to a more quietist postmillennialism. Bunyan linked the Isaiah text with a passage from the Song of Songs, in which the desire for heaven is described as one who is "sick with love" (Song 5:8).

[95] Edgar Page Stites, "Beulah Land" (c. 1876), in *The Complete Book of Hymns*, by William J. Petersen and Ardythe Peterson (Carol Stream, Ill.: Tyndale House, 2006), 438–39. For evangelicals like Stites, Beulah represented the link not only between God and Israel but between the present and the future.

nonconformist religion that Blake found insufficient not because of its idealized pietism but because he believed that it depended on a diminished and individualistic account of the self.[96] So chapter 1 of *Jerusalem* concludes with a prayer by the daughters of Beulah:

> Descend, O Lamb of God, & take away the imputation of Sin
> By the Creation of States & the deliverance of Individuals
> Evermore,
>   Amen.[97]

Blake's poem describes the unfolding of these states leading ultimately to redemption through participation in the Heavenly Canaan, which at the center, he says, has not individual consciousness but "eternal states."[98] The Beulah of Blake's *Jerusalem* is not the happy land of the converted waiting for death. It is the psychic realm of the subconscious, the liminal space between time and eternity, the gateway and threshold state of being connecting this world with the world beyond, the place of rest and renewal for the imagination, the realm of dreams and visions of the New Jerusalem where Christ and his angels speak.[99] And it is a place of erotic imagination, for, there in the sleep of Beulah's night, men and women, though sexually divided, are free to "wander in dreams of bliss among the Emanations."[100] It seems fitting, then, that Blake's marker lies in the central courtyard of Bunhill Fields facing Bunyan's monument, ever gesturing toward the "excellent things" to be found on the journey to that holy land.[101]

---

[96] "Beulah Land" became a popular trope that was transmitted through evangelical Christianity, as is evident in the compositions of Charles Ives (1874–1954), who frequently quoted lines from the hymn in his compositions. See James Wm. McClendon Jr., *Biography as Theology: How Life Stories Can Remake Today's Theology* (Nashville: Abingdon, 1974), 132–34.

[97] Blake, *Jerusalem*, 25.12–13, in *Blake Complete Writings*, 648.

[98] Blake, *Jerusalem*, 71.9, in *Blake Complete Writings*, 709.

[99] Blake, *Jerusalem*, 17.28, 36.22, 42.32, 63.37, in *Blake Complete Writings*, 639, 663, 670, 698. Samuel Foster Damon, *A Blake Dictionary* (Boulder, Colo.: Shambhala, 1979), 42.

[100] Blake, *Jerusalem*, 79.74, in *Blake Complete Writings*, 721.

[101] When Good Will opened the door at the wicket gate, he pointed Christian the way to the House of Interpreter, who would show him "excellent things" that would be a help on his journey. Bunyan, *Pilgrim's Progress*, 23–24.

BUILDING UP JERUSALEM

Blake's most well-known thoughts on Jerusalem are found not in his long epic poem on the city but rather in the short poem from the preface to his epic work on *Milton*. Looking at England with a prophetic gaze, he wonders:

> And did the Countenance Divine,
> Shine forth upon our clouded hills?
> And was Jerusalem builded here,
> Among these dark Satanic Mills?[102]

The crushing wheels of these mills are driven by none other than Satan himself, the "Miller of Eternity," whose all-powerful hand is ever present "to turn the Mills day and night."[103] His factories are driven by the "Wheel of Religion" and minded by "the dark Preacher of Death."[104] Like earlier dissenters, Blake looked at the world through an apocalyptic lens that perceived the established expressions of church and society to be dominated by satanic powers, so that "the Beast & the Whore rule without control."[105] Though the structures and expressions of his world were not those that his dissenting forebears resisted, he nevertheless saw the old powers inhabiting new forms of domestication and sovereignty. But where this false religion enslaves its followers into the service of Antichrist, Jerusalem above is free, and she is the mother of all (Gal 4:26). And where this natural religion proclaims only death, "Jesus is the bright Preacher of Life." Through Jesus, the Lamb of God, "Hell is open'd to Heaven," and "the dungeons burst

---

[102] Blake, *Milton*, 1.17, in *Blake Complete Writings*, 481.

[103] Blake, *Milton*, 1.3–4, in *Blake Complete Writings*, 483.

[104] Blake, *Jerusalem*, 77.13–18, in *Blake Complete Writings*, 718.

[105] Blake, "Annotations to *An Apology for the Bible*" (by R. Watson), in *Blake Complete Writings*, 383. Blake was criticizing Bishop Watson of Landaff, who published his apology for the Bible addressed to Thomas Paine. Blake exclaimed, "To defend the Bible in this year 1798 would cost a man his life." He suggested that "Paine has not attacked Christianity" but rather that "Watson has defended Antichrist" (383). He continued, "The Bishop never saw the Everlasting Gospel any more than Tom Paine" (394). Blake similarly denounced R. J. Thornton's "New Translation of the Lord's Prayer" (1827) as "a most malignant and artful attack on the kingdom of Jesus," characterizing its classical learning as Antichrist. Blake (786).

and the Prisoners set free."[106] The vision of the heavenly city arouses in those that see its beauty the desire for the liberty of its inhabitants to be spread throughout the earth, and it calls out for all the Lord's people to be its prophets, mounting chariots of fire and fighting with the weapons of transformed imagination for the building of Jerusalem in this world.[107] Only the gospel of Jesus can free the people of this troubled earth, and only in Jerusalem can a free people truly live, for Jerusalem is human community redeemed and renewed in wholeness.

Blake's most complete thoughts on the subject are in his epic poem *Jerusalem*, which he composed over a period of almost two decades (1804–1820). Jerusalem is not only its theme and title. It is literally the first and final word.[108] The sweeping arc of the poem renarrates the whole biblical story in an English context, from fall and struggle to redemption and apocalypse.[109] Like Bunyan's allegory, Blake's *Jerusalem* explores a series of dream-visions, though his symbols are much darker. Both are epics for "strangers and pilgrims on the earth" (Heb 11:13), and the end of the journey for those who embark as pilgrims is the same—the celestial city, Jerusalem above. But Blake's eschatology is more extreme than Bunyan's. It is apocalyptic. It is about a new creation that lies beyond the desolation of all things.[110] It incorporates the millenarian vision of the New Jerusalem being built on earth that was common among radial dissenters. Those who listen to Blake's song (as he called his poem) are struck as much by the imaginative beauty of its images as the lyric quality of its verses. The nature of his poetry is more emblematic than referential, and its patterns are more circular

---

[106] Blake, *Jerusalem*, 77.21, 34–35, in *Blake Complete Writings*, 718.

[107] Blake, *Milton*, 1.17, in *Blake Complete Writings*, 481.

[108] Blake's *Jerusalem* contains one hundred plates divided into four chapters of twenty-five pages, and each chapter begins with a preface addressed to a different audience: chap. 1 to *the Public*, chap. 2 to *the Jews*, chap. 3 to *the Deists*, and chap. 4 to *the Christians*.

[109] Northrop Frye, *Fearful Symmetry: A Study of William Blake* (Princeton, N.J.: Princeton University Press, 1947), 357.

[110] G. A. Rosso argues that "Blake endeavors to recapture the spirit of early Christian eschatology and build Jerusalem in the England of his day," by unmasking the alliance of religion and empire, in *The Religion of Empire: Political Theology in Blake's Prophetic Symbolism* (Columbus: Ohio State University Press, 2016), 53.

than linear. Unlike his illustrations of *The Pilgrim's Progress* that closely follow Bunyan's narrative, the illuminations in Blake's *Jerusalem* are as much a suggestion of states of mind as they are graphic images of the text.

The visionary quality of Blake's images reflects his own religious experience, which from an early age included angelic visitations and conversations with the dead and was filled with dreams and visions.[111] He celebrated his return to London, after a brief hiatus in Felpham, where he could carry on his visionary studies, converse with friends in eternity, see visions, dream dreams, and prophesy and speak parables unobserved and free from the intrusion of doubters.[112] But just before leaving "the Vale of Felpham," Milton appeared to Blake in a dream and entered his left foot. As he journeyed like Bunyan's Christian, on pilgrimage to London, he continued "to walk forward thro' Eternity."[113] *Jerusalem* recounts the story of the fall and redemption of Albion, the name of ancient England, though in the poem Albion represents universal humanity. The narrative proceeds not along a linear plot line moving through time but on an inward journey filled with apocalyptic visions that open the windows of eternity, passing beyond time through states of consciousness. Yet the mythical reality that the sons and daughters of Albion inhabit is not entirely *in illo tempore*, but instead it imagines the same world in which all the sons and daughters of earth live, although depicted in spiritual rather than natural terms.[114] It is, then, a realm in which the logic of Locke and the mechanics of Newton do not apply. Indeed, it is through this elaborate mythology that the spiritual subverts the natural.

Jerusalem opens with Jesus calling out to Albion, but, instead of focusing his attention on Jesus, Albion turns away in jealously, hiding Jerusalem to prevent Jesus from taking her as his bride. In his rejection

---

[111] Bentley, *Blake Records*, 10–11.

[112] William Blake, Letter to Thomas Butts (April 25, 1803), in *Blake Complete Writings*, 822–23.

[113] Blake, *Milton*, 21.1–14, in *Blake Complete Writings*, 503.

[114] Mircea Eliade, *The Sacred and the Profane: The Nature of Religion* (New York: Harcourt, 1959), 94–95. The phrase *in illo tempore* (lit. "in that time") denotes the sacred time of myth. It references the primordial (not historical) time of beginnings, *ab origine*.

of Jesus, Albion (like Adam) falls away, becoming alienated from himself and fragmenting into four Zoas, or life forms, which resemble the four living creatures that the apostle John sees surrounding the throne of the Lamb in heaven (Rev 4:6-8) and the four cherubim the Prophet Ezekiel glimpses within the wheels of the fiery chariot that transports the throne of the LORD God Almighty (Ezek 1:4-14). Each form represents a human faculty and corresponds to one of the four basic elements: Earth-Tharmas-Body, Air-Urthona/Los-Imagination, Fire-Luvah-Emotions, and Water-Urizen-Reason.[115] Each human faculty has a corresponding female emanation, and each state has a specter or shadow further frustrating and dividing the self. Yet virtually absent from Blake's narrative of *Jerusalem* is the fiery red figure of Orc, who dominates the earlier prophesies, *America* and *Europe*.[116] Orc is wrath, the personification of revolution. He proclaims the bloody path to life, liberty, and the pursuit of happiness. He resists the powers of domestication, defiantly declaring, "Empire is no more."[117] Taking the form of the serpent, he becomes satanic, the "lover of wild rebellion and transgressor of God's Law."[118] His serpentine sway corrupts the church and spreads until all is consumed in his fierce flames. He is the ferocious tiger burning bright, the negation of the Lamb, the rejection of love and forgiveness.[119] He is bound with chains of jealousy.[120] But, in *Jerusalem*, Orc is silently coiled in the South with the dragon, Urizen (Your Reason), the jealous god of this world.[121]

Having seen the cruelty of political revolution, where the thirst for blood is never consumed and the attainment of liberty leads to

---

[115] Blake, *Jerusalem*, 36[32].25–42, in *Blake Complete Writings*, 663. See also William Blake, *Four Zoas*, 1.9, in *Blake Complete Writings*, 264; and especially the illumination for Blake, *Milton*, 32, in *Blake Complete Writings*, 523. The image of the four Zoas appears in plate 33 in the Keynes edition, but it is on plate 32 in Blake's original.

[116] Blake, *Jerusalem*, 1.3, in *Blake Complete Writings*, 634. This is the direct reference to Orc in *Jerusalem*, and he plays no active role in the narrative.

[117] Blake, *America*, 6.1–15, in *Blake Complete Writings*, 198. Orc utters the poetic paraphrase of the Declaration of Independence of the United States of America.

[118] Blake, *America*, 7.6, in *Blake Complete Writings*, 198.

[119] William Blake, "The Tyger," in *Blake Complete Writings*, 214.

[120] Blake, *Four Zoas*, 5.92–242, in *Blake Complete Writings*, 307–11.

[121] Blake, *Jerusalem*, 14.3, in *Blake Complete Writings*, 634.

new expressions of violence, Blake considers a different source of transformation—the apocalypse of the imagination. The instrument of change in this new social order is not Orc but his father Los, who personifies the faculty of imaginative creativity. He represents the poetic and prophetic voice of Blake himself. He perceives his great task as "to open the Eternal Worlds, to open the immortal Eyes Of Man inwards into the Worlds of Thought, into Eternity."[122] He is the agent of a spiritual revolution. Unlike his bloody son, the fires of Los are unleashed not to consume and destroy but rather to fuel the furnaces of creativity. His hammer is justice, which he swings with mercy and strikes with forgiveness.[123] Like earlier working-class dissenters who dreamed of building Jerusalem in England's green and pleasant land, Los is the prophet of the Lamb, a laborer like Blake who builds the great city of Golgonooza in his furnaces and on his anvil. Los resembles the "sectarian" Seraph Abdiel in Milton's *Paradise Lost*, who confronts Satan and his fallen host, "fearless, though alone, Encompass'd round with foes."[124] But like his son Orc, Los is also troubled by the specter of rationality, yet he works toward the redemption of Albion's wholeness. As he works, Los thinks of Jerusalem, wandering far away, outside the city. But in Ulro, the material world, the land below Beulah, the established churches are consumed and energized by spectral thoughts.[125] In this vision of horror, the "Loom of Locke" and the "wheels of Newton" supply the delusions of materiality that lead church and state to collude in the sacrifice of their children to the gods of war "in the Valley of the Sons of Hinnom."[126] Yet even though the shadow of Babylon

---

[122] Blake, *Jerusalem*, 5.18–19, in *Blake Complete Writings*, 623.

[123] Blake, *Jerusalem*, 88.49–50, in *Blake Complete Writings*, 734.

[124] Milton, *Paradise Lost*, V.875–76, in *John Milton Complete Poems and Major Prose*, ed. Merritt Y. Hughes (New York: Macmillan, 1957), 322. Paley makes the Los-Abdiel connection (*Continuing City*, 239–40). Abdiel later channels the voice of the dissenter and his sect over against the established and satanic established church before striking the first blow in the apocalyptic battle, declaring, "To thee not visible, when I alone / Seem'd in thy World erroneous to dissent / my Sect thou seest, now learn too late / How few sometimes may know, when thousands err." Milton, *Paradise Lost*, VI.145–48, in *John Milton Complete Poems*, 327.

[125] Blake, *Jerusalem*, 13.51–66, in *Blake Complete Writings*, 634. See also Blake, *Milton*, 37.15–42, in *Blake Complete Writings*, 528.

[126] Blake, *Jerusalem*, 15.15–34, in *Blake Complete Writings*, 636.

looms over the earthly city, the vision of Jerusalem still hovers on the horizon. There is only one hope, voiced by the daughters of Beulah, who plead for Jesus, the Lamb of God, to take away "the imputation of Sin" and to create states of consciousness for deliverance of humanity.[127]

The sons and daughters of Albion, however, are unable to experience the gospel of love and the forgiveness of Jesus because they are held under the controlling power of the Law. Blake addresses this captivity to the Law in his address "to the Jews," which presents the religion of Judaism as an essential step in the spiritual evolution of humanity, giving the gift of the inspired writings of the Hebrew Bible. Yet it is an immature stage, proceeding from a literal reading of the Scriptures rather than recognizing them to be "canopied with emblems" and "Spiritual Verse."[128] But, instead of seeking spiritual vision, Albion strives to build a new world based on the foundations of morality and law. From the vantage point of his secret seat, he observes the sinfulness of fallen humanity and declares himself to be "punisher and judge."[129] But in this cruel and unforgiving world, it is Albion's specter, Satan, who rules as god.[130] It was he who rent the Law from the Gospel, and it was he who "forg'd the Law into a Sword and spill'd the blood of mercy's Lord."[131] This spectral demigod is rationality personified. He is falsely worshipped as God by Christians and Jews. Yet he is not God. He is Urizen, the god of theism, the silent and invisible deity, the Father of Jealousy, the Spectrous Chaos, whom Blake mockingly calls Nobodaddy. He hides in the clouds and cloaks himself in darkness and obscurity.[132] He continually smites Albion with the sword of morality, until, like Job, Albion is "Cover'd with boils from head to foot."[133] The punishment of such merciless justice reduces Albion to despair, as he cries out, "Hope is banish'd from me."[134] Yet, again, it is the daughters of Beulah, hoping against hope, who lament

---

[127] Blake, *Jerusalem*, 25.12–13, in *Blake Complete Writings*, 648.

[128] Blake, *Jerusalem*, 48.7–8, in *Blake Complete Writings*, 677.

[129] Blake, *Jerusalem*, 28.4–5, in *Blake Complete Writings*, 652.

[130] Blake, *Jerusalem*, 33[29].17–18, in *Blake Complete Writings*, 659.

[131] Blake, *Jerusalem*, 52.17–20, in *Blake Complete Writings*, 683.

[132] William Blake, "To Nobodaddy," in *Blake Complete Writings*, 171.

[133] Blake, *Jerusalem*, 29[43].63, in *Blake Complete Writings*, 655.

[134] Blake, *Jerusalem*, 47.18, in *Blake Complete Writings*, 677.

"the terrible Separation" of Albion and Jerusalem.[135] They lift up their prayer as an offering: "Come, O thou Lamb of God, and take away the remembrance of Sin."[136]

Blake's condemnation of "the Jews" should not be mistaken for a gnostic-like critique of ancient Israel or even the Old Testament. He attacks a kind of natural religion exemplified by the sons of Albion, who are those that falsely call themselves Christians. They are the descendants of mythic Anglo-Israel that became the cultural Christianity of England. Blake scorns their religion that is captive to the power of moral law. It is animated by satanic forces, transforming it into a malicious and merciless caricature of the gospel. It is embodied in the cruel legalism wielded by the priest in "A Little Boy Lost," whose horrid god and king, like ancient Moloch and Chemosh, are smeared with the blood of innocents and demand child sacrifice for the heresy of expressing a desire for universal love. The poet asks, "Are such things done on Albion's shore?"[137] Indeed, such cruel things are done in the name of religion underwritten and established by the authority of the Law, as the history of dissent vividly and tragically displays. Legalistic religion is characterized by a mind-set of moral rigidity and self-righteous certainty. It is bound to an inflexible code as if it were inscribed on tablets of stone. Its abstractions and negations petrify the imagination. Blake describes this legalistic religion as enshrined in the "Druid Patriarchal rocky Temples" of Albion's ancient shore, but it is not ancient paganism he scorns.[138] It is the legalism embodied in the established church. It is a religion that can condemn and judge but one that cannot forgive. Such legalism is not the gospel of Jesus but a Satanic counterfeit. Jesus embodies a spiritual message that overthrows the moral law:

[135] Blake, *Jerusalem*, 47.26, in *Blake Complete Writings*, 678.
[136] Blake, *Jerusalem*, 32[46].14–15, in *Blake Complete Writings*, 658.
[137] William Blake, "A Little Boy Lost," in *Blake Complete Writings*, 218–19.
[138] Blake, *Jerusalem*, 50.24, in *Blake Complete Writings*, 681.

He laid His hand on Moses' Law;
The ancient Heavens, in Silent Awe
Writ with Curses from Pole to Pole,
All away began to roll.[139]

Here, Blake's antinomianism comes out in full force: there is "One Religion, The Religion of Jesus, the Most Ancient the eternal & the Everlasting Gospel."[140] This is the religion of love, which offers what law cannot—forgiveness.

But the Law is not the only power that holds religion captive. There is also the spectral power of reason separated from the imagination that corrupts the Christian faith.[141] It too is animated by Satan. It debases and degrades true religion, transforming it into a selfish surrogate. Though Blake addresses his third chapter "to the Deists," the religion he describes is not the classical deism that conceived of God as a cosmic watchmaker of a universe that runs on its own (with need for neither prayer nor providence) but the rational religion that had been widely assimilated into the Church of England in his day. Such religion is dominated by satanic powers. It allows "the Beast & the Whore rule without control."[142] "[Hu]Man[ity] must & will have Some Religion," Blake observed, "if he has not the Religion of Jesus, he will have the Religion of Satan & will erect the Synagogue of Satan, calling the Prince of this World, God, and destroying all who do not worship Satan under the Name of God."[143] Blake's Satan is not the Miltonic superfiend but rather a conscious state of sheer selfishness and will to power that preaches morality while attacking liberty. This apostate religion is named Rahab, the Erastian civil religion that has turned against the gospel of forgiveness revealed in Jesus. The poet resists the religion of the beast and the whore by continuing to imagine the building of the great city, with the hope that it might

---

[139] William Blake, "The Everlasting Gospel," e.1–14, in *Blake Complete Writings*, 754.

[140] Blake, *Jerusalem*, 27, in *Blake Complete Writings*, 649.

[141] Blake, *Jerusalem*, 74.10–11, in *Blake Complete Writings*, 714.

[142] Blake, "Annotations to *An Apology for the Bible*" (by R. Watson), in *Blake Complete Writings*, 383.

[143] Blake, *Jerusalem*, 52.pref., in *Blake Complete Writings*, 682.

give expression to Jerusalem, which is called "Liberty."[144] Yet the fall of Albion continues its degenerative journey, as the building of the earthly city goes on and the false religion of its established church ritually binds its citizens in the chains of jealously and hatred.

Though Blake regarded the Church of England to have been founded by true Christians following the everlasting gospel, he thought it had fallen into error and corruption.[145] The great cathedral cities professed the false gospel of state religion, declaring, "What is a Church & What Is a Theatre? Are they Two & not One? Can they Exist Separate? Are not Religion & Politics the Same Thing?"[146] This assertion by the state-established churches is not the true faith. They worship at the altar of the god of empire. Theirs is a civil religion of priest and king, where "every blak'ning Church appalls" and "runs in blood down Palace walls."[147] Albion flees from this vision of the corrupt church, falling into the furrow of a new nation, plowed under by his own specter while the nations rage in Satan-inspired war. Even the song of the Lamb himself cannot arouse Jerusalem to bestow the gift of liberty upon the people enslaved by Satan.[148] For the religion of the established churches serves the beast. It is called Rahab, manifested as "Babylon the Great, the Abomination of Desolation" (Rev 17:4-5), whose false religion has trampled and destroyed Jerusalem the true bride of Christ. Rahab and her monstrous state-established churches are "Religion hid in War, a Dragon red & hidden Harlot."[149] Yet just when all hope seems to be lost, something unexpected happens. Jesus breaks through, opening "Eternity in Time & Space . . . to awake the Prisoners of Death, to bring Albion again into light eternal in his eternal day."[150]

[144] Blake, *Jerusalem*, 54.5, in *Blake Complete Writings*, 684. Rosso explains that Blake "associates Locke's moralism and Newton's cosmology with Milton's Satan to show that the new world system, reaching from the 'uppermost' regions of the cosmos to the 'innermost recesses' of the mind is fundamentally satanic." Rosso, *The Religion of Empire*, 107.

[145] William Blake, "Joseph of Arimathea," in *Blake Complete Writings*, 604.

[146] Blake, *Jerusalem*, 57.8, in *Blake Complete Writings*, 689.

[147] Blake, "London," 10, 13, in *Blake Complete Writings*, 216.

[148] Blake, *Jerusalem*, 60.10–37, in *Blake Complete Writings*, 692–93.

[149] Blake, *Jerusalem*, 75.19–20, in *Blake Complete Writings*, 716.

[150] Blake, *Jerusalem*, 76.22–26, in *Blake Complete Writings*, 716.

The poet envisions hope of freedom, but not through the appropriation of human constructions by moralizing or reasoning. These have become corrupt powers animated by demonic forces. Liberty is possible not through law or reason but only by deliverance from these powers and their false god in which church and nation trust and by participation in God through friendship and love. Blake offers an invitation, much as Bunyan did, to follow him on a journey of transformed understanding toward liberty:

> I give you the end of a golden string,
> Only wind it into a ball,
> It will lead you in at Heaven's gate
> Built in Jerusalem's wall.[151]

The false religions of legality and rationality offer only death. They preach a false gospel. There is, Blake announces, "no other Christianity and no other Gospel than the liberty both of body & mind to exercise the Divine Arts of Imagination."[152] This is Christian liberty. This is Jerusalem. Jesus came to bring this liberty to all, but he was crucified because he resisted the devouring sword turned by the wheel of natural religion. As Blake narrates his account of the story's end, the sons of Albion who call themselves Christians oppose the Lamb of God and Jerusalem, the poet's vision of a redeemed society. Instead, they serve Rahab as queen of all the earth.[153] Antichrist is revealed as the Covering Cherub, signaling the end of time. He is satanic, "the majestic image of Selfhood" and "a Human Dragon terrible," but, within the belly of manifest evil, Jerusalem is hidden awaiting the fullness of time.[154] Finally, the apocalypse comes. Jesus appears, and Albion awakes from his sleep. The appearance of Jesus is the likeness of Los, his prophetic

---

[151] Blake, *Jerusalem*, 77.pref., in *Blake Complete Writings*, 716. Bunyan states in his apology: "It will direct thee to the Holy Land / If thou wilt its Directions understand." Bunyan, *Pilgrim's Progress*, 6.

[152] Blake, *Jerusalem*, 77.pref., in *Blake Complete Writings*, 716.

[153] Blake, *Jerusalem*, 78.16, in *Blake Complete Writings*, 719.

[154] Blake, *Jerusalem*, 89.9–11, 43–44, in *Blake Complete Writings*, 734–35. The phrase appears in Ezek 28:16 and is understood by patristic theologians as a reference to Satan—viz., Tertullian, *Against Marcion*, II.10, in *The Ante-Nicene Fathers* (Grand Rapids: Eerdmans, 1978), 3:305–6.

voice.[155] Seeing Jesus and recognizing his divinity, Albion confesses Jesus to be the Lord and sees in Jesus the likeness of his friend Los.[156] With the Covering Cherub overshadowing them, Jesus declares the simple message of faith, saying, "Fear not Albion: unless I die thou canst not live; But if I die I shall arise again & thou with me."[157] Albion dies and is raised by Christ to share in the new humanity.[158] Antichrist is destroyed.[159] Humanity in its alienated and fragmented states of consciousness is reconciled and reunited. And everything is restored in a social and psychic *apocatastasis* of being.

The spiritual imagination of Blake's poem was guided by the biblical vision of the heavenly Jerusalem, which signifies the true church (Gal 4:26), not the false worship of empire religion. This is the social location where those who have been liberated by the gospel of Jesus discover what it means to be free. There is an old tradition among the Jewish rabbis that the Mosaic Law bestows freedom. The writing of God was "graven [*haruth*] upon the tables" (Exod 32:16), but as Joshua ben Levi attested, "Read not *haruth* (graven) but *heruth* (freedom), for thou findest no freeman excepting him that occupies himself in the study of the Law."[160] According to this tradition, the descendants of Hagar rejected the Law and therefore lost their freedom. The apostle Paul adapted this traditional understanding for the purpose of his argument, setting up "an allegory" (Gal 4:24). In this Christian misprision, Hagar represents the observance of the Law that leads her children into slavery, but Sarah is the Jerusalem above, the true church. She is free together with her children. It draws from the apocalyptic vision of a heavenly Jerusalem, awaiting to descend from heaven at the end time (e.g., Isa 54:10-12; 65:17-19; 1 Enoch 90:28-29; Rev 3:12; 21:2, 10). But, in this new figural reading, Sarah represents the eschatological city of God, who as spiritual mother is in the fullness of time giving birth to true believers. Just as the rabbis believed one received freedom

---

[155] Blake, *Jerusalem*, 96.7, in *Blake Complete Writings*, 743.
[156] Blake, *Jerusalem*, 96.22, in *Blake Complete Writings*, 743.
[157] Blake, *Jerusalem*, 96.14–15, in *Blake Complete Writings*, 743.
[158] Blake, *Jerusalem*, 96.35, in *Blake Complete Writings*, 744.
[159] Blake, *Jerusalem*, 98.6, in *Blake Complete Writings*, 745.
[160] *Aboth* 6:2, in *The Mishnah*, trans. Herbert Danby (London: Oxford University Press, 1983), 459.

in Torah observance, so Paul argued that Christians gain freedom by participation in the New Jerusalem, for "Jerusalem above is free, and she is our mother" (Gal 4:26).[161]

Blake's poem was animated by the apocalyptic imagination that reached back to previous generations of dissenters and earlier readings of the New Jerusalem like Arthur Dent's *The Ruine of Rome* and Thomas Brightman's *Apocalypsis Apocalypseos*.[162] It was a vision that stirred the dreams of social revolutionaries and prophetic voices from Gerrard Winstanley and the Diggers to Anna Trapnel and the Fifth Monarchists.[163] It was the apocalyptic hope of building the New Jerusalem that inspired the English Civil War and guided the visionary politics of Cromwell's Commonwealth, but it was an outlook that became politically dangerous and intellectually suspicious after the restoration of the monarchy.[164] Bunyan reframed the apocalyptic conflict as an inner psychological struggle of sin and grace. Boehmenists and Swedenborgians similarly turned inward, conceiving the apocalypse of the New Jerusalem in mystical terms.[165] Blake was surely influenced by these esoteric readings, but his *Jerusalem* revived a millenarianism akin to Joseph Mede's *Clavis Apocalyptica*, which looked to an imminent coming of the New Jerusalem and the return of Christ to reign with the saints on earth for a thousand years.[166] Mede proposed

---

[161] J. Louis Martyn, *Galatians*, Anchor Yale Bible (New Haven: Yale University Press, 1997), 447–57.

[162] Arthur Dent, *The Ruine of Rome* (London: W.I. for Simon Waterson & Richard Banckworth, 1607); and Thomas Brightman, *Apocalypsis Apocalypseos, a Revelation of the Apocalypse* (Amsterdam: Iudocus Hondius and Hendrick Laurenss, 1611).

[163] Winstanley, "Watch-Word to the City of London," in *Works of Gerrard Winstanley*, 315–17; Anna Trapnel, *The Cry of a Stone* (London, 1654), in Freeman, *Company of Women Preachers*, esp. 432–39; and Thomas Venner, *The Last Speech and Prayer and Other Passages of Thomas Venner* (London, 1660).

[164] Harold Fisch, *Jerusalem and Albion: The Hebraic Factor in Seventeenth-Century Literature* (New York: Schocken, 1964), 11–15.

[165] Nils Thune, *The Behmenists and Philadelphians: A Contribution to the Study of English Mysticism in the Seventeenth and Eighteenth Centuries* (Uppsala: Almqvist & Wiksell, 1948); and Hindmarsh, *Rise and Progress of the New Jerusalem Church*.

[166] Joseph Mede, *The Key of the Revelation*, trans. Richard More (London: R. B., 1643), part 2, 122–23. Sklar builds on Paley's work, showing the fuller incorporation of Mede's appropriation of visionary theater. Paley suggests that, in his *Jerusalem*, Blake

seeing Revelation holistically (or synchronically) as well as sequentially, so that related but apparently separate scenes are meant to be conflated as a simultaneous vision. He further indicated that it should be read typologically (or diachronically) as "apocalyptique theater" by superimposing visions of Revelation onto history.[167] Mede's work thus suggests how Blake might have conceived that the hermeneutical key to understanding *Jerusalem* lay in seeing its visions not only *sequentially* but *synchronically* (like in a painting) and *dramatically* (as on a stage).[168]

This spiritual vision guides Blake's prophetic imagination.[169] Yet as he looks at the London in which he lives, on South Molton Street, he does not see the lovely image of Jerusalem. Instead he gazes on a ruined city that is "blind & age-bent, begging thro' the Streets of Babylon, led by a child."[170] It is the London of the *Songs of Experience*, a city full of soot-covered buildings and filled with faces marked by weakness and woe, a wretched place where the winding worm of mortality devours the innocents like Moloch and Chemosh of old. Its inhabitants are a people in exile, having exchanged their faith in the one true God for the false religion of Rahab, whose hands approvingly turn the dehumanizing spindles of industry that have transformed them into cruel and heartless creatures who refuse to hear the cries of the poor. But as Blake like Los looks again through the eyes of the creative imagination, he sees a city in need of renewal. He envisions the New Jerusalem descending from heaven (Rev 21:2).[171] Yet his vision of Jerusalem is not a remote and otherworldly figure. Like earlier millenarians, who expected Jerusalem to come on earth, Blake also sees the building of Jerusalem as a spiritual possibility that can become an earthly reality. It is his prophetic task to imagine the building of a spiritual city. Like

---

followed a millenarian view similar to Mede. Paley, *Continuing City*, 124. Sklar, *Blake's "Jerusalem" as Visionary Theatre*, 20–23.

[167] Mede, *Key of the Revelation*, part 1, 130–37. Mede came to his notion of apocalyptic theater by typologically correlating the vision of the heavenly throne (Rev 4:2-11) with the "ancient encamping of God with Israel in the wilderness" (Num 1:52–2:34).

[168] Paley, *Continuing City*, 287; and Sklar, *Blake's "Jerusalem" as Visionary Theatre*, 23.

[169] Rowland, *Blake and the Bible*, 9.

[170] Blake, *Jerusalem*, 83.85–84.16, in *Blake Complete Writings*, 729.

[171] Blake, *Jerusalem*, 85.22–86.32, in *Blake Complete Writings*, 730–31.

Los, he must build it. Yet such a task is only possible because of psychic and social redemption that comes in Jesus. His love unshackles the chains of reason and law that bind the imagination, liberating captives to live free. In him humanity is risen anew to participate in his body, free to live as one people and share a common humanity. The social embodiment of this one-peoplehood is Jesus, the Lamb of God. He is in all, and all are in him.[172] He is the last Adam, who makes possible the new creation. In Blake's vision of the building of a spiritual city, the inward turn of Bunyan and the outward reach of Defoe are reunited in the apocalyptic redemption of soul and society.

Though in many ways Blake stood virtually alone among his contemporaries, he heard a voice calling to him: "Awake! awake O sleeper in the land of shadows."[173] The call awakened in him the wild energy of dissent that arose from his slumbering imagination and that like the burning brightness of the tiger could not be tamed or domesticated.[174] It was the prophetic spirit of dissenters long past arising to speak anew. In his critique of the apostate national church and his vision of the reform and restoration of Christian faith, he was standing on the shoulders of earlier dissenters.[175] Like his forbears, Blake believed that the reform of Christianity required conversion in "the passage through Eternal Death! And of the awakening to Eternal Life."[176] His epic poem *Jerusalem* is not the gnostic speculation of a mythical humanist. It is an apocalyptic vision of a dissenting Christian who believed that only a complete transformation of thinking could return Christianity to the religion of Jesus. It is more apocalyptic than esoteric. Yet the apocalypse as Blake conceived it is revelatory, not linear. It is a matter not of charting out the future but about learning to live in the light of a revelation that illumines the world in an entirely new way. It is not an otherworldly vision but a vision of this world renewed and redeemed.

---

[172] Blake, *Jerusalem*, 38[34].14–26, in *Blake Complete Writings*, 664–65.

[173] Blake, *Jerusalem*, 4.6, in *Blake Complete Writings*, 622.

[174] Blake, "The Tyger," in *Blake Complete Writings*, 214.

[175] Robert M. Ryan, *The Romantic Reformation: Religious Politics in English Literature 1789–1824* (Cambridge: Cambridge University Press, 1997), 44–79.

[176] Blake, *Jerusalem*, 4.1–2, in *Blake Complete Writings*, 622.

This *apocatastasis* of the imagination is accomplished through the incarnation of God in Jesus—an incarnation so profound that the humanity of God becomes visible for all to see. So he says to all, "Within your bosoms, I reside, and you reside in me."[177] This is no cliché of a new humanism. It is the hope of a redeemed humanity participating in the life of God through the human-God Jesus. "God becomes as we are," Blake exclaimed, "that we may be as he is."[178] Here, he echoed the patristic doctrine of *theosis*,[179] and he gestured to something like what Karl Barth finally admitted late in life, that the deity of God eternally included humanity and that this humanity became incarnate in Jesus.[180] Blake is no eccentric theologian. He is a highly centric Christian for whom Christ is the center and love is the circumference. He is no esoteric kabbalist. He is an apocalyptic Christian. And, in this unshakable hope, Blake lived unto death sustained in the conviction, as he put it, "I still & shall to Eternity Embrace Christianity and Adore him who is the Express image of God."[181] He rightly deserves to be remembered not only as a great poet and artist but as a prophetic voice of Christian dissent. Yet it was not long before memory of him faded away and was in danger of being forgotten.

[177] Blake, *Jerusalem*, 4.19, in *Blake Complete Writings*, 622.

[178] William Blake, "There Is No Natural Religion," 2nd series, in *Blake Complete Writings*, 98.

[179] Athanasius affirmed that "[God] assumed humanity that we might become God." Athanasius of Alexandria, *On the Incarnation*, §54 (Crestwood, N.Y.: St. Vladimir's, 1944), 93. Irenaeus made a similar point that "the Word of God, our Lord Jesus Christ, who did, through his transcendent love, become what we are, that he might bring us to be even what he is himself." Irenaeus of Leon, *Against Heresies*, V.pref., in *The Ante-Nicene Fathers* (Grand Rapids: Eerdmans, 1979), 1:526. Rosso suggests that Blake's account of the atonement invokes the classical Christus Victor tradition of Christian orthodoxy, which emphasizes Christ's defeat of Satan, to counter Milton's Arianism and other theologies that "deny the value of the Saviour's blood." Rosso, *Religion of Empire*, 101–3; Blake, *Milton*, 22.54, in *Blake Complete Writings*, 506.

[180] Karl Barth, *The Humanity of God* (Atlanta: John Knox, 1960), 45–46.

[181] William Blake, Letter to Thomas Butts (November 22, 1802), in *Blake Complete Writings*, 814–15.

ALL GOD'S PEOPLE AS PROPHETS

Blake was buried in Bunhill Fields on Friday, August 16, 1827. The day before his interment, one copy of his poem *Jerusalem* was delivered to William Young Ottley, an amateur art collector and curator at the British Museum.[182] It was one of only five copies printed during Blake's lifetime, of which only two originals have survived, and only a single copy was ever "finished."[183] Through his innovative technique of relief etching, he created words and images in a single process, enabling him to paint rather than engrave the copper plates. And because each plate was hand colored, every page of an illuminated book was unique. Illuminated printing for Blake was a performance art, not merely a means of mass production. Yet his decision to use this medium significantly limited the availability of his work. Unlike Bunyan's *Pilgrim's Progress* and Defoe's *Robinson Crusoe*—which were conventionally printed by presses in large quantities, making the cost of a book affordable and readily accessible—copies of Blake's *Jerusalem* were scarce, and the reception history is more complicated.[184] As Blake's first biographer observed, his illuminated writings "were in the most literal sense *never published* at all" but rather were "simply engraved by his own laborious hand."[185] Apart from a small circle of friends, who called themselves "the Ancients," his work went largely unappreciated in his lifetime.[186] Some collectors sought out his rare prints, and a few contemporary artists and poets respected him as a wildly creative genius. After seeing a version of Blake's *Jerusalem*, Robert Southey described it as "a perfectly mad poem."[187] William Wordsworth concurred, saying that "there is no

---

[182] Bentley, *Blake Records*, 464.

[183] Paley, *Continuing City*, 7–8.

[184] Paley, *Continuing City*, 7–12.

[185] Gilchrist, *Life of William Blake*, 1:2; emphasis in original.

[186] Ackroyd, *Blake*, 338–40. The "Ancients" included Samuel Palmer, Edward Calvert, George Richmond, Francis Finch, Frederick Tatham, and John Giles. The early reception history has been well documented by Deborah Dorfman, in *Blake in the Nineteenth Century: His Reputation as a Poet from Gilchrist to Yeats* (New Haven: Yale University Press, 1969).

[187] Robinson, *Diary, Reminiscences, and Correspondence of Henry Crabb Robinson*, ed. Thomas Sadler (Boston: Houghton, Mifflin, 1898), 217 (July 24, 1811); Bentley, *Blake Records*, 310.

doubt this poor man was mad," but, he added, "there is something in the madness of this man which interests me more than the Sanity of the Lord Byron & Walter Scott!"[188] Samuel Taylor Coleridge regarded Blake as "a man of Genius" and "a *Mystic*" whose poetry and painting is "apocalyptic" even "anacalyptic."[189]

Others were far less charitable. One critic mocked Blake as "an unfortunate lunatic, whose personal inoffensiveness secures him from confinement," and who "fancies himself a great master" but "has painted a few wretched pictures, some of which are unintelligible allegory, others an attempt at sober character by caricature representation, and the whole 'blotted and blurred,' and very badly drawn."[190] Blake was sensitive to and perhaps even complicit in fostering the perceptions of his critics, describing his work as "cried down as eccentricity and madness."[191] Henry Crabb Robinson put the matter succinctly, as he wondered, "Shall I call him Artist or Genius—or Mystic—or Madman?" To which he answered, "Probably he is all."[192] It was easy for polite society to dismiss him as a working-class visionary, an extreme enthusiast with an overheated brain, or a disorderly and heterodox dissenter. But to most of Blake's contemporaries, his creative work was virtually unknown, and so it would have remained had it not been for Andrew Gilchrist's biography, *The Life of William Blake*, in which

---

[188] Henry Crabb Robinson, *Reminiscences* (1832), in Bentley, *Blake Records*, 693.

[189] 1114: To [Reverend] Henry Francis Cary (February 6, 1818) and 1116: To Charles Augustus Tulk (February 12, 1818), in Samuel Taylor Coleridge, *Collected Letters*, ed. Earl Leslie Griggs (Oxford: Clarendon, 1956–1971), 4:832–34, 835–38; emphasis in original. The terms "apocalyptic" and "anacalyptic" are near synonyms, both denoting an "unveiling," though the latter in the sense of the Old Testament as a prefiguration of the New Testament. David M. Baulch says that both words suggest "the expression of a passionate, enthusiastic, and multifaceted mind that presents itself as having both an unbounded interest in the poetic imagination and a stubborn awareness of the theological and political stakes in a critical utterance." Baulch, "Reading Coleridge Reading Blake," *Coleridge Bulletin*, n.s. 16 (2000): 5–14.

[190] Robert Hunt, *The Examiner* (September 17, 1809), in Bentley, *Blake Records*, 282–83.

[191] William Blake, *A Descriptive Catalogue of Pictures, Poetical and Historical Inventions*, in *Complete Poetry and Prose of William Blake*, 537–38.

[192] Robinson, *Diary, Reminiscences, and Correspondence of Henry Crabb Robinson* (December 10, 1825), 24; Bentley, *Blake Records*, 420.

Gilchrist characterized Blake as *Pictor Ignotus* (the Unknown Paint-er).[193] Gilchrist sought to show that Blake's artistic work had discerning admirers and that their admiration was deserved. The two-volume project rendered Blake's material both verbally and visually. It was a magnificent achievement. As a recent study has described it, Gilchrist's *Life* was "sympathetic but not uncritical."[194] There is no question that Gilchrist and his circle of friends single-handedly recovered Blake from literary oblivion. But rather than becoming a "classic" biography, it aroused new interest in Blake studies and stimulated fresh waves of publication that superseded it.[195]

The recovery of Blake extended primarily to the poetical works. The prophetical books, including *Jerusalem*, were still largely ignored. Then, in 1916, Sir Hubert Parry composed a musical setting for Blake's short poem "Jerusalem." It became an immediate success as a patriotic hymn, bolstering support for the war effort at the time. And though Blake was a nonconformist and a republican, his poem ironically became a defining hymn for the Church of England and an unofficial national anthem sung lustily at political meetings, civic gatherings, social affairs, and sporting events.[196] But the "green and pleasant Land" of Parry's hymn that became a theme song of the empire was a tamed and domesticated version of dissent, not the disturbing apocalyptic vision of the New Jerusalem that Blake imagined. Beyond this popular reception, Blake had his cultured despisers, like T. S. Eliot, who praised his "peculiar honesty, which, in a world too frightened to be honest, is peculiarly terrifying." Yet Eliot explained Blake's creativity like "an ingenious piece of home-made furniture" put together by a "resourceful Robinson Crusoe." In the end, Eliot suggested that Blake should be regarded as "a poet of genius" who suffered from a "confusion of thought, emotion, and vision."[197] It is a familiar refrain, con-

---

[193] Gilchrist, *Life of William Blake*.

[194] Heather J. Jackson, *Those Who Write for Immortality: Romantic Reputations and the Dream of Lasting Fame* (New Haven: Yale University Press, 2015), 174.

[195] Jackson, *Those Who Write for Immortality*, 177–78.

[196] Jeremy Dibble, *C. Hubert H. Parry: His Life and Music* (New York: Oxford University Press, 1992), 483–85.

[197] T. S. Eliot, *Selected Essays*, new ed. (New York: Harcourt, Brace, & World, 1960), 275–80.

descendingly repeated by high church Royalists about working-class dissenters, who were legally prevented from obtaining the university education that would have rendered them more pleasant. But it simply proved once again Defoe's observation that the real division has always been the church and the dissenter.[198]

Yet the unpleasantness of Blake's vision of Jerusalem was more terrifying than even Eliot could bring himself to admit, as N. T. Wright, the former Bishop of Durham, recognized. Speaking in 2007 at the Cathedral Church on the occasion of the 175th anniversary of the founding of the University of Durham, Wright reflected on Blake's hymn, which was to be sung at the end of the service. Playing Blake for a fool, Wright suggested that the poet was badly misguided by mythic understandings: the feet of Jesus never walked on England's mountains green, nor was the Holy Lamb of God on England's pleasant pastures ever seen, nor did the countenance divine shine forth upon its clouded hills, nor was Jerusalem built among its dark satanic mills. Of course, Wright knew better: it is a spiritual vision. Only a fool could mistake Blake's rhetorical questions as history in a literal sense. But the bishop recognized something much more disturbing in Blake's imagery. The "dark Satanic Mills," he noted, were not simply references to the soot-covered factories of the Industrial Revolution, but rather, as he perceptively observed:

> [t]hey were the great churches, like Westminster Abbey and St Paul's Cathedral, which Blake saw as being hopelessly in thrall to the follies of the world, follies he saw all too clearly in the great thinkers of what was already calling itself the "enlightenment."[199]

---

[198] Daniel Defoe, *A New Test of the Church of England's Loyalty* (London, 1702), 3.

[199] Nicholas Thomas Wright, "Where Shall Wisdom Be Found?" homily at the 175th anniversary of the founding of the University of Durham (June 23, 2007), http://ntwrightpage.com/sermons/Durham_Wisdom.htm (accessed April 14, 2016). Wright mistakenly ascribed the hymn to Blake's epic poem *Jerusalem*, though it appears in the preface to *Milton*. Blake actually regarded the Gothic architecture of Westminster Abbey to be a monument to creative imagination, though he saw St. Paul's Cathedral as a shrine of natural religion and Newton's Pantocrator. In plate 32 of *Jerusalem*, St. Paul's is associated with Vala, while Westminster Abbey is connected with Jerusalem. Paul S. Fiddes, *Freedom and Limit: A Dialogue between Literature and Christian Doctrine* (Macon, Ga.: Mercer University Press, 1999), 88.

Indeed, Blake inveighed against the "Schools & Universities of Europe" that were under the tyrannical sway of "the Loom of Locke" and "the Water-wheels of Newton" with their mechanistic and reductive modes of thinking.[200]

Wright correctly described Blake's deep suspicion of what he regarded to be a satanic alliance between the rationalistic forces of natural religion in the university and the powers of the beast working in collusion with the whore of the state-established church. These domesticating agents of empire were familiar targets of dissenter criticism. But the difference between Wright and Blake is more fundamental. Wright views the powers as instruments of God's justice to which Christians are called to submit (Rom 13), while Blake sees them as forces animated by the diabolical beast from the abyss that Christians must seek to subvert (Rev 13). Consequently, Wright is apprehensive not only of Blake's apocalypticism but of all apocalyptic visions—even biblical ones.[201] In defense of state establishment, Wright reconfigures the entire biblical narrative as a story of God and God's covenant people Israel, which he construes in continuity with England and its established church.[202] He rightly perceives that the danger of Blake's poem lies not in its naked honesty but in its terrifying prophecy that imagines England's great cathedrals and the grand universities, like even the temple in Jerusalem, being destroyed in an apocalyptic conflagration—as Jesus once said, "not one stone will be left here upon another; all will be thrown down" (Matt 24:2). Such a vision, if true, is so subversive, so unimaginable, and so threatening to

---

[200] Blake, *Jerusalem*, 15.14–16, in *Blake Complete Writings*, 636.

[201] That N. T. Wright is suspicious not only of Blake's apocalypticism but of all apocalyptic is clear in his treatment of Ernst Käsemann's account of apocalyptic in the apostle Paul. In response to the critique, Käsemann warned that Wright's covenantal approach may actually be a retrojection of Anglicanism into the New Testament. Wright, *Paul and His Recent Interpreters* (Minneapolis: Fortress, 2015), 50–55, esp. 54n87.

[202] Wright echoes earlier voices following Thomas Brightman, who envisioned England as playing an instrumental role in consummating the reformation and leading to the ultimate fulfillment of God's redemptive purpose on earth. See "The Apocalyptic Imagination" in chap. 1 above. William Haller mistakenly attributed this theology of England as elect nation to John Foxe. Haller, *Foxe's Book of Martyrs and the Elect Nation* (London: Jonathan Cape, 1963), 18 and 109.

the comfortable culture of Anglican Christendom that it could only be mocked as the imprecations of an enthusiast.[203]

If the English were prone to be suspicious of Blake, the Americans by virtue of their participation in a revolutionary war and the subsequent adoption of a republican government were inclined to be more receptive. Blake's poetry and prophetic writings were received into the canon of literature to be studied in universities.[204] New interpretations of Blake emerged in America and beyond from this wealth of scholarship. One is a portrait of Blake as a *radical revolutionary* fostered by the work of Jacob Bronowski and David Erdman, rendering Blake particularly relevant to university students and others open to revolutionary political ideas during the 1960s and early 1970s.[205] Others portrayed

[203] Wright's view of Blake stands in stark contrast to former Archbishop of Canterbury Rowan Williams, who offered a more positive assessment, suggesting that "there's no more moral poet in the English language than William Blake" (http://rowanwilliams.archbishopofcanterbury.org/articles.php/1752/rowanwilliams-on-poetry [accessed December 12, 2016]). Williams further argues that "some aspects of Blake's understanding of the divine image are more closely connected than might initially appear with the classical theological picture of [the] self-dispossessing God . . . the God who is . . . neither conditioned by the world nor imaginable apart from divine engagement with it." Williams, "'The Human Form Divine': Revelation and Orthodoxy in William Blake," in *Radical Christians Voices and Practice*, ed. Zoë Bennett and David B. Gowler (Oxford: Oxford University Press, 2012), 147. Rosso makes a similar observation about the continuity-discontinuity of early Christianity and the established church, suggesting that John Howard Yoder's anti-Constantinian politics in *The Politics of Jesus* resembles Blake's apocalyptic critique of empire religion, whereas Oliver O'Donovan's *The Desire of Nations* is more like the ecclesial politics of Rahab. Rosso, *Religion of Empire*, 48–53. It parallels the argument above that Wright's rejection of Blake is rooted in a realized eschatology that supports the politics of establishment, whereas Williams' sympathy for Blake's vision arises from a suspicion of an overrealized ecclesial eschatology.

[204] The reception and growth of Blake studies has resulted in a rich harvest of scholarly resources that include G. E. Bentley Jr.'s exhaustive *Blake Records* (1969/1988), S. Foster Damon's *A Blake Dictionary* (1979), and David Erdman, *The Complete Poetry and Prose of William Blake* (1970/1988). For summaries of the history of critical interpretation of *Jerusalem*, see Paley, *Continuing City*, 12–32; and Sklar, *Blake's "Jerusalem" as Visionary Theatre*, 8–15.

[205] Jacob Bronowski, *A Man without a Mask* (New York: Haskell House, 1967); Bronowski, *William Blake and the Age of Revolution* (New York: Harper & Row, 1965); and David Erdman, *Blake: Prophet against Empire* (1954/1977). Rosso follows this line

Blake as an *eclectic mythmaker*, like the English poet and critic Kathleen Raine, who set him in conversation with the Neoplatonic and hermetic tradition, describing him as symbolist channeling the perennial philosophy, and conceiving of him as "Christian polytheist."[206] Still others have described him as a *mystical poet*.[207] Northrop Frye explored the psychological aspects that drove Blake's mystic thinking, noting that, in the final prophetic writings, Blake's allegiance shifted from Orc (revolution) to Los (imagination). Frye was followed in this line of analysis, though very differently, by Harold Bloom, who linked Blake's prophetic writings with the Hebrew prophets and *Jerusalem* with Merkabah mysticism. A. L. Morton and E. P. Thompson both saw connections between Blake's prophetic vision and the antinomian tradition of dissenters in the seventeenth century.[208] Yet none of these approaches enables readers to understand Blake—not primarily as a radical revolutionary, a mystical prophet, or a perennial philosopher, but as a *Christian prophet*, for whom the Bible was a generative source of a subversive imagination.[209]

Blake draws from apocalyptic images familiar to those in the dissenter tradition in his strategy of resistance, though differently than Bunyan and Defoe had done. Bunyan sought to resist the domestication of empire by turning the apocalyptic struggle into a battle within the soul. Defoe resisted domestication by appropriating a realized eschatology that accommodated itself to the politics of the new market economy through the acquisition of wealth and social influence.

---

of thought of Blake as a prophet against empire. His astounding interpretation of Rahab as the portrayal of the monstrous union of empire and religion counters assertions by postcolonial critics, who argue that Blake was complicit with empire. Rosso convincingly shows Blake's apocalyptic outlook to be anti-imperial. Rosso, *Religion of Empire*, 10–11.

[206] Raine characterizes Blake as a "Christian polytheist." Raine, *Blake and Tradition*, 1:xxx, 1:73–74, 2:101–4.

[207] Frye, *Fearful Symmetry*; and Harold Bloom, *Blake's Apocalypse: A Study in Poetic Argument* (Garden City, N.Y.: Doubleday, 1963).

[208] Morton, *Everlasting Gospel*.

[209] Christopher Rowland adds to an understanding of the biblical roots of Blake's spiritual vision by placing him in conversation with prophetic and apocalyptic literature as well as the Jewish world from which Christianity emerged. Rowland, *Blake and the Bible*.

Blake saw both of these strategies as subject to the corruption of spectral powers, and he recognized that the realization of true liberty required transformation of both the spiritual world of the imagination and the social world of habitation. The apocalyptic salvation Blake envisioned included both the psychic consciousness of Bunyan and the evangelicals and the social reform of Defoe and the liberals. Nothing short of an apocalyptic deliverance through the death and resurrection of Jesus could triumph over the beastly powers and renew the mind to the imaginative and creative task of building Jerusalem. Only by participating in this new social reality where forgiveness and love are freely given and received can there truly be liberty for all. For when all God's people take up their prophetic mantle, mount up their chariots of fire, and lift up their gifts of a creative imagination, then and only then will Jerusalem come down from heaven to earth. And when Jerusalem comes down, the sons and daughters of earth will be set free from the chains that bind them—set free to love and forgive, set free to build and create things of beauty, set free to wonder and imagine, set free to struggle for justice and peace, set free to give and receive the gifts of life, liberty, and laughter that belong to all the sons and daughters of earth.

Several examples of retrieving Blake as a guide for Christians in this work of building Jerusalem are worth noting. One is Malcolm Muggeridge, an agnostic journalist and former spy, who became a celebrated Christian convert. Muggeridge regarded Blake to be a prophet of a third Testament.[210] He suggested that Blake's central insight was seeing the only reality in life as a spiritual one. It was no wonder, Muggeridge opined, that Blake's contemporaries, who measured the world in quantitative terms, considered him to be mad. Muggeridge thought that Blake foresaw that the end of modernity with its myth of self-sufficiency—however well intentioned and good natured—led inevitably to decadence and violence. Rather than giving rise to the flourishing of the human condition, modernity resulted in bondage—poisoning the air, polluting the water, flattening the

---

[210] Malcolm Muggeridge, *A Third Testament* (Boston: Little, Brown, 1976), 85–117. Muggeridge names six prophets of the *Third Testament*: St. Augustine, Blaise Pascal, William Blake, Søren Kierkegaard, Leo Tolstoy, and Dietrich Bonhoeffer.

landscape, destroying art, and smothering the imagination. Blake saw that the false god of reason, whom Blake playfully named Urizen, offered no hope of escape, but he saw that salvation was possible only through the transformation of the imagination, embodied in Jesus, the Lamb of God. For Muggeridge, Blake made known the everlasting gospel of love as "a bright rainbow shining across a stormy sky, keeping alive the hope of deliverance from dark Satanic Mills of every variety, and all their lies and pollution."[211] And as God's spy, Blake guided Muggeridge back safely across enemy lines into the historic Christian faith and, ultimately, into full communion with the church Catholic.

Another retrieval of Blake as a Christian prophet was Thomas Altizer, for whom Blake was not a voice calling for a return to historic Christianity but the herald of a new form of faith brought about by the death of God.[212] As Altizer put it, "God has died in *our* time, in *our* history, in *our* existence."[213] The death of God, he argued, was a historical and ontological event.[214] For the Blake of Altizer's account, Jesus is not the message of the everlasting gospel but rather the messenger of the gospel of Christian atheism. Altizer contended that Blake, long before Nietzsche's celebrated announcement by the madman, recognized that the transcendent and wholly other God of Christianity is not eternal. When Jesus died, the Christian God died with him. But Altizer asserted that just as the total presence of God was with Jesus in the incarnation, so in Jesus' death God became kenotically incarnate in the life and suffering of all humanity. This apophatic absence of God in the world, Altizer believed, called for an apocalyptic faith,

---

[211] Muggeridge, *Third Testament*, 19–20.

[212] Thomas J. J. Altizer, "William Blake and the Role of Myth in the Radial Christian Vision," in *Radical Theology and the Death of God*, by Thomas J. J. Altizer and William Hamilton (New York: Bobbs–Merrill, 1966), 171–91. Altizer's essay contains selections from chapters 1 ("Fall"), 3 ("History"), and 4 ("Apocalypse") of his then unpublished book *The New Apocalypse: The Radical Christian Vision of William Blake* (East Lansing: Michigan State University Press, 1967).

[213] Thomas J. J. Altizer, "Theology and the Death of God," in Altizer and Hamilton, *Radical Theology*, 95; emphasis in original.

[214] The death of God is not a psychological event, as Altizer's collaborator William Hamilton explained: "We are not talking about the absence of the experience of God, but about the experience of the absence of God." Hamilton, "The Death of God Theologies Today," in Altizer and Hamilton, *Radical Theology*, 28.

which enables immediate participation in the kingdom of God. It is important to recognize that Altizer did not so much show Blake to be a prophet of the new atheism but rather revealed his own anxiety about Blake's apocalypse and showed himself to be clever in employing Hegel's dialectic to deliberately misread Blake. Altizer's misprision was a theological act to remythologize Blake's apocalypse for the purpose of speaking to a world where he thought the reality of God was no longer acknowledged.

This rhetorical sleight of hand was not lost on Thomas Merton, who pointed out that any supposed connection between Blake and Hegel is merely superficial. Merton worried that although the Hegelian negation of negation may result in the death of the villainous god of church establishment, the glib embrace of its secular contrary ignores the possibility that the next negation may just as easily be a totalitarian regime of the Marxist or capitalist variety. Merton expressed deep suspicion about joyfully embracing Antichrist, as Altizer urged readers to do. If God becomes incarnate in suffering, Merton wondered whether Antichrist at Auschwitz and other manifestations of such horrific human suffering can also be embraced with joy. The result, as Merton suggested, is that Altizer's god is not the God of the historic Christian faith, whom Blake honored, but Nobodaddy, a satanic negation, a god of historical process and human construction. Nor was Altizer's secular eschatology, which totally integrates God and humanity in Christ, in Merton's view, a Christian eschatology, because there is no final reversal that brings redemption to a fallen world.[215] Altizer made a move similar to that of the Quakers who claimed that the body of Jesus ascended not into heaven but into the hearts of the saints. But Altizer proposed that the risen body of Jesus descended into the life of the world. In so doing, he inverted the apocalyptic movement described at the end of *Jerusalem*, where Blake's final move is not *downward* in *kenosis* as the transcendent God becomes incarnate in humanity but *upward* in *theosis* as humanity is drawn to participate in life with the risen Lord.

---

[215] Thomas Merton, "Blake and the New Theology," in *The Literary Essays of Thomas Merton*, ed. Patrick Hart (New York: New Directions, 1985), 3–11.

At least one Baptist theologian, Paul Fiddes, has drawn on Blake's apocalyptic vision in developing an account of universal participation in God through the body of Christ.[216] But the most sustained yet over-looked retrieval of Blake for a Christian imagination in recent times is surely Wendell Berry—novelist, poet, environmental activist, cultural critic, and farmer. Berry is widely recognized as a Christian writer, less so as a Baptist. He refers to himself simply as "a person who takes the Gospel seriously."[217] He is also a critic of ways in which Christians have been complicit in the travails of the earth. Little discussed, however, is the deep connection of Blake as a source and guide in Berry's thinking. The reliance on Blake is so profound and pervasive in Berry's creative and critical work that he seldom steps back to point it out. Yet occasionally he does. In his essay "Two Economies," Berry draws attention to one of the dominant themes of what he calls "the Great Economy," which promises to put all things under *control*. He explains that the image of "control" by which the global market economy operates is the oppositional turning that Blake called "Satanic wheels," which he described in *Jerusalem*:

> And there behold the Loom of Locke, whose Woof rages dire,
> Wash'd by the Water-wheels of Newton: black the cloth
> In heavy wreathes folds over every nation: cruel Works
> Of many Wheels I view, wheel without wheel, with cogs tyrannic,
> Moving by compulsion each other, not as those in Eden, which,
> Wheel within Wheel, in freedom revolve in harmony & peace.[218]

Newton's wheels, like the great sun and planet gear at Albion Mills, converted reciprocating energy to rotary motion by a set of gears that turned inward, forcing one another to move, not drawn by gravitational forces like planets orbiting the sun, but in a tyrannical opposition. The cruel works of these unnatural and violent movements are what Blake called a "wheel without wheel." Yet Blake saw another natural and peaceable motion, a "wheel within wheel" that freely revolves

---

[216] Fiddes, *Freedom and Limit*, 94–103.

[217] Wendell Berry and Wen Stephenson, "The Gospel according to Wendell Berry," *Nation*, March 23, 2015.

[218] Blake, *Jerusalem*, 15.15–20, in *Blake Complete Writings*, 636.

around the arc of time in harmony with all living things.[219] Blake's simple image of natural versus mechanical motion becomes for Berry a root metaphor for understanding the basic order—and, indeed, economy—of things.[220]

When a group of American intellectuals put together a collection of essays after September 11, 2001, entitled *Dissent from the Homeland*, it was not surprising that Berry was one of the contributors. He offered a series of theses that explored the underlying economic and social currents driving the politics of fear that have dominated American public life since 9/11.[221] Berry suggests that the deep pathology in America has become manifest in the "environmental crisis," which exists, he explains, because "the human household or economy is in conflict at almost every point with the household of nature."[222] People have become enslaved to a life of consumption by giving their political and economic proxies to corporations and governments, which promise to produce and provide everything that people need. Addressing the crisis, Berry argues, requires a change of both heart and practice, for, as long as people continue to be passive consumers, they will be driven like cogs in the wheels of the machine of the Great Economy, which Jesus called Mammon. Berry advocates resistance to the powers of the free market by establishing local economies that rest on the principles of neighborhood and subsistence. The failure to build such communities is, he concludes, "a profound failure of imagination."[223] And so, like Albion, the *consciousness* of human beings must be awakened if there is to be a *conscience* of the economy. Redemption for Berry, as for

---

[219] Wendell Berry, "Two Economies," in *The Art of the Commonplace*, ed. Norman Wirzba (Washington, D.C.: Shoemaker & Hoard, 2002), 219–235.

[220] The connection between economics and mechanics is not as strained as one might imagine given that Adam Smith (1723–1790), the "father" of market economics, was the mentor and friend of the inventor and industrialist James Watt, who, with the help of associate William Murdoch, invented the sun-and-planet gear for the rotary steam engine.

[221] Wendell Berry, "Thoughts in the Presence of Fear," in *Dissent from the Homeland*, ed. Stanley Hauerwas and Frank Lentricchia (Durham, N.C.: Duke University Press, 2003), 37–42; also published in Berry, *In the Presence of Fear: Three Essays for a Changed World* (Great Barrington, Mass.: Orion Society, 2001).

[222] Wendell Berry, "The Idea of a Local Economy," in *In the Presence of Fear*, 12.

[223] Wendell Berry, "In Distrust of Movements," in *In the Presence of Fear*, 38.

Blake, requires an apocalyptic *apocatastasis* of human consciousness. Such a vision inspires the building of Jerusalem in those places and communities called home, and in doing so to become free from the forces that otherwise would determine the destiny of the sons and daughters of earth.

Here, Berry is not simply imitating Blake's prophetic example and imagery. He has heard and answered the call to be a prophet in the building up of Jerusalem—or, to be more precise, in the building up of Jerusalem in Henry County, Kentucky. He has followed a calling to cultivate the disciplines of the domestic arts, from farm and forest to open table shared with friends and strangers. And, in so doing, he has become not just a prophet against empire but a prophet for a community of gladness. This vocation follows the direction of divine desire, which Blake inscribed at the end of his preface to *Milton*, immediately following his hymn to Jerusalem: "Would to God that all the Lord's people were Prophets" (Num 11:29). The calling to a prophetic life is to see the brokenness of the world as Blake saw it through the eyes of Los, to lift the sighs and tears of humanity into the furnaces of the imagination and forge them into joy and laughter, to lay open hidden hearts and work their red-hot sorrow on the resolute anvil of creativity, to strike the hammer of justice with blows of mercy and forgiveness until the world is transformed anew. This is how Jerusalem must be built. Such an office, if it is an office, is a call not solely to "speak truth to power"[224] but simply to speak truth—for the sort of prophecy Blake described was not about predicting the end of the world but about telling the truth as best as one can about what one sees, strengthened by insight and conviction that, with struggle, things can change for the better.[225] Such a vocation requires attentiveness to voices beyond oneself or, as Blake observed, not pretending "to be any other than the

---

[224] The phrase was probably coined by civil rights leader Bayard Rustin, but it was popularized by the book *Speak Truth to Power: A Quaker Search for an Alternative to Violence* (Philadelphia: American Friends Service Committee, 1955).

[225] Christopher Rowland, "William Blake: A Visionary for Our Time," *Open Democracy*, November 27, 2007, https://www.opendemocracy.net/article/arts_culture/literature/william_blake_visionary (accessed April 21, 2016).

Secretary," because "the Authors are in Eternity."[226] Attentiveness to the spiritual requires a transformed imagination that peers through the fog of experience into a subversive reality that lies beyond the looms of logic and the spindles of reason where turn wheels outside wheels, a reality that is accessible only through spiritual perception of the imagination where there are wheels within wheels, and visions of creatures, and chariots, and thrones, and angels, and where eternity breaks through from behind the curtains of time.

The freedom that the prophetic imagination envisions is mimetic, not mechanical. The cruel works that drive the economic machinery of empire and its gods assert themselves as defenders of liberty, but instead they subject humanity to the bondage of market forces in a culture of consumption that reduces freedom to mere choice, which as it turns out is more illusory than real. This state of existence is unnatural. The structure of its thinking is imposed by the ideology of empire, which closes the mind's eye to the new creation. It is driven by narratives of reversion from human creatureliness, rupture of social wholeness, and refusal of spiritual transformation.[227] It signifies the brokenness that has long been the lot of the sons and daughters of earth, who dwell in the land east of Eden. The Christian imagination looks instead to that which, even after humanity's fall, continues to be directed toward the new that has come in Christ. This new world is not expressed in abstract ideas, nor can it be reduced to universal principles. It is revealed in the vision of a city that exists beyond the horizon of history. Yet this city comes in space and time as it is constructed by prophets whose minds have been liberated to envision the earth as redeemed, repaired, and raised. The prophetic imagination fixes its gaze on the new creation by linking up with the natural rather than the unnatural, all the while remembering that the ultimate goal of this vision is a spiritual reality that lies beyond the natural.[228] The patterns of spiritual reality that are

---

[226] William Blake, Letter to Thomas Butts (July 6, 1803), in *Blake Complete Writings*, 825.

[227] James Wm. McClendon Jr., *Doctrine: Systematic Theology*, vol. 2 (Waco, Tex.: Baylor University Press, 2012), 130–35.

[228] Dietrich Bonhoeffer, *Ethics*, ed. Eberhard Bethge (New York: Macmillan, 1965), 144.

embedded within nature, though hidden from view, become visible in following the way of Jesus by living and forgiving, by loving and being loved, by giving and receiving. This spiritual vision is open for all sons and daughters of earth, calling them to mount their chariots of fire and take up their vocation in the prophethood of all God's people. It is a place where the weary find rest and liberty is shared by all who dwell therein. The name of this place is Jerusalem.

5

POSTAPOCALYPTIC DISSENT

The church now is the primitive church and the church on judgment day; the obedience and liberty of the followers of Jesus of Nazareth is our liberty, our obedience, till time's end.[1]

Cotton Mather began the final book of his *Magnalia Christi Americana*, published in 1702, by telling the story of a windmill in the Netherlands that turned so wildly during a violent storm its grinding stone became overheated, causing the mill to catch fire and setting the entire town ablaze. Mather went on to claim that the whole country of America was once set on fire by a man with the rapid motion of a windmill in his head. This man with an overheated brain was Roger Williams, whom Mather described as having "zeal, but not according to knowledge," with "less light than fire in him."[2] Mather's negative view of Williams is not surprising, given that his maternal grandfather, John Cotton, was Williams' chief antagonist. When he arrived in New England in 1631, Williams declined an invitation by the congregation in Boston to serve as their minister, explaining later, "I durst not officiate

---

[1] James Wm. McClendon Jr., *Ethics: Systematic Theology*, vol. 1 (Waco, Tex.: Baylor University Press, 2012), 30; emphasis in original.

[2] Cotton Mather, *Magnalia Christi Americana: The Ecclesiastical History of New England*, VII.II.7 (London: Thomas Parkhurst, 1702), 7.

to an unseparated people."[3] He spent the next several years with the more separated churches of Plymouth and Salem. When John Cotton came to New England two years later, he was appointed teacher of the Boston church. The two men engaged in a public exchange of letters that grew from a doctrinal disagreement into a theological controversy, with Williams writing *The Bloudy Tenent of Persecution for Cause of Conscience*, John Cotton replying with *The Bloudy Tenent, Washed, and Made White in the Bloud of the Lambe*, and a rejoinder by Williams entitled *The Bloody Tenent Yet More Bloody*.[4]

Had Williams' disagreements been limited to theological disputes with church leaders, he might have continued his work unimpeded by his opponents, but he quickly ran into difficulty with the magistrates of the Massachusetts Bay Colony. In a letter to Governor John Winthrop, Williams disputed the colony's claim to the land. He argued that the patent issued by England was invalid and that they had no right to settle there unless they compensated the Indian people. When the letter came to the attention of authorities in Boston, they examined it and condemned its author. On October 9, 1635, the General Court banished Williams for having "broached and divulged diverse new and dangerous opinions."[5] John Cotton defended the practice of banishment, contending that society must be protected from the contamination of undomesticated dissenters like Williams whose "Errors be Fundamentall, or seditiously and turbulently promoted."[6] Williams responded that compelling the conscience of those who differ amounts

---

[3] Roger Williams, Letter to John Cotton, of Plymouth, March 25, 1671, in *The Complete Writings of Roger Williams* (New York: Russell and Russell, 1963; repr., Paris, Ark.: Baptist Standard Bearer, 2005), 6:356.

[4] Cotton, *A Letter of Mr. John Cotton*; Williams, *Mr. Cotton's Letter Lately Printed, Examined and Answered*; Cotton, *John Cotton's Answer to Roger Williams*; Williams, *Bloudy Tenent of Persecution*; Williams, *The Bloody Tenent Yet More Bloody*, in Williams, *Complete Writings*, vols. 1–4.

[5] Nathaniel E. Shurtleff, ed., *Records of the Governor and Company of Massachusetts Bay in New England* (Boston: William White, 1853), 1:160–61. No mention was made of his question about the patent, nor is it referred to in the final sentence of banishment.

[6] John Cotton, *The Bloudy Tenent, Washed, and Made White in the Bloud of the Lambe* (London: Matthew Symmons, 1647), 2.3.

to "soul-rape,"[7] and he declared that any religion "which needs such instruments of violence to uphold it" cannot be true.[8] After being exiled from Massachusetts, Williams set out to establish a colony at Providence as "a shelter for persons distressed of conscience."[9] He acquired land by customary law, agreeing to a fair purchase price with the tribal leaders. The Royal Charter of Rhode Island and Providence Plantation, finally obtained from England in 1663, ensured religious liberty for all its residents—it proclaimed,

> Noe person within the sayd colonye, at any tyme hereafter, shall bee anywise molested, punished, disquieted, or called in question for any differences in opinione in matters of religion and doe not actually disturb the civill peace of our sayd colony; but that all and everye person and persons may, from tyme to tyme, and at all tymes hereafter, freelye and fullye have and enjoye his and theire owne judgments and consciences, in matters of religious concernments.[10]

The charter echoed the earlier declaration by Charles II to allow "liberty to tender consciences" and to respect "differences of opinion in matter of religion, which do not disturb the peace of the kingdom."[11]

The experience of Roger Williams stands in sharp contrast to Thomas Weld, who immigrated to America in 1632 and served as the minister in the congregation in Roxbury, Massachusetts. Writing to members in his former church, who were concerned about the state of affairs in New England, Weld did not merely assure them of his safety. He went on to celebrate the freedom he and other English

---

[7] Williams, *Bloudy Tenent of Persecution*, in *Complete Writings*, 3:182, 219.

[8] Williams, *Bloudy Tenent of Persecution*, in *Complete Writings*, 3:139.

[9] "Confirmatory Deed of Roger Williams and his wife, of the lands transferred by him to his associates in the year 1638," in *Records of the Colony of Rhode Island and Providence Plantations* (Providence, R.I.: A. Crawford Greene & Brother, 1856–1865), 1:22–25.

[10] The Charter of Rhode Island and Providence Plantation, in Benjamin Perley Poore, *Federal and State Constitutions, Colonial Charters, and Other Organic Laws of the United States*, 2nd ed. (Washington, D.C.: Government Printing Office, 1878), 2:1596–1597. Full charter 2:1594–1603.

[11] Charles R., The Declaration of Breda (April 4, 1660), in *The Constitutional Documents of the Puritan Revolution 1628–1660*, ed. Samuel Rawson Gardiner (Oxford: Clarendon, 1889), 351–52.

colonists were experiencing: *freedom from* oppression and influence of the wicked and *freedom for* righteousness and religion. He exclaimed,

> Mine eyes blessed be God do see such administration of justice in civil government. All things so righteously so religiously and impartially carried. . . . And I profess if I might have my wish in what part of the world to dwell, I know no other place on the whole globe of the earth where I would be rather than here. . . . Here are none of the men of Gibea the sons of Belial knocking at our doors disturbing our sweet peace or threatening violence. Here, blessed be the Lord God forever, our ears are not beaten nor the air filled with oaths, swearers nor railers, nor our eyes and ears vexed with the unclean conversation of the wicked.[12]

Given the story of dissent from Bunyan to Blake, the treatment of Roger Williams might not be surprising, except that Weld and John Cotton were also Protestant dissenters, though not yet formally separated from the Church of England, which would soon enough separate from them.[13] They were committed, as was Williams, to the further reformation of Christianity, having embarked on a mission of building the New Jerusalem in the New World.[14] Yet their social vision of a new heaven in a new earth, unlike that of the founders of Rhode Island,

[12] Thomas Weld, Letter to his former parishioners at Terling, Essex, 1632, in *Letters from New England: The Massachusetts Bay Colony, 1629–1638*, ed. Everett Emerson (Amherst: University of Massachusetts Press, 1976), 97.

[13] The term "dissenter" is a flexible term and is difficult to apply in the 1630s. From the time of his arrival in Boston, Williams was a separatist in his ecclesiology, whereas many of the New England ministers like John Cotton still affirmed their connection to the Church of England. By the restoration of the monarchy in 1660, Congregationalists in America were regarded as nonconformists and dissenters along with Presbyterians, Baptists, and Quakers.

[14] Francis J. Bremer, *Building a New Jerusalem: John Davenport, a Puritan in Three Worlds* (New Haven: Yale University Press, 2012), 167–80. Theodore Dwight Bozeman maintains—against the predominant outlook among scholars who attribute a future-oriented outlook to puritanism—that millennial thinking was not a puritan obsession. He contends that their larger theological agenda was more about a restoration of the past than about the anticipation of a new eschatological world. And to the extent that puritans were interested in millennial ideas, they were tied to the primitivist priorities. Bozeman, *To Live Ancient Lives: The Primitivist Dimension in Puritanism* (Chapel Hill: University of North Carolina Press, 1988), 18.

had little if any room for dissent. There was simply no place in their social world for undomesticated dissenters like Roger Williams.

Forgotten Errand—Lively Experiment

Puritans who came to the new world expected a great coming apocalypse that was just on the horizon. In the opening chapter of his *Magnalia*, Mather expressed the conviction that, when Christ returned to reign on earth with the saints for a thousand years, New England would be the New Jerusalem of his millennial kingdom.[15] It was this hope that drew John Winthrop, members of the Massachusetts Bay Company, and a company of saints across the Atlantic to build before the watching eye of the world a community that would be "a Citty upon a Hill." Yet Winthrop reminded his companions that they would succeed in their mission not by harrying out sinners and smiting evildoers but by upholding "a familiar commerce together in all meekeness, gentlenes, patience and liberality," and delighting "in eache other." He urged them to make the condition of one another their own, to "rejoice together, mourne together, labour and suffer together," and always to remember their "commission and community in the worke, as members of the same body." By loving and caring for one another, Winthrop explained, they would "keepe the unitie of the spirit in the bond of peace." And, in so doing, the Lord would be their God and delight to dwell among them, as God's own people, and would command a blessing upon them in all their ways.[16] The warrant for this hope was more than the charter of the Massachusetts Bay Company. What grounded their commission was the conviction that they were a people joined in covenant with God and one another for this work.[17]

---

[15] Mather, *Magnalia Christi Americana*, I.I.1, 4.

[16] John Winthrop, "A Model of Christian Charity," in *The Puritans: A Sourcebook of Their Writings*, ed. Perry Miller and Thomas H. Johnson (New York: Harper, 1963), 1:198–99.

[17] Winthrop, "Model of Christian Charity," Miller and Johnson, *Puritans*, 1:198–99; Francis J. Bremer, *John Winthrop: America's Forgotten Founding Father* (New York: Oxford University Press, 2003), 174–84; and Edmund S. Morgan, *The Puritan Dilemma: The Story of John Winthrop* (Boston: Little, Brown, 1958). Bozeman argues that Winthrop's sermon pertains, not as an thesis for an eschatological mission as Miller and

Believing the great migration of the 1630s to be a new exodus of the saints and New England to be a New Israel, the Massachusetts Bay Christians regarded the Ten Commandments as a summary statement of their national covenant, which they understood to be composed of two tables. The first four commandments prescribed the right worship of God. The last six pertained to civil matters. Both tables were regarded to be binding on all people. One of the "dangerous opinions" of Roger Williams cited by the General Court was that he insisted "the magistrate ought not to punish the breach of the First Table."[18] Williams argued forcefully in *The Bloudy Tenent* that civil magistrates were restricted to affairs of "law" named in the second table,[19] and that they had no "power over the Soules or Conscience of their Subjects, in the matters of God," stipulated in the first table.[20] The Massachusetts Bay authorities justified the application of both tables by arguing that the magistrate fulfilled the kingly office in God's covenant with Israel, so that foremost among the terms of the covenant was the preservation and protection of true religion.[21] Officers of government, who exercised this enforcing role, were regarded as agents of God. Against this theocratic understanding of government, Williams argued that Israel was a type of Christ's church, not the puritan commonwealth or any other civil government, thus obliterating the basis for any union of church and state based on the Old Testament.[22] For Williams, soul liberty was forever established

---

others aver, but rather as a successful model of continuing reformation. Bozeman, *To Live Ancient Lives*, 90–93.

[18] Winthrop, July 8, 1635, *Journal of John Winthrop 1630–39*, ed. Richard S. Dunn and Laetitia Yeandle, abridged ed. (Cambridge, Mass.: Belknap, 1996), 82. When the General Court considered Williams' case, Winthrop, who was on friendly terms with Williams and considered him to be a "godly minister," was no longer governor and could not guide the process to a peaceful resolution. Bremer, *John Winthrop*, 249–52.

[19] Williams, *Bloudy Tenent of Persecution*, 46–47, in *Complete Writings*, 3:150–55.

[20] Williams, *Bloudy Tenent of Persecution*, 7, in *Complete Writings*, 3:76.

[21] Williams, *Bloudy Tenent of Persecution*, 109, in *Complete Writings*, 3:312; and Cotton, *Bloudy Tenent, Washed, and Made White*, 35.76.

[22] Perry Miller, *Roger Williams: His Contribution to the American Tradition* (Indianapolis: Bobbs-Merrill, 1953), 33–38.

by the divine kingship of Jesus Christ, making government interference in matters of faith disobedience to Christ.[23]

New England theocrats were unpersuaded by alternative biblical interpretations, and they continued to pursue their social vision through a policy of forced uniformity. Their intolerance toward dissenters and schismatics, especially Baptists, did not escape the notice of fellow Independents in England, who sent a letter to the Massachusetts Bay General Court urging them "to suspend all corporall punishment or restraint on persons that Doe Dissent from you and practice the principall of their Dissent without Danger or Disturbance to the Civill peace."[24] Henry Jessey, one the most leading Independent ministers in London and long a friend of Winthrop, also wrote the officers of the churches in New England, criticizing their "smiting of fellow servants and Persecution for Conscience sake."[25] The New Englanders, however, ignored appeals for tolerance. In their Standing Order, the Congregational churches instructed civil authorities to restrain and punish "idolatry, blasphemy, heresy, venting corrupt and pernicious opinions that destroy the foundation, open contempt of the word preached, profanation of the Lord's day, disturbing the peaceable administration and exercise of the worship and holy things of God, and the like." They also advised magistrates to apply coercive power "as the matter shall require" to control schismatical churches that "walk incorrigibly or obstinately in any corrupt way of their own."[26] New England Congregationalists had

[23] Williams, *Bloudy Tenent of Persecution*, 119, in *Complete Writings*, 3:346–47. On Williams' use of typology, see James P. Byrd Jr., *The Challenges of Roger Williams: Religious Liberty, Violent Persecution, and the Bible* (Macon, Ga.: Mercer University Press, 2002), 31–52.

[24] Thomas Goodwin and others, "To the Massachusetts General Court," in *Winthrop Papers*, by John Winthrop, 5 vols. (Boston: Massachusetts Historical Society, 1929–1947), 5:23–25. Thirteen of the most prominent Independent ministers in England signed the letter, including Thomas Goodwin, John Owen, George Cokayn, Anthony Palmer, George Griffiths, John Bowe, John Lodiwick, John Collins, John Carey, Simon Moore, Cornelius Thelens, and Thomas Blake.

[25] Philip J. Anderson, "Letters of Henry Jessey and John Thombes to the Churches of New England," *Baptist Quarterly* 28, no. 1 (1979): 30–39. Jessey wrote his letter on June 22, 1645, seven days prior to his (re)baptism and conversion to the Baptists.

[26] *The Cambridge Platform of Church Discipline*, 17.8–9 (Cambridge, Mass.: Synod of Congregational Churches, 1648), 85.

no interest in fostering religious liberty. They were "deliberately, vigorously, and consistently intolerant" of any and all whose views on church or state differed from theirs.[27] Roger Williams was not the last to be punished by the Massachusetts General Court. Anne Hutchinson was banished two years later for her role in the Antinomian controversy, and Mary Dyer was hanged for her Quaker beliefs in 1660. It took a royal directive in 1661 to stop the execution of dissenters, and it required the revocation of the old charter and the issuing of a new one to put an end to the theocracy in Massachusetts.

But, in reality, this policy of state-sponsored religious uniformity was doomed from the outset given that in other colonies like Rhode Island "justice did at greatest offenders wink."[28] It was simply impossible to discipline everyone judged to be in violation of the national covenant.[29] The failure to achieve the goal of a holy commonwealth, however, did give rise to the important American rhetorical tradition of the jeremiad, sermons that lamented unfaithfulness to the covenant and warned of coming judgment.[30] In his election-day message, delivered forty years after the landing of the Massachusetts Bay colonists, Samuel Danforth asked his audience to consider whether they had not forgotten their errand into the wilderness.[31] He urged them to strengthen their resolve and pursue their original mission with renewed commitment so that God's blessings might continue to be on them. Danforth framed his reconsideration of their commission with the words that Jesus directed to the crowds about John the Baptist: "What went ye out into the Wilderness to see?" (Matt 11:7). In his sermon, the "wilderness" was transformed into a type addressed to

[27] Perry Miller, *Errand into the Wilderness* (Cambridge, Mass.: Belknap, 1956), 5.

[28] Benjamin Thompson, "New Englands Crisis," in Miller and Johnson, *Puritans*, 2:639.

[29] Sidney E. Mead, *Lively Experiment: The Shaping of Christianity in America* (New York: Harper, 1963), 27.

[30] Perry Miller, *The New England Mind: From Colony to Province*, 2 vols. (Cambridge, Mass.: Belknap, 1953), 1:27–39; Miller, *Errand Into the Wilderness*, 1–15; and Sacvan Berecovitch, *The American Jeremiad* (Madison: University of Wisconsin Press, 1978), 3–30.

[31] Samuel Danforth, *A Brief Recognition of New-Englands Errand into the Wilderness* (Cambridge, Mass.: S. G. and M. J., 1671), 9.

descendants of the founders, and the "errand" became a trope for their collective calling. Considering their mission in this figural sense raised anew the subjects of conversion and covenant as it forced future generations to ask how they might make this story their own and pressed them to imagine what it might look like to build a good and just society in the American wilderness.

Yet alongside the narrative of remembering the errand stands the story of Roger Williams and the charge "to hold forth a lively experiment that a flourishing civil state may stand and be best maintained with full liberty in religious concernments."[32] Both images flow from the same tradition shared by religious dissenters in England like Bunyan, Defoe, and Blake, but on the American landscape the errand and the experiment thrived together as never before. Winthrop and the Massachusetts Bay Colony provided America with the sense of a national vocation aimed at creating a good society held together by bonds of trust, and the conviction of respect for the sacred space of conscience and the corollary virtue of religious liberty championed by Williams gave rise to the receptive generosity that became a fundamental feature of American democracy.[33] In the lively experiment of Rhode Island, these basic liberties extended not just to Baptists, Quakers, and other Christians but to Jews, Muslims, and adherents of no religion equally. Williams rejected the colonial ideology that regarded the indigenous people as "savages" without rights or property.[34] Instead, he obtained land from the Indians by customary law and treated them not only as

[32] The Constitution of Rhode Island, in Poore, *Federal and State Constitutions*, 2:1604.

[33] This tension between independence and interdependence in American culture was the subject of Robert N. Bellah et al., eds., *Habits of the Heart: Individualism and Commitment in American Life*, updated ed. (Berkeley: University of California Press, 1996); and Bellah et al., *The Good Society* (New York: Vintage Books, 1992). Bellah initially attributed this tension to John Winthrop, but he later proposed that a stronger candidate for "the first Puritan who contained our whole destiny . . . is Roger Williams." Bellah, "Religion and the Shape of National Culture," *America*, July 31–August 2, 1999, 11; and Bellah, "Is There a Common American Culture?" *Journal of the American Academy of Religion* 66, no. 3 (1998): 613–25.

[34] John Winthrop, Letter to John Endecott, in *Winthrop Papers*, 3:149; and Winthrop, "General Considerations for the Plantations in New England, with an Answer to Several Objections," in *Winthrop Papers*, 2:120.

human beings with basic rights but as mutual partners in the experiment of radical democracy. Challenging the racially biased stereotypes upon which colonial Christianity depended, Williams described the Indians as "remarkably free and courteous." He portrayed them as a generous and hospitable people who "invite all Strangers in; and if any come to them upon any occasion they request them to come in, if they come not in themselves."[35] Williams experienced this kindness firsthand, for, without the generosity of the Narragansett during the "sorrowful Winters flight" after his banishment, he might well have perished.[36]

The revolutionary vision of an all-inclusive society was voiced by Thomas Jefferson and the founders in the declaration "that all men are created equal." These words, however, struck Hannah Lee Corbin as insufficiently representative, given that the self-evident truth of human equality did not extend to women. The Lees were a prominent Virginia family of the planter aristocracy and members of the established Episcopal Church. When her husband died, Hannah, as a widow, was legally prohibited from inheriting her husband's estate. She received no sympathy or support from her sister Alice, who apparently had "a mean opinion of the Babtist [sic] religion," to which Hannah had converted.[37] Her appeal was met with a more receptive hearing from her brother, Richard Henry Lee, a delegate of the Second Continental Congress and a signatory of the Declaration of Independence. Hannah made her case for the rights of widows, even arguing in favor of women's suffrage.[38] The call of fidelity to the vision of a good society combined with openness to a widening in the scope of participation has created a constant tension and struggle. The hopes of this lively experiment found expression in the First Amendment to the Constitution of the United States, which acclaimed that "Congress shall

[35] Williams, *A Key into the Language of America*, in *Complete Writings*, 1:96.

[36] Williams, *Mr. Cotton's Letter Lately Printed, Examined and Answered*, in *Complete Writings*, 1:315.

[37] Hannah Lee to Her Sister Alice, in *Stratford Hall: The Great House of the Lees*, ed. Ethel Armes (Richmond, Va.: Garrett & Massie, 1936), 205.

[38] Richard Henry Lee, Letter to Hannah Lee Corbin (March 17, 1778), in *The Letters of Richard Henry Lee*, ed. James Curtis Ballagh, 2 vols. (New York: Macmillan, 1911–1914), 1:392–93. Lee replied that he saw no reason to prohibit widows that owned property from voting, even though there was no precedent in England or America.

make no law respecting an establishment of religion, or prohibiting the free exercise thereof."[39] It made space in America for both church and dissent, communal goods and individual differences.

There is no evidence that Thomas Jefferson or James Madison drew from the writings of Williams or the Rhode Island experiment in producing the basic documents of American democracy.[40] But when Jefferson and Madison introduced state and federal legislation protecting religious liberty for all, they had strong support from the Baptists, Presbyterians, and other dissenters, who thrived without state support.[41] As this Jeffersonian-Madisonian doctrine got parsed out, individuals were free to make up their own minds about religion. Civil magistrates could not compel worship or require support for churches. Everyone was entitled to an opinion about religion, and the right to this opinion was held to be "unalienable," entitling each individual to follow the dictates of conscience. Churches, or "voluntary societies" as Jefferson (following Locke) called them, were free to determine the criteria for membership and fellowship, but these requirements were binding on members only. Every person had a constitutionally protected right to hold private religious ideas and beliefs, but public expression of those ideas and beliefs, particularly when expressed

[39] Amendments to the Constitution of the United States of America, Amendment 1. The application of the First Amendment to the states has a complicated and contested history, which was settled somewhat in the mid-twentieth century. See T. Jeremy Gunn, "The Separation of Church and State versus Religion in the Public Square: The Contested History of the Establishment Clause," in *No Establishment of Religion: America's Original Contribution to Religious Liberty*, ed. T. Jeremy Gunn and John Witte Jr. (New York: Oxford University Press, 2012), 15–44.

[40] Perry Miller, "Roger Williams: An Essay in Interpretation," in Williams, *Complete Writings*, 7:10; and William G. McLoughlin, *New England Dissent, 1630–1833*, 2 vols. (Cambridge, Mass.: Harvard University Press, 1971), 1:8.

[41] Thomas Jefferson, A Bill for Establishing Religious Freedom, published in 1777 but not approved by the Virginia legislature until 1786, in *The Papers of Thomas Jefferson*, vol. 2, *1777 to June 18, 1779*, ed. Julian P. Boyd (Princeton, N.J.: Princeton University Press, 1950), 545–47; and James Madison, The Bill of Rights, Amendments 1–10 of the U. S. Constitution, ratified in 1791. For Madison's thinking on religious liberty, see "Memorial and Remonstrance against Religious Assessment" (June 20, 1785), in *The Papers of James Madison*, vol. 8, *March 10, 1784 to March 28, 1786*, ed. Robert E. Rutland and William M. E. Rachal (Chicago: University of Chicago Press, 1984), 295–306.

in association with others, was limited and subject to regulation. Yet Jefferson was deeply suspicious of the apocalyptic imagination of dissenters, describing the visions of the book of Revelation as "merely the ravings of a maniac, no more worthy nor capable of explanation than the incoherences of our own nightly dreams."[42] Like his hero Locke and the English Whigs, Jefferson sought to draw support from religious dissenters while at the same time seeking to domesticate their enthusiasm. The upshot of his account was to authorize the government to restrict *public* but not *private* religion.

With the passing of the Bill of Rights, Americans saw the world as they knew it come to an end and a new world come into being. They were no less the children of John Winthrop, who imagined his covenanted community as "a city upon a hill," than they were the spiritual offspring of Roger Williams, who favored religious liberty for all people including "Papists, Protestants, Jews, and Turks."[43] But as the experiment has grown livelier over the years, the sense of a shared errand seems ever more distant and the perception of religious experience increasingly individualistic. Yet this new account, though incorporating protections of liberty, did not come without a price. What earlier generations of English nonconformists understood as a *common matter* shared by all "experienced Christians" became a *private matter* increasingly enigmatic to others.[44] This view of religion as a private experience of individuals in their solitude is no longer a contested

---

[42] Thomas Jefferson, Letter to Alexander Smyth (January 17, 1825), in *The Writings of Thomas Jefferson*, 20 vols. (Washington, D.C.: Taylor & Maury, 1854), 7:395. Jefferson expressed no confidence or interest in the religion or literature of the Apocalypse: "I cannot so far respect them as to consider them as an allegorical narrative of events, past or subsequent. There is not coherence enough in them to countenance any suite of rational ideas. You will judge, therefore, from this how impossible I think it that either your exploration, or that of any man in 'the heavens above, or on the earth beneath,' can be a correct one. What has no meaning admits no explanation; and pardon me if I say, with the candor of friendship, that I think your time too valuable, and your understanding of too high an order, to be wasted on these paralogisms."

[43] Roger Williams, "Ship of State Letter, to the Town of Providence" (January 1654/55), in *The Correspondence of Roger Williams*, ed. Glenn W. LaFantasie (Hanover, N.H.: University Press of New England, 1988), 2:423–24.

[44] See "The Experience of Grace" in chap. 2, pp. 55–62.

concept. It is an unquestioned presupposition.[45] Membership in voluntary associations (once thought to be crucial to the flourishing of robust communities of virtue, what Tocqueville called "habits of the heart") is on decline, leading to the erosion of civic life and social disengagement.[46] It is a loss with roots in the decline of the Winthropian vision of the common good combined with the Jeffersonian stress on individual religion. As a result of this emphasis on privacy, Americans have lost touch with the value of their interdependence on one another.[47] With such emphasis on privacy and so little consciousness of common goods, the notion of dissent would seem to be tenuous if not incoherent, for, if all experience is unique, every personal experience might reasonably be understood as dissent, or at least the grounds of dissent, from the experiences of others. And with so little sense of a common life, the basic practices of democracy that undergirded the American experiment would now seem to be in question.

BELOVED COMMUNITY—KINGDOM OF GOD

Mather's *Magnalia* registered bewilderment, confusion, and chagrin that the mission to establish a city on a hill before a watching world was yet unrealized, but there was no surrender in its summons.[48] Its narrative laments the gradual declension from the godliness that he believed marked the founders, and thus it tells the story of a failed errand. Yet like the jeremiad tradition upon which he drew, Mather invited his audience not only to engage in the cathartic purge of their

[45] William James, *Varieties of Religious Experience* (New York: Collins, 1960), 50.

[46] Tocqueville coined the phrase "the habits of the heart" to describe "the whole moral and intellectual condition of a people." Alexis de Tocqueville, *Democracy in America*, trans. Phillips Bradley (New York: Vintage, 1945), 310. Robert Putnam famously suggested that the erosion of civic life and social disengagement is nowhere more evident than in the fact that, from 1980 to 1993, the total number of people bowling in the United States increased by 10 percent, but the number of people involved in league bowling decreased by 40 percent. Putnam, "Bowling Alone: America's Declining Social Capital," *Journal of Democracy* 6, no. 1 (1995): 65–78.

[47] Bellah et al., *Habits of the Heart*, 142–63; Bellah et al., *Good Society*; and Barry Alan Shain, *The Myth of American Individualism: The Protestant Origins of American Political Thought* (Princeton, N.J.: Princeton University Press, 1994), 10–11.

[48] Miller, *Errand into the Wilderness*, 15.

many failings but to ponder the history of America and behold in it the wondrous works of God. His chronicle attends to the blessing that rested on the first generation who journeyed across the Atlantic to settle in a wilderness land, but its focus is on the continued wonders of providence, which he thought signified that the blessing did not depart from subsequent generations despite their unfaithfulness to God's promise. The pages of its "history" are crowded with accounts of "remarkables" that testify to God's unfailing presence and call for subsequent generations of Americans to declare that they have come thus far by the Lord's help. Mather's *Magnalia* might well be described as an Ebenezer (1 Sam 7:12), raised as a memorial to American civil religion.[49] Yet his calls for greater reformation went largely unheeded, and, as his hope of ongoing reform was unrealized, Mather's focus became increasingly otherworldly. Still, his vision was grounded in the conviction that the greatest challenges ahead lay not in the wilderness itself but within the collective soul of its people, thus linking the question of national identity with the pursuit of national mission. The upshot of such self-reflection over time was that the pressing question became less a determination about why the American errand failed and more a matter of asking how it might be fulfilled anew.

Popular perceptions of the puritan errand stem less from Mather's tendentious narrative than from the domesticated myth proliferated in Felicia Dorothea Hemans' highly anthologized poem "The Landing of the Pilgrim Fathers," which was commonly read and recited in American classrooms and churches through the mid-twentieth century. Hemans' romanticized elegy praises the New England colonists for seeking not "the wealth of seas" or "the spoils of war" but "faith's pure shrine." It concludes with these lines:

---

[49] John Higginson, Attestation, in Mather, *Magnalia Christi Americana*, A2. The reference to "civil religion" is deliberate and follows the basic definition of Bellah as a religion of ethical principles that transcends the nation and is differentiated from the religion of churches, synagogues, and mosques. Robert N. Bellah, "Civil Religion in America," in *Beyond Belief: Essays on Religion in a Post-traditionalist World* (Berkeley: University of California Press, 1991), 168.

They have left unstain'd what there they found—
Freedom to worship God.[50]

Such an astounding assertion would no doubt have come as a surprise to Roger Williams, Anne Hutchinson, or Mary Dyer, who suffered for their religious convictions at the hands of those very Christians that sought a more pure faith, not to mention the indigenous people, whose blood stained the soil claimed by the colonies. Contrary to this idealized account, the legacy of the puritan founders was not the gift of religious liberty but a prophetic vision of the kingdom of God that stood above and sometimes against the American dream.[51] Yet Mather's vision of a new world, even though fixed on seeking the kingdom of God in history, was too restrictive to include those who differed. Subsequent voices of American civil religion like Jefferson and Madison questioned the failure to create a good society implicit in the founding mission and to imagine a new world with liberty *for all*. Their account expanded the lively experiment of Rhode Island envisioned by Roger Williams and other dissenters, creating space for soul freedom on a national scale. But even their version of the American dream, despite its more inclusive scope, still fell short, failing to make room for all.

In his oration delivered on December 22, 1820, at the Plymouth bicentennial, Daniel Webster, an influential statesman and an eloquent

---

[50] Felicia Dorothea Hemans, "The Landing of the Pilgrim Fathers in New England," in *The Poetical Works of Mrs. Hemans* (London: Frederick Warne, n.d.), 491. Though this idealized account of the American story has been shown to be more hagiography than history, it has been propagated in this immensely popular book by Peter Marshall and David Manuel: *The Light and the Glory* (Old Tappan, N.J.: Revell, 1977). Marshall and Manuel offer their jeremiad based on a revisionist account, arguing that America was founded as a Christian nation with a special calling from God to be a light to the world. They contend that though it has fallen away and forgotten its mission, America can return to God and embrace God's plan. More recently, Eric Metaxas perpetuates the myth of a Christian America when he states that "since the Pilgrims came to our shores in 1620, religious freedom and religious tolerance have been the single most important principle of American life." Metaxas, *If You Can Keep It: The Forgotten Promise of American Liberty* (New York: Viking, 2016), 70.

[51] H. Richard Niebuhr, *The Kingdom of God in America* (New York: Harper & Row, 1937; repr., Middletown, Conn.: Wesleyan University Press, 1988), 10.

rhetorician, drew from the jeremiad tradition to reexamine the national mission. His speech, like those in a long line before it, suggested that America was chosen as a heavenly instrument for a historic purpose. Near the conclusion, Webster declared,

> We are bound to maintain public liberty, and, by example of our own systems, to convince the world that order and law, religion and morality, the rights of conscience, the rights of persons, the rights of property, may all be preserved and secured, in the most perfect manner, by a government purely elective.[52]

Failure, he argued, would support the argument that government can rest only on power and control. Webster's vision reached back to earlier voices like Winthrop, Williams, and Jefferson, but he also looked forward, pointing to a larger problem that had to be addressed—the African slave trade. Describing the slave trader as "a pirate and a felon" and "an offender far beyond the ordinary depth of human guilt," Webster called on Americans to cooperate with the laws of humanity and the justice of heaven to abolish this abominable practice.[53] His appeal rose to a crescendo, urging that the land of the pilgrims could bear this shame no longer. He drew his listeners to hear the sounds of the hammer and the smoke of the furnaces that forge the manacles and fetters for human limbs. He exclaimed that he could see the faces of those who "by stealth and at midnight labor in this work of hell, foul and dark, as may become the artifices of such instruments of misery and torture."[54] And he urged them to purify this spot and to "let it be put out of the circle of human sympathies and human regards, and let civilized [hu]man[ity] have no communion with it."[55] It was a powerful and persuasive petition. Yet Webster himself grew weary in the mission, later turning his back on abolitionists as extremists and radicals.[56]

---

[52] Webster, "First Settlement of New England," in *The Works of Daniel Webster*, 6 vols. (Boston: Charles C. Little & James Brown, 1851), 1:44–45. See also Craig R. Smith, *Daniel Webster and the Oratory of Civil Religion* (Columbia: University of Missouri Press, 2005), 57–63.

[53] Webster, *Works of Daniel Webster*, 1:45.

[54] Webster, *Works of Daniel Webster*, 1:46.

[55] Webster, *Works of Daniel Webster*, 1:46.

[56] Webster, "The Constitution and the Union," Speech to Congress, Washington, D.C. (March 7, 1850), in *Works of Daniel Webster*, 5:331–32.

Fulfilling the errand so that the covenant extended to all people regardless of race led to "a great civil war." The call "to finish the work" and "to bind up the nation's wounds" after its apocalyptic struggle issued from the mouth of an odd sort of prophet, the unchurched son of a hardshell Baptist layman named Abraham Lincoln.[57] Like others before him, he was a voice crying to prepare a way in the wilderness. Yet the way was not prepared, nor the work finished, and almost a century passed before another prophet suddenly appeared like a root out of dry ground from the American South. He continued the call to fulfill the errand and bring about a new reformation for civil rights, which began not by nailing ninety-five theses on the great door of a grand castle church but by addressing an overflow crowd at a commodious sanctuary in a run-down section of town. On the evening of December 5, 1955, when at the unlikely age of twenty-six Martin Luther King Jr. stepped onto pulpit of the Holt Street Baptist Church in Montgomery, Alabama, he gave voice to a movement of tired and weary souls "reaching out for the daybreak of freedom and justice and equality." It was the end of the world, and the beginning of a new one. King began by addressing the assembly as "American citizens" who have a "love for democracy," but he reminded them that "the great glory of American democracy is the right to protest for right." Even those who knew him were amazed at his prophetic transformation that evening. Yet he did not stand alone. He stood with Rosa Parks and all the folks who were "tired of being trampled over by the iron feet of oppression." But he also stood in a long line of dissenters like John Bunyan, Daniel Defoe, William Blake, and the unnamed and unremembered who also knew what it meant to be "tired of going through the long night of captivity."[58]

[57] Abraham Lincoln, Second Inaugural Address (March 4, 1865), in *The Collected Works of Abraham Lincoln*, ed. Roy P. Basle (New Brunswick, N.J.: Rutgers University Press, 1953), 8:332–33; Mark A. Noll, *America's God: From Jonathan Edwards to Abraham Lincoln* (New York: Oxford University Press, 2002), 427–28.

[58] Martin Luther King Jr., MIA Mass Meeting at Holt Street Baptist Church Montgomery, Ala. (December 5, 1955), in *King Online Encyclopedia*, http://kingencyclopedia.stanford.edu/encyclopedia/documentsentry/mia_mass_meeting_at_holt_street_baptist_church/ (accessed June 22, 2016); and Richard Lischer, *The*

One of the enduring images King infused into the American consciousness was "the beloved community," a lovely phrase he borrowed from the philosopher Josiah Royce.[59] It was a vision of a new world to come after the passing of the old one. In King's imagination, the beloved community was a reality that would emerge as a result of nonviolent action. Its means is love, and its end is reconciliation and redemption.[60] But the weapons aimed at defeating the evil forces of segregation and creating the conditions for the coming of the beloved community were human, not divine. King began to question such an idealistic outlook, which failed to grasp the human tendency and capacity for evil. In his chastened imagination, the beloved community was replaced by the kingdom of God, which envisioned God's transformational activity that lies hidden behind the veil of history.[61] One of the most powerful moments of this prophetic vision came in his address before the Lincoln Memorial on August 28, 1963, at the March on Washington, where he told about his dream of a new age. There he stood with Danforth and Lincoln, calling America to finish the errand, "to hew out of the mountain of despair a stone of hope."[62] But on other occasions he stood with Bunyan and Blake, where his vision of the New Jerusalem was preceded by a glimpse of Beulah land, in which, like the prophet Moses, he ascended to the mountaintop, looked over, and saw the promised land of freedom, knowing that he might not

Preacher King: Martin Luther King Jr. and the Word That Moved America (New York: Oxford University Press, 1995), 85–89.

[59] Josiah Royce, _The Problem of Christianity_, 2 vols. (New York: Macmillan, 1913), 1:xxv, 172–73, 183, 278, 299, 344–45, 347, 350, 351–52, 356, 359–60, 400, 406–7, 410. See also Gary Herstein, "The Roycean Roots of the Beloved Community," _Pluralist_ 4, no. 2 (2009): 91–107.

[60] See King, "The Power of Nonviolence" and "An Experiment of Love," in _A Testament of Hope: The Essential Writings and Speeches of Martin Luther King, Jr._, ed. James Melvin Washington (San Francisco: HarperCollins, 1986), 12, 18.

[61] Martin Luther King Jr., "Pilgrimage to Nonviolence," in _Testament of Hope_, 35–40; and Lischer, _Preacher King_, 234.

[62] Martin Luther King Jr., "I Have a Dream," in _Testament of Hope_, 219. David L. Chappell takes this eschatological image to capture the outlook and philosophy of the civil rights movement. Chappell, _Stone of Hope: Prophetic Religion and the Death of Jim Crow_ (Chapel Hill: University of North Carolina Press, 2004), 1.

get there but that God's people would enter that place of rest.[63] King's apocalyptically illumined consciousness became the source of his prophetically awakened conscience. It was this eschatological imagination, so prominent in the tradition of dissenting Christians, that refreshed the religious cup of meaning that had been slowly draining away for generations. Yet not all apocalyptically guided imaginations have inspired such a transformational social vision.

There seems to be something about the tradition of dissent that is easily drawn to the extremist features of eschatology. And there is good reason to worry that this apocalyptic vision can run amok as it misled those militant Anabaptists in 1534 to insist that Münster was the New Jerusalem, or the Fifth Monarchy movement to believe that their revolt in 1661 would hasten the return of King Jesus, or Nat Turner's visions of the apocalypse that resulted in the 1831 slave revolt in Southampton, Virginia, or William Miller's disappointing predictions of the cleansing of the earth in 1843, or J. N. Darby's dispensational scheme and inventive rapture teaching that propagated the great premillennial myth and spawned exuberant apocalyptic speculation. All of these attempts to project the eschatological timetable have one thing in common: they were wrong. Yet there is a bigger problem: their millennial schemes are full of apocalyptic content, but they lack an ethical mandate. Everything in the apocalyptic vision gets pushed into the future to the end of history. This diminished sense of the ethical may be one reason why so many of these apocalyptic visions are imminently squeezed into the present. For millennialists, eschatology is all about the things that come last, but it has nothing to say about the things that last in the here and now. It was the anarchic expression of the eschatological imagination that Bunyan sought to transform by turning inward to the struggle of the soul. But this evangelical move has too often produced an ethically domesticated dissent that is socially indifferent, doing nothing to lift the prophetic gaze to the masses of the poor, the marginalized, and the disinherited with whom Jesus identified.[64]

---

[63] Martin Luther King Jr., "I See the Promised Land," in *Testament of Hope*, 286.

[64] Social gospel theologians commonly criticized dispensationalism as socially pessimistic. Timothy P. Weber, *Living in the Shadow of the Second Coming: American*

As a Baptist preacher, King was deeply influenced by evangelical conversion theology that grew out of the Bunyan tradition, but
he recognized that a religion based on individual salvation had too
few resources to resist evil or to struggle for justice. He was initially
drawn to the social gospel, which called for the present social order "to
transform human society into the kingdom of God by regenerating all
human relations and reconstituting them in accordance with the will
of God."[65] The social gospel was particularly critical of millennialism,
which applied the kingdom of God exclusively to the future and not to
the present.[66] Its theological outlook stressed that the kingdom of God
is the highest ideal for human life and looked to modern democracy as
offering the best mechanisms and institutions to Christianize the social
order.[67] But the social gospel was also biased against the apocalyptic
vision, which was regarded as "unreal, unhistorical, and mechanical,"
and even dangerous.[68] The eschatology of the social gospel did enable

---

Premillennialism, 1875–1925 (Chicago: University of Chicago Press, 1987), 65–66.
Southern Presbyterians were critical of dispensationalism, characterizing it as socially
irresponsible, particularly on the issue of racial segregation. R. Todd Mangum, *The
Dispensational-Covenantal Rift: The Fissuring of American Evangelical Theology from
1936 to 1944* (Milton Keynes: Paternoster, 2007), 104. Feminist theologian Catherine
Keller makes similar observations about the social implications of dispensationalism.
Keller, *Apocalypse Now and Then* (Minneapolis: Fortress, 2005), 63. Tony Campolo put
the matter sharply: "The implication of dispensationalism is that there is no point to
working toward peace, social justice, the end of poverty, and the like, on the basis that
such projects are ultimately futile. John Nelson Darby, Tim LaHaye, Jerry Jenkins
all emphasize that the church should not engage in such tasks. The church, they say,
should concentrate all of its efforts on one thing—getting people 'saved.' Converting
people so that they are ready for the rapture is all that matters to them. They argue
that preachers who call the church to work for justice on behalf of the poor and
oppressed are, at best, wasting their time and, at worst, leading people into erroneous
secular humanism. They argue that social-gospel preachers can be accused, whether
they realize it or not, of being agents of the anti-Christ." Campolo, *Letters to a Young
Evangelical* (Philadelphia: Basic Books, 2006), 112.

[65] Walter Rauschenbusch, *Christianity and the Social Crisis* (New York: Macmillan, 1907), xxxvii.

[66] Walter Rauschenbusch, *A Theology for the Social Gospel* (New York: Macmillan,
1917), 211.

[67] Walter Rauschenbusch, *Christianizing the Social Order* (New York: Macmillan,
1913), 83.

[68] Rauschenbusch, *Theology for the Social Gospel*, 216.

Christians to grapple with the eternal realities that last, though it was little concerned about the things that come last. Bigger still, social gospelers, no less than millennial evangelicals, seemed to have things neatly figured out, identifying the kingdom of God with democracy. Yet, as King observed, these progressive dreams could not deal with the human capacity to inflict brutality and violence, especially against the sons and daughters of earth who came out of Africa.[69]

But when it comes to the vision of the future, the eschatological outlook of both millennialism and the social gospel proved to be inversely inadequate. What one lacks in ethical content, it makes up in apocalyptic realism, and what is absent in the other with respect to apocalyptic fullness is offset in ethical richness.[70] Despite these shortcomings, millennialists and social gospelers glimpsed something of lasting significance in their vision of the future, even if both failed to grasp the nature of what and how they were seeing. King perceived these deficiencies and desired an eschatological vision that was both apocalyptically full and ethically rich.[71] An example of the sort of synthetic vision King described was tested out by Clarence Jordan, an obscure Baptist farmer-preacher, who in 1942 established an interracial community in southwest Georgia called Koinonia Farm as "a demonstration plot for the Kingdom of God."[72] The Koinonia community

[69] King, "Pilgrimage to Nonviolence," in *Testament of Hope*, 37.

[70] I have adapted this schematic of apocalyptic fullness and ethical richness from Cyril O'Regan, *Theology and the Spaces of Apocalyptic* (Milwauke, Wis.: Marquette University Press, 2009).

[71] King expressed that his preferred outlook would be a synthesis between neoorthodoxy and liberalism. Though he never moved in this direction, he surely knew that theologians at Yale Divinity School and Union Theological Seminary were already gesturing toward a "new and chastened liberalism." Robert L. Calhoun, "A Liberal Bandaged but Unbowed," *Christian Century*, May 31, 1939, 701–4; and William Hordern, "Young Theologians Rebel," *Christian Century*, March 12, 1952, 306–7.

[72] Andrew S. Chancey, "'A Demonstration Plot for the Kingdom of God': The Establishment and Early Years of Koinonia Farm," *Georgia Historical Quarterly* 75, no. 2 (1991): 321–53; and Dallas Lee, *The Cotton Patch Evidence* (New York: Harper & Row, 1971), 19–34. Koinonia Farm was an intentional Christian community committed to living faithfully to the radical reality of God's economy. In 1968 a new plan led to the expansion that was named Koinonia Partners. Habitat for Humanity was founded in 1976 by Koinonia partners Millard and Linda Fuller, who applied the economic

sought to make a life together following the postapocalyptic pattern of the early church in the book of Acts where all things were held in common, distribution was according to need, and there was complete equality and freedom regardless of race. Rather than the traditional language of the "Kingdom of God," Jordan typically referred to "the God Movement," which he understood as a radical transcending and transforming work of God in the world, and he looked to the Sermon on the Mount as the manifesto of the movement.[73] Jordan maintained that being part of the God Movement was not simply a matter of "getting saved" or engaging in "social action." He considered the religion of do-good liberals as deficient as the faith of feel-good evangelicals. What the gospel demands, Jordan declaimed, is to become "participants in the faith, not merely spectators."[74] Participating in the God Movement requires joining up in a process that is already ongoing, bearing in mind that the kingdom of God is always *at hand* but never fully *in hand*.[75]

Jordan produced a colloquial translation of the New Testament with a Southern accent, which he appropriately called *The Cotton Patch Version*. He gave his rendering of the book of Ephesians the title *The Letter to the Christians in Birmingham*, an allusion to King's well-known "Letter from Birmingham Jail."[76] Jordan's lesser-known *Letter* addressed black Christians in Birmingham, where four young

---

principles of the God Movement to the alleviation of poverty housing, beginning in Sumter, County Georgia. Millard Fuller, *No More Shacks* (Waco, Tex.: Word, 1986). The vision of life together at Koinonia Farm differed significantly from the brief utopic community of Brook Farm, founded by George Ripley in 1841 just outside of Boston. The Brook Farm experiment was brief, collapsing in 1847, in large measure because it failed to enact a sense of life shared by all members that was present in Koinonia. Sterling Delano, *Brook Farm: The Dark Side of Utopia* (Cambridge, Mass.: Harvard University Press, 2009).

[73] Clarence Jordan, "The God Movement," in *The Substance of Faith and Other Cotton Patch Sermons*, ed. Dallas Lee (Eugene, Ore.: Cascade, 2005), 57–99.

[74] Clarence Jordan, introduction to *The Cotton Patch Version of Paul's Epistles* (New York: Association Press, 1968), 7.

[75] Christopher Morse, *The Difference Heaven Makes: Rehearing the Gospel as News* (London: T&T Clark, 2010), 6.

[76] Martin Luther King Jr., "Letter from Birmingham Jail" (1963), in *Testament of Hope*, 289–302.

girls at the Sixteenth Street Baptist Church had been killed by a white supremacist. He reminded them that though they had been denied their rights by supposed believers (like Bull Connor, the local commissioner of public safety) and treated as if the gospel did not apply to them, God had changed the world in Christ. Jordan exclaimed that God had integrated humanity "and abolished the segregation patterns which caused so much hostility" (Eph 2:16). The "secret" that God revealed in Christ, Jordan continued, "is that the Negroes are fellow partners and equal members, co-sharers in the privileges of the gospel of Jesus Christ" (Eph 3:6).[77] The hermeneutical vision Jordan deployed is dipolar, holding together two vectors of sight, past and future, in one field: "this is that," a sense that those participating in the God Movement are an apostolic community in which the commands of Jesus are addressed to contemporary believers; and "then is now," a conviction that the God Movement is an end-time people, a new humanity anticipating the consummation of the blessed hope.[78]

For Jordan, as for King, the life, death, and resurrection of Jesus Christ marked the end beyond the ends of history. Ages come and go, but there is an end toward which all things move. And, in seeing the world from the end, they were able to envision the present age that was passing away (1 Cor 7:31) and the new creation that would endure (Gal 6:15). This was good news. It meant that God had delivered the world from the destructive forces that otherwise would have determined humanity for ruin, that the human race was not fated to live in bondage to the forces of racial prejudice, because humanity has been freed from the powers to live freely and fully in the world made new through Jesus Christ, though the struggle continues against the forces that resist the coming of the new creation. The glittering images of this vision cannot

---

[77] Jordan, *Cotton Patch Version of Paul's Epistles*, 107–8.

[78] McClendon, *Ethics*, 30; and James Wm. McClendon Jr., *Doctrine: Systematic Theology*, vol. 2 (Waco, Tex.: Baylor University Press, 2012), 45–46. McClendon treated Jordan as an exemplar of this hermeneutical theory he would later call "the baptist vision," deliberately utilizing the lower case "b" to denote its application to the wide range of baptist groups in the Free Church Protestant tradition, which in this study have been called Protestant dissenters or nonconformists. McClendon, *Biography as Theology: How Life Stories Can Remake Today's Theology* (Nashville: Abingdon, 1974), 112–39.

be plotted out on millennial charts or reduced to universal moral principles. It can be lived out only through incarnate faithfulness. It is an old lesson that has sustained the faithful for millennia, but it must be relearned and renewed. When the Goths sacked Rome on August 24, 410, it anticipated the ending of the age of Roman Christianity, but, in the prophetic imagination of Christians like Augustine of Hippo, it was neither a sign of the coming apocalypse nor the end of the Christian era. For, beyond the temporal age, they saw the New Jerusalem and the hand of providence bringing history to its appointed end.[79] Living faithfully in this earthly pilgrimage requires the sense of an ending full enough to disclose what endures beyond the fall of empires and the passing of ages. It demands attending to *what lasts* by seeing *what comes last*.[80] For only a vision that perceives the end of history in resurrection light can imagine a world beyond the end.

CONVICTION, CONSCIENCE, COMMUNITY

The narrative of this book has traversed the globe, following the message of dissent as it spread through the life and literature it produced. The story now returns where it began, at Bunhill Fields in London, where Bunyan, Defoe, and Blake lie together in memoriam with the cloud of witnesses that surround them. Yet they are also linked with the many in other places where the vision of dissent inspired the hopes and dreams of those who have struggled for liberty and against tyranny. These three are not simply creative authors of important literary works whose roots can be traced to earlier dissenters. They are themselves voices of the basic beliefs and convictions of a historic tradition and are, indeed, significant agents of its transmission and dissemination. The story told here is not narrowly about the reception of Bunyan, Defoe, and Blake. Rather, it shows how the message of dissent was welcomed in societies around the world, especially where the bloody tenet of persecution was supported by state and church. But it was particularly suited for the emergent democracy of America. There,

---

[79] Augustine, *City of God*, 15.20, trans. Henry Bettenson (New York: Penguin Books, 1984), 630.
[80] McClendon, *Doctrine*, 75.

the convictions of dissent gave expression to the founding vision and continued to exert influence on its development throughout history, calling for the inclusion of all to share in its liberties and privileges. Some would even argue that dissent in America has fueled the engines of progress.[81] Yet apocalypticism is not only the origin of democracy. As the powers that be rightly worried, it is also a source of anarchy. The lingering question that remains is whether the voices of dissent still have valuable contributions to make to the completion of the errand and the extension of the experiment.

The heirs of historic communities of dissent seeking to further the ongoing reception of their tradition would do well to focus on telling the Christian story from the standpoint of their identifying *convictions* of dissent.[82] In particular they might begin by recovering a rich and textured account of what it has meant for dissenting Christians to confess Jesus as Lord. For generations of dissenters, this confession had radically political implications that forced them to determine the obligations of their loyalty to Christ and the limits of their allegiance to king, unlike Christians in established churches for whom such clarification was not a pressing matter. In telling the Christian story, dissenters learned to see their lives in continuity with the lives of the apostles and martyrs for whom the baptismal confession that "Jesus is Lord" (Rom 10:9-10) was rooted in the conviction that Jesus, not Caesar, is king.[83] They identified with stories, like the apostle John con-

---

[81] Ralph Young, *Dissent: The History of an American Idea* (New York: New York University Press, 2015), 522. Young's claim that dissent has fueled social progress in America seems more about the social value of contrarian points of view, whatever those may be, than the tradition of religious dissent traced out in these chapters.

[82] Here, I am using the term "conviction" in a technical way, as "a persistent belief such that if X (a person or community) has a conviction, it will not easily be relinquished and it cannot be relinquished without making X a significantly different person (or community) than before." James Wm. McClendon Jr. and James M. Smith, *Convictions: Defusing Religious Relativism*, rev. ed. (Valley Forge, Penn.: Trinity International, 1994). 5; and McClendon, *Ethics*, 22–23.

[83] In the tradition of English dissent, Foxe's *Book of Martyrs* was widely read and conveyed this narrative. For the connection of the confession of "Jesus as Lord" and Christian baptism, see Gregory Dix and Henry Chadwick, eds., *The Apostolic Tradition of St. Hippolytus*, 2nd ed. (London: Alban, 1992), xxi.12–18; 36–37; and John Norman Davidson Kelly, *Early Christian Creeds*, 3rd ed. (New York: Longman, 1972), 113–19.

fronting Emperor Domitian at the imperial court with the declaration that Christ would return in judgment to reign as the true king over all the people of the earth. And they were challenged by the faithfulness of John, who survived a cauldron of boiling oil, a cup of deadly poison, and exile on the island of Patmos.[84] Such stories served as models to those who confess Jesus as Lord of what it might mean to be faithful even unto death.[85]

The importance of learning to tell the Christian story in this way gave Christian leaders like Martin Luther King and Clarence Jordan strength and insight to resist the powers of segregation. But it also inspired fifteen-year-old Carolyn McKinstry and thousands of other young people like her to march down the front steps of the Sixteenth Street Baptist Church in Birmingham, Alabama, and across the street to Kelly Ingram Park on May 2, 1963, where they were met by Bull Connor ordering them to "Go home!" Even when they were blasted with water cannons, beaten with batons, and attacked with dogs, they stood their ground, singing over and over:

Oh, freedom!
Oh, freedom!
Oh, freedom over me!
And before I'd be a slave

---

[84] James A. Kelhoffer, *Miracle and Mission: The Authentication of Missionaries and Their Message in the Longer Ending of Mark* (Tübingen: Mohr Siebeck, 2000), 459–65. It is an amazing story of resisting the powers—maybe even a little too amazing, given that the fourth-to-fifth century account from the *Acts of John in Rome* contains echoes of the longer ending of the Gospel of Mark about drinking deadly poison and healing the sick as miraculous signs of the apostolic preaching (Mark 16:18). But, in a more basic sense, the story fits the warning that Jesus had given the apostles: that they would "be dragged before governors and kings" because of him, "as a testimony to them and the Gentiles" (Matt 10:18). Yet the story of John appearing before Domitian rings true to other accounts like the apostle Paul's trial before Herod Agrippa II as told in the Acts of the Apostles (Acts 26). That John first survived being boiled in oil before drinking poison is told by John Foxe, in *The Acts and Monuments of John Foxe: A New and Complete Edition*, ed. Stephen Reed Cattley, 7 vols. (London: Seeley & Burnside, 1837–1841), 1:104–5.

[85] Karl Barth, *The Christian Life, Church Dogmatics*, IV/4, Lecture Fragments (Grand Rapids: Eerdmans, 1981), §78.

I'll be buried in my grave
And go home to my Lord and be free.

Though some might wonder what gave them strength to stand up to tanks, dogs, and cannons, it is no mystery. It was just the natural thing to do. They were simply following Jesus as they had learned in telling the story. It was their shared conviction.[86]

Yet something significant has changed that makes the retrieval of the dissenting tradition more pressing. From Cotton Mather to Martin Luther King, the prevailing assumption has been that completing the errand would somehow further the christianization of America. Even dissenters from Roger Williams to John Leland believed that extending the lively experiment would foster the thriving of religious communities that had been suppressed. It is now clear that the cultural establishment of Christianity in America, which held sway for so long, is now weakening as the number of Christians continues to decline and the ranks of the nonreligious grow.[87] But this development is not an isolated phenomenon. It is part of the wider process of secularization that has settled over the cultures in the global North, resulting not simply in the legal separation of church and state or even the cultural decline of Christianity but in a reality where faith is simply "one human possibility among others."[88] Secularization is bringing an end to a world where

---

[86] Carolyn McKinstry, *While the World Watched: A Birmingham Bombing Survivor Comes of Age during the Civil Rights Movement* (Carol Stream, Ill.: Tyndale House, 2011), 130–45.

[87] "America's Changing Religious Landscape," Pew Research Center (May 12, 2015), http://www.pewforum.org/2015/05/12/americas-changing-religious-landscape/ (accessed July 12, 2013). For a thick account on the changing social arrangements of Christianity in America, see Robert Wuthnow, *The Restructuring of American Religion* (Princeton, N.J.: Princeton University Press, 1988).

[88] Charles Taylor, *A Secular Age* (Cambridge, Mass.: Belknap, 2007), 1–3. The secular age is not characterized by unbelief. Rather, it is a world where a shared belief structure is no longer the default position of the whole society. All beliefs are contested and contestable. For a constructive engagement with Taylor's account of the secular age, see James K. A. Smith, *How (Not) to Be Secular: Reading Charles Taylor* (Grand Rapids: Eerdmans, 2014). Harvey Cox, a Baptist dissenter, much earlier came to terms with Taylor's first two stages of secularization. Drawing from Bonhoeffer's vision of a "religionless Christianity" in a "world come of age," Cox predicted that secularization would eventually marginalize religion, but he suggested that Christians

Christianity, though legally disestablished, is still culturally dominant. This emerging secular age will not be void of religion, but it will be a time when faith is a radical optional. In such a context, the church will be a minority presence. Yet, even in a secular age, it is conceivable that the faith can flourish through vital communities of believers. In this way, the habits of dissent could become an important ecumenical strategy, not merely a sectarian tactic. Retelling the story of dissent, then, is a reminder that followers of Christ must learn to live in a perpetual state of tension with the status quo, regardless of what it is.[89] Stripped of privileged standing and majority status, Christians perhaps may again become the salt of the earth.[90]

Becoming spiritual i for the world, however, will demand more than retrieving basic *convictions* of dissent. It will also require fostering the formation of *conscience* that informs prophetic awareness. It is reasonable to ask what Christians that seek to put dissent into practice are actually supposed to do and how specifically they are to do it. Those looking for a book of procedures or a set of propositions or a list of

---

must learn to love the secular age "in its unremitting secularity." Cox, *The Secular City* (New York: Mcmillan, 1965), 3. Dietrich Bonhoeffer, *Letters and Papers from Prison*, rev. ed. (New York: Macmillan, 1967), 279–81, 324–28, passim. Cox's endorsement of secularization should be distinguished from the celebration of secularity in "the death of God" theology as represented by Thomas J. J. Altizer and William Hamilton, in *Radical Theology and the Death of God* (Indianapolis: Bobbs-Merrill, 1966). When Cox revisited the theme twenty years later in *Religion in the Secular City*, he discovered that religion sometimes proves amazingly resistant to secularity. Cox, *Religion in the Secular City* (New York: Simon & Schuster, 1984), 11–26. As it turns out, Christianity has not proven to be as resilient as Cox imagined.

[89] Rowan Williams, *On Christian Theology* (Oxford: Blackwell, 2000), 227–38. At the time he wrote the essay "Incarnation and the Renewal of Community," which offered a nuanced and qualified approval of church establishment, Williams was the Lady Margaret professor of Divinity at Oxford University. Nevertheless, it is significant to note that the future Archbishop of Canterbury, who was baptized a Presbyterian dissenter before becoming Anglican, shockingly declaimed that the church's existence is angular to the natural forms of human association. Thus, he argued, the church's collaboration with the state, the nation, or the family must always be seen as tentative and conditional on whether these existing patterns of belonging can collaborate with the transformed patterns of God's new creation.

[90] Cardinal Joseph Ratzinger, *Salt of the Earth: The Church at the End of the Millennium*, trans. Adrian Walker (San Francisco: Ignatius, 1997), 222.

principles will be disappointed, for no one can determine what faithful dissent might look like in any given context. There are no norms, no ideals, no principles to appeal to. There are only concrete settings in which faithfulness must be discerned.[91] The word often used by Christian dissenters to describe such reflection is "conscience," which denotes the habits of practical judgment (Rom 12:15).[92] Dissenters have regarded conscience not as an infallible guide, for it may err, but as an inviolable sanctuary, which must not be bound or coerced. The weak conscience, and even the faulty conscience, demands to be respected and must never be compelled by powers and authorities, civil or religious.[93] Indeed, to force anyone to act contrary to conscience is sin (1 Cor 8:12; Rom 14:23). And though conscience is present in a natural state, and thus possessed by all human beings, Christian conscience must be formed by faith through baptism and participation in the new humanity that has come in Jesus Christ (1 Pet 3:21; Gal 3:27; Eph 2:15). Through such formation, judgments of conscience become not a source of private opinion but an expression of the church's witness

---

[91] William Stringfellow, *Conscience and Obedience: The Politics of Romans 13 and Revelation 13 in Light of the Second Coming* (Waco, Tex.: Word, 1977), 24–25.

[92] E.g., William Perkins, *A Discourse of Conscience*, in *The Workes of That Famous and Worthy Minister of Christ in the Universitie of Cambridge, Mr. William Perkins*, 3 vols. (London: John Legatt, 1626), 1:515–54. Conscience played an important role in early pre-Protestant Wyclifites and Lollards. Conscience serves as the guide for Wille in William Langland's poem *Piers Plowman*, though, for Langland, Christian conscience must be informed by faith. Derek Pearsall, *Piers Plowman: A New Annotated Edition of the C-text* (Exeter: University of Exeter Press, 2008), XX.9ff.; and David Aers, *Beyond Reformation? An Essay on William Langland's Piers Plowman and the End of Constantinian Christianity* (Notre Dame, Ind.: University of Notre Dame Press, 2015), 5. Langland described the conscience as the "constable" of the church, which enables ordinary people to exercise moral discernment. Pearsall, *Piers Plowman*, XXII.214; and Norman Doe, *Fundamental Authority in Late Medieval English Law* (Cambridge: Cambridge University Press, 1990), chap. "Conscience and the Common Law," 132–54.

[93] Thus, Thomas Helwys asserted that "the king has no more power over their consciences than over ours, and that is none at all." He argued that the judgments of conscience must be respected regardless of whether they are "heretics, Turks, Jews, or whatsoever, it appertains not to the earthly power to punish them in the least measure." Helwys, *A Short Declaration of the Mystery of Iniquity* (1611/1612), ed. Richard Groves (Macon, Ga.: Mercer University Press, 1998), 53. Roger Williams made a similar claim; see above, p. 201.

and advocacy.[94] To put it simply, conscience is a way of talking about how Christians in communion with one another exercise the mind of Christ (Phil 2:5). But for *conscience* to be aroused, *consciousness* must be awakened. Spiritual formation, then, must attend to the renewal of the mind so that Christians learn to resist conforming to the fragile contingencies of the present age that will not endure and learn to begin imagining the world as it could be if it were shaped toward God's good, acceptable, and perfect will (Rom 12:1-2).

Stated differently, dissent is simply another word for the stance of resisting accommodation to the way things are. Christian dissenters serve the whole church and the wider society as a check against the tyranny of the majority and the domination of the powerful.[95] Christian dissent, however, is not simply a matter of adopting a contrarian outlook toward what most people think.[96] The Christian dissenter is not merely a maverick who resists conventional wisdom but rather a prophet who tells the truth. Yet the powers that be are never comfortable with allowing dissenters free exercise of conscience. They seek to domesticate them, while dissenters look for ways to resist domestication. This struggle is poignantly illustrated in the life of Bill Moyers, who served as special assistant to President Lyndon Johnson. Moyers was an ordained Baptist minister with a conscience that had been formed by firm commitments to peace and a deep conviction to tell the truth. He became Johnson's closest advisor, a prophet who guided the president in imagining the new world that was to become the Great Society. But when Moyers expressed reservations about the president's intention to escalate the Vietnam War, their relationship was irreparably strained. Johnson allowed him to remain in his position as a "domesticated dissenter" as long as he agreed not to voice his concerns to outsiders and to keep his criticism within the bounds of acceptable deviation. Johnson reminded Moyers of his changed

---

[94] Stringfellow, *Conscience and Obedience*, 101–2.

[95] My account of dissent here is indebted to the excellent essay by Cass Sunstein: *Why Societies Need Dissent* (Cambridge, Mass.: Harvard University Press, 2013).

[96] Wendell Berry's poem "The Contrariness of the Mad Farmer" suggests that contrariness as a strategy of dissent can be more than a reflex reaction to take the opposite point of view. Berry, *The Mad Farmer Poems* (New York: Counterpoint, 2008), 4.

status by typically greeting him with these words: "Well, here comes Mr. Stop-the-Bombing."[97] Eventually, the burden on his conscience became too much to bear, leading Moyers to resign and return to his calling in journalism, where he could tell the truth without the domesticating constraints of power.[98]

For the heirs of dissenting Christianity to contribute to the building of a just and good society in the world today, it will demand fostering *conscience* and recovering *convictions*, but it will also depend on cultivating *communities* of resistance. Such communities grasp that seeing the world apocalyptically is not about predicting the future but about living in the light of a revelation that causes the world they inhabit to appear in an entirely new way.[99] They promote the habits of an imagination that equips members with the capacity to see the world through the lens of the life, death, and resurrection of Jesus Christ.[100] They read history backward, seeing their own lives retrospectively in continuity with the story of Israel's God and God's servant Jesus.[101] They understand God's disruptive action in Christ not as a future

---

[97] Irving L. Janis, *Groupthink: Psychological Studies of Policy Decisions and Fiascoes*, 2nd ed. (Boston: Houghton Mifflin, 1982), 114–17. Janis describes Moyers as a "domesticated dissenter."

[98] Moyers has for the most part resisted talking about his break with Johnson. In a recent interview he opened up, saying, "Lyndon B. Johnson . . . had a passion for power but suffered violent dissent in the ranks of his own personality. He could absolutely do the right thing at the right time—the reassuring grace, if you will, when he was thrust into the White House after Kennedy's assassination; the Civil Rights Act of 1964; the Voting Rights Act of 1965. But when he did the wrong thing—escalating the Vietnam War—the damage was irreparable." "Bill Moyers on Saving Our Democracy, 'Selma' and LBJ," Interview with Karin Kamp, in Moyers and Company (January 14, 2015), http://billmoyers.com/2015/01/14/whats-bills-mind/ (accessed July 18, 2016).

[99] Christopher Rowland, *The Open Heaven: A Study of Apocalyptic in Judaism and Early Christianity* (New York: Crossroad, 1982), 2; Joshua B. Davis and Douglas Harink, *Apocalyptic and the Future of Theology* (Eugene, Ore.: Cascade, 2012), 1–45; and J. Lewis Martyn, *Theological Issues in the Letters of Paul* (Nashville: Abingdon, 1997), 89–110.

[100] Richard B. Hays, *The Conversion of the Imagination: Paul as Interpreter of Israel's Scripture* (Grand Rapids: Eerdmans, 2005), 1–24.

[101] Richard B. Hays, *Echoes of Scripture in the Gospels* (Waco, Tex.: Baylor University Press, 2016), 358–59.

event but as a reality that is always present and ever new.[102] They do not withdraw into sectarian enclaves of homogeneity or accommodate to institutional structures of secularity but seek a life together that participates in the new creation and exemplifies what God in Christ intends for all humanity.[103] They recognize that they do not bring God's reign in history but reach out to meet the new world that is on its way.[104] They do not simply mirror the secular politics of left or right but seek to practice the politics of Jesus through forgiveness and friendship.[105] They refuse to regard distinctions of race, class, gender, or sexuality as determinative of standing in society but see only one new humanity in Christ.[106] They seek the peace of the earthly city, telling the truth about what they see and advocating for the healing of its brokenness, but they recognize that their citizenship is in heaven.[107] They see themselves as pilgrims in this secular age, answerable to the law of another city toward which they journey by faith on the wings of the love of God and neighbor.[108]

---

[102] J. Lewis Martyn, *Galatians* (New York: Doubleday, 1997), 104. David W. Congdon, "Eschatologizing Apocalyptic: An Assessment of the Present Conversation on Pauline Apocalyptic," in Harink and Davis, *Apocalyptic and the Future of Theology*, 131–36. See also Ben C. Blackwell, John K. Goodrich, and Jason Maston, eds., *Paul and the Apocalyptic Imagination* (Minneapolis: Fortress, 2016).

[103] Karl Barth, *Church Dogmatics* (Edinburgh: T&T Clark, 1958), IV/2§67.4, 719; Karl Barth, *The Epistle to the Romans*, 6th ed. (London: Oxford University Press, 1977), 5:12–21; J. Lewis Martyn, "The Gospel Invades Philosophy," 13–33, in *Paul, Philosophy, and the Theopolitical Vision*, ed. Douglas Harink (Eugene, Ore.: Cascade, 2010), 28–33; Martyn, *Galatians*, 97–106.

[104] John Howard Yoder, Stone and Morgan Lectures; cited in James Wm. McClendon Jr., *Witness: Systematic Theology*, vol. 3 (Waco, Tex.: Baylor University Press, 2012), 15–16.

[105] John Howard Yoder, *The Politics of Jesus* (Grand Rapids: Eerdmans, 1972); and McClendon, *Ethics*, 222–32.

[106] John Howard Yoder, "The New Humanity as Pulpit and Paradigm," in *For the Nations* (Grand Rapids: Eerdmans, 1997), 37–50.

[107] Stanley Hauerwas and William H. Willimon, *Resident Aliens: Life in the Christian Colony* (Nashville: Abingdon, 1989), 69–92; see also Tertullian, *Against Marcion*, 3.25, in *The Ante-Nicene Fathers* (Grand Rapids: Eerdmans, 1978), 3:342.

[108] Augustine, *Sermons on the Psalms*, 149.3, in *Nicene and Post-Nicene Fathers*, 1st ser. (Grand Rapids: Eerdmans, 1979), 8:678; and Rowan Williams, "Resident Aliens:

Cultivating communities of resistance shaped by the reality of the new that has come in Christ has been instrumental in nurturing dissenting voices in the past. In the fall of 1964, as the United States was escalating its military presence in Vietnam, Thomas Merton hosted a three-day retreat at his hermitage in the Gethsemani Abbey, in search of spiritual roots to nurture an authentic Christian witness against violence. Among the participants were Daniel and Philip Berrigan (Catholic priests and peace activists), Jim Forest (editor of the *Catholic Worker*), John Howard Yoder (a young Mennonite theologian), A. J. Muste (an established leader of the Fellowship of Reconciliation), and Merton. In prayer, study, and conversation, they gathered spiritual seeds of dissent from the Catholic, Protestant, and Free Church traditions. Over the years, they planted and cultivated communities of resistance that yielded an amazing harvest of prophetic protest and Christ-imitating discipleship that showed the world an alternative to the way of violence and war.[109] Together they fostered a Christian witness that was capable of resisting the domesticating powers of what Philip Berrigan called "American empire."[110] If the current heirs of religious dissent seem to have little to say that is truthful for the wider culture or fail to exemplify a way of life that is threatening to the powers that be, perhaps it is because their dissent has become domesticated.

Yet it is unlikely that even the most domesticated dissenter who has learned to reside comfortably in the shadow of American empire will remain comfortable for long. The growing specter of secularization and the decline of Christian culture present new challenges that call for changes. Some will be tempted to return to the more secluded spaces of their own fellowship and refrain from engaging the wider church and culture. As they retreat into the fortresses of familiarity in their own separated communities, the boundaries between their sectarian gatherings and the world will become less permeable, the pathways

---

The Identity of the Early Church," in *Why Study the Past? The Quest for the Historical Church* (Grand Rapids: Eerdmans, 2005), 32–59.

[109] Gordon Oyer, *Pursuing the Spiritual Roots of Protest* (Eugene, Ore.: Cascade, 2014).

[110] Philip Berrigan, foreword to *The Criminality of Nuclear Deterrence*, by Francis A. Boyle (Atlanta: Clarity, 2002), 12.

of cooperation with other Christians will be more limited, and their relevance to the culture will be further reduced. Others may choose a path driven by the aspiration to reverse their diminishing influence by transferring the energy of the Christian vision into the service of political processes and market forces. Yet it is not clear that such an approach can sustain a free and faithful Christian witness without being overwhelmed by social and economic influences that do not share its transcendent goal. Neither of these alternatives offers a strategy adequate to resist the forces of domestication. A third approach is needed, one that does not desire the privilege of social influence or demand the security of fixed boundaries, but one that cultivates communities of resistance by building cathedrals of hope founded on the confession of faith in a God who is made visible through the windows of love. The nature of the emerging world order is too challenging for anything short of such a radical strategy.

The world that contemporary Christianity inhabits is dominated by empire. It is not the old empire of colonialism or even sovereign nation-states pitting East against West. The age of old empires has passed. The empire that dominates the lives of people today and exerts sovereignty over its domain uses more subtle powers of influence. This new empire is supranational and global. It has no boundaries, neither territorial nor temporal, for this empire sees itself at the end of history. It does not possess a central apparatus of rule, but it exercises authority through market forces and imposes its policy with police action. Yet its greatest power of control is not by external force but through internal regulation. Its influence stretches far and wide in web-like fashion, controlling by connecting. Like Leviathan in John's Apocalypse, it has many heads and crowns, yet it is one, for it is animated by ideas and values shared by each and all. This beast is no totalitarian tyrant, though it uses its seductive charm to ventriloquize its surrogates and manipulate its puppets. It does not rely on the power of spectacle to display its sovereignty but exercises control through a vast network of surveillance. Its subjects willingly submit to its rule. It uses the force of law and democracy to exercise its influence and domesticate its subjects. This global empire with such enormous powers and control is not a vast right-wing or left-wing conspiracy. It transcends even these boundaries. And, though it may seem more sympathetic than sinister, it does not serve God or the Lamb, and it punishes those who do.[111] It is understandable that after the conviction of religious liberty was preserved in the U.S. Constitution and the rights of conscience were protected by the force of law, many Christians found it tempting to think about the institutions of democratic society more as instruments of God's justice than as beasts from the abyss. Yet, as communities of resistance seek ways of witnessing to the new creation in the age of emergent empire, it will require a capacity to see the world in Christ not only as redeemed but as a new social reality in which all that is Antichrist will be vanquished.[112] A moral imagination suited for a vocation of dissent in this new context will likely be found not by exploring the established patterns of Romans 13 but by seeing the world through the subversive imagery of Revelation 13.[113] Though both accounts represent opposing tendencies of sociopolitical reality, envisioning history through the aperture of John's Apocalypse may prove especially useful, not only for clarifying *what is*, but for imagining *what can be*.[114]

The freedom of the new creation is not merely the freedom of choice or even the political freedom to live without the coercive domination of others. It is freedom to be a new humanity reconciled in Christ, who liberates all the sons and daughters of earth from the powers that would determine their lives and who opens up the space in

---

[111] Michael Hardt and Antonio Negri, *Empire* (Cambridge, Mass.: Harvard University Press, 2000), xi–41.

[112] Walter Benjamin, *Theses on the Philosophy of History*, VI, in *Illuminations*, ed. Hannah Arendt, trans. Harry Zohn (New York: Schocken Books, 1969), 255.

[113] Stringfellow, *Conscience and Obedience*, 9–20. John Paul Lederach describes the concept of "moral imagination" as the capacity to recognize turning points and decisive opportunities to venture down uncertain paths and generate possibilities that do not yet exist. Lederach, *The Moral Imagination* (Oxford: Oxford University Press, 2005), 3–30.

[114] McClendon describes this sort of perception as "picture-thinking" (*Doctrine*, 75–77). Both John Howard Yoder and Karl Barth see Rom 13 and Rev 13 as providing two opposite tendencies in political realities. Yoder, *The Christian Witness to the State* (Scottdale, Penn.: Herald, 1964), 76–77; and Barth, *The Knowledge of God and the Service of God according to the Teaching of the Reformation*, 4th ed. (London: Hodder & Stoughton, 1960), 226.

which it is possible to live as free people.[115] The most determinative act for a witness of dissent may then simply be to listen to the voice that calls out from the heavens—"See, I am making all things new" (Rev 21:5)—and then to imagine the world through this vision as it can become when fully reconciled and renewed. For the new age is ultimately beyond the reach of human effort. It breaks into history as God's gift. Prophetic imagination can envision it descending and call fellow pilgrims to journey toward it. Seeing what comes last in light of the new in Christ opens blind eyes to enduring realities that outlast the fragile contingencies that will not endure the ends of history. Only such a transformed vision can imagine the building of a world that gestures to the life beyond.

[115] Martyn, *Galatians*, 97–106.

BIBLIOGRAPHY

Abrahams, Peter. *Jamaica: An Island Mosaic*. London: Her Majesty's Stationary Office, 1957.

Ackroyd, Peter. *Blake*. New York: Ballantine Books, 1995.

Aers, David. *Beyond Reformation? An Essay on William Langland's Piers Plowman and the End of Constantinian Christianity*. Notre Dame, Ind.: University of Notre Dame Press, 2015.

Albion Mill: State of Facts. London, 1791.

"The Albion Mills on Fire." London: C. Sheppard, March 10, 1791.

Alger, Horatio, Jr. *Ragged Dick*. Philadelphia: John C. Winston, 1868.

Altizer, Thomas J. J. *The New Apocalypse: The Radical Christian Vision of William Blake*. East Lansing: Michigan State University Press, 1967.

Altizer, Thomas J. J., and William Hamilton. *Radical Theology and the Death of God*. Indianapolis: Bobbs-Merrill, 1966.

"America's Changing Religious Landscape." Pew Research Center. May 12, 2015. http://www.pewforum.org/2015/05/12/americas-changing-religious-landscape/. Accessed July 12, 2013.

Ames, William. *Conscience, with the Power and Cases Thereof*. London, 1639.

Anderson, Philip J. "Letters of Henry Jessey and John Thombes to the Churches of New England." *Baptist Quarterly* 28, no. 1 (1979): 30–39.

Andrews, Lancelot. *Ninety-Six Sermons*. 5 vols. Oxford: John Henry Parker, 1841.

Armes, Ethel, ed. *Stratford Hall: The Great House of the Lees*. Richmond, Va.: Garrett & Massie, 1936.

Ashton, Robert, ed. *The Works of John Robinson: Pastor of the Pilgrim Fathers*. London: John Snow, 1851.

Aspinwall, William. *An Explication and Application of the Seventh Chapter of Daniel.* London: R. ., 1654.

Assheton, William. *Toleration Disapprov'd and Condemn'd.* London: Francis Oxlad Sen., 1670.

Athanasius of Alexandria. *On the Incarnation.* Crestwood, N.Y.: St. Vladimir's, 1944.

Atherton, Ian, and David Como. "The Burning of Edward Wightman: Puritanism, Prelacy, and the Politics of Heresy in Early Modern England." *English Historical Review* 120, no. 489 (2005): 1215–50.

Augustine of Hippo. *City of God.* Translated by Henry Bettenson. New York: Penguin Books, 1984.

———. *On Christian Doctrine.* Translated by Marcus Dods. In *Nicene and Post-Nicene Fathers,* 1st series, vol. 2. Grand Rapids: Eerdmans, 1979.

———. *Sermons on the Psalms.* In *Nicene and Post-Nicene Fathers,* 1st series, vol. 8. Grand Rapids: Eerdmans, 1979.

Backscheider, Paula R. *Daniel Defoe: His Life.* Baltimore: Johns Hopkins University Press, 1989.

Bacon, Nathaniel. *Relation of the Fearful Estate of Francis Spira in the Year 1548.* London: I[ohn] L[egat], 1638.

Bale, John. *Select Works of John Bale.* Edited by Henry Christmas. Cambridge: Cambridge University Press, 1849.

Barber, Daniel Coluccielo. *Deleuze and the Naming of God.* Edinburgh: Edinburgh University Press, 2014.

Barbour, Hugh. *The Quakers of Puritan England.* New Haven: Yale University Press, 1964.

Barlow, William. *The Summe and Substance of the Conference.* London: V[alentine] S[immes], 1604.

Barrington, John Shute. *An Account of the Late Proceedings of the Dissenting Ministers at Salters-Hall.* London: J. Roberts, 1719.

Barrow, Henry. *The Writings of Henry Barrow.* Edited by Leland H. Carlson. Vol. 3 of *Elizabethan Nonconformist Texts.* London: Allen & Unwin, 1962.

Barry, John M. *Roger Williams and the Creation of the American Soul: Church, State, and the Birth of Liberty.* New York: Viking, 2012.

Barth, Karl. *The Christian Life, Church Dogmatics,* IV/4. Lecture Fragments. Grand Rapids: Eerdmans, 1981.

———. *Church Dogmatics.* Edinburgh: T&T Clark, 1958.

———. *The Epistle to the Romans.* 6th ed. London: Oxford University Press, 1977.

———. *The Humanity of God.* Atlanta: John Knox, 1960.

———. *The Knowledge of God and the Service of God according to the Teaching of the Reformation.* 4th ed. London: Hodder & Stoughton, 1960.

Baston, Jane. "History, Prophecy, and Interpretation: Mary Cary and Fifth Monarchism." *Prose Studies* 21, no. 3 (1998): 1–18.

Baukham, Richard. *Tudor Apocalypse: Sixteenth Century Apocalypticism, Millenarianism, and the English Reformation.* Abingdon, Oxford: Sutton Courtenay, 1978.

Baulch, David M. "Reading Coleridge Reading Blake." *Coleridge Bulletin*, n.s. 16 (2000): 5–14.

Baxter, Richard. *The Practical Works of the Rev. Richard Baxter*. London: James Duncan, 1830.

Bebbington, David. *Evangelicalism in Modern Britain: A History from the 1730s to the 1980s*. Grand Rapids: Baker, 1992.

Becker, Adam H. *Revival and Awakening: American Evangelical Missionaries in Iran and the Origins of Assyrian Nationalism*. Chicago: University of Chicago Press, 2015.

Bellah, Robert N. *Beyond Belief: Essays on Religion in a Post-traditionalist World*. Berkeley: University of California Press, 1991.

———. "Is There a Common American Culture?" *Journal of the American Academy of Religion* 66, no. 3 (1998): 613–25.

———. "Religion and the Shape of National Culture." *America*, July 31–August 2, 1999, 9–14.

Bellah, Robert N., Richard Madsen, Stephen Tipton, William Sullivan, and Ann Swidler. *The Good Society*. New York: Vintage Books, 1992.

———. *Habits of the Heart: Individualism and Commitment in American Life*. Updated ed. Berkeley: University of California Press, 1996.

Bender, John. *Imagining the Penitentiary: Fiction and the Architecture of Mind in Eighteenth-Century England*. Chicago: University of Chicago Press, 1987.

Benjamin, Walter. *Illuminations*. Edited by Hannah Arendt. Translated by Harry Zohn. New York: Schocken Books, 1969.

Bentley, Gerald Eades, Jr. *Blake Records*. 2nd ed. New Haven: Yale University Press, 2004.

Berecovitch, Sacvan. *The American Jeremiad*. Madison: University of Wisconsin Press, 1978.

Berkhof, Hendrik. *Christ and the Powers*. Scottdale, Penn.: Herald, 1962.

Berne, Eric. "The Psychological Structure of Space with Some Remarks on *Robinson Crusoe*." *Psychoanalytic Quarterly* 25, no. 4 (1956): 549–67.

Berrigan, Philip. Foreword to *The Criminality of Nuclear Deterrence*, by Francis A. Boyle. Atlanta: Clarity, 2002.

Berry, Wendell. *The Art of the Commonplace*. Edited by Norman Wirzba. Washington, D.C.: Shoemaker & Hoard, 2002.

———. *In the Presence of Fear: Three Essays for a Changed World*. Great Barrington, Mass.: Orion Society, 2001.

———. *The Mad Farmer Poems*. New York: Counterpoint, 2008.

Berry, Wendell, and Wen Stephenson. "The Gospel according to Wendell Berry." *Nation*, March 23, 2015.

The Bible and Holy Scriptures. Geneva: Rouland Hall, 1560. Reprint, Madison: University of Wisconsin Press, 1969.

Blackwell, Ben C., John K. Goodrich, and Jason Maston, eds. *Paul and the Apocalyptic Imagination*. Minneapolis: Fortress, 2016.

Blackwood, Christopher. *The Storming of Antichrist*. London: S. N., 1644.

Blair, Robert. *The Grave*. London: Printed for M. Cooper, 1743.

Blake, William. *Blake Complete Writings*. Edited by Geoffrey Keynes. London: Oxford University Press, 1969.

———. *The Complete Poetry and Prose of William Blake*. Edited by David V. Erdman. Berkeley: University of California Press, 2008.

Bleby, Henry. *Death Struggles of Slavery*. London: Hamilton, Adams, 1853.

Bloom, Harold. *The Anxiety of Influence: A Theory of Poetry*. 2nd ed. New York: Oxford University Press, 1997.

———. *Blake's Apocalypse: A Study in Poetic Argument*. Garden City, N.Y.: Doubleday, 1963.

———. *The Complete Poetry and Prose of William Blake*, by William Blake. Edited by David V. Erdman. Berkeley: University of California Press, 2008.

———, ed. *William Blake*. New York: Chelsea House, 1985.

Boardman, Eugene Powers. *Christian Influence on the Ideology of the Taiping Rebellion, 1851–1864*. Madison: University of Wisconsin Press, 1952.

Bogue, David, and James Bennett. *History of Dissenters: From the Revolution to the Year 1802*. 2nd ed. London: F. Westley and A. H. Davis, 1833.

Bolam, Charles Gordon, Jeremy Goring, H. L. Short, and Roger Thomas. *The English Presbyterians*. London: Allen & Unwin, 1968.

Bonhoeffer, Dietrich. *Ethics*. Edited by Eberhard Bethge. New York: Macmillan, 1965.

———. *Letters and Papers from Prison*. Rev. ed. New York: Macmillan, 1967.

Booth, Wayne C. *The Rhetoric of Fiction*. 2nd ed. Chicago: University of Chicago Press, 1983.

Boreham, Frank W. *A Handful of Stars*. New York: Abingdon, 1922.

Boswell, James. *Life of Johnson*. Edited by George Birkbeck Hill. 6 vols. New York: Harper, 1891.

Boyle, Francis A. *The Criminality of Nuclear Deterrence*. Atlanta: Clarity, 2002.

Bozeman, Theodore Dwight. *To Live Ancient Lives: The Primitivist Dimension in Puritanism*. Chapel Hill: University of North Carolina Press, 1988.

———. *The Precisionist Strain: Disciplinary Religion and Antinomian Backlash in Puritanism to 1638*. Chapel Hill: University of North Carolina Press, 2004.

Bradford, William. *Bradford's History "Of Plimouth Plantation" from the Original Manuscript with a Report of the Proceedings Incident to the Return of the Manuscript to Massachusetts*. Boston: Wright & Potter, 1899.

Braithwait, Richard. *The English Gentleman*. London: John Haviland, 1630.

Brauer, Jerald C. "Conversion: From Puritanism to Revivalism." *Journal of Religion* 58, no. 3 (1978): 227–43.

Bremer, Francis J. *Building a New Jerusalem: John Davenport, a Puritan in Three Worlds*. New Haven: Yale University Press, 2012.

———. *John Winthrop: America's Forgotten Founding Father*. New York: Oxford University Press, 2003.

Brenner, Robert. *Merchants and Revolution: Commercial Change, Political Conflict, and London's Overseas Traders, 1550–1653*. New York: Verso, 2003.

Brigham, Clarence S. "Bibliography of American Editions of *Robinson Crusoe* to 1830." *American Antiquarian Society* (October 1957): 137–83.

Brightman, Thomas. *Apocalypsis Apocalypseos, a Revelation of the Apocalypse.* Amsterdam: Iudocus Hondius & Hendrick Laurenss, 1611.

Bronowski, Jacob. *A Man without a Mask.* New York: Haskell House, 1967.

———. *William Blake and the Age of Revolution.* New York: Harper & Row, 1965.

Brooks, Peter. *Reading for the Plot: Design and Intention in Narrative.* Cambridge, Mass.: Harvard University Press, 1984.

Brothers, Richard. *A Description of Jerusalem: Its Houses and Streets, Squares, Colleges, Markets, and Cathedrals.* London: George Diebau, 1801.

———. *A Revealed Knowledge of the Prophecies and Times.* London, 1794.

Brown, Louise Fargo. *The Political Activities of the Baptists and Fifth Monarchy Men in England during the Interregnum.* Washington, D.C.: American Historical Association, 1912.

Brown, Raymond. *The English Baptists of the Eighteenth Century.* London: Baptist Historical Society, 1986.

Brueggemann, Walter. *The Prophetic Imagination.* Philadelphia: Fortress, 1978.

Bunhill Fields Burial Ground: Proceedings in Reference to its Preservation. London: Hamilton, Adams, 1867. Reprint, London: Forgotten Books, 2015.

Bunker, Nicholas. *Making Haste from Babylon: The Mayflower Pilgrims and Their World.* New York: Vintage, 2011.

Bunyan, John. *Ai Tukutuku Kei Vulgai-Lako: A Ya Nai Tukutuku Ni Nona Lako Mai Na Vuravura O Qo Ki Ka Vuravura Ena Muri Mai: Sa Volai Me Vaka Sa Dua Na Tadra. E Vola Taumada.* Translated by Ko Misa Joni Puniyani. Sa Laveti Ki Na vosa Vaka-Viti. Sa Tabaki Mai Londoni, E Peritani, 1867.

———. *Bedangweri Ya Balondo O Mundi Ma Wasi Na O Mu Mu Mapo: The Pilgrim's Progress.* Translated into Dualla by J. J. Fuller. London: Alexander & Shepheard, 1885.

———. *Bunyan's Pilgrim's Progress.* First part. Translated into Sinhalese. Colombo: The Christian, 1907.

———. *Bunyan's Pilgrim's Progress.* Part 1. Translated by Sarah Judson. Maulmain: American Baptist Mission Press, 1840.

———. *Bunyan's Pilgrim's Progress.* Abridged and translated into Hindi by Rev. W. Buyers. Calcutta: Baptist Missionary Press, 1835.

———. *Bunyan's Pilgrim's Progress.* Translated into Sgau Karen by Jonathan Wade. Rangoon: Printed at the Mission Press; published by the Burmah Bible and Tract Society, 1863.

———. *Cherita Darihal Orang Yang Menchari Selamat* [*The Story of One Seeking Salvation*]. Translated by R. A. Blasdell. Singapore: Malaya Publishing House, 1955.

———. *Chrita Orang Yang Chari Slamat* [*One Who Seeks Salvation*]. Translated by William G. Shellabear. Singapore: American Missionary Press, 1905.

———. *Grace Abounding to the Chief of Sinners.* Edited by W. R. Owens. London: Penguin, 1987.

————. *Kristian Vân Ram Kawng Zwh Thu.* Translated into Lushai. London: Religious Tract Society, n.d.

————. *The Miscellaneous Works of John Bunyan.* Edited by W. R. Owens. Oxford: Clarendon, 1994.

————. *The Pilgrim's Progress.* Part 1, translated by Shem Sahu. Part 2, translated by Ghanu Shyam Naik. Cuttack: Religious Tract Society and the Orissa Tract Society, 1873.

————. *The Pilgrim's Progress.* Abridged by John Wesley. Newcastle: John Gooding, 1743.

————. *The Pilgrim's Progress.* Edited by N. H. Keeble. New York: Oxford University Press, 1984.

————. *The Pilgrim's Progress.* London: Religious Tract Society, 1903.

————. *The Pilgrim's Progress.* Part 1. Translated into Bengalee by F[elix] Carey. Serampore: Mission Press, 1821.

————. *The Pilgrim's Progress.* Translated into Urdu. n.p.: P.R.B.S., 1889.

————. *The Pilgrim's Progress from This World to That Which Is to Come.* Part 1. Calcutta: Printed at the Baptist Mission Press, for the Calcutta Tract and Christian Book Society, 1835.

————. *The Pilgrim's Progress, Illustrated by a Chinese Artist.* Translated by George Piercy in Canton vernacular. n.p., 1871.

————. *The Works of John Bunyan.* Edited by George Offor. 3 vols. Glasgow: W. G. Blackie and Son, 1854. Reprint, Carlisle, Penn.: Banner of Trust, 1991.

Burgess, Walter H. *John Robinson, Pastor of the Pilgrim Fathers: A Study of His Life and Times.* New York: Harcourt, Brace & Howe, 1920.

Burke, Edmund. *Reflections of the Revolution of France.* London: James Dodsley, 1790.

Burrage, Champlain. *The Early English Dissenters in Light of Recent Research.* 2 vols. Cambridge: Cambridge University Press, 1912.

Butterfield, Herbert. *The Whig Interpretation of History.* New York: Scribner, 1951.

Butterfield, L. H. "Elder John Leland." *Proceedings of the American Antiquarian Society* 62 (1952): 155–242.

Butterworth, Joseph, and Son. *A General Catalogue of Law Books.* 6th enlarged ed. London: Butterworth, 1819.

Byrd, James P., Jr. *The Challenges of Roger Williams: Religious Liberty, Violent Persecution, and the Bible.* Macon, Ga.: Mercer University Press, 2002.

Caldwell, Patricia. *The Puritan Conversion Narrative: The Beginnings of American Expression.* Cambridge: Cambridge University Press, 1983.

Calendar of State Papers, Domestic, 1653–1654. London: Longmans, 1875–1876.

Calhoun, Robert L. "A Liberal Bandaged but Unbowed." *Christian Century*, May 31, 1939, 701–4.

Callahan, James Patrick. "*Claritas Scripturae*: The Role of Perspecuity in Protestant Hermeneutics." *Journal of the Evangelical Theological Society* 39, no. 3 (1996): 353–72.

Calvin, John. *Commentary on the Book of Psalms.* Translated by James Anderson. Grand Rapids: Eerdmans, 1949.

————. *Commentary on Daniel.* Grand Rapids: Eerdmans, 1948.

————. *Institutes of the Christian Religion.* Edited by John T. McNeill. Translated by Ford Lewis Battles. Philadelphia: Westminster, 1960.

The Cambridge Platform of Church Discipline. Cambridge, Mass.: Synod of Congregational Churches, 1648.

Campolo, Tony. *Letters to a Young Evangelical.* Philadelphia: Basic Books, 2006.

Canipe, Lee. *Loyal Dissenters: Reading Scripture and Talking Freedom with 17th-Century English Baptists.* Macon, Ga.: Smyth & Helwys, 2016.

Capp, Bernard S. *The Fifth Monarchy Men: A Study in Seventeenth-Century English Millenarianism.* Totowa: Rowman & Littlefield, 1972.

Carey, S. Pearce. *William Carey.* London: Hodder & Stoughton, 1926.

Cary, Mary. *The Little Horns Doom and Downfall; or, A Scripture-Prophesie of King James, and King Charles, and of This Present Parliament, Unfolded.* London, 1651.

Catalogue of Books Imported from London in the Ships Sterling, Jane, and Cornplanter, and for Sale by C. and A. Conrad & Co. Pennsylvania: C. & A. Conrad, 1807.

Catalogue of Novels and Romances, Being Part of an Extensive Collection for Sale by M. Carey and Son, Corner of Chestnut and Fourth Streets. Philadelphia: M. Carey & Son, 1817.

Catalogue of Novels and Romances, for Sale by John Conrad & Co. No. 30, Chestnut-Street. Philadelphia: M. & J. Conrad, 1804.

Certeau, Michel de. *The Practice of Everyday Life.* Translated by Steven F. Rendall. Berkeley: University of California Press, 1984.

Chalmers, George. *The Life of Daniel De Foe.* London, 1790. Reprint, Oxford: D. A. Talboys, 1841.

Chancey, Andrew S. "'A Demonstration Plot for the Kingdom of God': The Establishment and Early Years of the Koinonia Farm." *Georgia Historical Quarterly* 75, no. 2 (1991): 321–53.

Chappell, David L. *Stone of Hope: Prophetic Religion and the Death of Jim Crow.* Chapel Hill: University of North Carolina Press, 2004.

Chesterton, Gilbert K. *Orthodoxy.* New York: Image/Doubleday, 1959.

Child, John. *A Second Argument for a More Full and Firm Union amongst All Good Protestants.* London: J. How, 1684.

Christianson, Paul. *Reformers and Babylon: English Apocalyptic Visions from the Reformation to the Eve of the Civil War.* Toronto: University of Toronto Press, 1978.

Clark, John, W. Dendy, and J. M. Phillippo. *The Voice of Jubilee: A Narrative of the Baptist Mission, Jamaica.* London: John Snow, 1865.

Clarke, John. *Memorials of Baptist Missionaries in Jamaica.* London: Yates & Alexander, 1869.

Clarke, William. *The Clarke Papers.* Edited by Charles Harding Firth. 4 vols. London: Camden Society, 1891.

Coffey, John. *John Goodwin and the Puritan Revolution.* Woodbridge, Suffolk: Boydell, 2006.

————. *Persecution and Toleration in Protestant England, 1558–1689.* New York: Longman, 2000.

Coleridge, Samuel Taylor. *Collected Letters*. Edited by Earl Leslie Griggs. Oxford: Clarendon, 1956–1971.

———. *The Collected Works of Samuel Taylor Coleridge*. Princeton, N.J.: Princeton University Press, 1969–2002.

Collins, Wilkie. *The Moonstone: A Romance*. New York: Harper, 1874.

Collinson, Patrick. *The Elizabethan Puritan Movement*. Oxford: Clarendon, 1967.

———. *From Cranmer to Sancroft*. New York: Hambledon Continuum, 2006.

———. "The Jacobean Religious Settlement: The Hampton Court Conference." In *Before the English Civil War: Essays in Early Stuart Politics and Government*, edited by Howard Tomlinson, 27–51. New York: St. Martin's, 1984.

Como, David R. *Blown by the Spirit: Puritanism and the Emergence of an Antinomian Underground in Pre-Civil-War England*. Stanford: Stanford University Press, 2004.

Como, David R., and Peter Lake. "'Orthodoxy' and Its Discontents: Dispute Settlement and the Production of 'Consensus' in the London (Puritan) 'Underground.'" *Journal of British Studies* 39, no. 1 (2000): 34–70.

Congar, Yves. *The Meaning of Tradition*. New York: Hawthorn Books, 1964. Reprint, San Francisco: Ignatius, 2004.

Congdon, David W. "Eschatologizing Apocalyptic: An Assessment of the Present Conversation on Pauline Apocalyptic." In *Apocalyptic and the Future of Theology: With and beyond J. Louis Martyn*, edited by Douglas Harink and Joshua Davis, 118–36. Eugene, Ore.: Cascade, 2012.

Constitutions and Canons Ecclesiastical. 2nd ed. London: Robert Baker, 1604.

Coppe, Abiezer. *A Fiery Flying Roll*. London, 1649.

Cotton, John. *The Bloudy Tenent, Washed, and Made White in the Bloud of the Lambe*. London: Matthew Symmons, 1647.

Coughlin, Margaret Morgan. "Strangers in the House: J. Lewis Shuck and Issachar Roberts, First American Baptist Missionaries in China." PhD diss., University of Virginia, 1972.

Cox, Harvey. *Religion in the Secular City*. New York: Simon & Shuster, 1984.

———. *The Secular City*. New York: Macmillan, 1965.

Crispe, Tobias. *Christ Alone Exalted in the Perfection and Encouragement of the Saints*. 2nd ed. London: M. S., 1646.

Crosby, Thomas. *The History of the English Baptists*. London: The Editor, 1738.

Culross, James. *William Carey*. London: Hodder & Stoughton, 1881.

Cunningham, Valentine. "Daniel Defoe." In *The Blackwell Companion to the Bible in English Literature*, edited by Rebecca Lemon, Emma Mason, Jonathan Roberts, and Christopher Rowland, 345–58. Malden, Mass.: Wiley-Blackwell, 2009.

Curtis, Mark H. "The Hampton Court Conference and Its Aftermath." *History* 46, no. 156 (1961): 1–16.

Dabney, William Pope. "President Madison and the Baptist Preacher." *Harper's New Monthly Magazine*, August 1881, 446–48.

Damon, Samuel Foster. *A Blake Dictionary*. Boulder: Shambhala, 1979.

Danforth, Samuel. *A Brief Recognition of New-Englands Errand into the Wilderness.* Cambridge, Mass.: S.G. & M.J., 1671.

Darwin, Charles. *The Origin of Species.* London: John Murray, 1859. Reprint, Chicago: Encyclopaedia Britannica, 1952.

Darwin, Erasmus. *The Collected Letters of Erasmus Darwin.* Edited by Desmond King-Hele. Cambridge: Cambridge University Press, 2007.

Davies, David. *Vavasor Powell: The Baptist Evangelist of Wales in the Seventeenth Century.* London: Alexander & Shepheard, 1896.

Davies, Keri. "William Blake's Mother." *Blake: An Illustrated Quarterly* 33 (1999): 36–50.

Davis, Ellen F. *Imagination Shaped: Old Testament Preaching in the Anglican Tradition.* Valley Forge, Penn.: Trinity, 1995.

Davis, Joshua B., and Douglas Harink, eds. *Apocalyptic and the Future of Theology.* Eugene, Ore.: Cascade, 2012.

Defoe, Daniel. *The Consolidator.* London, 1705.

———. *A Dialogue between a Dissenter and the Observator, Concerning "The Shortest Way with the Dissenters."* London, 1703.

———. *An Enquiry into Occasional Conformity.* London, 1698.

———. *An Essay on the History and Reality of Apparitions.* London: J. Roberts, 1727.

———. *The Farther Adventures of Robinson Crusoe.* London: W. Taylor, 1719.

———. *The History of the Devil.* 2nd ed. London: T. Warner, 1727.

———. *A Hymn to the Pillory.* London, 1703.

———. *Jure Divino: A Satire in Twelve Books.* London, 1706.

———. *A Letter to a Dissenter from His Friend at the Hague Concerning the Penal Laws and the Test, Shewing that the Popular Plea for Liberty of Conscience is not Concerned in that Question.* Tot de Hague: Gedrunckt door Hans Verdraeght, 1688.

———. *A Letter to the Dissenters.* London: J. Wright, 1719.

———. *A Letter to Mr. How By Way of His Considerations to the Preface to "An Enquiry in to the Occasional Conformity of Dissenters."* London, 1701.

———. *The Life and Strange Surprising Adventures of Robinson Crusoe, of York, Mariner.* New York: R. H. Russell, 1900.

———. *New Family Instructor.* London: T. Warner, 1727.

———. *A New Test of the Church of England's Loyalty.* London, 1702.

———. *The Novels and Miscellaneous Works of Daniel De Foe.* Bohn's Standard Library. London: George Bell, 1894–1899.

———. *The Novels and Miscellaneous Works of Daniel De Foe.* Oxford: D. A. Talboys, 1840.

———. *Robinson Crusoe.* Norton Critical Edition. Edited by Michael Shinagel. New York: W. W. Norton, 1994.

———. *A Second Volume of the Writings of the Author of the True-Born Englishman.* London, 1705.

———. *Serious Reflections during the Life and Surprising Adventures of Robinson Crusoe.* London: W. Taylor, 1720.

————. *Serious Reflections during the Life and Surprising Adventures of Robinson Crusoe.* Philadelphia: Samuel Keimer, 1725.

————. *The Shortest Way with the Dissenters and Other Pamphlets.* Oxford: Blackwell, 1974.

————. *The Shortest-Way with the Dissenters; or, Proposals for the Establishment of the Church.* London, 1702.

————. *The True-Born Englishman: A Satyr.* London, 1701.

————. *The Wonderful Life and Surprising Adventures of the Renowned Hero, Robinson Crusoe.* New York: Hugh Gaine, 1774.

Delano, Sterling. *Brook Farm: The Dark Side of Utopia.* Cambridge, Mass.: Harvard University Press, 2009.

Dell, William. *Several Sermons and Discourses.* London: J. Sowle, 1709.

Denne, Henry. *The Man of Sin Discovered.* London: John Sweeting, 1646.

Dent, Arthur. *The Plaine Mans Path to Heaven.* 15th ed. Belfast: North of Ireland Book & Tract Depository, 1859.

————. *The Ruine of Rome.* London: W.I. for Simon Waterson & Richard Banckworth, 1607.

Diamond, Jared. *Guns, Germs, and Steel: The Fates of Human Societies.* New York: W. W. Norton, 1999.

Dibble, Jeremy. *C. Hubert H. Parry: His Life and Music.* New York: Oxford University Press, 1992.

Dilley, Andrea Palpant. "The World the Missionaries Made." *Christianity Today* 58, no. 1 (2014): 34–41.

A Discovery of the Most Dangerous and Damnable Tenets That Have Been Spread Within This Few Years By Erronious, Heretical, and Mechannick Spirits. London, 1647.

Dix, Gregory, and Henry Chadwick, eds. *The Apostolic Tradition of St. Hippolytus.* 2nd ed. London: Alban, 1992.

Dixon, David N. "The Second Text: Missionary Publishing and Bunyan's *Pilgrim's Progress.*" *International Bulletin of Missionary Research* 36, no. 2 (2012): 86–90.

Documentary History of the Constitution. Washington, D.C.: Department of State, 1905.

Doe, Norman. *Fundamental Authority in Late Medieval English Law.* Cambridge: Cambridge University Press, 1990.

Dorfman, Deborah. *Blake in the Nineteenth Century: His Reputation as a Poet from Gilchrist to Yeats.* New Haven: Yale University Press, 1969.

Dorrien, Gary. *The Making of American Liberal Theology: Idealism, Realism, and Modernity, 1900–1950.* Louisville: Westminster John Knox, 2003.

Dryden, John. *The Poetical Works of John Dryden.* Edited by George Gilfillan. New York: D. Appleton, 1857.

Drysdale, Alexander Hutton. *History of the Presbyterians in England: Their Rise, Decline, and Revival.* London: Presbyterian Church of England, 1889.

Dunning, Robert. *The Monmouth Rebellion: A Guide to the Rebellion and Bloody Assizes.* Wimborne, U.K.: Dovecote, 1984.

Durso, Keith E. *No Armor for the Back.* Macon, Ga.: Mercer University Press, 2007.

Edwards, John. *Some Thoughts concerning the Several Causes and Occasions of Atheism.* London: J. Robinson, 1695.

Edwards, Thomas. *Gangraena: The First and Second Part.* 3rd ed. London: Ralph Smith, 1646.

Eire, Carlos. "Calvin and Nicodemism: A Reappraisal." *Sixteenth Century Journal* 10, no. 1 (1979): 45–69.

———. "Prelude to Sedition: Calvin's Attack on Nicodemism and Religious Compromise." *Archiv fur Reformationsgeschichte* 76 (1985): 120–45.

Eliade, Mircea. *The Sacred and the Profane: The Nature of Religion.* New York: Harcourt, 1959.

Eliot, Thomas Stearns. *Selected Essays.* New ed. New York: Harcourt, Brace, & World, 1960.

Emerson, Everett, ed. *Letters from New England: The Massachusetts Bay Colony, 1629–1638.* Amherst: University of Massachusetts Press, 1976.

Emerson, Ralph Waldo. *The Complete Writings of Ralph Waldo Emerson.* New York: Wm. H. Wise, 1929.

Emerson, William Richard. *Monmouth's Rebellion.* New Haven: Yale University Press, 1951.

Erdman, David V. *Blake: Prophet against Empire; A Poet's Interpretation of the History of His Own Times.* 3rd ed. Princeton, N.J.: Princeton University Press, 1954/1977.

Evans, Caleb. *British Constitutional Liberty.* Bristol: William Pine, 1775.

———. *Letter to the Rev. Mr. John Wesley.* New ed. Bristol: William Pine, 1775.

———. *Political Sophistry Detected; or, Reflections on the Rev. Mr. Fletcher's Late Tract Entitled "American Patriotism."* Bristol: William Pine, 1776.

Fannin, Jordan Rowan. "The Promise and Temptation of Allegory: Reading the Possibility of Pilgrimage in (Baptist) Bunyan and (Catholic) O'Connor." *American Baptist Quarterly* 33, nos. 3–4 (2014): 267–89.

Farrell, Michael. *Blake and the Methodists.* New York: Palgrave Macmillan, 2014.

Feake, Christopher. *A Beam of Light, Shining in the Midst of Much Darkness and Confusion.* London: J.C., 1659.

Ferguson, Niall. *Empire: The Rise and Demise of the British World Order and Lessons for Global Power.* New York: Basic Books, 2004.

Fiddes, Paul S. *Freedom and Limit: A Dialogue between Literature and Christian Doctrine.* Macon, Ga.: Mercer University Press, 1999.

———. *Tracks and Traces: Baptist Identity in Church and Theology.* Carlisle, U.K.: Paternoster, 2003.

Fielding, Henry. *The History of Tom Jones, a Foundling.* 4 vols. London: C. Cooke, 1792.

Firth, Katharine R. *The Apocalyptic Tradition in Reformation Britain, 1530–1645.* Oxford: Oxford University Press, 1979.

Fisch, Harold. *Jerusalem and Albion: The Hebraic Factor in Seventeenth-Century English Literature.* New York: Schocken, 1964.

Fisher, Edward. *The Marrow of Modern Divinity.* London: J.S., 1658.

Foucault, Michel. *Discipline and Punish.* New York: Vintage Books, 1977.

———. *Discipline and Punish*. Translated by Alan Sheridan. 2nd ed. New York: Vintage Books, 1995.

Fox, George. *The Works of George Fox*. 8 vols. Philadelphia: Marcus T. C. Gould, 1831.

Foxe, John. *Acts and Monuments*. London: John Day, 1563.

———. *The Acts and Monuments of John Foxe: A New and Complete Edition*. Edited by Stephen Reed Cattley. 7 vols. London: Seeley & Burnside, 1837–1841.

Franklin, Benjamin. *Autobiography: An Authoritative Text, Contexts, Criticism*. Edited by Joyce E. Chaplin. New York: W. W. Norton, 2012.

———. *The Papers of Benjamin Franklin*. Edited by Leonard W. Labaree et. al. 41 vols. New Haven: Yale University Press, 1959–2014.

———. *The Way of Wealth*. New York: Random House, 1930.

Freeman, Curtis W., ed. *A Company of Women Preachers: Baptist Prophetesses in Seventeenth-Century England*. Waco, Tex.: Baylor University Press, 2011.

———. "Last Heretic and/or First Baptist? Reflections on the Burning of Edward Wightman in 1612." In *Mirrors and Microscopes: Historical Perspectives of Baptists*, edited by C. Douglas Weaver, 74–86. Milton Keynes: Paternoster, 2015.

———. "Roger Williams, American Democracy, and the Baptists." *Perspectives in Religious Studies* 34, no. 3 (2007): 267–86.

Freeman, Thomas S. "A Library in Three Volumes: Foxe's 'Book of Martyrs' in the Writings of John Bunyan." *Bunyan Studies* 5 (1994): 47–57.

Frye, Northrop. *The Collected Works of Northrop Frye*. Edited by Alvin A. Lee. 30 vols. Toronto: University of Toronto Press, 1996.

———. *Fearful Symmetry: A Study of William Blake*. Princeton, N.J.: Princeton University Press, 1947.

———. *Northrop Frye in Conversation*. Edited by David Cayley. Concord, Ont.: Anansi, 1992.

———. "William Blake." In *The English Romantic Poets and Essayists*, edited by Lawrence Houtchens and Carolyn Houtchens, 1–35. New York: Modern Language Association, 1957.

Fowler, Edward. *The Design of Christianity*. London: R. Royfton, 1761.

———. *Dirt Wip't Off; or, A Manifest Discovery of the Gross Ignorance, Erroneousness and Most Unchristian Wicked Spirit of One John Bunyan, Lay-Preacher in Bedford*. London: Richard Royston, 1672.

Fuller, Andrew. *The Complete Works of Rev. Andrew Fuller*. Edited by Joseph Belcher. 3 vols. Philadelphia: American Baptist Publication Society, 1845. Reprint, Harrisonburg, Va.: Sprinkle, 1988.

Fuller, Millard. *No More Shacks*. Waco, Tex.: Word, 1986.

Furbank, Philip Nicholas, and W. R. Owens. *The Canonization of Daniel Defoe*. New Haven: Yale University Press, 1988.

———. *A Political Biography of Daniel Defoe*. London: Pickering & Chatto, 2006.

Gallie, W. B. "Essentially Contested Concept." In *The Importance of Language*, edited by Max Black, 121–46. Englewood Cliffs, N.J.: Prentice-Hall, 1962.

Gardiner, Samuel Rawson, ed. *The Constitutional Documents of the Puritan Revolution 1628–1660*. Oxford: Clarendon, 1889.

Gates, Henry Louis. *The Signifying Monkey: A Theory of African-American Literary Criticism.* New York: Oxford University Press, 1989.

Gaustad, Edwin Scott. *Dissent in American Religion.* Rev. ed. Chicago: University of Chicago Press, 2006.

General Catalogue, of the Theological and Literary Book-store, Kept by William W. Woodward, No. 52, South Second Street. Philadelphia: William W. Woodward, 1812.

Gilchrist, Alexander. *The Life of William Blake, "Pictor Ignotus."* London: Macmillan, 1863.

Gill, John. *A Body of Doctrinal Divinity.* London: M. & S. Highman, 1839.

Girard, Renè. *The Scapegoat.* Translated by Yvonne Freccero. Baltimore: Johns Hopkins University Press, 1986.

Golder, Harold. "Bunyan and Spenser." *PMLA* 45, no. 1 (1930): 216–37.

Goodwin, Philip. *The Mystery of Dreames, Historically Discoursed.* London, 1658.

Goodwin, John. *Anticavalierism; or, Truth Pleading as Well the Necessity as the Lawfulnesse of This Present Warre for the Suppressing of that Bloody Butcherly Brood of Cavaliering Indecencies.* London: Henry Overton, 1643.

Goodwin, Thomas. *The Works of Thomas Goodwin.* 12 vols. Edinburgh: James Nichol, 1861–1866.

Gordon, Alexander. *Addresses Biographical and Historical.* London: Lindsey Press, 1922.

———. *Heads of English Unitarian History.* London: Philip Green, 1895.

Gordon, Shirley C. *God Almighty Make Me Free: Christianity in Preemancipation Jamaica.* Indianapolis: Indiana University Press, 1996.

Greaves, Richard L. *Glimpses of Glory: John Bunyan and English Dissent.* Stanford: Stanford University Press, 2002.

———. "John Bunyan and the Fifth Monarchists." *Albion* 13, no. 2 (1981): 83–95.

———. "The Puritan-Nonconformist Tradition in England." *Albion* 17, no. 4 (1985): 449–86.

———. *Secrets of the Kingdom: British Radicals from the Popish Plot to the Revolution of 1688–89.* Stanford: Stanford University Press, 1992.

Green, Martin Burgess. *Dreams of Adventure, Deeds of Empire.* New York: Basic Books, 1979.

Greenwood, John, and Henry Barrow. *The Writings of John Greenwood 1587–1590, together with the Joint Writings of Henry Barrow and John Greenwood 1587–1590.* Edited by Leland H. Carlson. Vol. 4 of *Elizabethan Non-conformist Texts.* London: Allen & Unwin, 1962.

Gregory, Brad S. *Salvation at Stake: Christian Martyrdom in Early Modern Europe.* Cambridge, Mass.: Harvard University Press, 1999.

Griffiths, John, ed. *Homilies Appointed to Be Read in Churches.* London, 1623. Reprint, Brynmill, U.K.: Preservation Press, 2006.

Gunn, T. Jeremy. "The Separation of Church and State versus Religion in the Public Square: The Contested History of the Establishment Clause." In *No Establishment of Religion: America's Original Contribution to Religious Liberty*, edited by T. Jeremy Gunn and John Witte Jr., 15–44. New York: Oxford University Press, 2012.

Gutteridge, Thomas. *The Universal Elegy; or, A Poem on Bunhill Burial Ground*. London, 1735?.

Gwyn, Douglas. "The Early Quaker Lamb's War: Secularism and the Death of Tragedy in Early Modern England." In *Towards Tragedy / Reclaiming Hope: Literature, Theology and Sociology in Conversation*, edited by Pink Dandelion, 33–56. Aldershot, U.K.: Ashgate, 2004.

Ha, Polly, and Patrick Collinson, eds. *The Reception of Continental Reformation in Britain*. New York: Oxford University Press, 2010.

Halévy, Elie. *The Birth of Methodism in England*. Translated by Bernard Semmel. Chicago: University of Chicago Press, 1971.

———. *A History of the English People in the Nineteenth Century*. Translated by E. I. Watkin and D. A. Baker. London: Ernest Benn Limited, 1912.

Hall, David D. *The Antinomian Controversy, 1636–1638: A Documentary History*. 2nd ed. Durham, N.C.: Duke University Press, 1990.

Hall, Joseph. *Contemplations Upon the Principal Passages of the Holy Story*, vol. 2. London: H. L[ownes], 1614.

Hall, Robert [Jr.]. *The Works of Robert Hall*. 6 vols. London: Henry G. Bohn, 1851.

Hall, Robert [Sr.]. *Help to Zion's Travelers*. Bristol: William Pine, 1781.

Haller, William. *Foxe's Book of Martyrs and the Elect Nation*. London: Jonathan Cape, 1963.

———. *The Rise of Puritanism*. New York: Columbia University Press, 1957.

Hardt, Michael, and Antonio Negri. *Empire*. Cambridge, Mass.: Harvard University Press, 2000.

Harper, George Mills. *The Neoplatonism of William Blake*. Chapel Hill: University of North Carolina Press, 1961.

Harris, Tim. *Restoration: Charles II and His Kingdoms, 1660–1685*. London: Penguin, 2005.

Harrison, Robert, and Robert Browne. *The Writings of Robert Harrison and Robert Browne*. Edited by Albert Peel and Leland H. Carson. Vol. 2 of *Elizabethan Nonconformist Texts*. London: George Allen & Unwin, 1953.

Hatch, Nathan. *The Democratization of American Christianity*. New Haven: Yale University Press, 1989.

Hauerwas, Stanley. "The Past Matters Theologically: Thinking Tradition." In *Theologies of Retrieval: An Exploration and Appraisal*, edited by Darren Sarisky. London: T&T Clark, 2017.

Hauerwas, Stanley, and Frank Lentricchia, eds. *Dissent from the Homeland*. Durham, N.C.: Duke University Press, 2003.

Hauerwas, Stanley, and William H. Willimon. *Resident Aliens: Life in the Christian Colony*. Nashville: Abingdon, 1989.

Haymes, Brian. "On Religious Liberty: Re-reading *A Short Declaration of the Mystery of Iniquity* in London in 2005." *Baptist Quarterly* 42, no. 3 (2007): 197–217.

Hays, Richard B. *The Conversion of the Imagination: Paul as Interpreter of Israel's Scripture*. Grand Rapids: Eerdmans, 2005.

————. *Echoes of Scripture in the Gospels.* Waco, Tex.: Baylor University Press, 2016.

Helwys, Thomas. *A Short Declaration of the Mystery of Iniquity.* Edited by Richard Groves. Macon, Ga.: Mercer University Press, 1998.

Hemans, Felicia Dorothea. *The Poetical Works of Mrs. Hemans.* London: Frederick Warne, n.d.

Hempton, David. *Methodism and Politics in British Society, 1750–1850.* Stanford: Stanford University Press, 1984.

Herstein, Gary. "The Roycean Roots of the Beloved Community." *Pluralist* 4, no. 2 (2009): 91–107.

Hicks, Edward. *Memoirs of the Life and Religious Labors of Edward Hicks.* Philadelphia: Merrihew & Thompson, 1851.

Hill, Christopher. *The Collected Essays of Christopher Hill.* 3 vols. Amherst: University of Massachusetts Press, 1986.

————. *Milton and the English Revolution.* Harmondsworth: Penguin, 1979.

————. *Society and Puritanism in Pre-revolutionary England.* 2nd ed. New York: Schocken Books, 1967.

————. *A Turbulent, Seditious, and Factious People: John Bunyan and His Church, 1628–1688.* Oxford: Oxford University Press, 1998.

————. *The World Turned Upside Down.* London: Penguin, 1972.

Hill, Christopher, and Edmund Dell, eds. *The Good Old Cause: The English Revolution of 1640–1660.* New York: Routledge, 2012.

Hill, Christopher, with Barry Reay and William Lamont. *The World of the Muggletonians.* London: Temple Smith, 1983.

Hindmarsh, Robert. *Rise and Progress of the New Jerusalem Church.* Edited by Rev. Edward Madeley. London: Hodson & Son, 1861.

Hinton, John Howard. *Memoir of William Knibb.* London: Houlston & Stonemen, 1847.

Hobbes, Thomas. *Leviathan; or, The Matter, Forme and Power of a Common Wealth Ecclesiastical and Civil.* London: Andrew Crooke, 1651. Reprint, Chicago: University of Chicago Press, 1952.

Hofmeyr, Isabel. "Bunyan: Colonial, Postcolonial." In *The Cambridge Companion to Bunyan,* edited by Anne Dunan-Page, 162–76. Cambridge: Cambridge University Press, 2010.

————. *The Portable Bunyan: A Transnational History of "The Pilgrim's Progress."* Princeton, N.J.: Princeton University Press, 2004.

Hopkins, James K. *A Woman to Deliver Her People: Joanna Southcot and English Millenarianism in an Era of Revolution.* Austin: University of Texas Press, 1982.

Hordern, William. "Young Theologians Rebel." *Christian Century,* March 12, 1952, 306–7.

Horst, Irvin Buckwalter. *The Radical Brethren: Anabaptism and the English Reformation.* Nieuwkoop: B. De Graaf, 1972.

Howe, John. *The Works of the Rev. John Howe.* Edited by J. P. Hewlett. 3 vols. London: William Tegg, 1848. Reprint, Ligonier, Penn.: Soli Deo Gloria, 1990.

Hughes, Ann. *Gangraena and the Struggle for the English Revolution.* Oxford: Oxford University Press, 2004.

Hunter, J. Paul. *The Reluctant Pilgrim: Defoe's Emblematic Method and Quest for Form in "Robinson Crusoe."* Baltimore: Johns Hopkins Press, 1966.

The Inscriptions Upon the Tombs, Grave-Stones, &c. in the Dissenters Burial-Place Near Bunhill-Fields. London: E. Curll, 1717.

Irenaeus of Leon. *Against Heresies.* In *Ante-Nicene Fathers,* vol. 1. Grand Rapids: Eerdmans, 1979.

Itzkin, Elissa S. "The Halévy Thesis: A Working Hypothesis? English Revivalism: Antidote for Revolution and Radicalism 1789–1815." *Church History* 44, no. 1 (1975): 47–56.

Ivimey, Joseph. *A History of the English Baptists.* 4 vols. London: Isaac Taylor Hinton, Warwick Square, and Holdsworth & Ball, St Paul's Church-Yard, 1811–1830.

Jackson, Heather J. *Those Who Write for Immortality: Romantic Reputations and the Dream of Lasting Fame.* New Haven: Yale University Press, 2015.

James R[ex]. *A True Relation of the Commissions and Warrants for the Condemnation and Burning of Bartholomew Legatt and Thomas Withman [sic].* London: Michael Spark, 1651.

James, William. *Varieties of Religious Experience.* New York: Collins, 1960.

Janis, Irving L. *Groupthink: Psychological Studies of Policy Decisions and Fiascoes.* 2nd ed. Boston: Houghton Mifflin, 1982.

Jauss, Hans Robert. "Literary History as a Challenge to Literary Theory." *New Literary History* 2, no. 1 (1970): 7–37.

——. *Toward an Aesthetic of Reception.* Translated by Timothy Bahti. Minneapolis: University of Minnesota Press, 1982.

Jefferson, Thomas. *The Papers of Thomas Jefferson.* Princeton, N.J.: Princeton University Press, 1950.

——. *The Writings of Thomas Jefferson.* 20 vols. Washington, D.C.: Taylor & Maury, 1854.

Jesse, Jennifer G. *William Blake's Religious Vision: There's a Methodism in His Madness.* Plymouth, U.K.: Lexington Books, 2013.

Jessey, Henry. *The Exceeding Riches of Grace Advanced.* London: Matthew Simmons, 1647.

Jordan, Clarence. *The Cotton Patch Version of Paul's Epistles.* New York: Association Press, 1968.

——. *The Substance of Faith and Other Cotton Patch Sermons.* Edited by Dallas Lee. Eugene, Ore.: Cascade, 2005.

Judson, Adoniram. "Obituary—Mrs. Sarah B. Judson." *Baptist Missionary Magazine* 26, no. 2 (1846): 41–44.

Judson, Emily C. *Memoir of Mrs. Sarah B. Judson.* New York: Colby, 1849.

Juster, Susan. "Mystical Pregnancy and Holy Bleeding: Visionary Experience in Early Modern Britain and America." *William and Mary Quarterly* 57, no. 2 (2000): 249–88.

Kadane, Matthew. "Anti-Trinitarianism and the Republican Tradition in Enlightenment Britain." *Republic of Letters* 2, no. 1 (2010): 38–54.

Keeble, N. H., ed. *John Bunyan: Conventicle and Parnassus; Tercentenary Essays*. Oxford: Clarendon, 1988.

———. *The Restoration: England in the 1660s*. Oxford: Blackwell, 2002.

Kelhoffer, James A. *Miracle and Mission: The Authentication of Missionaries and Their Message in the Longer Ending of Mark*. Tubingen: Mohr Siebeck, 2000.

Keller, Catherine. *Apocalypse Now and Then*. Minneapolis: Fortress 2005.

Kelly, John, and Norman Davidson. *Early Christian Creeds*. 3rd ed. New York: Longman, 1972.

Kennedy, Fred W. *Daddy Sharpe: A Narrative of the Life and Adventures of Samuel Sharpe*. Kingston, Jamaica: Ian Randle, 2008.

Kiffen, William. *The Humble Apology of Some Commonly Called Anabaptists*. London: Henry Hills, 1661.

King, Martin Luther, Jr. *A Testament of Hope: The Essential Writings and Speeches of Martin Luther King, Jr.* Edited by James Melvin Washington. San Francisco: HarperCollins, 1986.

King Online Encyclopedia. The Martin Luther King Jr. Research and Education Institute, Stanford University, http://kingencyclopedia.stanford.edu/encyclopedia/documentsentry/mia_mass_meeting_at_holt_street_baptist_church/. Accessed June 22, 2016.

Knott, John R. *Discourses of Martyrdom in English Literature, 1563–1694*. Cambridge: Cambridge University Press, 1993.

Kreitzer, Larry. *Kissing the Book: The Story of Sam Sharpe as Revealed in the Records of the National Archives at Kew*. Oxford: Regent's Park College, 2013.

Kyi, Aung San Suu. "Aung San Suu Kyi in Washington." September 18, 2012. http://asiasociety.org/video/policy/aung-san-suu-kyi-washington-complete?page=1. Accessed November 11, 2015.

Lachman, David C. *The Marrow Controversy*. Edinburgh: Rutherford House, 1988.

Lake, Peter. *Anglicans and Puritans? Presbyterianism and English Conformist Thought from Whitgift to Hooker*. London: Unwin Hyman, 1988.

———. *The Boxmaker's Revenge: "Orthodoxy," "Heterodoxy" and the Politics of the Parish in Early Stuart London*. Stanford: Stanford University Press, 2001.

Lamont, William. *Last Witnesses: The Muggletonian History, 1652–1979*. Burlington, Vt.: Ashgate, 2006.

Laqueur, Thomas W. *The Works of the Dead: A Cultural History of Mortal Remains*. Princeton, N.J.: Princeton University Press, 2015.

Latourette, Kenneth Scott. *History of the Expansion of Christianity*. 7 vols. New York: Harper & Row, 1937–1945.

Laws, Curtis Lee. "Convention Sidelights." *Watchman-Examiner*, July 1, 1920, 834–35.

The Leacherous Anabaptist; or, The Dipper Dipt'. London, 1681.

Lederach, John Paul. *The Moral Imagination*. Oxford: Oxford University Press, 2005.

Lee, Dallas. *The Cotton Patch Evidence*. New York: Harper & Row, 1971.

Lee, Richard Henry. *The Letters of Richard Henry Lee*. Edited by James Curtis Ballagh. 2 vols. New York: Macmillan, 1911–1914.

Lee, Sidney. *Oxford Dictionary of National Biography*. Edited by Leslie Stephen, Sidney Lee, and Christine Nicholls. Oxford: Oxford University Press, 2004–2014.

Leith, John H., ed. *Creeds of the Churches*. New York: Anchor Books, 1963.

———, ed. *Creeds of the Churches*. 3rd ed. Louisville, Ky.: Westminster John Knox, 1982.

Leland, John. *The Writings of the Late Elder John Leland*. Edited by L. F. Greene. New York: G.W. Wood, 1845. Reprint, New York: Arno, 1969.

Levens, Laura Rogers. "'Reading the Judsons': Recovering the Literary Works of Ann, Sarah, Emily, and Adoniram Judson for a New Baptist Missionary History." *American Baptist Quarterly* 32, no. 1 (2013): 37–73.

Lilburne, John. *The Free-Mans Freedome Vindicated*. London, 1646.

Lincoln, Abraham. Second Inaugural Address (March 4, 1865). In *The Collected Works of Abraham Lincoln*, edited by Roy P. Basler, 8:332–33. New Brunswick, N.J.: Rutgers University Press, 1953.

Lischer, Richard. *The Preacher King: Martin Luther King Jr. and the Word That Moved America*. New York: Oxford University Press, 1995.

Locke, John. *A Letter concerning Toleration*. Indianapolis: Liberty Fund, 2010.

———. *The Works of John Locke*. 10 vols. London: Thomas Tegg, 1823.

Lowenstein, David. "The War of the Lamb: George Fox and the Apocalyptic Discourses of Revolutionary Quakerism." In *The Emergence of Quaker Writing: Dissenting Literature in Seventeenth-Century England*, edited by Thomas N. Corns and David Lowenstein, 25–41. London: Frank Cass, 1995.

Lumpkin, William Latane. *Baptist Confessions of Faith*. Valley Forge, Penn.: Judson, 1959.

Macaulay, Lord Thomas Babington. *The History of England from the Accession of James II*. Edited by Charles Harding Firth. London: Macmillan, 1913. Originally published in 1848.

Machor, James, and Philip Goldstein, eds. *Reception Study: From Literary Theory to Cultural Studies*. New York: Routledge, 2001.

MacIntyre, Alasdair. *After Virtue: A Study in Moral Theory*. Notre Dame, Ind.: University of Notre Dame Press, 1981.

———. *Three Rival Versions of Moral Enquiry: Encyclopaedia, Genealogy, and Tradition*. Notre Dame, Ind.: University of Notre Dame Press, 1990.

Madison, James. *The Papers of James Madison*. Edited by Robert E. Rutland and William M. E. Rachal. Chicago: University of Chicago Press, 1984.

Mangum, R. Todd. *The Dispensational-Covenantal Rift: The Fissuring of American Evangelical Theology from 1936 to 1944*. Milton Keynes: Paternoster, 2007.

Marlowe, Christopher. *The Complete Plays*. Edited by J. B. Steane. Harmondsworth: Penguin, 1969.

Marsden, George M. *Understanding Fundamentalism and Evangelicalism*. Grand Rapids: Eerdmans, 1991.

Marshall, John. "Locke, Socianism, 'Socinianism,' and Unitarianism." In *English Philosophy in the Age of Locke*, edited by M. A. Stewart, 111–82. Oxford: Clarendon, 2000.

Marshall, Peter, and David Manuel. *The Light and the Glory*. Old Tappan, N.J.: Revell, 1977.

Marshall, Stephen. *A Sacred Panegyrick, or a Sermon of Thanksgiving*. London, 1644.

Martyn, J. Lewis. *Galatians*. Anchor Yale Bible. New Haven: Yale University Press, 1997.

———. *Galatians*. New York: Doubleday, 1997.

———. "The Gospel Invades Philosophy." In *Paul, Philosophy, and the Theopolitical Vision*, edited by Douglas Harink, 13–33. Eugene, Ore.: Cascade, 2010.

———. *Theological Issues in the Letters of Paul*. Nashville: Abingdon, 1997.

Marx, Karl. *Capital*. Translated by Samuel Moore and Edward Aveling. Great Books of the Western World. Chicago: Encyclopaedia Britannica, 1952.

Mather, Cotton. *Magnalia Christi Americana: The Ecclesiastical History of New England*. London: Thomas Parkhurst, 1702.

McCalman, Iain. *Radical Underworld: Prophets, Revolutionaries and Pornographers in London, 1795–1840*. Cambridge: Cambridge University Press, 1988.

McClendon, James Wm., Jr. *Biography as Theology: How Life Stories Can Remake Today's Theology*. Nashville: Abingdon, 1974.

———. *Doctrine: Systematic Theology*. Vol. 2. Nashville: Abingdon, 1994. Repr. with a new introduction by Curtis W. Freeman. Waco, Tex.: Baylor University Press, 2012.

———. *Ethics: Systematic Theology*. Vol. 1. Nashville: Abingdon, 1986. 2nd ed., rev. and enlarged. Nashville: Abingdon, 2002. Repr. with a new introduction by Curtis W. Freeman. Waco, Tex.: Baylor University Press, 2012.

———. *Witness: Systematic Theology*. Vol. 3. Nashville: Abingdon, 2000. Repr. with a new introduction by Curtis W. Freeman. Waco, Tex.: Baylor University Press, 2012.

McClendon, James Wm., Jr., and James M. Smith. *Convictions: Defusing Religious Relativism*. Rev. ed. Valley Forge, Penn.: Trinity, 1994.

McKinstry, Carolyn. *While the World Watched: A Birmingham Bombing Survivor Comes of Age during the Civil Rights Movement*. Carol Stream, Ill.: Tyndale House, 2011.

McLachlan, H. John. *Socinianism in Seventeenth-Century England*. London: Oxford University Press, 1951.

McLoughlin, William G. *New England Dissent, 1630–1833*. 2 vols. Cambridge, Mass.: Harvard University Press, 1971.

Mead, Sidney E. *Lively Experiment: The Shaping of Christianity in America*. New York: Harper, 1963.

Mede, Joseph. *The Key of the Revelation*. Translated by Richard More. London: R. B., 1643.

Mellvill, James. *The Autobiography and Diary of Mr. James Mellvill*. Edited by Robert Pitcairn. Edinburgh: Woodrow Society, 1842.

Merton, Thomas. "Blake and the New Theology." In *The Literary Essays of Thomas Merton*, edited by Patrick Hart, 3–11. New York: New Directions, 1985.

—. *The Seven Storey Mountain: An Autobiography of Faith.* New York: Harcourt, 1948.

Metaxas, Eric. *If You Can Keep It: The Forgotten Promise of American Liberty.* New York: Viking, 2016.

Michael, Franz, ed. *The Taiping Rebellion: History and Documents.* 3 vols. Seattle: University of Washington Press, 1971.

Miller, Perry. *Errand into the Wilderness.* Cambridge, Mass.: Belknap, 1956.

—. *Jonathan Edwards.* New York: William Sloan, 1949. Reprint, Lincoln: University of Nebraska Press, 2005.

—. *The New England Mind: From Colony to Province.* 2 vols. Cambridge, Mass.: Belknap, 1953.

—. *Roger Williams: His Contribution to the American Tradition.* Indianapolis: Bobbs-Merrill, 1953.

Miller, Perry, and Thomas H. Johnson, eds. *The Puritans: A Sourcebook of Their Writings.* 2 vols. New York: Harper, 1963.

Milton, John. *John Milton Complete Poems and Major Prose.* Edited by Merritt Y. Hughes. New York: Macmillan, 1957.

The Mishnah. Translated by Herbert Danby. London: Oxford University Press, 1983.

Montgomery, Helen Barrett. *The Bible and Missions.* West Medford, Mass.: Central Committee on the United States of Foreign Missions, 1920.

Moore, LeRoy, Jr. "Roger Williams and the Historians." *Church History* 32 (1963): 432–51.

Morden, Peter J. *Communion with Christ and His People: The Spirituality of C. H. Spurgeon.* Oxford: Regent's Park College, 2010.

—. *Offering Christ to the World: Andrew Fuller (1754–1815) and the Revival of Eighteenth Century Particular Baptist Life.* Carlisle, U.K.: Paternoster, 2003.

More, Henry. *A Modest Enquiry into the Mystery of Iniquity.* London: James Flesher, 1664.

—. *Synopsis Prophetica; or, The Second Part of the Enquiry Into the Mystery of Iniquity.* London: James Flesher, 1664.

Morgan, Edmund S. *The Puritan Dilemma: The Story of John Winthrop.* Boston: Little, Brown, 1958.

—. *Visible Saints.* New York: New York University Press, 1963.

Morse, Christopher. *The Difference Heaven Makes: Rehearing the Gospel as News.* London: T&T Clark, 2010.

Mortimer, Sarah. *Reason and Religion in the English Revolution: The Challenge of Socinianism.* Cambridge: Cambridge University Press, 2010.

Morton, Arthur L. *The Everlasting Gospel: A Study in the Sources of William Blake.* New York: Haskell House, 1966.

Moyers, Bill. "Bill Moyers on Saving Our Democracy, 'Selma' and LBJ." Interview with Karin Kamp. In Moyers and Company. January 14, 2015. http://billmoyers.com/2015/01/14/whats-bills-mind/. Accessed July 18, 2016.

Muggeridge, Malcolm. *A Third Testament.* Boston: Little, Brown, 1976.

Nackenoff, Carol. "The Horatio Alger Myth." In *Myth America: A Historical Anthology*, 2nd ed., edited by Patrick Gerster and Nicholas Cords, 2:72–76. St. James, N.Y.: Brandywine, 2006.

A Narrative of the Apprehending, Commitment, Arraignment, Condemnation, and Execution of John James. London, 1662.

Naylor, James. *The Lambs Warre against the Man of Sinne*. London: Thomas Simmons, 1657.

Newman, John Henry. *Apologia Pro Vita Sua*. Edited by David J. DeLaura. New York: W. W. Norton, 1968.

Newton, John, and William Cowper. *The Olney Hymns*. Bucks, U.K.: Arthur Gordon Hugh Osborn for the Cowper & Newton Museum, 1979. Facsimile from the 1st ed. at Cowper & Newton Museum, published in 1779.

Ney, Julius. *Geschichte des Reichstages zu Speyer im Jahre 1529: Mit einem Anhange ungedruckter Akten und Briefe*. Hamburg: Angentur des Rauhen Hauses, 1800.

Nicolson, Adam. *God's Secretaries: The Making of the King James Bible*. New York: Harper Collins, 2003.

Niebuhr, H. Richard. *The Kingdom of God in America*. New York: Harper & Row, 1937. Reprint, Middletown, Conn.: Wesleyan University Press, 1988

Noll, Mark A. *America's God: From Jonathan Edwards to Abraham Lincoln*. New York: Oxford University Press, 2002.

Norvig, Gerda S. *Dark Figures in the Desired Country: Blake's Illustrations to "The Pilgrim's Progress."* Berkeley: University of California Press, 1993.

Nuttall, Geoffrey F. *The Holy Spirit in Puritan Faith and Experience*. Oxford: Basil Blackwell, 1946.

O'Brien, Glen. "John Wesley's Rebuke to the Rebels of British America: Revisiting the *Calm Address*." *Methodist Review* 4 (2012): 31–55.

O'Regan, Cyril. *Theology and the Spaces of Apocalyptic*. Milwaukee, Wis.: Marquette University Press, 2009.

Owens, William Robert. "Bunyan and the Millennium." In *John Bunyan and His England, 1628–88*, edited by Anne Laurence, W. R. Owens, and Stuart Sim. London: Hambledon, 1990.

Oxford Dictionary of National Biography. Oxford: Oxford University Press, 2004–2014.

Oyer, Gordon. *Pursuing the Spiritual Roots of Protest*. Eugene, Ore.: Cascade, 2014.

Paine, Thomas. *Rights of Man*. London: J. S. Jordan, 1791.

Paley, Morton D. *The Continuing City: William Blake's Jerusalem*. Oxford: Oxford University Press, 1983.

———. *William Blake*. New York: E. P. Dutton, 1978.

Papias. *Fragments*. In *The Ante-Nicene Fathers*, vol. 1. Grand Rapids: Eerdmans, 1979.

Parish Law: Being a Digest of the Law Relating to Parishes. Cambridge: Cambridge University Press, 1830.

Parker, Henry. *A Discourse concerning Puritans*. 2nd ed. London: Printed for Robert Bostock, 1641.

Parker, Samuel. *A Discourse of Ecclesiastical Politie.* 3rd ed. London: John Martyn, 1671.

Patrick, Simon. *A Continuation of the Friendly Debate.* London: R. Royston, 1669.

———. *A Friendly Debate between a Conformist and a Non-conformist.* London: R. Royston, 1669.

———. *A Further Continuation and Defense; or, A Third Part of the Friendly Debate.* London: E.G. & A.C., 1670.

Pattison, Robert. *The Great Dissent: John Henry Newman and the Liberal Heresy.* New York: Oxford University Press, 1991.

Paul, Thomas. *Some Serious Reflections on That Part of Mr. Bunion's Confession of Faith: Touching Church Communion with Unbaptized Persons.* London: Francis Smith, 1673.

Payne, Ernest A. "John Linnell, the World of Artists and the Baptists." Edited by Roger Hayden. *Baptist Quarterly* 40, no. 1 (2003): 22–35.

———. *Thomas Helwys and the First Baptist Church in England.* 2nd ed. London: Baptist Union of Great Britain, 1966.

Pearsall, Derek. *Piers Plowman: A New Annotated Edition of the C-text.* Exeter: University of Exeter Press, 2008.

Pelikan, Jaroslav. *The Christian Tradition: A History of the Development of Doctrine.* Vol. 1, *The Emergence of the Catholic Tradition (100–600).* Chicago: University of Chicago Press, 1971.

Penn, William. *No Cross, No Crown.* 8th ed. Leeds: James Lister, 1743. Originally published in 1668.

Perkins, William. *The Works of That Famous and Worthy Minister of Christ in the Universitie of Cambridge, Mr. William Perkins.* 3 vols. London: John Legatt, 1626.

———. *The Work of William Perkins.* Edited by Ian Breward. Appleford, Abingdon: Sutton Courtenay, 1970.

Phillippo, James M. *Jamaica: Its Past and Present State.* London: John Snow, 1843.

Poore, Benjamin Perley. *Federal and State Constitutions, Colonial Charters, and Other Organic Laws of the United States.* 2nd ed. 2 parts. Washington, D.C.: Government Printing Office, 1878.

Pope, Robert, ed. *T&T Clark Companion to Nonconformity.* London: T&T Clark, 2013.

Porter, Andrew. *Religion versus Empire: British Protestant Missionaries and Overseas Expansion, 1700–1914.* Manchester: Manchester University Press, 2004.

Portier-Young, Anthea E. *Apocalypse Against Empire: Theologies of Resistance in Early Judaism.* Grand Rapids: Eerdmans, 2011.

Powell, Vavasor. *The Bird in the Cage Chirping.* London: L. C., 1661.

———. *Common-Prayer-Book No Divine Service.* London: Livewell Chapman, 1660.

———. *Spirituall Experiences, of Sundry Beleevers.* London: Robert Ibbitson, 1653.

Price, E. O. *Animal Domestication and Behavior.* New York: CABI, 2002.

Putnam, Robert. "Bowling Alone: America's Declining Social Capital." *Journal of Democracy* 6, no. 1 (1995): 65–78.

Raboteau, Albert. *Slave Religion: The Invisible Institution in the Antebellum South.* Oxford: Oxford University Press, 1978.

Rack, Henry D. *Reasonable Enthusiast: John Wesley and the Rise of Methodism*. 3rd ed. London: Epworth, 2002.

Raine, Kathleen. *Blake and the New Age*. London: George Allen, 1979.

———. *Blake and Tradition*. 2 vols. Princeton, N.J.: Princeton University Press, 1968.

Raithby, John, ed. *Statutes of the Realm*. 9 vols. London: G. Eyre & A. Strahan, 1819.

Rapp, John A. "Clashing Dilemmas: Hong Renan, Issachar Roberts, and a Taiping 'Murder' Mystery." *Journal of Historical Biography* 4, no. 4 (2008): 27–58.

A Ra-Ree Show. London: For B.T., 1681.

Rathbun, Robert C., and Martin Steinmann Jr., eds. *From Jane Austen to Joseph Conrad*. Minneapolis: University of Minnesota Press, 1958.

Ratzinger, Cardinal Joseph. *Salt of the Earth: The Church at the End of the Millennium*. Translated by Adrian Walker. San Francisco: Ignatius, 1997.

Rauschenbusch, Walter. *Christianity and the Social Crisis*. New York: Macmillan, 1907.

———. *Christianizing the Social Order*. New York: Macmillan, 1913.

———. *A Theology for the Social Gospel*. New York: Macmillan, 1917.

Reckord, Mary. "The Jamaica Slave Rebellion of 1831." *Past & Present* 40, no. 3 (1968): 108–25.

Records of the Colony of Rhode Island and Providence Plantations. Providence, R.I.: A. Crawford Greene & Brother, 1856–1865.

Reed, Charles. *History of the Bunhill Fields Burial Ground*. London: Charles Skipper & East, 1893.

Reid, C. Sam. *Samuel Sharpe: From Slave to National Hero*. Kingston, Jamaica: Bustamante Institute, 1988.

Reilly, Thomas H. *The Taiping Heavenly Kingdom: Rebellion and the Blasphemy of Empire*. Seattle: University of Washington Press, 2004.

Reis, Elizabeth. "Seventeenth-Century Puritan Conversion Narratives." In *Religions of the United States in Practice*, edited by Colleen McDannell, 1:22–31. Princeton, N.J.: Princeton University Press, 2001.

"The Religion of Robinson Crusoe: Belief in Providence Was Its Outstanding Feature." *Current Opinion* 67, no. 3 (1919): 177–78.

Rivera, Luis N. *A Violent Evangelism: The Political and Religious Conquest of the Americas*. Louisville, Ky.: Westminster John Knox, 1992.

Robert, Dana L., ed. *Converting Colonialism: Visions and Realities in Mission History, 1706–1914*. Grand Rapids: Eerdmans, 2008.

Roberts, Jonathan, and Christopher Rowland. "William Blake." In *The Blackwell Companion to the Bible in English Literature*, edited by Rebecca Lemon, Emma Mason, Jonathan Roberts, and Christopher Rowland, 373–83. Malden, Mass.: Wiley-Blackwell, 2009.

Robinson, Henry Crabb. *Diary, Reminiscences, and Correspondence of Henry Crabb Robinson*. Edited by Thomas Sadler. Boston: Houghton, Mifflin, 1898.

Robinson, H. Wheeler. "Hebrew Psychology." In *The People and the Book*, edited by Arthur S. Peake, 353–82. Oxford: Clarendon, 1925.

Robinson, John. *The Works of John Robinson*. London: John Snow, 1851.

Rogers, Edward. *Some Accounts of the Life and Opinions of a Fifth Monarchy Man*. London: Longmans, 1867.

Rogers, Pat, ed. *Defoe: The Critical Heritage*. London: Routledge & Kegan Paul, 1972.

Rolt, Lionel Thomas Caswell. *James Watt*. New York: Arco, 1963.

Rosso, G. A. *The Religion of Empire: Political Theology in Blake's Prophetic Symbolism*. Columbus: Ohio State University Press, 2016.

Rowland, Christopher. "Blake and the Bible: Biblical Exegesis in the Work of William Blake." In *Biblical Interpretation: The Meanings of Scripture—Past and Present*, edited by John M. Court, 168–84. London: T&T Clark, 2003.

———. *Blake and the Bible*. New Haven: Yale University Press, 2010.

———. *The Open Heaven: A Study of Apocalyptic in Judaism and Early Christianity*. New York: Crossroad, 1982.

———. "William Blake: A Visionary for Our Time." *Open Democracy*, November 27, 2007. https://opendemocracy.net/article/arts_culture/literature/william_blake_visionary. Accessed April 21, 2016.

Royce, Josiah. *The Problem of Christianity*. 2 vols. New York: Macmillan, 1913.

Russell, Horace O. *Samuel Sharpe and the Meaning of Freedom: Reflections on a Baptist National Hero of Jamaica*. Oxford: Regent's Park College, 2012.

Ryan, Robert M. *The Romantic Reformation: Religious Politics in English Literature 1789–1824*. Cambridge: Cambridge University Press, 1997.

Said, Edward W. *Culture and Imperialism*. New York: Knopf, 1993.

———. *Orientalism*. New York: Vintage Books, 1979.

Sandberg, Russell. *Law and Religion*. Cambridge: Cambridge University Press, 2011.

Sanneh, Lamin. "Christian Missions and the Western Guilt Complex." *Christian Century*, April 8, 1987, 331–34.

———. *Translating the Message: The Missionary Impact on Culture*. Maryknoll, N.Y.: Orbis, 1989.

Schleiermacher, Friedrich. *On Religion: Addresses in Response to Its Cultured Critics*. Translated by Terrence N. Tice. Richmond, Va.: John Knox, 1969.

Schuchard, Marsha Keith, and Keri Davis. "Recovering the Lost Moravian History of William Blake's Family." *Blake: An Illustrated Quarterly* 37 (2004): 36–43.

Scott, Christopher L. *The Maligned Militia: The West Country Militia of the Monmouth Rebellion, 1685*. Burlington, Vt.: Ashgate, 2015.

Séguenny, André, with Jean Rott and Martin Rothkegel, eds. *Bibliotheca Dissidentium*. Baden-Baden: Valentin Koerner, 1980–present.

Semple, Robert B. *A History of the Rise and Progress of the Baptists in Virginia*. Rev. ed. Richmond, Va.: Pitt & Dickinson, 1894.

Senior, Bernard Martin. *Jamaica: As It Was, as It Is, and as It May Be*. New York: Negro Universities Press, 1969. Originally published, London: T. Hurst, 1835.

Shain, Barry Alan. *The Myth of American Individualism: The Protestant Origins of American Political Thought*. Princeton, N.J.: Princeton University Press, 1994.

Shakespeare, William. *The Complete Works of Shakespeare*. Edited by David Bevington. Glenview, Ill.: Scott, Foresman, 1980.

Shannon, David T., ed. *George Liele's Life and Legacy: An Unsung Hero*. Macon, Ga.: Mercer University Press, 2012.

Sharrock, Roger. "Bunyan Studies Today: An Evaluation." In *Bunyan in England and Abroad*, edited by M. van Os and G. J. Schutte, 45–59. Amsterdam: VU University Press, 1990.

———. *John Bunyan*. New York: Macmillan, 1968.

Shenk, Wilbert R. "The 'Great Century' Reconsidered." In *Anabaptism and Mission*, edited by Wilbert R. Shenk, 158–77. Scottdale, Penn.: Herald, 1984.

A Short Relation of Some Part of the Sad Sufferings and Cruel Havock and Spoil, Inflicted on the Persons and Estates of the People of God, in Scorn Called Quakers. London, 1670.

Shriver, Frederick. "Hampton Court Re-visited: James I and the Puritans." *Journal of Ecclesiastical History* 33, no. 1 (1982): 48–71.

Shurtleff, Nathaniel E., ed. *Records of the Governor and Company of Massachusetts Bay in New England*. Boston: William White, 1853.

Sim, Stuart. "Bunyan and His Fundamentalist Readers." In *Reception, Appropriation, Recollection: Bunyan's "Pilgrim's Progress,"* edited by W. R. Owens and Stuart Sim, 213–28. Oxford: Peter Lang, 2007.

A Sketch of the History and Proceedings of the Deputies Appointed to Protect the Civil Rights of Protestant Dissenters. London: Samuel Burton, 1813.

Sklar, Susanne. *Blake's "Jerusalem" as Visionary Theatre: Entering the Divine Body*. New York: Oxford University Press, 2011.

Smith, Craig R. *Daniel Webster and the Oratory of Civil Religion*. Columbia: University of Missouri Press, 2005.

Smith, Francis. *An Account of the Injurious Proceedings of Sir George Jeffreys, Knt., Late Recorder of London, Against Francis Smith, Bookseller with His Arbitrary Carriage Towards the Grand-Jury at Guild-Hall, Sept. 16, 1680, Upon an Indictment Then Exhibited Against the Said Francis Smith, for Publishing a Pretended Libel, Entituled, An Act of Common-Council for Retrenching the Expences of the Lord Mayor and Sheriffs of the City of London, &c*. London: Francis Smith, 1681.

———. *Symptoms of Growth and Decay in Godliness*. London: Francis Smith, 1673.

———. *Vox Populi; or, The Peoples Claim to Their Parliaments Sitting, to Redress Grievances, and Provide for the Common Safety, by the Known Laws and Constitutions of the Nation Humbly Recommended to the King and Parliament at their Meeting at Oxford, the 21st of March*. London: Francis Smith, 1681.

Smith, James K. A. *How (Not) to Be Secular: Reading Charles Taylor*. Grand Rapids: Eerdmans, 2014.

Smith, John Thomas. *Nollekens and His Times*. London: Richard Bentley & Son, 1895 [1828].

Smith, Jonathan Z. "What a Difference a Difference Makes." In *"To See Ourselves as Others See Us": Christians, Jews, and "Others" in Late Antiquity*, edited by Jacob Neusner and Ernest S. Frerichs, 3–48. Chico, Calif.: Scholars Press, 1985.

Smith, Miles. "The Translators to the Reader." In *The Holy Bible: Conteyning the Old Testament, and the New*. London: Robert Barker, 1611.

Smith, Nigel. "Did Anyone Understand Boehme?" In *An Introduction to Jacob Boehme: Four Centuries of Thought and Reception*, edited by Ariel Hessayon and Sarah Apetrei, 98–119. New York: Routledge, 2014.

———. *Perfection Proclaimed: Language and Literature in English Radical Religion 1640–1660*. Oxford: Clarendon, 1989.

Smyth, John. *The Works of John Smyth*. Edited by W. T. Whitley. 2 vols. Cambridge: Cambridge University Press, 1915.

Sommerville, C. John. *The News Revolution in England*. New York: Oxford, 1996.

Song, Yuwu, ed. *Encyclopedia of Chinese-American Relations*. Jefferson, N.C.: McFarland, 2009.

Southey, Robert. *Common-Place Book*. Edited by John Wood Warter. 4 vols. London: Longman, Brown, Green & Longmans, 1849–1851.

——— [Espriella, Don Manuel Alvarez]. *Letters from England*. 3 vols. London: Longman, Hurst, Rees & Orme, 1814.

———. "The Life of John Bunyan." In *The Pilgrim's Progress*, by John Bunyan, edited by Robert Southey, 11–74. New York: Harper & Brothers, 1837.

Southworth, John. *Fools and Jesters at the English Court*. Stroud, Gloucestershire: History Press, 1998.

Sowerby, Scott. *Making Toleration: The Repealers and the Glorious Revolution*. Cambridge, Mass.: Harvard University Press, 2013.

Speak Truth to Power: A Quaker Search for an Alternative to Violence. Philadelphia: American Friends Service Committee, 1955.

Spence, Jonathan D. *God's Chinese Son: The Taiping Heavenly Kingdom of Hong Xiuquan*. New York: W. W. Norton, 1996.

Spenser, Edmund. *The Faerie Queene, Book I*. Edited by George A. Wauchope. Project Gutenberg, 2005.

Spurgeon, Charles H. "The Dumb Become Singers." In *Metropolitan Tabernacle Pulpit*, vol. 58, 589–600. London: Passmore, 1912. Reprint, Pasadena, Tex.: Pilgrim Publications, 1979.

———. *Pictures from Pilgrim's Progress*. Chicago: Fleming H. Revell, 1903.

———. *Spurgeon's Sermons*. New York: Sheldon, 1857–1860.

Stachniewski, John. *The Persecutory Imagination: English Puritanism and the Literature of Despair*. Oxford: Clarendon, 1991.

Stanley, Brian. *The Bible and the Flag: Protestant Missions and British Imperialism in the Nineteenth and Twentieth Centuries*. Leicester: Apollos, 1990.

———. "Christianity and the End of Empire." In *Missions, Nationalism, and the End of Empire*, edited by Brian Stanley, 1–11. Grand Rapids: Eerdmans, 2003.

———. *The History of the Baptist Missionary Society 1792–1992*. Edinburgh: T&T Clark, 1992.

Statutes of the Realm: Printed by Command of His Majesty King George the Third. 11 vols. London: Dawsons, 1963.

Stites, Edgar Page. "Beulah Land." In *The Complete Book of Hymns*, by William J. Petersen and Ardythe Peterson, 438–39. Carol Stream, Ill.: Tyndale House, 2006.

Stow, John, and Edward Howes. *Annales; or, Generall Chronicle of England*. London: Richard Meighen, 1631.

Stringfellow, William. *Conscience and Obedience: The Politics of Romans 13 and Revelation 13 in Light of the Second Coming*. Waco, Tex.: Word, 1977.

Sunstein, Cass. *Why Societies Need Dissent*. Cambridge, Mass.: Harvard University Press, 2013.

Sutherland, James. *The Restoration Newspaper and Its Development*. Cambridge: Cambridge University Press, 1986.

Swift, Jonathan. *A Modest Proposal for Preventing the Children of Poor People in Ireland from Being a Burthen to Their Parents or the Country*. London, 1729.

Synodis, Hilarius de. *An Account of the Pamphlets Writ This Last Year Each Side by the Dissenters*. London: James Knapton, 1720.

Tan, Bonny. "A Graphic Tale in Baba Malay: *Chrita Orang Yang Chari Slamat* (1905)." *Biblioasia*, October 2009.

Taylor, Charles. *A Secular Age*. Cambridge, Mass.: Belknap, 2007.

———. *Sources of the Self: The Making of Modern Identity*. Cambridge, Mass.: Harvard University Press, 1989.

Teng, Yuan Chung. *Americans and the Taiping Rebellion: A Study of the American-Chinese Relationship, 1847–1864*. Taipei: China Academy, 1982.

———. "Reverend Issachar Jacob Roberts and the Taiping Rebellion." *Journal of Asian Studies* 23, no. 1 (1963): 55–67.

Tertullian. *Against Marcion*. In *The Ante-Nicene Fathers*, vol. 3. Grand Rapids: Eerdmans, 1979.

Thompson, Edward Palmer. *Customs in Common*. New York: New Press, 1991.

———. *The Making of the English Working Class*. Middlesex: Penguin, 1970.

———. "The Moral Economy of the English Crowd in the Eighteenth Century." *Past and Present* 50 (1971): 76–136.

———. *Witness against the Beast: William Blake and the Moral Law*. Cambridge: Cambridge University Press, 1993.

Thompson, Martyn P. "The Reception of Locke's Two Treatises." *Political Studies* 24, no. 2 (1976): 184–91.

Thune, Nils. *The Behmenists and Philadelphians: A Contribution to the Study of English Mysticism in the Seventeenth and Eighteenth Centuries*. Uppsala: Almqvist & Wiksell, 1948.

Tilley, Terrence W. *Inventing Catholic Tradition*. Maryknoll, N.Y.: Orbis, 2000.

Tillich, Paul. *The Protestant Era*. Translated by James Luther Adams. Chicago: University of Chicago Press, 1957.

Tindall, William York. *John Bunyan: Mechanick Preacher*. New York: Columbia University Press, 1964.

Tocqueville, Alexis de. *Democracy in America*. Translated by Phillips Bradley. New York: Vintage, 1945.

Todd, Dennis. *Defoe's America*. Cambridge: Cambridge University Press, 2010.

Tolmie, Murray. *The Triumph of the Saints: Separate Churches in London 1616–1649.* Cambridge: Cambridge University Press, 1977.

Toon, Peter. *Puritans, the Millennium, and the Future of Israel.* Cambridge: James Clarke, 2003.

Tracy, David. *Analogical Imagination: Christian Theology and the Culture of Pluralism.* New York: Crossroad, 1981.

Trapnel, Anna. *The Cry of a Stone.* London, 1654.

———. *A Legacy for Saints.* London: T. Brewster, 1654.

———. *Poetical Addresses or Discourses Delivered to a Gathering of "Companions" in 1657 and 1658.* London?, 1659?.

Trevelyan, George Otto. *The Life and Letters of Lord Macaulay.* 8 vols. New York: Harper & Brothers, 1876.

A True and Plaine Genealogy or Pedigree of Antichrist. London: For Samuell Rande, 1634.

Turner, Mary. *Slaves and Missionaries: The Disintegration of Jamaican Slave Society 1787–1843.* Urbana: University of Illinois, 1982.

Turner, Victor. *The Ritual Process.* Ithaca, N.Y.: Cornell University Press, 1969.

Underhill, Edward Bean. *The Life of James Mursell Phillippo, Missionary in Jamaica.* London: Yates & Alexander, 1881.

———, ed. *The Records of a Church of Christ, Meeting in Broadmead Bristol, 1640–1685.* London: J. Haddon, 1847.

———. *Tracts on Liberty of Conscience and Persecution, 1614–1661.* New York: Burt Franklin, 1966.

Underwood, A. C. *A History of the English Baptists.* London: Carey Kingsgate, 1956.

Underwood, Ted Leroy, ed. *The Acts of the Witnesses: The Autobiography of Lodowick Muggleton and Other Early Muggletonian Writings.* Oxford: Oxford University Press, 1999.

———. *Primitivism, Radicalism, and the Lamb's War: The Baptist-Quaker Conflict in Seventeenth-Century England.* New York: Oxford University Press, 1997.

Vallance, Ted. Review of *The Acts of the Witnesses: The Autobiography of Lodowick Muggleton and Other Early Muggletonian Writings,* ed. Ted L. Underwood. *H-Albion,* November 2001. https://networks.h-net.org/node/16749/reviews/17647/vallance -underwood-acts-witnesses-autobiography-lodowick-muggleton-and.

Venner, Thomas. *The Last Speech and Prayer and Other Passages of Thomas Venner.* London, 1660.

Wade, Jonathan. "The First Seventy Years of the Mission to the Karens of Burma." Handwritten manuscript in Jonathan Wade Papers. American Baptist Historical Society Archives. Atlanta, Georgia.

Wagner, Rudolf. *Re-enacting the Heavenly Vision: The Role of Religion in the Taiping Rebellion.* Berkeley: University of California Press, 1982.

Wakefield, Gordon Stevens. *Bunyan the Christian.* London: Harper Collins, 1992.

Wakefield Master. *Second Shepherd's Play.* Adapted by Ian Borden. Vancouver: Revelry Theater, 1991.

Walker, Graham B., Jr. "Building a Christian *Zayat* in the Shade of the Bo Tree." *American Baptist Quarterly.* 32, no. 1 (2013): 13–36.

Walsh, J. D. "Elie Halévy and the Birth of Methodism." *Transactions of the Royal Historical Society*, 5th series, 25 (1975): 1–20.

Walsham, Alexandra. *Charitable Hatred: Tolerance and Intolerance in England 1500–1700.* Manchester, U.K.: Palgrave, 2006.

Walzer, Michael. *The Revolution of the Saints: A Study in the Origins of Radical Politics.* Cambridge, Mass.: Harvard University Press, 1965.

Watts, Michael. *The Dissenters.* Vol. 1, *From the Reformation to the French Revolution.* Oxford: Clarendon, 1978.

———. *The Dissenters.* Vol. 2, *The Expansion of Evangelical Nonconformity.* Oxford: Clarendon, 1995.

Weber, Max. *The Protestant Ethic and the Spirit of Capitalism.* Translated by Talcott Parsons. New York: Charles Scribner's Sons, 1958.

Weber, Timothy P. *Living in the Shadow of the Second Coming: American Premillennialism, 1875–1925.* Chicago: University of Chicago Press, 1987.

Webster, Daniel. *The Works of Daniel Webster.* 6 vols. Boston: Charles C. Little & James Brown, 1851.

Wesley, John. *A Calm Address to Our American Colonies.* Bristol: Bonner and Middleton, 1775.

———. *The Works of John Wesley.* Nashville: Abingdon, 2011.

West, Richard. *The Life and Strange Surprising Adventures of Daniel Defoe.* New York: Harper Collins, 1997.

White, Barrington Raymond. *The English Baptists of the Seventeenth Century.* Didcot: Baptist Historical Society, 1996.

———. *The English Separatist Tradition: From the Marian Martyrs to the Pilgrim Fathers.* London: Oxford University Press, 1971.

Whitefield, George. *The Works of the Reverend George Whitefield.* 4 vols. London: Edward & Charles Dilly, 1771.

Whiting, Charles E. *Studies in English Puritanism from the Restoration to the Revolution, 1660–1688.* New York: Macmillan, 1931.

Whitley, William Thomas. *The Baptists of London, 1612–1928.* London: Kingsgate, 1928.

Wilkinson, John. *An Exposition of the 13: Chapter of the Revelation of Iesus Christ.* Amsterdam: G. Thorp, 1619.

———. *The Sealed Fountaine Opened to the Faithfull, and Their Seed.* London, 1646. First published in 1613.

Williams, E. Neville, ed. *The Eighteenth Century Constitution, 1688–1815.* Cambridge: Cambridge University Press, 1960.

Williams, Roger. *The Complete Writings of Roger Williams.* 7 vols. New York: Russell & Russell, 1963. Reprint, Paris, Ark.: Baptist Standard Bearer, 2005.

———. *The Correspondence of Roger Williams.* Edited by Glenn W. LaFantasie. Hanover, N.H.: University Press of New England, 1988.

Williams, Rowan. "'The Human Form Divine': Revelation and Orthodoxy in William Blake." In *Radical Christians Voices and Practice*, edited by Zoë Bennett and David B. Gowler, 151–64. Oxford: Oxford University Press, 2012.

———. *On Christian Theology*. Oxford: Blackwell, 2000.

———. *Why Study the Past? The Quest for the Historical Church*. Grand Rapids: Eerdmans, 2005.

Wilson, Walter. *The History and Antiquities of Dissenting Churches and Meeting Houses in London, Westminster, and Southwark*. 4 vols. London: Printed for the Author, 1808–1814.

———. *Memoirs of the Life and Times of Daniel Defoe*. 3 vols. London: Hurst, Chance, 1830.

Wink, Walter. *Engaging the Powers: Discernment and Resistance in a World of Domination*. Minneapolis: Fortress, 1992.

Winslow, Edward. *Hypocrisie Unmasked: A True Relation of the Proceedings of the Governor and Company of the Massachusetts against Samuel Gorton of Rhode Island*. London: Rich. Cotes, 1646. Repr., New York: Burt Franklin, 1968.

Winstanley, Gerrard. *The Works of Gerrard Winstanley*. Edited by George H. Sabine. Ithaca, N.Y.: Cornell University Press, 1941.

Winterbotham, William. *The Commemoration of National Deliverance and the Dawning Day: Two Sermons, Preached November 5th and 18th, 1792*. London: William Winterbotham, 1794.

———. *The Trial of Wm. Winterbotham, assistant preacher at How's Lane meeting, Plymouth before the Hon. Baron Perryn, and a special jury, at Exeter; on the 25th of July, 1793, for seditious words*. 2nd ed. London: William Winterbotham, 1794.

Winthrop, John. *Journal of John Winthrop 1630–39*. Edited by Richard S. Dunn and Laetitia Yeandle. Abridged ed. Cambridge, Mass.: Belknap, 1996.

———. *Winthrop Papers*. 5 vols. Boston: Massachusetts Historical Society, 1929–1947.

Wolf, Edwin, II. "The Reconstruction of Benjamin Franklin's Library: An Unorthodox Jigsaw Puzzle." *Papers of the Bibliographical Society of America* 56, no. 1 (1962): 1–16.

Wolf, Edwin, II, and Kevin J. Hayes. *The Library of Benjamin Franklin*. Philadelphia: American Philosophical Society, 2006.

Woo, Kenneth Joseph. "'Newter'-ing the Nicodemite: Reception of John Calvin's *Quatre Sermons*." ThD diss., Duke University, 2015.

Wood, Gordon S. *The Americanization of Benjamin Franklin*. New York: Penguin, 2005.

———. *The Radicalism of the American Revolution*. New York: Vintage Books, 1993.

Woodberry, Robert D. "The Missionary Roots of Liberal Democracy." *American Political Science Review* 106, no. 2 (2012): 244–74.

———. "The Shadow of Empire: Christian Missions, Colonial Policy, and Democracy in Postcolonial Societies." PhD diss., University of North Carolina, Chapel Hill, 2004.

Wright, David F. "Why Was Calvin So Severe a Critic of Nicodemism?" In *Calvinus Evangelii Propugnator*, edited by David F. Wright, A. N. Lane, and Jon Balserak, 66–90. Grand Rapids: CRC Product Services, 2006.

Wright, Nicholas Thomas. *Paul and His Recent Interpreters*. Minneapolis: Fortress, 2015.

———. "Where Shall Wisdom Be Found?" Homily at the 175th anniversary of the founding of the University of Durham. June 23, 2007. http://ntwrightpage .com/2016/03/30/where-shall-wisdom-be-found/. Accessed April 14, 2016.

Wuthnow, Robert. *The Restructuring of American Religion*. Princeton, N.J.: Princeton University Press, 1988.

Wylie, James Aitken. *History of Protestantism*. London: Cassell, 1800.

Yoder, John Howard. *The Christian Witness to the State*. Scottdale, Penn.: Herald, 1964.

———. *For the Nations*. Grand Rapids: Eerdmans, 1997.

———. *The Politics of Jesus*. Grand Rapids: Eerdmans, 1972.

Young, Ralph. *Dissent: The History of an American Idea*. New York: New York University Press, 2015.

SCRIPTURE INDEX

GENERAL INDEX